CODING DEMOCRACY

CODING DEMOCRACY

HOW HACKERS ARE DISRUPTING POWER, SURVEILLANCE, AND AUTHORITARIANISM

MAUREEN WEBB

FOREWORD BY CORY DOCTOROW

THE MIT PRESS   CAMBRIDGE, MASSACHUSETTS   LONDON, ENGLAND

This book was set in ITC Stone and Avenir by Toppan Best-set Premedia Limited. Printed and bound in the United States of America.

Library of Congress Cataloging-in-Publication Data

Names: Webb, Maureen, author. | Doctorow, Cory, writer of foreword.
Title: Coding democracy : how hackers are disrupting power, surveillance,
     and authoritarianism / Maureen Webb.
Description: Cambridge, MA : MIT Press, [2020] | Includes bibliographical
     references and index.
Identifiers: LCCN 2019018826 | ISBN 9780262043557 (hardcover : alk. paper)
Subjects: LCSH: Hacktivism. | Cyberspace--Political aspects. |
     Internet--Social aspects. | Hacktivism. | Computer security. |
     Internet--Social aspects. | Democratization.
Classification: LCC HV6773 .W427 2020 | DDC 364.16/8--dc23 LC record available
at https://lccn.loc.gov/2019018826

10 9 8 7 6 5 4 3 2 1

To those in precarious situations

CONTENTS

FOREWORD: THERE ARE TWO KINDS OF PEOPLE

Cory Doctorow

When you're small, you're taught that there are two kinds of people:

1. good ones, and
2. bad ones.

As you get older, if you're lucky enough to have the right kinds of teachers and the right opportunities for learning, you realize that there are indeed two kinds of people:

1. people who think there are two kinds of people ("good ones" and "bad ones"), and
2. people who think that people are pretty much a mixed bag, prone to venality and capable of nobility, fallible and self-deceiving; and that the goodness or badness of a person from moment to moment has more to do with the structures we build to act as a check on fallibility than it does with the intrinsic virtues or wickedness of any one of us.

The name for the systems we build to elevate virtue and check vice is "politics," and, practiced correctly, it can produce a sum that is greater than the whole of its parts: a superhuman machine capable of superhuman feats. Literally: welding together more than one person to accomplish a common end enables outcomes that are more than one person could ever hope for. Superhuman.

For a quarter-century, dreamers, theorists, schemers, builders, optimists, pessimists, crackpots, and geniuses have run a series of experiments in connecting people using networked computers, experimenting with governance structures (ICANN, github, Unix file permissions, standards development organizations, Reddit upvotes, statutes, treaties, regulations), normative frameworks (manifesti, terms of service, moderator guidelines), tools (encryption, error correction, ranking algorithms), and businesses (eBay, Amazon, iTunes, Google Play, the Silk Road), trying to find ways to upregulate desirable behaviors and downregulate the bad ones.

The societal view of this project has been a mess: at first, it was widely dismissed as a distraction, a toy for nerds who believed that somehow their *Star Trek* message-boards had some political consequence. Then, in a hot second, the outside world pivoted to mock tech activists for their supposed "techno-optimism" and alleged indifference to the ways in which tech had become a dominant political force in the world.

These two points of view—tech doesn't matter versus tech matters too much to listen to nerds—have one thing in common: they're both most commonly evinced by people who don't understand tech very well. This is a book that aims to bridge that divide in understanding, and at this political moment that's an important contribution.

I don't mean that critics lack an appreciation of how tech *businesses* work (although many do), or of the human frailties of technologists themselves (these are often self-evident): I mean that, at a nuts-and-bolts level, they tend not to understand what's going on when they sit in front of a computer and make it do things, or have things done to them. When better-informed activists point out the technical incoherence of some critiques (e.g. "Why can't YouTube just use an algorithm to block hate speech?"), they are accused of a mulish intransigence dressed up as technical objections. All too often, the answer to "that's just not possible," is "NERD HARDER!"

The thing is, technology activists are, in fact, enthusiastic about technology. They really do believe that with technology, we can create structures that upregulate the angels of our better nature and downregulate the venal, cowardly, and unworthy impulses. If that was all that tech activists believed, then it would be totally fair to call them monsters of hubris, the unwitting handmaidens of technological oppression through ubiquitous surveillance and control.

But that's not all tech activists believe. They believe that *everything could be so great* but only *if we don't screw it up*. After all, if you're an information security person, your whole job is to sit around and think of how terrible people will abuse the systems you're charged with protecting. If you're an information security specialist, you have to both love and fear tech—the way that a demolitions expert loves and fears dynamite.

The hacker way has its problems: "move fast and break things" was always self-serving bullshit fronted by overgrown toddlers who wanted to grift their way to millions (billions!) without adult supervision.

But the way hackers do policy—deploying deep, hard-won technical expertise to build and modify systems with some real concern for systems' societal effects and an approach that reduces how much agreement we need before we can work together—is admirable. It is animated by a profound understanding of the perils of tech gone wrong as much as by an exuberance at the transformative power of tech.

This is a book about hackers and hacker politics: the nuts-and-bolts and the big picture. The people who appear in it (including, briefly, me) are, like our fellow human beings—deeply flawed, cracked vessels who struggle to contain bad impulses and to let the pure water of our noble ones pour out freely.

Hacker politics are anti-authoritarian because hackers know that authorities are just as damaged as they are. Hacker politics are pluralistic because hackers know that unchecked power is a catastrophe in the making, because without those checks, the bugs in the system will run wild and brick the device before you even know there's something wrong there. It is a political ethos that accounts for the fallibility of human beings as much as for their unlimited potential. It is designed to avoid making things worse, even if doesn't always know how to make them better.

Hacker politics may not solve our problems, but as this book makes clear, they are going to be part of the solution.

AUTHOR'S NOTE

As this book was well into production, in August 2019, a series of allegations began to emerge against a number of people and institutions featured in the text. These allegations linked sex offender Jeffrey Epstein to MIT and to Harvard, and also to faculty and donors at those institutions, including MIT Media Lab Director Joi Ito and MIT professor Marvin Minsky (now deceased). In early September, *The New Yorker* reported that Ito had accepted numerous donations to the Media Lab from Epstein after the latter's conviction in 2008 for soliciting prostitution from a minor, as well as more than $1 million for Ito's own personal investments. It alleged that Ito had concealed the donations. Around the same time, the President of MIT, Rafael Reif, admitted that he had approved a donation from Epstein to a University faculty member in 2012 and had signed a thank-you note to him. Marvin Minsky, meanwhile, was accused of sexually exploiting a 17-year-old female (more than 55 years his junior) allegedly trafficked by Epstein.

LinkedIn cofounder and MIT Media Lab donor Reid Hoffman defended Ito, and Free Software Foundation founder and MIT research scientist Richard Stallman defended Minsky in ways that drew immediate public condemnation and disgust. In September, Ito resigned as Director of the Media Lab, and Richard Stallman resigned from his positions at the Free Software Foundation and MIT's Computer Science and Artificial

Intelligence Lab (CSAIL). The allegations against Ito and the Media Lab led to the departures of associate professor Ethan Zuckerman and visiting scholar J. Nathan Matias from the Lab, who stated that they could no longer be associated with the institution. Ito's failure to respond, and Hoffman's defensive response when questioned by Anand Giridharadas, led to the resignation of that journalist and author from the board overseeing the Media Lab Disobedience Award.

I first started reading about these stories huddled in a tent at the 2019 Chaos Communication Camp, the freezing black night illuminated only by the light of the news articles displayed on my cell phone. It was a lot to take in over the high-decibel punk music and partying that were shaking the ground outside.

Dismay was my initial emotion. My book reports, among many other things, on these individuals' contributions to the history of hacking. What was the proper course of action? Even if I could have excised passages about the impugned individuals entirely from the book at that late stage of the production process, I would not have done it. I don't believe it's fair or wise to erase people and their accomplishments from history in order to serve one's own professional interests. We miss the opportunity to process difficult lessons when we self-righteously rush to scrub someone from the face of an institution, a movement, a profession, or the public record. And as a lawyer I believe that each individual's case must be examined and judged on its own set of facts in the appropriate forums. Everyone is entitled to due process.

Granted, each individual may be judged, too, in the forum of public opinion. But when we make our own judgments we need to think, not just about individual culpability but about the systems in which individuals are embedded, too.

For me, these stories underline the overwhelming gender imbalance in the computing and high-tech worlds. It's an imbalance that poses real challenges for holistic tech solutions for our societies. The stories show the danger of universities being corrupted by private and corporate money, and losing sight of their public mandates. They show privileged elites making terrible decisions. By their depressing mulitiplicity, the stories suggest a general moral crisis. In my view the takeaway is clear: *we need to rebuild our societies and institutions with a new ethos of distributed power. It is our collective responsibility.* That is what this book is about.

At this time, too, it is important to mention that Julian Assange is in prison in the United Kingdom, having been turned out of his sanctuary at the Ecuadorian Embassy in London and forcibly extracted from the building by police. Sweden's investigation against him for sexual crimes has been dropped, reopened by prosecutors, and recently put on hold by a Swedish court, but he is now serving prison time in the United Kingdom for skipping bail (in 2012) and might be extradited to the United States. There is heavy disapprobation of him in the hacker scene. I experienced this firsthand at the recent Chaos Communication Camp in 2019. However, regardless of what one thinks of each of Assange's many actions, his personality, his mental state, his motivations, and his treatment of other people, especially women, over the years, it is important to recognize that his case is, above all, a case about press freedom. *What the UK and US governments decide to do with him will set the course for press freedom in this century.* In that respect we should all be speaking up and getting involved in the matter because as this book describes, we won't be living in democracies if we don't have a free press.

I imagine many more developments will unfold before and after the publication of this book to highlight the pressing relevance of its subject matter. My one hope is that you will feel that you understand what's going on better once you've read it. That is the public service I have aimed to provide.

In solidarity,

Maureen Webb
Fall 2019
Vancouver

ACKNOWLEDGMENTS

This book was truly a journey, and many people helped me on my way.

First, I would like to thank all of the people I interviewed: Andy Müller Maguhn, Peter from Sweden, Andrew Clement, Lucy Suchman, Christian Heck, Harry Halpin, Sacha van Geffen, Cindy Cohn, Corrado Primier, Matteo Ruina, Gianluca Gilardi, Andreas Ghirardini, Matteo Flora, Simona Levi, Rubén Sáez, Maddalena Falzoni, Alfa Sanchez, Sergio Salgado, Danilo Toninelli, Riccardo Fraccaro, John Richardson, Samer Hassan, and Yochai Benkler. Meeting each of you and learning about your contributions to the contemporary democratic struggle was like stepping onto new land. "O brave new world, That has such people in't," enthuses Miranda in act 5 of Shakespeare's *Tempest*. I feel the same way.

Warm thanks to the many other wonderful people I spoke with who gave me important leads, insights, and introductions: Wolfgang Kaleck, Gabriella Coleman, Guillaume Rochefort, Amir Attaran, Holger Krekel, Markus Beckedahl, Irina Bolyshevski, Sean O'Brien, Paul Allen (of Toronto), Kate Milberry, Andrea Neuman, the Fellows and librarians at the American Academy in Rome, Peter Benson Miller, director at the American Academy, and Ilaria Loquenzi, to name a few. Thanks to Silvia Virgulti for translation at the Cinque Stelle offices.

There are people I did not interview but whose work I cover in the book at some length because of its power in the genealogy of hacker ideas. Thank you to Larry Lessig for his exposition of the insight that code is law, Eben Moglen for his affecting oratory, John Clippinger for his thoughts on a digital common law, John Perry Barlow for his poetic intuition, and Richard Stallman, for his vision in starting the free software movement.

I must thank Richard Stallman, too, for his generosity in reading this book's manuscript. His patience in offering information and clarifications was critical to improving the final text.

Special thanks for the altruism of other people who read and vetted parts of the manuscript: to the anonymous reviewers whose valuable comments helped me to articulate the intent of the book and to recalibrate when I went astray in the vast geography of disciplines I was foolhardy enough to traverse; to the interviewees who reviewed their chapters, several of whom painstakingly explained technical matters so that I could write about them intelligently; and to David Weinberger (Senior Researcher at Harvard's Berkman Klein Center), Patrick Henry Winston (Ford Professor of Artificial Intelligence and Computer Science at MIT), Ellen Hoffman (Director of Communications at the MIT Media Lab), and Janine Liberty, Chia Evers and Joi Ito at MIT Media Lab for their fact-checking and comments on chapter twelve. In May 2019, as this book was going into copyediting, I had the opportunity to interview Joi Ito, then Director of the MIT Media Lab, by telephone and would like to thank him for his time and graciousness.

Harry Halpin was like a Hermes to me, appearing as a magical guide at the Chaos Communication Camp and reappearing months later to point out the continuation of the path; he did not let me down despite his heavy travel schedule. Andrew Clement, my fellow Canadian, set me straight on a lot of technical and tonal matters. And it was lovely to start the book in a friendly place, with the warmth of his and Lucy Suchman's hospitality in the Gulf Islands. Andy Müller Maguhn and Christian Heck were also generous with their time and technical advice, Christian taking time away from his own family to help. Thank you to Simona Levi, Sergio Salgado, and the other members of XNet for eloquently describing the social implications of hacking. Any errors or misconceptions lingering in the text are my own.

I would like to thank Heidi Boghosian and Peter Prontzos, who each gave me great support and encouragement in the early stages of this project—Heidi, in New York, for reading and commenting generously on outlines and draft chapters, and traveling to Germany despite her fear of flying; Peter, in Vancouver, for his articles as well as for his love and hugs. Thanks to Greg Ruggiero for suggesting a book about hackers.

I owe the largest debt of gratitude to two women without whom this book would not have happened. Gita Devi Manaktala, the MIT Press's editorial director, picked up the proposal for the book within days of receiving it, when only a handful of chapters had been drafted, and she did not waver in her support of it. In a world that is hurtling along at high speed these days, it was a brave choice. She knew much could change between the time of writing and the time of publication, and yet the topic urgently needed to be covered. Her advice, assistance, and sheer goodness over the course of this project have been a boon to me. Jackie Kaiser, president of Westwood Creative Artists and the other person without whom this book would not have happened, picked me up as a writer and gave me help and attention I will always be grateful for. Working at the top of the book industry for many years she is an alchemical miracle of business acumen and book love, professionalism and heart. Always taking account of my circumstances, she was there at each turn to smooth the way and allow me to write. I have been lucky to have her as my agent.

Thank you to Tessa McWatt for her generous introduction to Jackie. Thanks to Liz Culotti, Pia Singhal and the other staff at Westwood Creative Artists. Thank you to Alex Shultz, a consummate editor. It was a pleasure and privilege to work with you and a comfort to rely on your good taste and unerring judgment.

The Massachusetts Institute of Technology and the MIT Press are institutions that are woven like gold thread throughout the fabric of this book's story. Their part in the genealogy of innovation and civic acts I describe reminds one of the importance of public institutions. I would like to acknowledge the MIT Press's institutional support of me as an author and also that of the American Academy in Rome and the Canada Council for the Arts. The latter gave me a grant at a crucial point to travel down to Boston and Cambridge and write about what was happening there. Thanks to all the staff at the MIT Press, including the ever patient and positive Nhora Lucia Serrano (thanks, Nhora), Kyle Gipson, and those I worked with in the production and marketing process. Deborah Cantor-Adams and Rosemary Winfield were responsible for the final copyediting and fine polishing of the manuscript, a task they executed deftly and with amazing speed. Susan Clark wrote wonderful copy for the catalog.

Writer friends—Monia Mazigh, Rick Salutin, Mark Danner, and Stephanie Young—thank you for your camaraderie and influence. And thank you to friends Professor Mary Chapman for her discerning advice offered generously over so many years and her network intelligence, Gail Davidson (for her example), Tom Sandborn (for his example), Lori Kozub Hodgkinson (for her tips on audio books) and Jose Rodrigues (for his insights into the political complexity of the Catalan independence movement).

Thank you to my dear family, Connie Webb, and Michael and Joanne Webb, who have always been there for me. And thank you to my brothers and sisters in the labor movement, and at the Hospital Employees' Union in particular. This struggle to recover our dignity as citizens has many links with the struggle for dignity in work.

To my children: You have put up with the extra burden of this book's writing for four years with sterling kindness. Thank you for that. I know it has not always been easy. Michele, my sweet son, you gave me insights on memes and fake news that I had not heard elsewhere. You are the digital native and philosopher of the family. Lucia, my light, thank you for taking an interest, now you are grown, in what I've been writing. There could be no better reward for the effort, especially as I watch you begin to formulate your own ideas about the world.

Reader, thank you. As we go forward, let us make it a sweet habit of solidarity to call each other citizen.

1

THE HACKER ETHIC
Germany's Chaos Computer Club
and the Genealogy of the Hacker Ethos

IN BERLIN

Berlin still has many bombed-out lots. If you peer in behind the mesh fences, you see deep craters that sink precipitously under a cover of decades-old trees. These holes seem to perforate the psyche as well as the landscape of the city. Some are the size of city blocks, some the size of small neighborhoods, and some are just green spaces where large tracts of city and inhabitants have ceased to exist as geographic facts.

In photos of the postwar period, the Reichstag building is often visible, with Germans picking their way around its large, defeated hulk on foot and on bicycles, the road a track of mud. The seat of German democratic government in Berlin, the Reichstag was notoriously set on fire in 1933, then scorned by Adolf Hitler (he never used it), and badly bombed by Allied planes. The Germans left it unreconstructed until well into peacetime, living with its wreckage until it was finally patched up for use in the 1960s and fully renovated in the 1990s. The dome of the renovated Reichstag echoes the burned-out, twisted dome of the old building and is encased in glass—a symbol, perhaps, of both contrition and transparency.[1]

Walking around the bomb sites, the broken wall, and the sooty, uncared-for imperial buildings of Berlin, a visitor might wonder whether these two values, contrition and transparency, can exorcise the dark history of the place, which in the twentieth century went through multiple paroxysms—two wars of aggression, wild excess and inflation, mass deportations and murder, totalitarian surveillance, and a grim physical division. Despite a new German narrative of economic recovery and openness, Berliners still live amid the ruins of their elites' many bad decisions. They tend to be people with few illusions.

It's no coincidence that a strong hacker culture has taken root here and flourished.

GETTING TO THE CHAOS COMMUNICATION CAMP

The Chaos Communication Camp happens every four years. The trouble is, every four years its attendance seems to double. In 2015, its organizers are struggling to accommodate 4,500 camping hackers. The website of the Chaos Computer Club (CCC), the group that organizes the camp, still says,

> ~~The Chaos Communication Camp is an international, five-day open-air event for hackers and associated life-forms. It provides a relaxed atmosphere for free exchange of technical, social, and political ideas. The Camp has everything you need: power, internet, food and fun. Bring your tent and participate!~~

But it also says:

> ~~Verpeiler friends' request? If you don't get your ticket on Friday, you will have one very last, very tiny chance. Go to the ticket system and convince us that you are one of our dearest verpeiler friends. There won't be many of those tickets available. Also you need to be very patient waiting for a reply~~ ... **We are sold out!**

I've come to Berlin on the fly. I've failed to obtain tickets to the camp by any means, but through an American lawyer I know, who knows a prominent German lawyer, who knows one of the main organizers of the camp, I've managed to score a ride this late afternoon of the first day of the event, and that's a relief.

I'm here to do research, to talk to people in the hacking world, and I'm keenly aware I'm starting this book project with only a moderate amount of knowledge about what hacking and code are. I wrote a book on mass surveillance, *Illusions of Security: Global Surveillance and Democracy in the*

Post-9/11 World (2007), which came out six years before Edward Snowden made his disclosures of highly classified National Security Agency (NSA) materials. The book predicted much of what Snowden's leaks revealed about the scope of government and private-sector surveillance and its dangers for democracy. At the time, I had hoped constitutions in Western democracies would be strong enough to roll back these abuses once they were uncovered. But lately, I've become convinced this is not going to happen. When you take stock of the pervasive illegality states and corporations are engaged in with their uses of digital tech, it is manifest the law is collapsing.

In this era of rising instability, a digital revolution is unleashing forces that are not well understood by citizens and their elected officials. As the mass surveillance, concentrations of power, and authoritarianism enabled by digital tech grow around the globe, millions have begun to worry where this new century is taking us. Can societies hold onto and, indeed, "build out" democracy into cyberspace in the digital age?

Code, more than law, will soon determine what kind of societies we live in and whether they end up resembling democracies at all. Yet code is incomprehensible to most people, myself included. Computer users, for the most part, are at the mercy of the code makers.

Who controls code? This is the urgent civics question that's spurred the journey I am about to make through the world of hackers and hacking, a journey that, before I am done, will take me to Berlin and the Chaos Communication Camp and also to Barcelona, Rome, Boston, Cambridge, San Francisco, Vancouver, and the Gulf Islands in the Salish Sea. In many respects, it is an everyperson's journey, and I am that everyperson—not a hacker, technologist, or academic who studies hackers but rather a labor and constitutional lawyer, a Canadian, a trade unionist, a parent trying to raise children and hold down a regular job, and one of millions of ordinary citizens in Western countries concerned about our democracies in this new century. Although this journey might prove challenging for someone like myself without tech expertise, I'm convinced it's a journey every citizen must make to understand what is happening to democracy in the twenty-first century.

A struggle is taking place right now as corporations, states, criminal elements, and parts of civil society vie to build the coded environment around us. Hackers are savants in this world. But their identity is protean.

Sought after for their talents, almost folkloric in status, they've been recruited and reviled, celebrated and thrown into prison.

I'm familiar with the stereotype of hackers as dangerous, nihilistic elements in society who are capable of bringing down critical infrastructure and sowing strife between nations. These are real threats, not to be minimized. Yet I know enough to believe hackers might also be vital disruptors in the emerging digital environment, with its dystopic, antidemocratic tendencies. There is an astounding array of hacker experiments underway right now that could fundamentally change the current political economy.

More than this, I see hacking becoming a practice, an ethos, and a metaphor for a growing social movement in which ordinary citizens are taking things into their own hands when reform seems out of sight. At a time when people's faith in elites to govern has never been lower, I see hacking inspiring a new wave of activism, a new way of thinking and acting, as citizens fight to take back their democracies.

As I wait on the sidewalk for the ride that will take me to the hacker camp this summer day in Berlin, I feel strongly that I'm writing this book for tech insiders as well, for them to reflect on where hacking has come from and where it might be going, and on the processes by which the knowledge they possess might urgently be transferred to the mind of the ordinary citizen. My intent on this journey is not to valorize the hacker, Silicon Valley visionary, counterculture guys' club, Harvard professor, or MIT hotshot—necessary as it is to situate their remarkable stories and credit their innovations in the genealogy of hacking. My intent is to celebrate the hacking ethos, the collective intelligence of people, and the spirit in all of us to resist domination and unfairness. The stories at the heart of this book will be about citizen hackers who are inventing new forms of distributed democracy. Its central question will be how we ordinary citizens and tech insiders go forward together to accomplish the hard work of democracy in the digital age. It won't be easy, but we've got to try.

My ride today is with Andy Müller-Maguhn. People have told me that Andy is the *ur* German hacker—meaning the earliest, the original, the prototypical German hacker. He pulls up behind the wheel of a black diplomatic series Mercedes sedan, complete with automated curtains on the windows. He doesn't stop right at the curb but askew to it, like someone on the move. He's wearing a vinyl version of a hipster's pork pie hat. The man beside him in the passenger seat introduces himself as Peter, from Sweden. I climb in and am immediately enveloped by the Mercedes's sound system, pulsing with '90s techno music.

The Chaos Computer Club, which Andy has been associated with since its early days, was founded in 1982. It has been involved in all the major digital tech debates of the last four decades, and its role in the unfolding story of hacking in the early part of the twenty-first century is central. The club began, so the story goes, around a table that once belonged to the notorious counterculture group Kommune 1. A communal group in West Germany in the 1960s, Kommune 1 practiced performance politics, free sex, and experimental drug use, attracting a glamorous entourage that included the late Jimi Hendrix. The table belonged to the German Green Party at one point, and by the time it entered the self-conscious mythology of the hacker group, it was in the rooms of the progressive newspaper *Die Tageszeitung*. The Chaos Computer Club's founder, Herwart Holland-Moritz, also known as Wau Holland, wrote occasionally for the paper and was an early digital rights pioneer in Germany.

The CCC's first annual Congress was held, aptly, in 1984. A few hundred people were present. Today, the Chaos Computer Club is Europe's largest association of hackers, and close to ten thousand people attended its congress in 2014.[2] Like Nelson Mandela's African National Congress, its reputation has morphed over time from suspected criminality to fashionable respectability.

Andy, Peter from Sweden, and others have been working for the past year to organize the camp, but Andy doesn't like camping and will not be staying over. Tough-minded and politically sophisticated, Andy has been in the thick of things for a long time. Just how much in the thick, I sense, he might not want to say, and it might be bad form to ask.

FIRST-WAVE HACKERS: HACKING CULTURE IN THE US FROM THE LATE 1950S, INCLUDING THE HANDS-ON IMPERATIVE AND OTHER PRINCIPLES OF A HACKER ETHOS

Hacker culture's earliest origins were not in Europe but in the United States, where hacker culture began in the 1950s at academic institutions that had early, mainframe computers. That might seem a long-ago place to start a story about contemporary hacking, but hacking is a story about a genealogy of ideas as much as anything—ideas as they are lived, distilled, built on, repurposed, and disseminated by hackers, just as code is. In this chapter, I give a brief history of the beginnings of hacking and the hacking ethos in the United States and Europe from the 1950s through the 1990s and attempt to leave the reader with a first impression of the Chaos Communication Camp, too.

The story begins at the Massachusetts Institute of Technology (MIT). *Wired* magazine journalist Steven Levy wrote a seminal book in the mid-1980s on the history of hacking called *Hackers: Heroes of the Computer Revolution*.[3] It is a dense yet entertaining book that everyone who hacks or writes about hacking references yet seldom revisits and unpacks. Levy's descriptions of the early MIT hackers and the ethic he ascribed to them are worth recounting in detail because Levy's distillation of that ethic has been picked up, *verbatim*, by progressive political hacker scenes in the twenty-first century, including the burgeoning scene coalescing around the Chaos Computer Club. While Levy's distillation may not be universally subscribed to, it's been very influential in contemporary hacking. Insiders who know the early history of American hacking, which Levy recorded, may want to skip forward to my exposition of early hacking in Europe or to my detailed account later in this chapter of the Chaos Computer Club's history. But for ordinary computer users trying to understand contemporary hacking, the next few pages will be foundational.

Levy described how a hacking culture first grew at MIT among engineering and physics students coalescing around a club that built an elaborate model train set in MIT's Building 20. As the electronic routers the club designed became ever more complicated and the group scrounged around the halls of MIT at night looking for parts, they discovered early "keypunch" machines in the basement of Building 26. These machines produced the "punch cards" that were the programming medium for an early IBM 704 computer housed on the building's first floor. Thirty tons and nine feet tall, the IBM computer was off limits to students, but they managed to sneak into the basement room at night and play with the keypunch machines, inventing new "programming" solutions for their railway system. In 1959, when MIT offered the first computer programming course for freshmen, these enthusiasts signed up. What they really wanted was to get their hands on the IBM computer itself. But there was an elaborate bureaucratic system of rules around these bigger machines to keep tinkering-obsessed students from tampering with them.

The most proficient tinkerers in the model railroad club called themselves, self-deprecatingly, "hackers." They might call a clever patch they had made "a mere hack" or say that they were "hacking away" at the railway routing system—*hacking* in the dictionary sense meaning "to cut or sever with repeated irregular or unskillful blows; to cut or shape by, or as if by, crude or ruthless strokes; ... to play inexpert golf." Early radio geeks had called themselves "hackers," and there was a long tradition at MIT (which persists today) of students engineering elaborate, playful pranks, called "hacks" (such as covering the great dome of Building 10 with tin foil or building a police patrol car on the dome, replete with flashing lights and a box of donuts).

When one of the first transistor-run computers in the world, the TX-0, was loaned to MIT, it was housed on the second floor of Building 26, and the model railroad club hackers were allowed to sign up for time to work with the machine, which was run around the clock. As their obsession with the TX-0 deepened, they began calling themselves "TX-0 hackers." They discovered that the best hours to book, or "vulture," time on the machine were in the middle of the night. First, you used a machine called a Flexowriter to punch the programming instructions into a long, thin paper tape, and then you fed those instructions into the TX-0. The TX-0 made sounds as you did so—a kind of low, out-of-tune organ music that changed according to the data the machine was reading. You could hear what part of your program was going through—that is, if you could hear anything over the din of your friends' clacking Flexowriters, "which would make you think you were in the middle of a machine gun battle."[4] You got the results of your programming immediately. For these budding pioneer programmers, the process was addictive.

The culture that coalesced around the model railroad club and the TX-0 hackers embodied precepts that, although only silently agreed on among themselves, would be distilled by Steven Levy into a "hacker ethic":

1. *Access to computers—and anything that might teach you how the world works—should be unlimited and total. Always yield to the hands-on imperative!* "Hackers," Levy explained, "believe that essential lessons can be learned

about the systems—about the world—from taking things apart, seeing how they work, and using this knowledge to create new and more interesting things. They resent any person, physical barrier, or law that tries to keep them from doing this."

2. *All information should be free.* "If you [don't] have access to the information you [need] to improve things, how [can] you fix them? A free exchange of information ... [allows] for greater overall creativity."

3. *Mistrust authority. Promote decentralization.*"Bureaucracies, whether corporate, government, or university, are flawed systems, dangerous in that they cannot accommodate the exploratory impulse of true hackers ... [which these institutions] perceive ... as a threat."

4. *Hackers should be judged by their hacking, not by bogus criteria such as degrees, age, race, or position.* "Hackers [care] less about someone's superficial characteristics than they [do] about his potential to advance the general state of hacking, to create new programs to admire, to talk about that new feature in the system."

5. *You can create art and beauty on a computer.* "Code ... [holds] a beauty of its own." Among the TX-0 hackers, Levy explained, "A certain esthetic of programming style ... emerged. Because of the limited memory space of the TX-0 (a handicap that extended to all computers of that era), hackers came to deeply appreciate innovative techniques that allowed programs to do complicated tasks with very few instructions."

6. *Computers can change your life for the better.*"This belief was subtly manifest," Levy wrote. "Surely the computer had changed [these early hackers'] lives, enriched their lives, given their lives focus, made their lives adventurous. It had made them masters of a certain slice of fate."[5]

The professors who led the artificial intelligence (AI) work at MIT—Jack Dennis, John McCarthy, and Marvin Minsky—were early proselytizers of computers' potential to better the lot of the human race.[6] Minsky, more than others, understood the genius of the hacker approach and "encouraged hackerism in any way he could."[7] The "golden age" of hacking at MIT developed through the 1960s under Minsky's tutelage, with hackers like Bill Gosper, Richard Greenblatt, and Stewart Nelson joining the student ranks in the early part of the decade. This group of hackers worked on operating systems, programming language, distributed systems, and the theory of computation. They ate copious amounts of Chinese food, worked all hours, and led a monastic lifestyle. There were a few women programmers at MIT at the time, but they were not within the hacker ranks. Computing was then, and remains today, a field dominated by Western white males. (This demographic is certainly a concern, considering computing's profound effects on society. It is not a direct focus of this book, although in the second half I show that as hacking proliferates and merges with social movements, diversity and inclusiveness are seeping into the field and beginning to have their effects.)

Soon, the MIT hackers began working with a much more exciting machine—the PDP series. Joseph Weizenbaum, author of the well-known ethical treatise *Computer Power and Human Reason: From Judgment to Calculation*[8] and an MIT student during this time, vividly described hackers' fevered lifestyle:

> Bright young men of disheveled appearance, often with sunken glowing eyes, can be seen sitting at computer consoles. … They work until they nearly drop, twenty, thirty hours at a time. Their food, if they can arrange it, is brought to them: coffee, Cokes, sandwiches. If possible, they sleep on cots near the printouts. Their rumpled clothes, their unwashed and unshaven faces, and their uncombed hair all testify that they are oblivious to their bodies and to the world in which they move. These are computer bums, compulsive programmers.[9]

The "golden age" hackers were even more hard core in their embrace of the hacker ethic than their TX-0 predecessors had been. Fighting the university bureaucracy to gain access to systems and tools, they developed a transgressive approach to rules. Richard Stallman, who came to the AI group at the tail end of this era, not long after Minsky established it as the "AI Lab" in 1970, recalled later in an interview,

> I don't know if there actually is a hacker's ethic as such, but there sure was an M.I.T. Artificial Intelligence Lab ethic. This was that bureaucracy should not be allowed to get in the way of doing anything useful. Rules did not matter—results mattered. Rules, in the form of computer security or locks on doors, were held in total, absolute disrespect. We would be proud of how quickly we would sweep away whatever little piece of bureaucracy was getting in the way, how little time it forced you to waste. Anyone who dared to lock a terminal in his office, say because he was a professor and thought he was more important than other people, would likely find his door left open the next morning. I would just climb over the ceiling or under the floor, move the terminal out, or leave the door open with a note saying what a big inconvenience it is to have to go under the floor, "so please do not inconvenience people by locking the door any longer." … There is a big wrench at the AI Lab entitled "the seventh-floor master

key," to be used in case anyone dares to lock up one of the more fancy terminals.[10]

SECOND-WAVE HACKERS: COMPUTERS AND CODE FOR THE PEOPLE, INCLUDING THE PEOPLE'S COMPUTER COMPANY, THE WELL, HOMEBREW, SILICON VALLEY, RMS, AND FREE SOFTWARE

As Levy observed, the impetus of this first wave of North American hackers at MIT was to "ingest the magic of the computer; to absorb, explore and expand [its] intricacies."[11] But through the 1970s, a second wave of hacking was gathering force in and around Berkeley, California, and a place called Silicon Valley in the southern part of the San Francisco Bay Area. It was marked by a much greater social consciousness and outward orientation than the early MIT hacker culture. The inspiration of this second wave of hackers was to *bring computers to the people*. Tech insiders will know this history well and might want to skip over it. But many ordinary computer users do not and will find it critical background for understanding contemporary hacking and digital tech issues today.

In the early 1970s, Intel began manufacturing the first computer microchips, spurring the dream that people could own small computers themselves. The People's Computer Company proselytized the democratizing power of the personal computer in a counterculture publication, a newsletter called *People's Computer Company* that gave heady dispatches from the front lines of the revolution, and also ran a computer center that offered classes and computer time to anyone interested for fifty cents an hour.[12] The Community Memory Project brought computer message boards to people in the streets of Berkeley.

The Homebrew Computer Club, another well-known group from this era of hackers, ended up realizing the personal computer revolution. It formed in 1975 to tinker with the first build-your-own home computer kit, the Altair (built using Intel's new 8080 microcomputer chip). The Homebrew enthusiasts came together in the spirit of the original hacker ethos to present new prototypes for each other's feedback, test each other's source code, and share solutions. Experiments and inventions were shared even with nominal competitors.

These second-wave hackers were forging their way on a new frontier together. "We reinforced each other," Lee Felsenstein, who belonged to both the Community Memory group and the Homebrew Computer Club,[13] later explained to Steven Levy: "We provided support structure for each other. We bought each other's products. We covered each other's asses, in effect. There we were—the industrial [IBM] structure was paying no attention to us. Yet we had people who knew as much as anyone else did about this aspect of technology, because it was so new. We could run wild, and we did."[14]

The conditions proved perfect for innovation. Within a few years, many of the Homebrew Computer Club's members went on to become major designers and manufacturers of personal computers, including Steve Wozniak, who designed the Apple I. The Homebrew Computer Club's hacker newsletter was a formative influence in the emerging culture of Silicon Valley, where the silicon microchip manufacturers and many of the startups in the personal computer revolution came to be located. These companies understood the power of the hacker ethic because it was in their DNA. They recruited hackers, modeled their work processes after hackers' processes, and loosened corporate culture to emulate a more freewheeling hacker culture.[15]

But the tension between the hacker ethos and the commercial, for-profit ethos soon created rifts. Back at MIT, one such rift opened up in the hacker scene when one set of MIT hackers started a company called Symbolics, developing proprietary code for a machine that ran Lisp software in competition with a project they had been working on with a larger group. By the end of 1981, many of the MIT hackers were employed by Symbolics and were working mostly at its offices instead of at the AI Lab, although they continued to be involved with MIT projects. Proprietary code cannot be shared outside of a company. It is a trade secret. By working for a competing company, these hackers had abandoned a key principle of the hacker ethic—the hands-on principle, the free flow of information.[16] A great deal of rancor was generated over the split, and rooms that used to be full of hackers working late into the night emptied. Steven Levy described the AI Lab in the mid-1980s as a place where the flame of the original hacker ethos still flickered but only barely. The professors, students, and nonhacker researchers at the lab did not know (and did not want to know) how to take the guts out of machines and put them back together. The new programmers coming in did not want to tinker on things collectively. When they wrote new programs, they circulated them with a copyright notice, which was anathema to Richard Stallman. "I used to wander through the lab," he has said, "through rooms so empty at night where they used to be full and think, 'Oh my poor AI Lab! You are dying and I can't save you.' Everyone expected that if more hackers were trained, Symbolics would hire them away anyway, so it didn't even seem worth trying."[17] Stallman, Levy wrote, "grieved at the lab's failure to uphold the Hacker Ethic." He "considered himself the last true hacker left on earth."[18] "I'm the last survivor of a dead culture," Stallman told Levy.[19]

In fact, Stallman was a pivotal figure between the first wave and second wave of North American hackers. His instinct to rebel against any institution that would not make source code freely available for tinkering may have stemmed from the hacker's hands-on imperative, but Stallman, more than earlier hackers, was able to link this imperative to an outward-looking social vision, and he would pursue the implications of this for the rest of his working life.

In the early 1980s, Richard Stallman's inspiration was to *bring code to the people*. In January 1984, Stallman quit his job as a "system hacker" (developing software for MIT's operating systems) so that he could build a complete, Unix-like system that was "free." Unix was a widely used proprietary computer system in university computer science departments, and Stallman felt he could get the biggest uptake if he based his software on an interface already known to many people. He was compelled by his goals to quit MIT because if he had developed his software under MIT auspices, the institution could have claimed copyright on it and interfered with its distribution. A scientific atheist, Stallman has said the decision to start his project was prompted by the same altruistic spirit expressed in the famous aphorism attributed to the religious leader Hillel: "If I am not for myself, who will be for me? If I am only for myself, what am I? If not now, then when?"[20]

He called his software "free," explaining that he meant "free as in freedom, not price." Stallman had no problem with people selling free software, which might be necessary to make a living or fund development projects. To be "free software," he held, software had to comply with the "four essential freedoms." Users had to be

0. Free to run the program as they wished, for any purpose;

1. Free to modify the program to meet their needs, which entailed access to source code;

2. Free to redistribute copies, either without charge or for a fee; and

3. Free to distribute modified version of the program so that the community could benefit from one's improvements.[21]

Stallman's answer to the question "Who controls code?" was definitively "The user."

Stallman sent an open email to the unix-wizards listserv:

> Starting this Thanksgiving I am going to write a complete Unix-compatible software system called GNU (for Gnu's Not Unix), and give it away free [at no cost] to everyone who can use it. ... I may be able to hire a few people. ... The salary won't be high, but I'm looking for people for whom knowing they are helping humanity is as important as money ... So that I can continue to use computers without violating my principles, I have decided to put together a sufficient body of free software so that I will be able to get along without any software that is not free [in the sense of the "four freedoms"].[22]

Stallman and his collaborators made a list of the programs needed to make a complete operating system, including command processors, assemblers, compilers, interpreters, debuggers, text editors, and mailers. Then they systematically "found, wrote, or found people to write everything on the list."[23] As his recruitment email stated, he called it GNU (Gnu's Not Unix), a recursive acronym, the kind of joke that hackers like. In 1985, Stallman published "The GNU Manifesto," a declaration of his intention, and started the Free Software Foundation, a charity for the development of free software.

FIRST-WAVE EUROPE: THE EARLY DEVELOPMENT OF EUROPEAN HACKER CULTURE IN THE 1970S AND 1980S

In Europe, hacker groups like the Chaos Computer Club developed later than hacker culture in the United States and not always with much consciousness of US hacker culture. The dawning of hacker culture in Europe aligned more with the advent of personal computing than with the development of early mainframe computing.

By the late 1970s in Europe, personal computers were beginning to enter people's lives, and governments there and in the USSR were promoting the technology, encouraging computer literacy in their populations with a range of initiatives. To bolster national economies in the slump of the 1980s, several governments supported the development of national computer industries, but these efforts were largely unsuccessful. Government support for Dutch Tulip, Swedish Compis, Yugoslav Lola, and Polish Meritum, for example, was insufficient for these companies to keep up with the rate of innovation by US companies.[24]

People on both sides of the Iron Curtain were embracing, experimenting with, and appropriating computer technology within their own political and social contexts. The user manuals were not necessarily published in their languages, and there was room and a need to experiment with the basic programming that came with commercially distributed computers.

In the Netherlands, computer tech was embraced quickly by a civic-minded, hobbyist culture. In Greece, where the early, Western-built gaming and personal computers provided nothing to help users adapt them to the Greek language, hacking software was imperative and became the norm. In Yugoslavia, which was an autonomous Communist state wedged between the USSR and Europe, the government promoted an autonomous, national computer industry, and the thriving hacker scene there was elitist rather than being motivated by counterculture politics.[25] Behind the Iron Curtain, Polish hackers had access to computer magazines and grassroots publications and maintained connections with clubs and periodicals in the West, despite Cold War restrictions. Also behind the Iron Curtain, Czech hackers, lacking a WiFi infrastructure, experimented successfully in sending beams of light containing data to each other. Usually red, these data beams could be seen stretching eerily across apartment-building courtyards and Prague rooftops at night. In Finland, the socialist culture that produced both Linus Torvalds (the instigator of the collectively produced Linux kernel) and the Angry Birds game, many hackers were part of a "demoscene" that treated hacking as a form of real-time, collectively produced art, creating "demonstrations" out of hacks of popular computer games. In France and Italy, politically conscious hacker groups sprang up that were aligned with the republican and anarchist traditions of those countries.

THE EARLY DAYS OF THE CHAOS COMPUTER CLUB

In Germany, yet another very specific set of social and political circumstances shaped hacker culture. In the 1970s, West Germany was still divided from East Germany, which formed part of the Communist bloc. West Germany had gone through the counterculture politics of the 1960s with the rest of Europe; East Germany had not. West Berlin was not contiguous with the rest of West Germany but was an island of heavily fortified democracy that had been saved from the encroaching Soviet army by the Americans' Berlin Airlift at the end of World War II. It was entirely surrounded by Communist East Berlin.

In Hamburg, West Germany, Wau Holland imbibed the ideas of the 1968 student revolution, which had erupted in international protests against state authority. He was anticapitalist, antistatist, and somewhat anti-American. He had studied electrical engineering, computer science, and politics and then worked in leftist bookstores for a while. But his ideas did not fit well within the leftist spectrum of the era. In Germany, countercultural movements had, for the most part, adopted a skepticism toward technology influenced by the Frankfurt School and were wary of technophiles.

Holland, having "no natural audience on the left … had to create one himself."[26] He felt the Green Party, for example, fought technological developments "with garlic, the cross and holy water."[27] In an instrumentalist, technology-driven world, he believed one should fight back with technology, humor, and ethics. It was a strategy he called "positive chaos."[28] His take on tech was somewhere between the utopian vision of the People's Computer Company in California, which saw computers as innately liberating and democratizing, and a more anarchist appropriation. In an influential article he published in the newspaper *Die Tageszeitung* (*taz*) in 1981, he invited fellow computer enthusiasts to "stop scurrying around" and meet with him to discuss important issues like data laws, encryption, and copyright. He convened a regulars' table at a local alternative bookstore.

In 1982, in *taz*, he announced the formation of the Chaos Computer Club. With its technophile bent, it diverged from conventional counterculture thinking, but the Chaos Computer Club was still, from its inception, a counterculture group. It is no coincidence that the Kommune

1 table, around which its inaugural meeting, real or apocryphal, was held, became the club's chosen transgressive icon—an object associated with a 1960s counterculture group so notorious in Europe that hackers thrilled to imagine what might have been done at or on top of it.

I did not ask Andy if he had ever been photographed at that table in a hagiographic image of club founders, but he most certainly got involved with the club around the time it began putting out its influential newsletter, *Datenschleuder*. After Holland announced the publication of *Datenschleuder* in *taz* in 1984, he immediately received a hundred advance orders. The publication was a hodgepodge of technical discussion, disclosures, political disquisition, and announcements of new projects. The group became a self-identified "vanguard" of the information society, and its preoccupations were state and corporate accountability, consumer protection, user empowerment, and a 1968-era concern about struggling against centralized, opaque systems, whether political or technical. Among its many outreach actions, the club showed people how to build their own modems, exposed security vulnerabilities, released the technical specifications for broadband networks and government protocols for shutting down telecommunications in times of emergency, and after the nuclear reactor meltdown at Chernobyl, discussed a project for monitoring radioactivity using personal computers.

Anyone could subscribe to the newsletter, but in order to become a member of the club, one had to demonstrate both technical prowess and playfulness: the entrance requirement was to program a "quine." A quine is like a recursive joke but in programming code. It is a piece of code that refers to itself in a way that causes it to keep reproducing itself. There is, in fact, a "recursion theorem" in programming (Kleene's) that "proves the existence of quines in every sufficiently strong programming language," but they are not easy to discover.[29]

In 1984, Holland and Steffen Wernéry, an important collaborator of Holland's and spokesperson for the Chaos Computer Club, announced the hack of the Bildschirmtext (Btx). The Btx was an early teletext system offered by Germany's federal mail service and main telecommunications provider, Deutsche Bundespost (DBP). The club had repeatedly warned the DBP that the Btx system was flawed. Btx had been introduced to a public that was already wary of large, opaque technical systems: West Germans had protested against nuclear energy production and against the 1981 population census, finally winning a novel right to "informational self-determination." The club did not like DBP because it held a government monopoly over telecommunications and controlled access to the system, including what kind of hardware could be used legally.

DBP ignored the club's repeated warnings and denied there were weaknesses in Btx. By hacking emails, the club discovered Btx users' passwords and began publishing them. Provoked into stronger action by DBP's dismissals, the club found the password for Hamburg's savings bank, Hamburger Sparkasse (HASPA), and used it to transfer 135,000 deutschmarks (DMs) to the club's bank account in just one night. The money was returned the next day, and Holland and Wernéry held a news conference to report the "robbery" to Hamburg's data protection commissioner.

The hack was the kind of performance politics Kommune 1 would have appreciated and a demonstration of the club's evolving tactics of "countercontrol" and "inverse panopticism." The BDP accused the hackers of malfeasance, but the media and public applauded.

Although at first the club's "hacktivist" stunts were received favorably by the public, by the late 1980s, the fleeting positive image of hackers that CCC had helped create was overtaken by news stories of very young hackers doing reckless stunts and cracking systems without much, if any, coherent political thought. The public's view of hackers as defenders of the public interest began to change. Increasingly, they were seen as trespassing hobbyists with dangerous criminal proclivities that the state was obliged to protect the public against. A series of high-profile attacks on US military complex targets—culminating in the "WANK" worm attack on the National Aeronautics and Space Administration (NASA) and contemporaneous attacks on EU targets—brought things to a head. In Europe, the hackers had apparently used a flaw in the VAX system, which was used by public authorities to access the computers of research facilities and companies. Companies alleged the hackers had copied and destroyed data in over a hundred machines. The perpetrators, out of their depth, anonymously contacted the Chaos Computer Club for help.

What assistance, if any, was given to these anonymous troublemakers, Andy might be able to tell. What is known publicly is that the club notified Germany's Federal Office for the Protection of the Constitution. Law enforcement agencies began a preliminary investigation to determine the hackers' identity. Other jurisdictions became involved, and Steffen Wernéry became one of the suspects. The media coverage against the club was harsh.

In 1987, there was a police raid at the club's Hamburg headquarters. When Wernéry was traveling to Paris in 1988 for a computer conference, he was arrested for computer crimes.[30] He was later released back to Germany after serving two months in a French prison for hacking the the code of the Dutch electronics multinational, Phillips.[31]

1989: A WATERSHED YEAR FOR GERMANY AND THE CCC

As Andy tells it, 1989 was a big year not just for Berlin and Germany but also for the Chaos Computer Club. In March 1989, nine months before the fall of the Berlin Wall, the KGB story broke.[32] Some youths affiliated with the club had hacked into computers in the US and EU and transferred source code and other documents to the KGB for money.

The KGB hack was a complete breach of what Wau Holland and others in the club considered "a decent way of hacking."[33] It created a big commotion within the European hacker community and forced the club to face the problem of dealing with its own wayward teenagers.

This was also the year of the first big international hackers' meeting, held in the Netherlands at the Paradiso, a large church converted into a meeting hall.[34] At this seminal gathering of hackers from all over the world, especially the US and EU, Wau Holland took the opportunity to make an example of the kids involved in the KGB hack. He pulled one of them up and conducted a public interview with him for the edification of everyone at the conference. It was an important moment in the oral, and moral, history of the hacker scene.

The fact that European hackers still talk about and recreate the event is indicative of the special influence Wau Holland and the Chaos Computer Club have exercised in the European hacking scene. In the interview, a transcript of which still exists,[35] Holland underlines the hacker ethic to which the CCC is committed. Like an Old Testament father figure, he lays down the principles in full for the eighteen-year-old, who went by the code name "Pengo." The principles Holland recites are the original hacker precepts distilled by Steven Levy in his book *Hackers: Heroes of the Computer Revolution.*

In the interview, Holland tells Pengo and the audience that he is angry and disappointed and that hackers need to trust each other. "We as hackers should be guided by a hackers' ethic as it was described in the 1984 Hackers Convention," he says and proceeds to enumerate the Levy list:

Number 1: Access to computers, as with anything that can teach you how the world works, should be unlimited and total. Always cling to the hands-on imperative.

Number 2: All information should be free.

Number 3: Distrust authorities, and promote decentralization.

Number 4: Hackers should be judged only by their hacking, not by bogus criteria such as age, race, position, or degrees.

Number 5: You can create beauty and art on a computer.

Number 6: Computers can change your life—for the better!

Holland tells Pengo and the audience, "I'm not saying that the hackers' ethic is an iron law; hackers always break laws, even their own, but what Pengo did was ignoring them altogether."

In the interview, Pengo himself confesses that, looking to make a profit, his group contacted the KGB with the expectation that an intelligence service would be interested in hacker knowledge and that thrill-seeking had led them along:

Intelligence services have always been interested in computer knowledge. And we thought of ourselves as the most ingenious people in the world so we didn't bother too much to question for which people we were working in the end.

At first we penetrated computers and didn't see the social consequences of our actions. Fascination with technology led more or less to fascination with power. Breaking into computers was a more or less ethereal pleasure. Making contact with this KGB agent was total life, very real indeed. Suddenly I became the star in an espionage movie. Hacking was just playing with a toy, contacting the KGB agent was real social interaction. Everything was a swirl.

"Well, you crossed the threshold you shouldn't have crossed," Wau Holland tells him: "You started out playing a game that you were too young to play, and now you are part of a game that secret services play, you are their prisoner … and if you don't have your own strong ethical standards, you will remain their plaything."

"It's an old question," Holland tells the hacker audience: "Who profits? Every time I deal with information, I have responsibilities. I can kill people with information. We've been thinking about this in the Chaos Computer Club. You can, for example, break into the control computer of an atomic reactor and provoke a catastrophe."

"Isn't that somehow fascinating?" the incorrigible Pengo interjects, and Holland continues resolutely:

> Yes, it is. But fascination is dangerous because you might not see the existing limitations. The Chaos Computer Club is not just a bunch of techno freaks: we've been thinking about the social consequences of technology from the very beginning and I think our strength derives in part from our moral standards. Everybody must face the question "What am I doing?" … We Germans already have such a bad reputation that one really couldn't be careful enough.

Driving fast down the Autobahn, Andy tells me that Pengo's group of young hackers was manipulated by criminal elements "who thought it was an easy deal to deliver these kids up, with their abilities, to people who had a use for them." There's a lull in the conversation as I take in this information. "That local hacker group seems to have had a lousy set of morals," Andy adds over his shoulder without taking his eyes off the road.

Not long after the Paradiso interview—on May 23, 1989—a body was found in a forest near Hanover. It was Karl Koch, a hacker from Pengo's group.

"He was found burned in a forest with his shoes and car keys removed and in bondage," Andy says. "But I'm sure you don't want the gory details. Officials said it was suicide. The case was never investigated." He shrugs. "He got in between German Interior Department, American, and Russian interests."

"The second time a kid got killed," Andy continues, and I hunch forward from the back seat now to be sure to catch his words, "I thought it was my duty to find out what had happened. You know, crying parents, and with such an event happening you have people who get scared.

It's not sexy. They come to play with their tech and then start to run away."

The second kid was a young hacker who went by the handle Tron and specialized in smart cards and video encryption. In 1998, he came under the influence of piracy groups, a situation that ended badly. "The same methods used to secure encrypted TV are also used to secure military satellite communications," Andy explains. "He was too young to understand the impact of his technology.

"At one point, a friend told us, 'You guys have a choice. You can either fall within the definition of a criminal organization, or you can incorporate.' So we became a limited liability, registered association."[36]

THE FALL OF THE WALL

A few months after the KGB affair broke, in November 1989, the Berlin Wall came down.

Many East Berliners put aside their daily undertakings and, taking no chances, walked straight over to West Berlin, leaving whole neighborhoods empty in East Berlin. The flux went the other way, too. The artists came from West Berlin into East Berlin right away. So did people like Andy.

It was chaotic, and the infrastructure was crappy. Some neighborhoods, like Spandauer Vorstadt, were in such bad repair that they were pretty much completely deserted. Some 130 buildings in East Berlin were occupied by squatters, mostly young people who created their own unified Germany before formal reunification in 1990.[37] The slogan "Wir sind das Volk" (We are the people), which was chanted at the GDR protests, quickly became "Wir sind ein Volk" (We are one people).[38] The graffiti that had been restricted to the west side of the Berlin Wall spread like a virus into East Berlin. It is still one of the most ubiquitous features of the urban landscape there.

This new squatter movement in Germany was in synch with a hacker group like the Chaos Computer Club, which played with the idea of ownership in the sphere of digital tech and tested notions of private property, equal access, and shared use. The Dutch slang word *kraken*, coined to mean both hacking and squatting, pointedly fused the physical and the cybersphere claims to common goods.[39]

A newly constituted version of the Chaos Computer Club also fused East and West. "The Chaos Computer Club became two groups melded," Andy explains: "A group from East Germany and a few guys, including me, from the West German hacker scene. The East German guys had their own way of dealing with reality and intelligence. The great news about the whole situation was, when the Wall fell, we had the most complete disclosure for any security agency on earth. The Stasi was the best documented security agency in history, and we had access to all their manuals, like 'How to Bring Distrust into Groups' and 'How to Destroy Political Movements,' and we discussed all these things in the club. If you look at what happened to Julian [Assange], it's in the manuals. So in the CCC, we have a bit of immunity from totalitarian structures in our attitude."

A good friend of Andy's, Wolfgang Kaleck—the person who arranged my ride with Andy to the camp—also came to East Berlin at that time. A criminal lawyer straight out of law school, Kaleck arrived in East Berlin to set up a small progressive law firm. The young lawyers tried to bring Stasi members to court, but it was difficult because the worst abuses—including torture—had happened decades earlier.

THE 1990s: HACKERDOM EXPANDS, SILICON VALLEY TAKES OFF, AND A SCHISM DEVELOPS BETWEEN THE PHILOSOPHIES OF PROPRIETARY SOFTWARE AND FREE SOFTWARE

In the United States in the 1990s, the question of who controls code, posed by Richard Stallman in 1983 with his launch of the free software movement, evolved into a philosophical schism. It is a schism well known to tech insiders, and ordinary computer users need to understand it, too.

In 1991, not long after the tumultuous events of 1989, Tim Berners-Lee launched the World Wide Web. By 1995, Berners-Lee's invention had become widely embraced by the public, and the internet as most people know it was born.

The internet brought hacker groups across countries into closer connection. The different scenes became even more aware of the statements and manifestos of their counterparts, especially across the Atlantic. Hackers developed a more unified, self-conscious philosophy and a shared language. To be sure, there were diverse lineages and strains of hacking: the origin story of hacking is more complicated than Levy made it seem, and his articulation of a singular hacker ethic was not adopted by all groups.[40] But ideas began to diffuse internationally, and important international relationships were built. Levy's articulation of a hacker ethic, as mentioned earlier, was adopted verbatim by the Chaos Computer Club,[41] and its tenets and the tenets of free software spread widely throughout the scene coalescing around CCC events.[42] At the same time, social activist groups began using the internet to organize and communicate, and the global social justice movement was built. A new net culture emerged, along with the ideas of digital rights and net citizenship.

The hacker world was expanding everywhere in the 1990s, in tandem with the spread of personal computers. The decade saw a proliferation of hacker fanzines, conferences, hacker spaces, and hackathons.

But by the 1990s, hacking was a complex terrain. Richard Stallman's "free software" principles profoundly influenced how the internet and then the World Wide Web were built and left unenclosed for anyone to use. At the start of the decade, around the same time the World Wide Web was invented, Stallman won a MacArthur "genius" award in the United States.[43] Someone was paying attention. In 1992, hackers in California, John Gilmore (a founding member of the Homebrew Computer Club) among them, founded the Electronic Frontier Foundation, an early advocate for users' rights and for the defense of hackers when they tangled with the law.

At the same time, digital tech by the 1990s was well on its way to becoming a multi-billion-dollar industry. The halcyon hacking days of the Homebrew Computer Club had been short-lived. Started in 1975, the club reached its peak in 1977 with the West Coast Computer Faire, an event Steven Levy called the Woodstock of the burgeoning California hacker scene.[44] Hundreds of people were still coming to the club's meetings, and fifteen thousand subscribed to its newsletter, but the core members who had gone on to start companies stopped attending and began to focus on their bottom lines, recreating the club culture within their own staffs and keeping their ideas to themselves. Silicon Valley giants like Apple incorporated the hacker ethic into their identity and production processes, understanding that the obsession, mastery, and collective problem solving of hackers were keys to their success. A proliferating startup culture also celebrated the hacker identity. But by the 1990s, the California computer culture had become deeply invested in secret, proprietary software and hardware.

Meanwhile, Richard Stallman, stalwart in his hacker ideals, ploughed on. By the early 1990s, GNU developers had put together a whole integrated operating system of free software, except for the "kernel," which is the program at the center of the operating system that allocates the machine's resources. In another large collaborative process, Linus Torvalds, the Finn, was working to create a kernel that could serve a modular system.[45]

In 1992, the Linux kernel was freed through a free software license (Richard Stallman's GNU General Public License, version 2, otherwise known as the GPLv2) that guaranteed free software's "four essential freedoms" for users. The story of the kernel's development, its founding developer Linus Torvalds, and its mascot (the Linux Penguin) are all widely known to most computer users. GNU's story is less well known, and its mascot (a geeky gnu) is perhaps not as cute as the penguin. Like the incredible incubator of the Homebrew Computer Club, both of these projects showed what could be achieved with open, collaborative hacker efforts and have since become widely studied precedents of cooperative processes.

Richard Stallman has said, "By the time Linux was started, Gnu was almost finished." It was good timing because by the time the GNU network of contributors got to the final step of developing the GNU kernel, called "Hurd," it had encountered technical difficulties. In the spirit of free software, users started putting together the GNU system with the newly available Linux kernel, and Stallman called the complete system GNU/Linux.[46]

GNU/Linux took off with users and programmers due to its clear practical and technical advantages over proprietary systems. But much to Stallman's chagrin, most people began referring to the GNU/Linux system—the first complete free software operating system in existence— simply as "Linux." As Stallman is at pains to reiterate, only the kernel was Linux. To add further confusion, users persisted in thinking that *free software* meant "without charge." Proponents' efforts to keep explaining that *free software* meant "free as in free speech, not as in free beer" did not seem to make much of a dent in popular understanding.

Throughout much of the 1990s, the two cultures—one of "proprietary" code and the other of "free software" code—coexisted without much overlap. Although tech companies had embraced hacker culture in the service of product innovation, they were wedded to the idea that secret, proprietary software was the best way of making a profit, and the hacker ideal of "free software" was not an obvious value proposition to them.

Then in 1997, Eric Raymond's essay (later turned into a book) "The Cathedral and the Bazaar" was published. Raymond's thesis was that "given enough eyeballs, all bugs are shallow." He called this "Linus's law." He argued that the more widely a program's source code was made available for scrutiny and tinkering by users, the faster its flaws could be discovered and fixed, and the more robust the program would become. By contrast, in a "closed," proprietary model, where only a few company developers had access to the code, it would take an immense amount of time to look for bugs, and the program would be less optimized.

Put to them as a commercial proposition, companies came around to embrace the idea. "Open source" became an important mode of commercial production. Meanwhile, companies and government agencies were also discovering the quality and versatility of free software products. GNU/Linux became ubiquitous. The Linux kernel became famous for its reliability and stability. It was widely recognized for its capacity to work on any chip in the world and manage the demands of many software programs at once.[47] NASA replaced large parts of its proprietary software with versions of GNU/Linux.[48] The Linux kernel was used by Google for the heart of its "Android" operating system (which by 2016 would corner 85 percent of the market share for smartphones, vastly more than Apple's iOS operating system for the iPhone).[49] Eventually, GNU and the Linux kernel would run on most of the internet's servers, on most of the world's supercomputers, on the New York Stock Exchange, and on the platforms of Google, Facebook, and Amazon. The US government would use the Linux kernel. It could found running on medical equipment, on drones, on warships, and in the burgeoning Internet of Things.[50]

Richard Stallman considered "open-source software" a cooption of the free software movement's work and a rejection of its values. As a product, he has said, open-source software is usually equivalent to free software (there are some licenses, not widely encountered, that qualify as open source but not as free software because of restrictions they contain), but it is amoral.[51] It adopts free software's method of development but drops its philosophy. It is not motivated by a commitment to freedom and giving users full control over their computing.

Today, there are many "distributions" (curated collections of programs) that contain "free" and "open source" and "closed proprietary" software together, and companies have donated significant amounts of money to further the development of the free Linux kernel. But the fact that most distributions with free software components also contain software components that are not free deprives users (including government users) of full control over their computing. Another practice, known as "tivoization", which locks up free software inside unfree software so that it cannot be accessed and modified, deprives users of the benefits of the free software altogether.

Stallman has tried to get at this last practice with a new license, the GPLv3, which adds a prohibition on tivoization, in addition to guaranteeing users the "four freedoms," but adoption has been uneven. (The point of the GPLv2 is to make middlemen pass along the "four freedoms" to end users. GPLv3 extends this by banning them from tivoizing.) Linus Torvalds has rejected the GPLv3 license for the Linux kernel. And recently, Google has threatened to remove the free Linux kernel at the heart of its Android operating system. It might replace it with a new open source kernel called Fuchsia, but without GPLv2 or GPLv3 protection, so that manufacturers will be allowed to make the versions they ship totally proprietary.[52] If this happens, there will be no smartphone device on the market that users can modify and control as they wish.[53] (Currently, five out of six of the leading smartphones on the market are powered by Google's Android operating system.)[54] Some people in the free software movement are complaining that companies leach the expertise of hackers and fail to pay back to the community by following the free software philosophy.

So "open source" or "open code" is *not* the same as "free software" or "free code." It is ironic that a man who wanted code—computer language—to be in the control of users has had his advocacy efforts frustrated by the semantics of the English language. Unfortunately, the ideas behind free software are simply more complicated than a single word or name can fully denote. Stallman is constantly trying to untangle the confusion: Linux was *not* the complete operating system that started the free software movement; free software does *not* mean software given away at no cost; open-source software is *not* the same thing as free software.

Even by the 1990s, it was becoming apparent that the world was being built with code. The microchips that ushered in the personal computer revolution had led to ubiquitous computing. Computer systems were not just sitting on people's desks; they were in everything. For those who reflected seriously on it, Stallman was a visionary in a world in which code was coming to control everything. His implicit question, "Who gets to control code?" was hugely significant.

In that light, Stallman's promulgation in 1985 of his GNU manifesto was a seminal moment. It marked the beginning of a great schism between free code (in the user's control) and proprietary code (not in the user's control) that now looms over the digital age in the twenty-first century.

Hackers and a few academics like Harvard's Larry Lessig understood the significance of Stallman's GNU manifesto. In the hacker community, the idea of free software would become as important an organizing principle as "liberty, fraternity, and equality" was for early Enlightenment democrats. In fact, free software is arguably the digital age descendant of those principles, if twenty-first century democrats could only realize it.

We've left the Autobahn and have been driving past tidy farmhouses built in the old style but with brand new materials. Their red roofs are glossy, and the whitewash fresh. A field of giant wind turbines comes into view on the slope of a hill ahead, their massive propellers circling gracefully.

I feel the pressure of trying to cover the whole hacking landscape in whatever interviews I can get over the next few days at the camp. I'm not an academic researcher with the luxury of time and the constraints of a discipline to help me—I must focus on what is most salient to my concerns as a citizen. I've been reading about revolutions lately in research for this book, and I think about what the Russian revolutionary Leon Trotsky once said about the German Social Democratic leader Ferdinand August Bebel. Bebel, Trotsky said, "personified the slow and stubborn movement of a new class that was rising from below … a class that gets its learning during its spare hours, values every minute, and absorbs voraciously only what is strictly necessary."[55] I am comforted by the thought that this might be as valid an approach for attacking an urgent political subject as any more circumscribed, academic method.

I wonder out loud what the present state of hacking is in the United States and in Europe. Where are the true hackers now? Where do hacker scenes even exist?

Andy glances in the rear-view mirror and changes lanes to avoid some roadwork. "The Chaos Computer Club France was run by a snitch until we found out and intervened. La Quadrature du Net is an important group. The Spanish are getting stronger. There's a small hacker scene in Switzerland and Austria. Italy and Holland are important. In the UK, there's no political space, and no culture for it. Their Parliament just voted in the worst of the worst cyberlaws."

And in the US?

"It's all commercialized there now," Peter says. "Defcon is a corporate event. Europeans don't think much is going on in the US now that's important, either politically or technically. Especially at the Defcon and the Black Hat conferences. These are the same people. They will sell their wares to anyone who pays. They had General Keith Alexander give the keynote at the Defcon conference in 2014!"[56]

Andy says, "John Gilmore [founding member of the Homebrew Computer Club and the Electronic Frontier Foundation] has always been about taking care of society—although John got a little afraid around the WikiLeaks stuff and backed off, maybe because he was surrounded by a bunch of anxious lawyers. Then you have the 2600 crowd,[57] who have not talked to each other in twenty years, and they are heavily infiltrated. They think it's okay to tell each other funny tech stories and don't mind if someone is a spook."

So is the Chaos Computer Club a leader when it comes to progressive hacking?

Andy is quick to squelch the idea that the Chaos Computer Club is a leader: "You're using a term that we can't accept. We don't like leaders. Yes, we like progress and people making cooperation, but go away with 'leaders.' I like the idea, rather, that we provide spaces where things can happen. The motto is to 'Always act in a way where you widen the options to act.' And the CCC has managed to provide a space where young people can learn and discuss things. But to be blunt, I wish the young people were more political than they are. You shouldn't put us up as heroes."

"Yes," Peter says. "How are we going to save the world when we also have jobs from nine to five, just like everyone else?"

FIRST IMPRESSIONS: BE EXCELLENT TO EACH OTHER

We've been driving on back roads through the countryside for a while now, the houses getting sparser, until finally we go down a long road and pull into a large, dusty parking lot with masses of tents pitched beyond it as far as one can see. The rest of our conversation is cut short as we climb out of the car, stretch, and survey the camp.

This year the Chaos Computer Club's Chaos Communication Camp is being held at the site of a large nineteenth-century factory that once supplied Berlin with its terracotta roof tiles. As we approach the box office gate, Andy and Peter, smiling wryly, say I'll have to argue for myself to get in. "Use anything you think might help you," jokes Peter. I walk over to the plywood ticket booth, ready to say I've just arrived with Andy, but they seem to have a policy that anyone who arrives at the gate can buy a day pass at a premium price. So I'm in, with only my wallet compromised.

Andy has meetings to attend, and I wander off into the camp unchaperoned.

It is vast and it looks chaotic, but in fact it is wonderfully organized. An elaborate electrical grid has been laid down along the dusty ground over the whole area of the camp, which covers about twenty acres. The grid serves the "hacker spaces"—large white tents open at all hours and filled with desks and outlets for hackers to congregate around. It serves the giant circus tents that are the main speaking venues for the camp's extensive and varied event schedule, and it serves the sparkling food tents that glitter in copses of trees, each with its own whimsical decorations, from the Töller paintings of the handmade-latke restaurant to the cutlery and teacups dangling from tree branches surrounding the vegan kiosk.

The electrical grid serves the "national" tents, sporting flags of Norway, Italy, and France, and it serves the warren of squares and stages rigged up by superkeen engineers who have spared no effort in building out their environment. It powers the wacky experiments on display here and there—from a computerized crêpe-flipping machine to gizmos lining the pathways surrounded by beer-drinking comrades who laugh and cheer on the people struggling to make their inventions work. The grid lights the friendly bars that look like the festive bars at tropical resorts and, always nearby, the huge caravan tents with multiple peaks sheltering homey arrangements of living room furniture, usually matching, including large white Naugahyde sectionals, orange sofa-and-recliner sets, and tasteful brown ensembles. And it powers the consoles where hackers are creating techno music on the spot. (Andy has told us the camp uses forty-five tons of sofas and loveseats, which the club stores during the four years between events, giving some idea of the effort that goes into staging them.)

The thick electrical cables are covered at crossroads, where bikes and baby buggies pass over them. A trolley train runs over the old tile factory's internal railroad tracks, trundling smiling families, bathers with towels around their necks, and gaggles of drink-sipping campers to where they want to go. There is a delightful small lake, I discover, where, from the fresh early morning until the silken hour of dusk, people and dogs jump into the water from docks and rafts. There are large tent villages, and someone tells me, "No one tells you where to put your tent. You just have to work it out with your neighbors." A couple of main arteries, wider dusty roads, divide the camp into quadrants.

There is something sweetly ingenuous about hacker culture. Small signs are affixed to tents that say "Be excellent to each other," a motto from the Keanu Reeves time-travel movie of the early 1990s, *Bob and Ted's Excellent Adventure.* Camping has never been this comfortable or convivial. You can strike up a conversation with anyone. Hackers don't make judgments about who you might be based on signs of status, your age, or your looks; they wait to see what you might say or do. The outdoor bars serving beer and the hackers' energy drink of choice, Clubmate, are staffed by charming people. Everyone brings their bottles back, there is no trash problem, even the washrooms stay orderly. People are indeed excellent to each other.

Photographs are forbidden, but it's hard not to want to take them because the light displays are beautiful. The techno music is entrancing. The camaraderie so apparent. The camp radiates a collective intelligence. It is a hive of peaceful, collaborative activity, like a science fiction vision of what the future with technology could be. There are a few families with children. It is mostly men, but there are many women too.

As dusk falls, the big rocket ship (yes, there is a fifty-foot-high mock-up of a rocket ship) is glowing and pulsating light in the middle of a large field, and people are relaxing and dancing around it.

The whimsy of it all reminds me of an early note of Julian Assange's, written by him in around 2007 to recruit students to his WikiLeaks project. Assange had been one of those teenage hackers (described earlier) who gave hackers a bad name in the 1980s. He joined the hacker underground in Melbourne and, with a group that included two other young hackers, conducted that series of cyberattacks against US and EU targets which were reported in newspapers in Germany.[58] *His* was the teenage hacking group that likely contacted the Chaos Computer Club for help in the late 1980s. After Assange was criminally charged, it took five years for his case to be finally resolved, in 1996.[59] The judge let him off with a fine, and he had gone back to school, attending Melbourne University's Math and Statistics Department, where he served as the puzzle master for a traditional start-of-academic-term treasure hunt.

A year after leaving the university, he used the school listserv to write the following note:

> Dear Puzzle Hunters ...
> Are you interested in being involved with a courageous project to reform every political system on earth—and through that reform move the world to a more humane state? We have only 22 people trying to usher in the start of a world-wide movement. We don't have time to reply to most reporters' emails, let alone the interview requests—and I leave for Africa in under a week! We need help in every area, admining, coding, sys admining, legal research, analysis, writing, proofing, manning the phone, standing around looking pretty, even making tea.[60]

It was the start of a brave new adventure that would cast hackers as central characters in the struggle for democracy in the twenty-first century.[61]

2

THE HACKER CHALLENGE

Cypherpunks on the Electronic Frontier

THIRD-WAVE HACKERS: THE CYPHERPUNKS

The publication of hacked US classified information by Julian Assange's WikiLeaks in 2010 and by Edward Snowden in 2013 are two of the most momentous stories in the short history of hacking. No book on the disruptive effects of hacking in Western liberal democracies would be complete without describing them in some detail, and they lay the ground for the bracing hacking experiments and collective citizen exploits that are the focus of the second part of this book.

But before getting to WikiLeaks and Snowden, it is important to know the fascinating story of a third wave of hackers, the cypherpunks, and the ideas they tested in the cryptowars of the 1990s. As I suggest at the outset of this book, hacking is as much about a genealogy of ideas as it is about code, and the cypherpunks' influence on Julian Assange and the contemporary hacker scene is an important piece of the contemporary hacker narrative that is overlooked by most commentators. Insiders to the hacker world know the story well and may wish to skip over the next two chapters. But, then again, they might find a certain satisfaction in seeing it retold.

When WikiLeaks's "Collateral Murder" video of gunsight footage from Iraq exploded in the news in 2010,[1] veteran insider Bruce Sterling (author of *Hacker Crackdown: Law and Disorder on the Electronic Frontier*) made a trenchant announcement only insiders could fully appreciate: "At last—at long last—the home-made nitroglycerin in the old cypherpunks' blast shack has gone off."[2]

The term *cypherpunk* was first used in the early 1990s by a group of Silicon Valley insiders. Tim May was a software engineer who retired at the age of thirty-four from Intel. While employed there, he had played an instrumental role in fixing a small but potentially disastrous glitch in the famous Intel microchip (the invention that spurred the personal computer revolution) where 1s and 0s in the code would flip unpredictably. He was a big, bearded guy with a ponytail who wore cowboy hats and leather. John Gilmore had been "number five" employee at Sun Microsystems and done very well by it. He was tall, also bearded with a ponytail. Eric Hughes, originally from Utah, was a programmer and mathematician. He had a red goatee, shared May's taste for cowboy hats, and also had a ponytail.

These three early cypherpunks were libertarians. There is in America a strain of virulent libertarianism that is hard for many who are not American to get their heads around. It is a worldview that speaks of the "dirt people clamoring for more hand-outs" and of coming decades in which there will be "a massive burn-off of useless eaters." Those, in fact, are the words of Tim May.[3] He was a hard-liner. It would be easy to dismiss him as a marginal crank if this strain of thinking did not appear in so much of American politics these days.

In any case, prophets are often cranky. What Tim May foresaw back in the late 1980s and early 1990s was that rapidly advancing technology would allow the state to achieve near total social control over individuals. To May, the future would be grim unless individuals seized the technological means to outwit the state.

When May first retired from Intel in his thirties, he thought he would retreat to his redoubt on the wild Pacific Coast and write science fiction, but his intellectual pursuits led him to the work of David Chaum, an academic widely admired as the godfather of cryptography. May came across old copies of Chaum's articles, and they set his brain on fire. Chaum's 1981 paper "Untraceable Electronic Mail, Return Addresses, and Digital Pseudonyms" and his 1985 article "Security without Identification: Transaction Systems to Make Big Brother Obsolete" laid the foundations for anonymous communications research. His work went beyond mere encryption. It recognized that encrypting information was not enough if the sender or seeker of the information could be identified.

Chaum, who had done his graduate work at the University of California at Berkeley in the 1970s, predicted even before the invention of the internet that surveillance and data mining would pose a severe danger to civil liberties, and he laid out what he intended to be a comprehensive set of solutions for protecting personal information from abuse in the digital age. He proposed the idea of "card computers," which were credit-card-size devices that would allow users to delink their identities from financial and credentialing transactions and thereby limit the amount of information that businesses and governments could collect about them. He proposed "mix networks" that would turn every node in a communications network into a shuffler of messages that would obscure the identity of the sender. He proposed "blind signatures" to verify the authenticity of digital currency without revealing its spender.

Tim May, the anarcho-capitalist libertarian, recognized in Chaum's work the darker potentialities of a digital world in which no transaction could be traced. Tax evasion, markets in illicit substances, trade in state secrets, even the operation of assassination hiring halls: anything that could be done digitally could be done freely. Whole economies of personal liberty could flourish.

Like a desert prophet building his eschatological vision of the world on the prophecies of his predecessor Chaum, Tim May wrote his own "Crypto-Anarchist Manifesto" in 1988:

> The State will of course try to slow or halt the spread of this technology … [but] just as the technology of printing altered and reduced the power of medieval guilds and the social power structure, so too will cryptologic methods fundamentally alter the nature of corporations and of government interference in economic transactions.[4]

May and Chaum, in short, foresaw the future and envisioned the technical solutions that would be needed to make societies "free" in the coming internet age—cryptography, remailers, onion routing, cryptocurrencies, leaks, and, for May, the illegal parts of the "dark net." Their early grasp of what was about to unfold was impressive, and they broadly defined the technical challenges that hackers would come to grapple with. When the internet finally came into widespread use in the mid-1990s, May's email signature read, "Anonymous networks, digital pseudonyms, reputations, information markets, black markets, collapse of governments."[5]

Tim May met Eric Hughes at a party thrown by their mutual friend John Gilmore. Hughes had worked for David Chaum, and he and May became close collaborators.[6] In September 1992, Hughes hosted a daylong gathering at his newly purchased house in Oakland. About twenty mostly ponytailed coders and cryptographers sat on the floor of Hughes's unfurnished living room, and May read his "Crypto-Anarchist Manifesto" to general approval. The morning was spent going over basics, and in the afternoon, people settled in to play a series of cryptogames to illustrate how cryptocurrency, information markets, and mix networks could work.[7] Chaum's concept of "mix networks" would later become one of the most influential ideas in shaping the technology of anonymous communications.

Sitting on Hughes's floor, the participants divided into two groups, one pretending to be ambassadors, corporations, and rebels trying to communicate securely with each other and the other pretending to be spies.[8] They put messages into envelopes, sealed them, and then sealed those envelopes inside other envelopes. Each envelope was addressed to a "friendly" remailer, and the idea was that each remailer could only open the envelope addressed to him and pass the enclosed envelope to the next addressee. Recipients did not know the identities of other people between whom the envelope had passed and therefore did not know who the original sender was. The original sender became untraceable in the schmozzle of envelopes circulating in random patterns. Even with some spies posing as "friends," the identity of the original sender could not be ascertained because each remailer possessed limited information.

Eric Hughes's girlfriend, Jude Milhorn, a well-known tech writer for *Mondo 2000*, suggested they call themselves *cypherpunks*, a play on the word *cyberpunk*,[9] the name coined by science fiction writer William Gibson for a certain kind of scrappy fictional hacker fighting authority from the margins of society.

John Gilmore offered his company's offices to host the group's monthly meetings. He also agreed to host a mailing list, which became active almost immediately after the first meeting.[10]

The dominant political voice on the new mailing list was Tim May's. By the time the listserv reached its height, however, cypherpunks were of many political stripes. Many were anarcho-capitalist, cryptoanarchist libertarians like May, but others were traditional Republicans, liberals, and even Maoists and Wobblies (members of the labor union the Industrial Workers of the World).[11] What they shared was a passion to fight for freedom in cyberspace. In 1994, May created an online compendium of cypherpunkdom titled "Cyphernomicon" that can still be found on the internet. It is divided into a multitude of numbered parts, answering questions like "What's the 'Big Picture'?"; "How do I get on— and off—the Cypherpunk list?"; and "Who runs the Cypherpunks?"[12] In "The Cyphernomicon," May described the mailing list participants' commonalities this way:

> 3.4.1. "Is there a set of beliefs that most Cypherpunks support?"
> + There is nothing official (not much is), but there is an emergent, coherent set of beliefs which most list members seem to hold:
> * that the government should not be able to snoop into our affairs
> * that protection of conversations and exchanges is a basic right
> * that these rights may need to be secured through _technology_ rather than through law
> * that the power of technology often creates new political realities (hence the list mantra: "Cypherpunks write code")
> + Range of Beliefs
> * Many are libertarian, most support rights of privacy, some are more radical in apppoach [sic]

The cypherpunks came together just as the US government was beginning to impose tougher restrictions on the civilian use of cryptography. Ever since World War II, in which cryptography played a vital role—most famously in the case of the Enigma code, which gave Germany its edge over Western Allied operations and which the British finally broke—the US government had treated cryptography like any other military armament and banned its export to foreign countries by civilians. But with rising civilian interest in cryptography and a growing availability of computer power for civilians to play with, the government decided it had to ban domestic use of cryptography, too. Senator Joe Biden was the legislator who proposed the fix. In a 1991 omnibus crime bill, he added the following provision: "It is the sense of Congress that providers of electronic communications services and manufacturers of electronic communications service equipment shall ensure that communications systems permit the government to obtain the plain text contents of voice, data, and other communications when appropriately authorized by law."

This seemingly innocuous provision was the beginning of what became known in the 1990s as the cryptowars. Tim May sounded the alarm in October 1992 about the government's plan to build a back door into all civilian cryptographic communications.[13] Law enforcement agencies referred to the plan as a necessary update to their existing powers to tap telephones. But any forward-looking person who understood the nature of digital communications knew that surveillance of this kind would be much more intrusive than phone tapping: it would be as if the government had a back door to your whole house and, indeed, to your mind. The cypherpunks waded headlong into the controversy, and it began to occupy most of their time.[14]

In April 1993, the newly elected Clinton administration announced a plan to offer strong encryption to the public through an NSA-developed encryption program called "Skipjack," implemented through a micro-chip that had a "back door" for law enforcement. The administration was calling it the "Clipper Chip." It sounded so sporting—a sail around Chesapeake Bay with a salt spray of Kennedy nostalgia and national pride for American know-how thrown in. The presentation of the Clipper Chip presaged the way that really useful but highly insidious applications have been marketed to the public by government and Silicon Valley ever since.

Expecting something like this, Eric Hughes had fired off the cypherpunks' first salvo in the cryptowars only a month before the Clipper Chip announcement. It was a new manifesto for user liberty—"A Cypherpunk Manifesto." As a call to arms, it was more egalitarian than May's earlier "Crypto-Anarchist Manifesto." It spoke to the "common good," called for all users' self-determination, and laid out the cypherpunks' central claim that "We write code":

A Cypherpunk's Manifesto[15]

Privacy is necessary for an open society in the electronic age. ...

We cannot expect governments, corporations, or other large, faceless organizations to grant us privacy out of their beneficence. ...

We must defend our own privacy if we expect to have any. We must come together and create systems which allow anonymous transactions to take place. People have been defending their own privacy for centuries with whispers, darkness, envelopes, closed doors, secret handshakes, and couriers. The technologies of the past did not allow for strong privacy, but electronic technologies do.

We the Cypherpunks are dedicated to building anonymous systems. We are defending our privacy with cryptography, with anonymous mail forwarding systems, with digital signatures, and with electronic money.

Cypherpunks write code. We know that someone has to write software to defend privacy, and since we can't get privacy unless we all do, we're going to write it. We publish our code so that our fellow Cypherpunks may practice and play with it. Our code is free for all to use, worldwide. We don't much care if you don't approve of the software we write. We know that software can't be destroyed and that a widely dispersed system can't be shut down. …

For privacy to be widespread it must be part of a social contract. People must come and together deploy these systems for the common good. Privacy only extends so far as the cooperation of one's fellows in society. We the Cypherpunks seek your questions and your concerns and hope we may engage you so that we do not deceive ourselves. We will not, however, be moved out of our course because some may disagree with our goals.

The Cypherpunks are actively engaged in making the networks safer for privacy. Let us proceed together apace.

Onward.
Eric Hughes <hughes@soda.berkeley.edu>
9 March 1993

Wired magazine's second issue featured the cypherpunks in a cover story titled "Crypto Rebels."[16] Written by none other than Steven Levy (author of *Hackers: Heroes of the Computer Revolution*), the article's banner line read, "It's the FBIs, NSAs, and Equifaxes of the world versus a swelling movement of Cypherpunks, civil libertarians, and millionaire hackers. At stake: Whether privacy will exist in the twenty-first century."

Stories about the cypherpunks appeared in the *New York Times*, *Whole Earth Catalog*,[17] and *Village Voice*. "We write code" became the mantra of their mailing list.[18] They had strong links to the newly formed advocacy group Electronic Frontier Foundation and the older Computer Professionals for Social Responsibility. They were ready to tangle.

FELLOW TRAVELERS, RELUCTANT HEROES, AND THE CRYPTOWARS OF THE 1990S

To tell the full story of the cypherpunks and the cryptowars of the 1990s, a few more *dramatis personae* are needed—two fellow travelers of the group and one reluctant hero. The fellow travelers were John Young and John Perry Barlow. The reluctant hero was Phil Zimmermann.

Tim May had been immune to 1960s counterculture when he enrolled at the University of California at Santa Barbara. But for John Young, John Perry Barlow, and Phil Zimmermann (and cypherpunk founder John Gilmore, too, for that matter), the '60s had been a life-changing experience.

John Young had been part of the student strikes and building occupations at Columbia University in 1968 and then went on to form Urban Deadline, a group that aimed to apply the urgency of the 1968 protests to architecture, education, and politics in the city of New York. "Even Anarchism was too organized for us," Young said.[19] Young discovered the cypherpunk mailing list in 1994, when he was a fifty-seven-year-old activist/architect, and he was hooked.[20] He did not participate in listserv discussions but instead started posting as a kind of news service, an activity which eventually morphed into a separate online site, Cryptome. Cryptome was a gutsy, sometimes bewilderingly pugnacious early web platform for anonymously leaked materials. Young is radical. Since launching Cryptome, he has posted a list of 2,619 Central Intelligence Agency informants, images of secure government facilities, the internal policies of Microsoft and Cisco, a photograph of the home of Bill O'Reilly when he was Fox News's biggest star, an aerial photo of Dick Cheney's secret bunker, and the names of 116 officials working with the United Kingdom's Secret Intelligence Service (known as MI6) and their movements across the world.[21]

John Perry Barlow, another cypherpunk fellow traveler, was a cattle rancher in Wyoming. He didn't just wear cowboy clothes: he was a cowboy. Barlow was also a poet and was instrumental in popularizing cypherpunk concerns within the technology, government, and user communities and in founding the Electronic Frontier Foundation.

As a poet, Barlow had the sensibility and language to convey the excitement of a new frontier and the stakes it represented. For Barlow, the frontier was cyberspace, a "global social space" that people were building where governments had no sovereignty.[22] Barlow was the first tech commentator to use the term *cyberspace*, gleaned from William Gibson's science fiction novels.[23] With the help of Barlow's poetic elucidation, cyberspace became a concept widely adopted in the 1990s to discuss a whole range of ideas and phenomena related to digital tech. The term was picked up by almost everyone, including bureaucrats, law enforcement agents, lawyers, and members of the media.

Barlow grew up on and then ran a large family cattle ranch in Wyoming, a state so sparsely populated that, he would later say, anonymity did not exist there; all the inhabitants knew each other's names and business.[24] Barlow also was a high school friend of a member of the psychedelic rock band the Grateful Dead. The talent for poetry Barlow honed in the solitude of Wyoming he put to use for the band, writing many of their most famous lyrics. Traveling frequently to the San Francisco area to connect with Deadhead friends, Barlow met Silicon Valley people there, became fascinated with computers, and took up computer journalism,[25] becoming an influential voice in publications like *Wired* magazine and the *New York Times*.[26] He even ran once for election as a Republican state senator.[27]

Like May, Hughes, and Gilmore, Barlow was a libertarian. "In Wyoming, the place where I was raised," he once said, "they don't like authority, because they can't see a good reason for it."[28]

In 1990, Barlow and other attendees of the Hackers Conference, held annually in California since 1984, came under suspicion for a hack of Apple. Someone had copied the small piece of Apple's proprietary software that controlled the Macintosh screen display and had mailed it to rival companies across the United States. The code was not useful, competitively, to Apple's rivals. Whoever hacked it meant the caper to be a poke in Apple's eye more than anything else. By this time, Steve Jobs, Steve Wozniak, and many of Apple's early Homebrew Computer Club hacker employees had moved on from Apple and some bad blood had developed as the enterprise had grown into a large corporation. The corporate types at Apple called the Federal Bureau of Investigation (FBI).[29]

Barlow received a visit in Wyoming from a local FBI agent. Mitch Kapor, the coinventor of the Lotus spreadsheet program, received a visit in Boston. Barlow posted a critique of the investigation on The WELL (the Whole Earth 'Lectronic Link), an early computer bulletin board run by *The Whole Earth Catalog* folks in Berkeley. The investigation appeared to be part of a series of law enforcement operations at the time that was fueled by exaggerated fears and stereotypes of hackers. The irony was that the regular attendees of the Californian Hackers Conference were not the underground teenage hackers then in the news. Conference regulars tended to be successful tech entrepreneurs, computer engineers, and commentators like Kapor, Barlow, and the cypherpunk crowd. Kapor was concerned. As he was being driven to the local FBI station to be fingerprinted, he brooded about the dangers of leaving computer users' civil liberties to be defined by the technologically unsophisticated.[30] Reading Barlow's post on The WELL a little later, he decided to visit him in Wyoming. Their conversations in Pinedale, Wyoming, population 1,195,[31] were the beginning of the Electronic Frontier Foundation (EFF).[32]

Barlow wrote—what else?—a founding manifesto, or at least a long article, titled "Crime and Puzzlement" in which he canvassed the kinds of crackdowns the authorities had been making on hackers and crackers of various stripes, finishing with a manifesto-style announcement about his intention to form a political organization with Kapor:

> Events are boiling up at such a frothy pace that anything I say about current occurrences surely will not obtain by the time you read this. The road from here is certain to fork many times. ...
>
> But as of today (in early June of 1990), Mitch and I are legally constituting the Electronic Frontier Foundation, a two (or possibly three) man organization which will raise and disburse funds for education, lobbying, and litigation in the areas relating to digital speech and the extension of the Constitution into Cyberspace.
>
> ... Mitch has received an offer from Steve Wozniak to match whatever funds he dedicates to this effort. (As well as a fair amount of abuse from the more institutionalized precincts of the computer industry.)
>
> The Electronic Frontier Foundation will fund, conduct, and support legal efforts to demonstrate that the Secret Service has exercised prior restraint on publications, limited free speech, conducted improper seizure of equipment and data, used undue force, and generally conducted itself in a fashion which is arbitrary, oppressive, and unconstitutional.
>
> In addition, we will work with the Computer Professionals for Social Responsibility and other organizations to convey to both the public and the policy-makers metaphors which will illuminate the more general stake in liberating Cyberspace.[33]

As Bruce Sterling, author of the 1990s chronicle *The Hacker Crackdown: Law and Disorder on the Electronic Frontier*, observed, "The sudden declaration of a coherent, politicized counter-strike from the ranks of hackerdom electrified the community."[34] Barlow was insisting on extending freedom and democracy out into cyberspace.

John Gilmore stepped forward to help launch the EFF.[35] A second meeting in San Francisco garnered even more supporters among the tech and philanthropic elite.[36]

Barlow later would say, "When we started the Electronic Frontier Foundation we called it the Frontier Foundation and not the Freedom Foundation because we knew that it would always be on the frontier— that for the rest of our lives technology was continuously going to make a new frontier that we would have to figure out how to live on."[37]

As a legal, policy, defense, and advocacy group for hackers' and users' rights, the EFF bore many similarities to the Chaos Computer Club, created eight years earlier in 1982, and like the Chaos Computer Club, it had some impeccable counterculture credentials (and not just in John Perry Barlow's participation). The Grateful Dead itself—"perhaps the most successful and long-lasting of the numerous cultural emanations from the Haight-Ashbury district of San Francisco, in the glory days of Movement politics and lysergic transcendence"[38]—also kicked in to support the organization. The band had a lot of money from its many years of successful touring and was known for funding worthy community causes.[39] It also had a formidable social network, with a lot of Deadheads in both high and low places. Bruce Sterling described the band as "a force to be reckoned with"[40]: "The symbols, and the realities, of Californian freak power," he wrote, "surround the Grateful Dead like knotted macrame."[41]

In this respect, the EFF was a distinctly American, Silicon Valley kind of organization: it was much better connected than the Chaos Computer Club and more lawyered up. It achieved a lot in its early days mostly by networking.

Again, Bruce Sterling describes it best: "By mid-'91 Kapor was the best-known advocate of his cause and was known *personally* by almost every single human being in America with any direct influence on the question of civil liberties in cyberspace. Mitch had built bridges, crossed voids, changed paradigms, forged metaphors, made phone-calls and swapped business cards to such spectacular effect that it had become impossible for anyone to take any action in the 'hacker question' without wondering what Mitch might think—and say—and tell his friends."[42] EFF became, in a sense, the advocacy arm of the cypherpunks and perhaps a more reputable institutional repository of their ideas. After only a year, it had a national office in Cambridge, Massachusetts, a growing grassroots membership base, loads of media coverage, and the keen support of a press of civil rights attorneys ready to defend the Constitution in cyberspace. The organization had launched defensive and offensive lawsuits in the courts, it successfully lobbied for legislative changes, and its media campaigns (as reported by its own publication, the *EFFector*) had "affected the climate of opinion about computer networking and begun to reverse the slide into 'hacker hysteria' that was beginning to grip the nation."[43]

By the time the US government began cracking down hard on the export and use of cryptography by civilians in 1993, EFF was battle-ready to defend the principles and the people at stake.

And that included Phil Zimmermann.

Not exactly a fellow traveler but more of a reluctant adoptee of the cypherpunks, Phil Zimmermann's great accomplishment was to bring usable cryptography to the people. He would become the hero of the 1990s cryptowars whom EFF and the cypherpunks were determined to defend.

Around the time Tim May had been reading Chaum's articles on the beaches of California, Zimmermann had been reading them in Boulder, Colorado. They had both read a 1977 *Scientific American* article, too, about a revolutionary new kind of encryption developed by three MIT researchers. It was called "public key" encryption.[44] The weakness with traditional encryption schemes had always been that they used a single key. If Alice, let's say, sends Bob an encrypted text and the key to decrypt it, anyone who intercepts that key can break the encryption, no matter how sophisticated it is. The stark beauty of the mathematical invention called "public key encryption" was that it used two keys and that a message encrypted with one key could be unencrypted only by the other. Alice could publish her "public key" so that anyone who wanted to send her an encrypted message could do so and keep the "private key" to herself so that only she could decrypt the message. No one had to send keys anywhere or entrust them to anyone else.

At the time, Zimmermann was active in the antinuclear movement and other political causes. He had heard Daniel Ellsberg speak on civil disobedience in Colorado in the 1980s, and that had been an inspiration for him.[45]

Ellsberg was the young military analyst employed at the RAND Corporation who, during the Vietnam War, copied and leaked classified documents exposing the fact that the government "had systematically lied, not only to the public but also to Congress"[46] about how it was prosecuting the war and whether it was winnable. The documents were damning to three successive administrations—Kennedy's, Johnson's, and Nixon's. Charged under the Espionage Act, Ellsberg would have served time in jail had a number of major newspapers not rallied around him and simultaneously published the classified documents, which became known as "the Pentagon Papers." Ellsberg had initially given his seven thousand photocopied pages to the *New York Times*, which published the first excerpts on June 13, 1971. The newspaper was then enjoined from publishing more under a court order obtained by the Nixon administration.[47] Ellsberg went underground and, on the run from the FBI, managed to distribute the documents further to the *Washington Post*, seventeen other newspapers, and a senator from Alaska. On June 29, the senator entered 4,100 pages into the record of the Subcommittee on Public Buildings and Grounds. On June 30, the United States Supreme Court ruled that the *New York Times* was free to publish further excerpts. It was a thrilling story of civil disobedience that seemed to revive a nation that was despairing about war and doubting its values, and the affair helped to establish the principle of press freedom in the United States.[48]

When Zimmermann read about public key encryption, he recognized quickly that this was the kind of tool that could protect political dissidents in their fights against repressive regimes. But the MIT researchers who invented it were running their invention on a giant mainframe computer. There was no usable public key for ordinary people. So Zimmermann decided he would like to build one.

Phil Zimmermann was not a Silicon Valley whiz kid, Stanford academic, or millionaire tech insider. He was a modest guy with a wife and kids and a nine to five job running a small computer business in the hinterland of the United States. But he had a purpose and some fire in his belly. Sometimes, that is enough to get important things done.

His opportunity came when another small businessman, Charlie Merritt, called him about some new software he was selling. It was an early prototype of public key encryption that was small enough to fit onto a personal computer. Zimmermann jumped on it with pure hobbyist joy. He picked Merritt's brain clean. Merritt soon resigned himself to the fact that this partnership was not going to be a money maker. More salient to his waning interest were the visits that poker-faced National Security Agency agents were making to his offices, warning him about the provisions of the International Traffic in Arms Regulations (ITAR).[49] This was the legislation that made it illegal to export cryptographic tools outside of the United States or Canada. Zimmermann's goal was to ship the technology to freedom fighters in places like Burma, El Salvador, and Eastern Europe. Yes, ITAR prohibited export, but Zimmermann was not interested in making money; he planned to ship the technology for free. How could the US government possibly care about that? Merritt dropped out, and Zimmermann kept going, determined to make a public key encryption tool that any ordinary person could use easily. In 1987, he published his work in progress in the prestigious engineering journal *IEEE Computer*. He called his tool Pretty Good Privacy (PGP), after the fictional Pretty Good Grocery in Garrison Keillor's folksy radio program *A Prairie Home Companion*.[50] In June 1991, Zimmermann put out his 1.0 version through community computer bulletin boards.[51]

"Like thousands of dandelion seeds blowing in the wind," he later wrote, PGP spread. People were downloading it within hours. "It was overseas the day after the release. I've gotten mail from just about every country on Earth."[52] One message read, "Phil, I wish you to know: let it never be, but if dictatorship takes over Russia your PGP is widespread from Baltic to Far East now and will help democratic people if necessary. Thanks."[53]

As Tim May recorded in "The Cyphernomicon,"

```
7.5.1. PGP 2.0 arrived at an important time
- in September 1992, the very same week the Cypherpunks had
their first meeting, in Oakland, CA. (Arthur Abraham printed
up professional-looking diskette labels for the PGO [sic] 2.0
diskettes distributed. A general feeling that we were forming
at the "right time.")
- just 6 months before the Clipper announcement caused a
firestorm of interest in public key cryptography.
```

What was so special about PGP? Tim May:

```
7.5.2. PGP has been the catalyst for major shifts in opinion
- has educated tens of thousands of users in the nature of
strong crypto
- has led to other tools, including encrypted remailers,
experiments in digital money, etc.
7.3.2. …
- A practical, usable, understandable tool. Fairly easy to
use. In contrast, many other developments are more abstract
and do not lend themselves to use by hobbyists and amateurs.
This alone ensures PGP an honored place (and might be an
object lesson for developers of other tools).
```

Zimmermann was summoned before a grand jury not long before the government made its Clipper Chip announcement in April 1993. With the release of PGP 2.0, he had become the public face of resistance in the unfolding cryptowars, and the government was going to make an example of him. The cypherpunks held a war council: they talked about organizing boycotts, waging media campaigns, and putting warning stickers on devices that said "Big Brother Inside."[54] Graffiti appeared on at least one garage door in San Francisco saying, "Stop the Clipper—Fuck the NSA."[55] EFF mobilized lawyers to help defend Zimmermann.

Zimmermann ran into Tim May several times during this period and "pleaded with him to tone down his antigovernment rhetoric."[56] He thought the cypherpunks' approach was counterproductive to the cause. "I saw them as angry young men in leather jackets, without children and with too much testosterone," he would later say.[57] Still, Zimmermann did not shrink from the role fate had thrust upon him. With the advice of a local Colorado criminal lawyer, he went on a media offensive, taking every interview that came his way and using it as an opportunity to sway the ordinary, law-abiding public. "Every last article was sympathetic to me," he would later say, "Not ninety-nine percent. One hundred point zero percent."[58]

Zimmermann had EFF and American Civil Liberties Union (ACLU) lawyers, as well as the Colorado lawyer he started out with, to defend him. Everyone except his Colorado lawyer was telling him he would lose.[59]

Then the cypherpunks thought of a strategy. What if they could get a book about cryptography past the ITAR regulators? Could they export the instructions and the code in print form with government approval and then turn around and use it as Exhibit A in Zimmermann's defense? They ran a test program. They tried submitting Bruce Schneier's book *Applied Cryptography: Protocols, Algorithms, and Source Code in C* to the State Department for prior export approval, and they got it. The book had an appendix full of code for the NSA's declassified encryption standard. Feeling their oats, the cypherpunks submitted the floppy disc version. Export permission was denied.[60] But the exercise had not been futile.

A little later, Zimmermann met an editor from the MIT Press at a conference. The editor, Bob Prior, was interested in publishing the user's manual that had accompanied Zimmermann's 1.0 release of PGP. Zimmermann seized on the opportunity: Could he publish the whole thing? The source code as well as the manual? Incredibly, MIT Press said yes. The code ran to nearly eight hundred pages, and the press published the whole thing in a machine-readable font that could be easily fed into a computer. Titled *PGP: Source Code and Internals*, it was sent it off to the State Department's export approval office. When the MIT Press did not receive a reply, it took silence for a barn door left open and courageously shipped the book to European bookstores with all the other titles for that publishing season.[61]

Three years after the Justice Department began its investigation of Zimmermann, it dropped its case against him without explanation. The first battle in the cryptowars was won, although it was unclear whether it was the MIT Press, public opinion, or just growing corporate and banking reliance on cryptographic communications that had been the critical factor.

By the mid-1990s, public opinion was tacking strongly against the Clipper Chip scheme. Even Bill Gates spoke out against it,[62] which carried weight because Silicon Valley by that time was a main driver of the US economy. The chip's "back door key" algorithm had been successfully hacked in testing,[63] and the National Research Council had put out an expert report, *Cryptography's Role in Securing the Information Society* (1996), that was surprisingly strong in its criticism of government policy and recommended relaxed export controls on cryptography and greater information security in the private sector.[64]

In 1996, the government finally withdrew its plans. Clipper Chip sank into the deep.

In a flush of success similar to the one that led neoliberals to predict the end of history and triumph of capitalism at the fall of the Berlin

Wall, John Perry Barlow, the poet laureate of the cypherpunks, penned one more hacker manifesto infused with an appropriate sense of history. As he later explained, "I was at the World Economic Forum the closing night. And the president of the US had signed into law the Communications Decency Law that presumed to tell everyone that they would be punished for using certain words on the Internet. I wanted to make the point that the Internet would be free in the same way that the mind is not the body. And I felt the mind was about to supersede all of the sovereignties that had hence been laid against it."[65]

With the heady title "A Declaration of the Independence of Cyberspace" (1996), the document was calculated to shape the future by imagining it in unabashedly utopian terms.[66] I reproduce Barlow's famous manifesto here almost in full because it is crammed with prescient passages—about how freedom and democracy might be preserved and extended in the digital world—to which I'll return throughout this book (along with some criticism of it in chapter 10). These include Barlow's references to popular sovereignty and the consent of the governed, to the commonweal and a common wealth, and to the effects of transformative technology on the whole superstructure of a society. Other prescient passages contain ideas about the normative force of law in the face of the self-executing norms of code and a self-ordering collective; the borderless nature of networks and its consequences for political organization; the emergence of a digital world ethics or civics; the metaphor of freedom as virus and contagion; and the significance of peer-based collective production, "zero-cost" replication, the organic, chaotic characteristics of code, and the role of hackers and digital natives as self-appointed defenders of the early ideals of the US Constitution. For the moment, however, I recommend that it be read and absorbed as poetry:

> Governments of the Industrial World, you weary giants of flesh and steel, I come from Cyberspace, the new home of Mind. On behalf of the future, I ask you of the past to leave us alone. You are not welcome among us. You have no sovereignty where we gather.
>
>   We have no elected government, nor are we likely to have one, so I address you with no greater authority than that with which liberty itself always speaks. I declare the global social space we are building to be naturally independent of the tyrannies you seek to impose on us. You have no moral right to rule us nor do you possess any methods of enforcement we have true reason to fear.

Governments derive their just powers from the consent of the governed. You have neither solicited nor received ours. We did not invite you. You do not know us, nor do you know our world. Cyberspace does not lie within your borders. Do not think that you can build it, as though it were a public construction project. You cannot. It is an act of nature and it grows itself through our collective actions.

You have not engaged in our great and gathering conversation, nor did you create the wealth of our marketplaces. You do not know our culture, our ethics, or the unwritten codes that already provide our society more order than could be obtained by any of your impositions.

You claim there are problems among us that you need to solve. You use this claim as an excuse to invade our precincts. ... Where there are real conflicts, where there are wrongs, we will identify them and address them by our means. We are forming our own Social Contract. This governance will arise according to the conditions of our world, not yours. ...

Ours is a world that is both everywhere and nowhere, but it is not where bodies live.

... We believe that from ethics, enlightened self-interest, and the commonweal, our governance will emerge. Our identities may be distributed across many of your jurisdictions. The only law that all our constituent cultures would generally recognize is the Golden Rule. ...

In the United States, you have today created a law, the Telecommunications Reform Act, which repudiates your own Constitution and insults the dreams of Jefferson, Washington, Mill, Madison, DeToqueville, and Brandeis. These dreams must now be born anew in us.

... In China, Germany, France, Russia, Singapore, Italy and the United States, you are trying to ward off the virus of liberty by erecting guard posts at the frontiers of Cyberspace. These may keep out the contagion for a small time, but they will not work in a world that will soon be blanketed in bit-bearing media.

Your increasingly obsolete information industries would perpetuate themselves by proposing laws. ... These laws would declare ideas to be another industrial product, no more noble than pig iron. In our world, whatever the human mind may create can be reproduced and distributed infinitely at no cost. The global conveyance of thought no longer requires your factories to accomplish.

These increasingly hostile and colonial measures place us in the same position as those previous lovers of freedom and self-determination who had to reject the authorities of distant, uninformed powers. ...

We will create a civilization of the Mind in Cyberspace. May it be more humane and fair than the world your governments have made before.

Davos, Switzerland

February 8, 1996

Barlow sent it out to his friends.[67] Within a few years it could be found on over twenty thousand websites.[68] Big ideas, it seems, have been and always will be spread by pamphleteers.

THE SMART-ASS ANTIPODEAN

By the mid-1990s, over a thousand people were on the cypherpunk mailing list, a stroppy young Australian hacker among them.

Julian Assange was a committed believer in the free software movement of Richard Stallman. He contributed to the development of NetBSD, a free and open-source computer operating system developed out of Berkeley.[69] For several years, he ran a local internet service provider company called Suburbia Public Access Network. When the Church of Scientology, in the midst of suing some of its critics, tried to get information from Suburbia about one of its user's accounts, Assange stood up to them. "He had titanium balls," the user would later tell Andrew Greenberg, author of the excellent book on leakers *This Machine Kills Secrets: Julian Assange, the Cypherpunks, and Their Fight to Empower Whistleblowers.*[70] For a reformed teenage hacker delinquent, these were respectable commitments to take on in the digital rights community. But Assange's participation on the cypherpunk mailing list would turn out to be a more formative influence on his ideas and action.

Assange contributed to the mailing list from December 1995 to June 2002, throughout the year his criminal prosecution for teenage hacking was finally being settled, up to the year before he went back to school at Melbourne University.[71] As the Australian political review *The Monthly* observed, "It must have been more than a little gratifying for a self-educated antipodean computer hacker, who had not even completed high school, to converse on equal terms with [the Californian cypherpunks who] ... saw themselves as Silicon Valley Masters of the Universe."[72] Where Assange was far on the periphery of both the US empire and its tech elite, the cypherpunks were certainly insiders—millionaire entrepreneurs, math professors, and some of the top coders and inventors in the world.

As the cypherpunks wrote about the future and envisioned the technical solutions for freedom, the cocky young contributor from Australia was learning at their knee and building his own versions of their ideas.

In 1997, for example, he built a program called Rubber Hose, which encrypted the contents of a computer in multiple layers, like a suitcase with a false bottom. It was designed to make it impossible for anyone trying to extract the keys from the owner to know if they had got them all. In 1998, before he left Australia to travel the world for two years, Assange asked if anyone could provide him with a complete archive of the mailing list to that date.[73] In 1999, he registered a domain name, leaks.org.[74]

Assange took on the California cypherpunks ideologically. Like them, he was staunchly antistate, but he was to the left of their libertarianism. On the mailing list, he gave spirited defenses of altruism, unions, toleration, and others' critiques of laissez-faire capitalism. His first post on the list began, "I am annoyed. ..."[75]

Increasingly, he took on the big guy himself. "Quoting Jews again, Tim?" Assange mocked, on catching Tim May quoting the son of laissez-faire economist Milton Friedman when May had previously made anti-Semitic comments.[76] Both Assange and May advocated user privacy, yet May believed that only elites who had the skill to control technology should prosper:

> 6.7.3. Crypto anarchy means prosperity for those who can grab it, those competent enough to have something of value to offer for sale; the clueless 95% will suffer, but that is only just. With crypto anarchy we can painlessly, without initiation of aggression, dispose of the nonproductive, the halt and the lame. (Charity is always possible, but I suspect even the liberal do-gooders will throw up their hands at the prospect of a nation of mostly unskilled and essentially illiterate and innumerate workers being unable to get meaningful [sic], well-paying jobs.)[77]

Assange answered May in one of his own final discussion posts to the mailing list in March 2002: "The 95% of the population which comprise the flock have never been my target and neither should they be [cypherpunks']; it's the 2.5% at either end of the normal that I find in my sights, one to be cherished and the other to be destroyed."[78]

3

A MANIFESTO FOR THE TWENTY-FIRST CENTURY

Privacy for the Weak, Transparency for the Powerful

CODE IS LAW, AND THE ONION ROUTER PROVES IT

While the cypherpunks were sparring throughout the 1990s in the rough discourse of their mailing list, in the more decorous environs of Yale and Harvard universities, law professor Larry Lessig was tuning in. His contribution to the development of hacker ideas is another antecedent that needs to be described before coming to the WikiLeaks and Snowden stories. Again, insiders know it well, but for ordinary computer users, Lessig's core idea might read like a blinding insight.

"Code," Lessig wrote, "is law."

Let me unpack that because it is a central premise of this book.

A guy who knew how to code (as a law clerk for the US Supreme Court, he improved their clunky printer system by hacking around its software), Lessig was skeptical of the net euphoria that was seizing the popular imagination in the 1990s. Utopian statements—like John Gilmore's widely accepted claim that "the Internet sees censorship as damage and routes around it"—were mildly irritating to him.[1] He thought this was wishful thinking. Code, he was coming to believe, could implement censorship and surveillance as well as forestall them: there was no magic place called cyberspace, only the cyberspace that people built.

In 1999, Lessig published *Code and Other Laws of Cyberspace*,[2] an important academic book that was in many ways a remix and development of the ideas of Richard Stallman and the cypherpunks. Recall that Richard Stallman advocated that code should be transparent and in the control of users (in the ways articulated by the "four freedoms"). And in "The Cyphernomicon" of 1994, Tim May said cypherpunks believed

```
* that … [individual] rights may need to be secured through_
technology_rather than through law
* that the power of technology often creates new political
realities.
```

In *Code and Other Laws of Cyberspace* and the article "Code Is Law,"[3] Lessig argued that computer code is the de facto regulator of cyberspace. Code, he said, "sets the terms on which life in cyberspace is experienced." Code determines how easy it is to protect privacy, to censor speech, or to access information: "In a host of ways that one cannot begin to see unless one begins to understand the nature of this code, the code of cyberspace regulates."[4]

But whereas May, the libertarian, had "very little faith in democracy,"[5] Lessig, the constitutional lawyer, was clearly a democrat[6] and concerned about preserving democratic values. Lessig warned that

> as this code changes, the character of cyberspace will change as well. Cyberspace will change from a place that protects anonymity, free speech, and individual control, to a place that makes anonymity harder, speech less free, and individual control the province of individual experts only. … Unless we understand how cyberspace can embed, or displace, values from our constitutional tradition, we will lose control over those values. The law in cyberspace—code—will displace them.[7]

As I understand it, Lessig's statement that "Code is law" means much more than "Code is like legislation." The words of statutes and constitutions are not sufficient in themselves to protect society's values. "Code is law" essentially means that code can supply *the* force of law. It can supply defined rights and duties (in the way that legislation does, say, in setting out what personal information can be accessed by whom and when and for what reason); it can supply the social norms that shape everyone's expectations of how to behave or what to demand from the market or from government; and it can supply the physical coercion to enforce rights and duties in case anyone does not want to comply (that is, the code is self-executing, and a digital tool that is widely adopted by users is difficult for governments and the corporate sector to shut down). Traditional legislation and constitutions are not irrelevant to the circumstances in which "code becomes law," but they play a secondary or supportive role.

To summarize, one might say that Lessig foresaw that code *more than law* would determine what kind of societies we live in and whether they end up resembling democracies at all. The rapid, widespread adoption of cryptography for civilian use that took place during the cryptowars—overcoming legislation that would prevent it—was one manifestation of the premise.

While Lessig was disseminating the idea that "Code is law" in academic circles, coders were busy working on another tool that would demonstrate it—the Onion Router, or Tor. When Alice sends Bob a message encrypted with public key encryption, the content is encrypted, and the keys are kept safe, but the fact that Alice is sending Bob a message, its timing, and information about Alice and Bob's respective locations are not safe. Metadata can expose and endanger Alice and Bob even more than the substance of what they are sending to each other. The Onion Router, or Tor, conceived of by Naval Research Laboratory researcher Paul Syverson and coded by two young MIT hacker types, was funded in 2001 through a three-year grant from the US Navy and the Defense Advanced Research Projects Agency (DARPA). It built out Chaum's idea of mix networks to solve the security problem of metadata in the real world and prove "Code is law" as it steadily became one of the most widely used "hacker" tools after Phil Zimmermann's PGP. It set the norms for law enforcement's ability to access information about users' communications before legislators had a chance to.

Roger Dingledine and Nick Mathewson had lived together as students in MIT's Senior House, a hacker microculture that in its day embraced the motto "Sport death" and a credo of anarchism, drugs, leather jackets, and polyamorous sex.[8] Like Julian Assange, Dingledine and Mathewson had "grown up" reading the cypherpunk mailing list and subscribed to the maxim "Cypherpunks write code."

Tor combined the idea of public key encryption with mix networks. The goal of Tor was to hide the metadata of messages—the identity and location of their senders and receivers, their routing, and their timing—by sending messages in random routes through the nodes of the internet. A message was sent into the Tor network with the metadata of its routing encrypted in multiple layers, like the sealed envelopes in Eric Hughes's parlor game or the multiple layers of an onion.

Rather than a crowd of people exchanging envelopes, however, Tor was more like sending a message down a rabbit hole. The sender sent the message down into the hole, and its content was wrapped in layers of encrypted addresses chosen randomly. These were addresses of people who volunteered to make their routers "nodes" in the Tor network. Each receiving node, or remailer, had only the key necessary to decrypt the next address. And when the remailer sent the message on, it would wipe out the metadata of the previous sender, as if wiping out the rabbit's tracks. No remailers knew where they were in the chain of remailers. Finally, the message would pop up from the last random remailer—say, a rabbit hole in Serbia—and be sent on to its final destination.

Spies watching the transaction could see the message enter the warren of tunnels but would not know where in the world the "exit" rabbit hole would be. If they were watching only a few entrance holes and the one exit hole, they might be able to deduce the origin of a message by the timing of its exit. But if messages were held for random periods of time to obscure timing and the number of paths and possible exit holes was large, it would be much, much harder to deduce the origin of messages. A spy watching the rabbit hole in Serbia would see messages exiting but would not know where they originated from. And the beauty of Tor was that what could be done to obscure the origin of messages could also be done to obscure the origin of browser requests, leaks, and the location of hidden services.

WIKILEAKS

Julian Assange took two ideas from his apprenticeship on the cypherpunk mailing list—John Young's Cryptome and Chaum's mix networks— and put them together with the progress made to that time on Tor to develop his own leaking system, WikiLeaks. It provided a spectacular demonstration of Larry Lessig's thesis that "Code is law."

In two blog essays he wrote not long before the launch of WikiLeaks, Assange explained his theory of leaking—his own contribution to the genealogy of hacker ideas. Leaking, he posited, was emancipatory not only because it exposed secrets to public scrutiny and resistance but also because it strangled the communication between the powerful that was necessary to effect their plans.

Assange started his first essay[9] with a quote from Theodore Roosevelt, the American president known for his "trust busting" in the early years of the twentieth century: "Behind the ostensible government sits enthroned an invisible government owing no allegiance and acknowledging no responsibility to the people. To destroy this invisible government, to befoul this unholy alliance between corrupt business and corrupt politics is the first task of statesmanship."

The thrust of Assange's theory was that in the current age, political elites and big business were again collaborating to deceive and dominate populations: "Schemes are concealed by successful authoritarian powers until resistance is futile or outweighed by the efficiencies of naked power. This collaborative secrecy, working to the detriment of a population, is enough to define their behavior as conspiratorial."[10] Earlier revolutionaries resisted authoritarian conspiracies by trying to cut the links between the most important players with assassination and other kinds of violence. But in the current age, Assange reasoned, the most effective disruptive strategy was to attack the cognitive ability of the conspiracy:

> A man in chains knows he should have acted sooner for his ability to influence the actions of the state is near its end. To deal with powerful conspiratorial actions we must think ahead and attack the process that leads to them since the actions themselves cannot be dealt with. We can deceive or blind a conspiracy by distorting or restricting the information available to it. We can reduce total conspiratorial power via unstructured attacks on links or through throttling and separating. A conspiracy sufficiently engaged in this manner is no longer able to comprehend its environment and plan robust action.[11]

Foreshadowing events that would take place in the preliminaries to the 2016 American presidential election, he continued: "For example, ... let us consider two closely balanced and broadly conspiratorial power groupings, the US Democratic and Republican parties":

> Consider what would happen if one of these parties gave up their mobile phones, fax and email correspondence—let alone the computer systems which manage their subscribers, donors, budgets, polling, call centres and direct mail campaigns?
>
> They would immediately fall into an organizational stupor and lose to the other. ...

An authoritarian conspiracy that cannot think is powerless to preserve itself against the opponents it induces. ... It falls, stupefied; unable to sufficiently comprehend and control the forces in its environment.[12]

Now Assange was in need of a service provider with titanium balls. He invited John Young, the cypherpunk fellow traveler and fearless owner of the early leaking platform Cryptome, to participate in the new project: "You knew me under another name from cypherpunk days. I am involved in a project that you may have a feeling for. I will not mention its name yet in case you feel you are not able to be involved. The project is a mass document leaking project that requires someone with backbone to hold the .org domain registration. We would like that person to be someone who is not privy to the location of the master servers which are otherwise obscured by technical means. ... Will you be that person?"[13]

Assange invited Daniel Ellsberg, the famous leaker of the Pentagon Papers, to be a member of the advisory board: "We have come to the conclusion that fomenting a world-wide movement of mass leaking is the most cost effective political intervention available to us. New technology and cryptographic ideas permit us to not only encourage document leaking, but to facilitate it directly on a mass scale." Never one to shy away from thinking on a grand scale, Assange added, "We intend to place a new star in the political firmament of man." Ellsberg wrote back, demurring: "Your concept is terrific and I wish you the best of luck with it."[14]

In its early days, WikiLeaks seemed to be pulling information flows from Tor exit nodes that were relaying sensitive documents stolen by Chinese hackers or spies. These included internal documents from foreign ministries, the United Nations, the US Council on Foreign Relations, the World Bank, and trade groups. The flood of information was so great that after one terabyte had been gathered, WikiLeaks stopped trying to store it.[15]

A giddy Assange wrote to John Young, "We're going to fuck them all ... crack the world open. ... and let it flower into something new."[16] But within weeks of joining the launch efforts, John Young fell out with Assange over Assange's proposal to approach the foundation of hedge fund owner George Soros for $5 million of funding. Following an expletive-laden exchange of email, Young leaked WikiLeaks's entire secret planning correspondence on his own site, Cryptome.[17]

Assange launched his WikiLeaks website in 2006 despite John Young's defection and a lack of uptake by his former Puzzle Hunt classmates at Melbourne University. Roaming between Africa, Iceland, and Europe over the next few years with a few helpers in each place, the project—staffed much of the time by only two full-time people, Assange and a serious young German engineer and Chaos Computer Club member, Daniel Domscheit-Berg—sometimes looked like it was held together with binder twine. Domscheit-Berg had volunteered for the adventure enthusiastically over internet relay chat (IRC), but he harbored hopes that WikiLeaks would one day be a respectable organization with offices and a stable budget. There was friction between the two partners from the start, and eventually it turned into outright contempt and rupture.

By late 2009, they had leaked a dizzying array of documents, including the emails of Sarah Palin; internet censorship lists from Australia; the "Climategate" emails; US intelligence reports on the battle of Fallujah; the Guantanamo Bay operational manuals; the loans book of the Icelandic bank Kaupthing; and documents that revealed tax avoidance by the Swiss bank Julius Baer, corruption in Kenya, an oil spill in Peru, and other scandals.[18] Their system had flaws, but no whistleblower's identity had been blown, no opponent had succeeded in suing WikiLeaks, and the group had won awards from *The Economist* in 2008 and from Amnesty International in 2009.[19] Nevertheless, Assange was disappointed with the impact they were making; the response by the media and the public was, he felt, middling to indifferent.[20]

When a disaffected young US lieutenant stationed in Iraq named Bradley Manning got in touch with WikiLeaks in 2010, Assange had the big leak that would send him simultaneously into the history books and the seven circles of hell.

As they planned the disclosure of 720,000 documents[21]—the largest cache of classified documents ever leaked from the US State Department and Defense Department—Bradley Manning (who was born male, and later underwent sex change therapy and changed her name to Chelsea Manning) and Assange met only by email.

A Hollywood movie and several indie films have been made about Assange, Manning, and Domscheit-Berg. In *We Steal Secrets*, Manning is typing a message to Assange on a black screen. The letters appear in bursts on the screen, forming words as Manning formulates her thoughts in this most intimate of mediums: "Hillary Clinton … diplomats around the world … are going to have a heart attack when they wake up one morning … and find an entire repository of classified foreign policy is … available to the public … it affects everybody … on earth. It's open diplomacy, world-wide anarchy … *it's beautiful, and horrifying.*"[22]

A NEW KIND OF CYPHERPUNK

The first decade of the new century saw a heightening of political awareness in hacking circles, and much of the energy was coming from the periphery of the American sphere—from the international rag-tag team of WikiLeaks led by Assange, the feisty Australian, and from Europeans, especially those linked to the Chaos Computer Club scene. The cypherpunk mailing list had been instrumental in galvanizing many of these hackers and bringing them together. During its time of operation in the 1990s and early 2000s, when Assange was participating on the list, French, Finnish, Dutch, and German hackers (Andy Müller-Maguhn of the Chaos Computer Club and Jérémie Zimmermann of La Quadrature du Net among them) were also participating on it. The list helped hackers, more than ever, to forge links across continents. And the personal and working relationships that resulted consolidated a new international community of politically progressive hackers. This new wave of hackers redefined what it meant to be a cypherpunk. They came together to play a number of interrelated roles in the WikiLeaks and Snowden stories, adjusting the mantle of the cypherpunks to fit their own shoulders.

During the 1990s and early 2000s, the Chaos Computer Club was very active. It was engaged in performance politics, much as Kommune 1 had been in the radical 1960s and 1970s, which it creatively blended with the kind of advocacy and litigation the Electronic Frontier Foundation was doing in the United States. This was not a stretch for German hackers: the CCC had been championing privacy, transparency, and user self-determination from its start. Moving on from its "hack of the Bildschirmtext" stunt and agitation against the national census in the 1980s, the club made itself known in the 1990s and 2000s for demonstrations of security risks in a range of software, including the software in SIM cards and computerized voting machines. It said the latter were so flawed they could be reprogrammed to play chess, and then it went ahead on a dare and made them play chess. The club also showed how votes could be manipulated on the machines, which led German courts to find that the machines were unconstitutional and the Dutch government to ban their use.[23]

In terms of style, the Chaos Computer Club was both less earnest and less dire than the American cypherpunks: the club's antiauthoritarian antics often contained a healthy dose of irreverent wit. To protest the government's use of biometrics in German passports and other identification documents, for example, they got their hands on the fingerprints of the German minister of the interior, Wolfgang Schäuble, and published them in a magazine, printed on plastic film that readers could use to impersonate Schäuble when going through ID checkpoints.[24] To celebrate CCC's twentieth birthday and commemorate its founder, Wau Holland, who had recently died, the group built a light installation, dubbed Project Blinkenlights, that turned a building in East Berlin into a giant interactive computer screen.[25]

Andy Müller-Maguhn was in the thick of the club's activities. In addition to being a Chaos Computer Club board member and spokesperson, in 2002 he cofounded European Digital Rights (EDRi), a European-wide version of EFF. He was elected by European internet users to be the European director of the Internet Corporation for Assigned Names and Numbers (ICANN). He did online journalism on the surveillance industry through the wiki buggedplanet.info; he started a company, CryptoPhone, that invented one of the first commercially available cryptographic voice phones; and he ran a consultancy business that specialized in network architecture.[26]

Julian Assange presented his WikiLeaks project at the Chaos Communication Camp in 2007. On our ride to the 2015 camp, Andy told me that he met Assange for the first time at that camp. "I thought at the time Julian might run into more trouble than he anticipated with that project," he added laconically as we sped through the German countryside.

The Chaos Computer Club provided Assange with important assistance when the Manning leak came and as subsequent events unfolded. Among the information Manning gave WikiLeaks was a video of an American military helicopter crew shooting down Iraqi civilians in cold blood. In the video, as crew members kill people below, they patter as if they are playing game, making it particularly disturbing to watch. Shrewdly, Assange decided that this was the leak to edit and package for the press. He and his team worked with supporters in Iceland to prepare it.[27] They called it the "Collateral Murder" video. A long-time veteran of the Chaos Computer Club, Dutch hacker Rop Gonggrijp,[28] went to Iceland to lend a hand. He and Assange then flew to Washington together, where Assange presented the video at the Press Club on April 5, 2010.[29]

The "Collateral Murder" video made WikiLeaks famous. Assange's idea that the group should be "the people's intelligence agency"[30] leapt into being, first with the incendiary video, illustrating the recklessness and lies of America's disastrous war in Iraq, and then with thousands of State Department cables that showed the American regime as cynical imperialists.

Domscheit-Berg finally walked away from WikiLeaks in late 2010, having completely broken with Julian Assange. He took with him its already published submissions, its recently improved submissions platform, and, allegedly, a slew of unpublished leaks.[31] Andy Müller-Maguhn mediated between Assange and Domscheit-Berg to arrange the return of the data and platform.

After being put off for nearly a year with unconvincing excuses, Andy got the published stuff back, and WikiLeaks mirrored it on other servers so that it would never again be vulnerable to being taken down from the internet.[32] But Andy felt he was getting the run-around on the other items and began to doubt Domscheit-Berg's integrity.[33]

At the 2011 Chaos Communication Camp, Domscheit-Berg launched a new leaking platform of his own, OpenLeaks. Although he refused to release the platform's code[34] (anathema to free-software-movement hackers), he asked camp attendees to bolster its credibility by testing its security. Speaking of Domscheit-Berg's presentation, Andy told an interviewer from *Der Spiegel* it was shameless: "We won't allow ourselves to be co-opted like this."[35] On the third day of the camp, Andy hand-delivered a letter to Domscheit-Berg at a party at around 3 a.m., expelling him from the Chaos Computer Club for exploiting the club's reputation.[36] His decision to exile Domscheit-Berg from hacker ranks was later reversed by the club, but Domscheit-Berg became a pariah in hacker circles: by then, many hackers suspected him of being a government informant, and his OpenLeaks platform of being controlled by intelligence agencies.[37]

By this time, the Chaos Computer Club was running the Wau Holland Foundation, which included collecting money for WikiLeaks among its activities. When PayPal and other financial institutions boycotted WikiLeaks, the foundation had its PayPal account cut off and lost its charitable status, although both were later reinstated.[38]

By January 2012, more roadblocks materialized to hinder the WikiLeaks cause. That month, Julian Assange was detained and jailed in the United Kingdom. He was held at Wandsworth Prison for seven days in the cell in which Oscar Wilde had been detained.[39] He was jailed not for his hacking activities but, like Wilde, for alleged sex crimes. Two women in Sweden had accused him of sexually assaulting them in the context of initially consensual relations, one when she was asleep and the other when he refused to use a condom.[40] These were troubling accusations that Assange and some of his supporters tried to brush off, but they ultimately clung to him like a moral rot, spreading with each minimization he made of them and each sexist, offensive thing he said. (Jake Appelbaum, another widely known personality in the hacker and digital rights community, associated with both Tor and WikiLeaks, also was accused of serious sexual misconduct and abuse of people around him, underlining the dismal fact that abuse of power is an issue in the so-called progressive milieu as much as it is in any other.)

Released on bail and facing extradition to Sweden, Assange was put under house arrest at the Norfolk estate of a wealthy friend.[41] Members of the WikiLeaks team stayed there with him. But in many ways, the group was imploding. Some supporters were angry at Assange for what they felt was his reckless release of the first tranche of material Manning had leaked from the Afghan War without redacting the names of people who could be put at risk.[42] Others were disturbed by his increasingly dictatorial style and outbursts.[43] But some were just freaked out by what WikiLeaks had taken on—the American empire and many other regimes that had the means to strike back against the group. The political virtue Assange said he valued most was courage. "Courage is contagious," he liked to say.[44] But Rop Gonggrijp told his colleagues at the Chaos Computer Club, "I guess I could make up all sorts of stories about how I disagreed with people or decisions, but the truth is that [during] the period that I helped out, the possible ramifications of WikiLeaks scared the bejezuz out of me. Courage is contagious, my ass."[45]

Still, Andy Müller-Maguhn visited Assange several times while he was under house arrest in England.[46] During this period, Müller-Maguhn, Assange, Appelbaum, and Jérémie Zimmermann, well-known representatives by this time of the new wave of politically progressive hackers, consciously redefined the cypherpunk mantle. In a conversation recorded for an RT television program and later published by them as a book with the title *Cypherpunks: Freedom and the Future of the Internet*,[47] the four hackers identified themselves as cypherpunks, acknowledging the influence the cypherpunk mailing list had had on their respective careers as activists. On the frontispiece of the book, there is a question ("What is a cypherpunk?"), and in the definition that follows, the hackers shed the earlier libertarian and extreme-right strains of the cypherpunk identity. "Cypherpunks," they state, "advocate for the use of cryptography and similar methods as ways to achieve societal and political change. Founded in the early 1990s, the movement has been most active during the 1990s Cryptowars and the following 2011 internet spring." In the book's introduction, the authors make their agenda plain: "Our task is to secure self-determination where we can, to hold back the coming dystopia where we cannot, and if all else fails, to accelerate its self-destruction."[48]

"It wasn't ... [the cypherpunks' view] that one should simply complain about the burgeoning surveillance state and so on, but that we can, in fact must, build the tools of a new democracy," Assange says at one point in the conversation recorded in the book: "We can actually build them with our minds, distribute them to other people and engage in collective defense. Technology and science are not neutral. There are particular forms of technology that can give us these fundamental rights and freedoms that many people have aspired to for so long."[49]

"Going far, far back to the old Cypherpunk mailing list with Tim May," Appelbaum reflects, "and reading Julian's old posts on the ... list, that's what started a whole generation of people to really become more radical-ized, because people realized that they weren't atomized anymore, that they could take some time to write some software which could empower millions of people."[50]

SNOWDEN

Even as these reinvented cypherpunks looked to the future to imagine what hacking could do for "a new democracy," the second most momentous story in the short history of hacking was unfolding. Unknown to them and the wider hacker community, a young contractor working in Hawaii for the US National Security Agency was methodically gathering, organizing, and writing explanatory notes for an estimated 1.7 million classified documents[51] on the agency's activities.[52]

In 2013 Edward Snowden revealed to the world that the United States was close to achieving an omniscient power of surveillance. In a Hong Kong hotel room littered with clothes and room service trays, where he had been hiding out for weeks, Snowden told American journalists Glenn Greenwald and Laura Poitras that the United States was "building a system whose goal [was] the elimination of all privacy, globally. To make it so that no one [could] communicate electronically without the NSA being able to collect, store and analyze the communication."[53]

The documents leaked by Snowden that Greenwald and others wrote about in June 2013 and over the following months proved his claims were not hyperbolic. Even the most informed tech activists were shaken. They revealed that the Foreign Intelligence Surveillance Act (FISA) court ordered the American telecom giant Verizon to turn over to the NSA, in bulk, millions of telephone records belonging to American customers. They revealed that the NSA had direct access to the servers of nine major US internet companies (AOL, Apple, Facebook, Google, Microsoft, PalTalk, Skype, Yahoo, and YouTube) and was looking at the content of emails, videos, photos, VoIP (voice over internet protocol) chats, social networking sites, stored data, and more. Snowden's leaked documents showed the agency's own estimates of how much metadata it had collected from computer and telephone networks across the globe, complete with maps and monthly tallies (97 billion pieces in March 2013 alone).

One month later, in July, articles in *Der Spiegel* and the Brazilian newspaper *O Globo* confirmed that the NSA had been spying on the metadata of *entire populations*, including the Germans and Brazilians, through a program that enlisted the foreign partners of US telecoms. Another story revealed that the underwater cables carrying the world's phone and internet communications across the Atlantic and other oceans were being tapped by the NSA's allied agency in the United Kingdom, the Government Communications Headquarters (GCHQ), in collaboration with the NSA and in its pay. With the flowing codename Operation Tempora, it was a "full take" program, sucking up both metadata and content. It had probes attached to over two hundred internet links under the seas, each transporting data at the speed of ten gigabits a second.

At the end of July, a number of articles exposed one of the NSA's most disturbing systems, XKeyscore. It was a desktop tool that allowed analysts to data mine the NSA's entire distributed system of digital information, including information collected by its "Five Eyes" allies. If an analyst had some identifying information about an individual, such as an email or internet protocol (IP) address, he or she could search the content and metadata of just about anything a person could do on the internet and could do so *in real time*. No warrant was required. The analyst needed only to fill out an online form. In his Hong Kong hotel room, Snowden had claimed that "I, sitting at my desk … [could] wiretap anyone, from you or your accountant, to a federal judge or even the president, if I had a personal email."[54]

At the end of the summer of 2013, newspapers revealed that the NSA had cracked the encryption codes that millions of users relied on for email, e-commerce, and financial transactions and had worked to weaken international encryption standards.

By then, it was clear to anyone who listened even sporadically to the news that the United States was spying on its own population and the populations of other countries and that no electronic information of any kind was necessarily private anymore. The situation was made plain by a leaked NSA document published in November 2013 in which the agency itself stated its end goal was to be able to access what it needed on "anyone, anywhere, anytime."[55]

The United States was, in effect, subjecting all of the world's civilian populations to a globalized system of mass, continuous surveillance. But it had also built an authoritarian system of control that could be turned against its own population any time that members of the American political class were feeble enough to allow it. The United States, Snowden warned, had created a surveillance infrastructure that would make "turn-key tyranny" possible: "A new leader will be elected, they'll flip the switch, say that because of the crisis, because of the dangers that we face in the world, you know, some new and unpredicted threat, we need more authority, we need more power. And there will be nothing the people can do at that point to oppose it … it will be turn-key tyranny."[56]

This is how at last—at long last, tech activists might say—the future that the cypherpunks had been warning about broke through the consciousness of the ordinary citizen. Snowden's great contribution was that he took a factually, politically, and technically complex matter and through strategic, incremental leaks induced a collective epiphany among ordinary people. The shock of Snowden's revelations as they sank in over the successive breaking news stories was not just that the state wanted to know everything but also how rapidly the technology had advanced in the last decade to allow it. With the Snowden revelations, people began viscerally to sense the "end of privacy"—the end of private thought, of ephemeral conversation, of uninhibited association. The state's ability to drill down, data mine, and network-analyze every floating piece of information about a person that existed spelled the end of "anonymity in the crowd," which, people realized, was the condition on which their modern liberal freedoms depended. A world in which the state collected everything and could pinpoint anything promised enhanced state security but at the price of greatly diminished individual security and autonomy.

The shock of Manning's and Assange's disclosures, by contrast, was that potentially everyone—including corporations, employers, identity thieves, organized crime, journalists, and any other person with a malign or well-intended will to know more about any individual—could know everything. This dystopia placed personal security and identity at the mercy of forces (predatory or simply intrusive) beyond the state. It also put institutions of all kinds in the position of having to function in a condition of complete transparency.

Even the ordinary person understood that a situation in which everything was potentially available to everyone was unstable and unpredictable. For the first time, perhaps, they began to grasp what digital technology had unleashed—a new cyber "arms race"; a new ecology of secrets and lies as various players vie to dominate or to defend themselves; a new economy with new players, new uses for the correlation of vast troves of data, new kinds of value and profit, new relationships of power between citizens, strangers, and the state. Emailing her message to Assange, Manning seemed to regard the imminent danger of such a rapid, radical destabilization of existing power relationships with awe: "It's beautiful, and horrifying."

A MANIFESTO FOR THE TWENTY-FIRST CENTURY AND THE CONCEPT OF POPULAR SOVEREIGNTY

This new wave of hackers, the reinvented cypherpunks and more broadly the contemporary hacker scene coalescing around the Chaos Computer Club, went on write its own manifesto, one that referred to and drew inspiration from the contributions of WikiLeaks and Snowden. The manifesto, "Privacy for the Weak, Transparency for the Powerful" is now ubiquitous in hacker circles. It is short—sound-bite short—as a manifesto for the twenty-first century must be. I have not been able to discover who the author is. It seems to have arisen from the leaderless collective.

As a constitutional lawyer, I can attest that it is decidedly a democratic manifesto. "Privacy for the Weak, Transparency for the Powerful" is used today by hackers and digital rights activists from a broad range of political persuasions to express a general belief in the basic democratic tenet of popular sovereignty.

It helps to know a little about the history of popular sovereignty to truly understand the concept and why hackers have embraced it. In the early, European way of thinking about democracy, the people ceded their power to their elected representatives, and democratic institutions were merely mixed with or balanced against older aristocratic and monarchical organs of government.[57] Popular sovereignty was a uniquely American contribution to the democratic canon of ideas. It emerged in American debates over the replacement of the Revolution's 1776 Articles of Confederation with a new Constitution.

Prior to the Revolution and continuing after it, the American people were used to taking things into their own hands. They were used to organizing "committees, conventions and other extralegal bodies in order to voice grievances and achieve political goals."[58] They were used to taking mob and vigilante action to do "quickly and effectively"[59] what state governments were often incapable of doing, such as stopping profiteering, controlling prices, and punishing Tories. As American historian Gordon S. Wood has observed, a long tradition of "the people out of doors,"[60] acting on their own behalf, effecting their will, "instruct[ing] and control[ling] the institutions of government," had led to a positive belief, "even a legal reality,"[61] that the American people, unlike the British, did not surrender their sovereign power to any political institution or collection of institutions.

At the Philadelphia Constitutional Convention of 1787, a patrician Federalist faction proposed a new Constitution that would create a new form of government. It gave a lot of power to the president and senate and created a single republican state in place of a confederation of states.[62] In the ensuing debates over ratification, the aristocratic Federalists had to explain how this structure of government would not end up working the same way as a monarchy, annihilating the sovereign power of individual state legislatures, and how two legislatures could, in fact, govern the same communities without either one of them being sovereign.

The Federalists did so (somewhat disingenuously) by appropriating Americans' belief in their own popular sovereignty. They said that sovereignty resided with the people at large. The election of representatives did not extinguish or eclipse this sovereignty. All powers of government were derived from the people and remained with the people, so that all elected parts of government were only ever partial agents or representatives of the people, and power was always recallable by the people.[63]

The Federalists' innovation was a whole new way of thinking about governments' relation to the governed that made earlier ways seem bankrupt. Over time, the American idea of popular sovereignty had such appeal that it crept into popular consciousness in other places, to such a degree that it has become a normative influence even in parliamentary democracies like those of Canada and the United Kingdom, where the monarch remains the head of state.

Bringing this history to bear on the current era, the contemporary hacker manifesto "Privacy for the Weak, Transparency for the Powerful" captures the two sides of the concept of popular sovereignty: government must be accountable to the people, and people do not have to account for themselves to government (except in specific legal situations and then with adequate protections like due process). When politically minded hackers talk about self-determination for the user, they are broadly evincing a belief in a digital order of popular sovereignty.

"Privacy for the Weak, Transparency for the Powerful" expresses a twenty-first-century hacker commitment to help citizens take back and enforce two rights that are fundamental to a functioning democracy—privacy (the guarantee of autonomy and security in one's personal sphere and thoughts) and access to information (the primary antidote to misguided or corrupt governance). If privacy and transparency are the minimal conditions people need for maintaining a functioning democracy, it may be hackers' contribution in the twenty-first century to provide these to them.

In a line that stretches from John Perry Barlow to Julian Assange, Edward Snowden, and beyond, hackers have become the self-appointed defenders of the early ideals of the American Revolution and Constitution. "From the glory days of American radicalism, which was the American Revolution, I think that Madison's view on government is still unequaled"—Julian Assange told *Rolling Stone* at the end of his year of house arrest, not long before he found sanctuary at the Ecuadorian embassy in London—"that people determined to be in a democracy, to be their own governments, must have the power that knowledge will bring—because knowledge will always rule ignorance. ... The question is, where has the United States betrayed Madison and Jefferson, betrayed these basic values on how you keep a democracy?"[64]

4

THE BURDEN OF SECURITY
The Challenges for the Ordinary User

It is the day after my first visit to the Chaos Communication Camp, and I'm sitting in a Weimar period café in Berlin drinking serial cups of coffee, trying to work out another layer of security for my laptop before I return to the camp by train in the evening. The few hacker-connected people I know have said that to have credibility at a hacker camp, I'll have to prepare my own computer security and show people I can use the basic tools.

Citizens need to know the history of hacker ideas, both technical and political, that have led up to the contemporary manifesto "Privacy for the Weak, Transparency for the Powerful" but what about the practical applications of those ideas? I can describe the concepts behind the tools hackers have developed to achieve privacy and transparency, but can I figure out how to use them? Few popular treatments of hackers grapple seriously with the nuts and bolts of hacker tools and their user interfaces. For that matter, few treatments describe the basic architecture and governance structures of cyberspace—the practical parameters that hackers working for privacy and transparency have to contend with. On this journey of discovery through the hacker world, I find myself searching for primers on how things work.

At the same time, I am developing the belief that insiders need to know how hard it is for the ordinary user to find, absorb, and master this practical knowledge. Insiders could benefit from the opportunity to experience their world from the perspective of a person who is not a technologist.

It is several hours past lunch, and the café is deserted. Berlin is a city of spies, I think. Gazing past my laptop to the empty cane-seated chairs clustered around the marble-topped tables, I imagine the betrayed, the marked, and the departed of this city fretting in cafés like this one shortly before their various fates overtook them. In 1931, American writer Paul Bowles recalled the mood of the city as Germany's biggest bank failed and the economic crisis deepened: "It was sinister because of the discrepancy between those who had and those who didn't, and you felt it all very intensely. ... You felt the catastrophe coming, which gave an uncomfortable tinge to everything that happened."[1]

Until the final days of Hitler's takeover of the chancellorship in early 1933, the intellectuals and bohemians who regularly congregated in the coffee houses of Berlin, many of them Jews, could not bring themselves to believe the endgame had begun—especially because the Nazis had recently fallen far short of a majority in the 1932 elections. In denial, they delayed their flight from the city until the last possible minute.[2] "Berlin ... your dancing partner is Death," civic health officials warned the public on posters at the end of World War I, not knowing how dreadfully apt those words would remain throughout the decades to come.[3]

Berlin is a long way from the Pacific Northwest Coast where I've come from. Only a month earlier, in July, I had taken a ferry out to the Gulf Island home of Andrew Clement and his partner, Lucy Suchman. Andrew, a computer science professor at the University of Toronto and long-time digital rights activist, was the only person I knew who could begin to show me how to set up a more privacy-secure laptop and also brief me on the basics of internet architecture and governance.

Unlike Berlin, whose atmosphere is thick with the history and deeds of men, the islands of the Pacific Northwest have a timeless quality. The black backs of whales occasionally break the surface of the Salish Sea and a serene mist veils the islands' successive silhouettes, which recede, ever more faintly, into the supposed horizon. On a rainy day, it can feel like the end of the earth, and cyberspace only an abstract construct of a distant civilization.

Andrew is originally from this place, and he and Lucy have built a simple house with a panoramic view of its beauty. Lucy is an anthropologist and the author of a seminal book on technical design, *Plans and Situated Actions: The Problems of Human Machine Communication*, which at the time it was written challenged conventional assumptions about the design of interactive systems. Lucy thought she would study corporate power as an anthropologist, went to Xerox, and ended up staying for twenty-two years, becoming a leader on computer design there.[4] She did her PhD at Berkeley in the late 1980s, where she cofounded Computer Professionals for Social Responsibility (CPSR).

An older, more staid organization than the Electronic Frontier Foundation, CPSR started in Palo Alto in 1981 as a discussion group of computer scientists at Xerox's Palo Alto Research Center. Members of the group were concerned about the "Star Wars" anti-ballistic missile defense system being promoted by the Reagan administration. CPSR was the adult voice in the techno-utopian atmosphere of Silicon Valley at the time, always warning against putting too much faith in complex computer systems. Lucy still evinces that premise: computers for her are not magical, and it should never be assumed they will provide magic solutions for societies.

Andrew was in the University of British Columbia's first computer science class in the 1960s and experienced the early mainframe days of computing, like the first generation of MIT hackers. In the 1980s, he did his PhD in computer science with Kelly Gotlieb, an early pioneer in Canadian computing. In 1952, Gotlieb was instrumental in bringing the first electronic computer (a huge piece of old tube technology) to Canada.[5]

But Andrew is a "second-wave" hacker. Inspired by the Community Memory Project set up by the People's Computer Company in Berkeley in the 1970s, he and others decided to clone it for Vancouver. Their computer bulletin board was funded by one of the Local Initiative Program (LIP) grants that Pierre Trudeau's government gave for socially innovative experiments and was located in a storefront in Kitsilano, a beach neighborhood popular with the counterculture.

Andrew is still hacking. His current project is to map the physical architecture of the internet—specifically, the pathways by which personal communications are routed and where they might be intercepted by the US National Security Agency (NSA). Named IXmaps ("IX" standing for "internet exchange"), the project uses an interactive mapping tool and website that encourages users to map the routing of their own communications and contribute to the compilation of a global routing map. The mapping might show, for example, how one email sent from the University of Toronto to a recipient just a few blocks away stays within the greater Toronto area but how another sent to someone just as close travels all the way down to New York or Chicago, primary cities of NSA surveillance, before reaching its destination.

Andrew, like Lucy, wants to demystify tech and address popular misunderstandings about it. His work emphasizes the fact that cyberspace—which, John Perry Barlow declaimed, "was everywhere and nowhere" actually has a concrete, physical infrastructure.

On the evening I arrived, as the three of us ate dinner in a restaurant near the ferry dock, I asked Andrew a question I had been turning over in my mind for some time. Why couldn't Canada have a fully sovereign, national internet, regulated in the public interest and accountable to the democratic process? Why couldn't our national government regulate everything in the interest of citizens?

He told me that in the 1990s, when the internet was still being called the "information superhighway," the question had been whether to regulate the internet at all, and the consensus among stakeholders was "hands off": regulation would stifle innovation. Andrew had been involved in the early hearings of the Canadian Radio and Telecommunications Commission (CRTC), which examined the issue. The CRTC agreed it would refrain from applying the Telecommunications Act and the Broadcasting Act. Andrew had argued that the internet should be regulated as a new public utility, with universal access. And indeed, for a short time, Industry Canada was talking about offering everyone in the Canadian maritime province of Prince Edward Island a publicly provided email address as part of a public physical infrastructure with universal public access.

But this approach did not win the day. Private companies took over the infrastructure for internet services, and most users ended up with addresses for services like Gmail or Yahoo. The fiber optic system became a public and private patchwork. In a few localities, there was a fully public architecture: Fredericton, New Brunswick, for example, had its own fiber optic network. It was originally built to connect the city's agencies, but WiFi routers were added to create a Fred-eZone, giving the public free internet access across large sections of the city. Toronto Hydro did the same thing in core parts of Toronto at one point but then sold its fiber optic system to the private sector. Now the vested corporate interests make a fully public architecture much harder to attain. This has been the story, more or less, in other countries, too. The infrastructure, even if it was originally public, has largely been privatized.

"If people could view the internet like they view the more familiar network infrastructures—where everyone can see the roadways, where connections are made and where they are not, and know who owns the lands they cross and who decides the routes they follow—then people would get a better intuitive sense of their personal and policy choices," Andrew explained.

His IXmaps project began in the wake of the early revelation during the George W. Bush era that the NSA was spying on internet traffic routed through and within the United States. That was in 2005. IXmaps's aim was to help people understand this secret surveillance and know whether their own communications were likely to be intercepted. Finding that a large proportion of domestic Canadian traffic (that is, communications with both ends in Canada) was routed through the United States and NSA surveillance sites heightened Andrew's concerns about democratic governance and Canadian sovereignty. (In fact, most global internet traffic flows through the United States.)[6] He was astonished to realize that the most important internet exchanges were often hiding in plain sight in giant, featureless buildings in the center of major cities. "Who owns this, the wires and the routers, and the real estate they sit on?" he wondered. "What are the business deals that determine these seemingly arbitrary patterns of traffic? Who makes the deals that, in effect, govern internet routing and therefore our security?"

At the very least, Andrew told me, we need to understand how the packets flow to be able to intervene and direct the design more in the public interest. If we make the infrastructure visible, it will reveal the interests at play and inform debate.

The next day, as we drank beer on the veranda of Andrew and Lucy's house, Andrew expanded on his observations from the night before. In addition to the routing infrastructure, he explained, the other physical infrastructure posing a risk to user security was "the cloud," the data storage infrastructure. As we looked down at the spectacular view of islands dotted across the wide blue sea, it seemed plausible that the cloud could be something ethereal and benign. But Andrew was telling me about Vincent Mosco's work on the marketing of the cloud—how companies have built an interconnected infrastructure of large data centers containing tens of thousands of servers; how these centers have a huge physical presence and carbon footprint; how companies were funneling everyone into them; how people were either fooled into thinking the cloud was magically immaterial and secure or put their data in it because they felt powerless to do otherwise; and how Canada, like Europe, had strong data protection laws, requiring informed consent, a right of access, and storage for limited purposes and periods of time, but the United States had a patchwork of data protection laws with weaker protections, especially for foreigners, which contributed to making the US a favored jurisdiction for locating data farms.

If national governments were not exerting control over the physical infrastructure of the internet to regulate it in the interests of citizens, then who ran it? Surely there had to be some standards. If it was a complete free-for-all, how could it work technically?

Andrew offered me another beer and gave me a short overview of how the internet was governed.

The three main governance bodies—the Internet Engineering Task Force (IETF), the World Wide Web Consortium (W3C), and the Internet Corporation for Assigned Names and Numbers (ICANN)—all use principles of consensus, he said. It is an oversimplification to say they "run by consensus," but laypeople should know that consensus is an important governing principle for all of them. The IETF establishes the protocols for the internet's operation; it governs the architecture of the internet. Its motto for decision making is "Rough consensus, running code." IETF working groups are open to anyone with the ability to attend meetings or to participate in email discussion groups. All participants are formally equal, and in practice all have equal access to at least the email part of the discussion, which includes written reports that summarize relevant discussions at IETF in-person meetings.

The private sector has financial stakes in many of the decisions made and can afford to maintain an active presence in deliberations year over year. So governance has increasingly been the domain of private-sector experts. Where industry does not agree with safeguards or where these do not exist, the individual user has had only hacker tools to work with, like Zimmermann's PGP and Tor.

Later that afternoon, as Andrew and I sat at the kitchen counter, fiddling with installing PGP on my laptop, he told me his own stories about the Chaos Computer Club and his brief connection with the various digital exiles living in Berlin who became close associates of the club. Andrew met Jacob Appelbaum, the Tor and WikiLeaks associate and one of the Berlin exiles, at the Citizen Lab, a research center at the University of Toronto with hacking know-how and a geopolitical angle on digital rights issues, and later when attending a conference in Berlin.

"So it's evening at the Chaos Computer Clubhouse, and a number of us are working on our laptops there and want to go out and eat."

"What does it look like?" I asked.

"It's dark and dingy! With run-down furniture and makeshift tables. There are young guys, mostly, scattered around, working intently on their laptops, and Jake is telling me that he takes his with him even when he goes to the bathroom. Then we leave for dinner, and a bunch of us are walking down the street when Jake comes running after us: 'You left your laptop open!'

"And I say, 'What do I have to be careful of?'

"'You have to protect it physically,' he says, and he's kind of upset with me, 'because something could be introduced into it while you're gone.'"

"He sometimes uses silver sprinkles on his own laptop, and tapes it up, then photographs the sprinkle pattern so that he can tell if it's been tampered with. You see, you have to be able to trust every element in the chain if you're going to achieve strong protection. Temperamentally, I can't work that way. Personally, I'm just too sloppy."

"It's high spycraft," I said.

"It's high spycraft," Andrew agreed, and we looked at each other for a few seconds, sharing the realization.

"So this is my cautionary tale," he continued. "Even if you don't see yourself at risk, you've got to learn to practice all this high security if you're afraid of compromising someone who really does rely on it."

Take, for example, the journalists and activists who are handling the Snowden documents. Andrew gave me a rough breakdown of the number of Snowden documents published by different newspapers—*Der Speigel*, 122; the *New York Times*, 17; *The Guardian*, 26. The *Washington Post* had published some, too

Glenn Greenwald and Laura Poitras had the whole collection of NSA documents Snowden had stolen, and they were publishing them incrementally in *The Intercept* (incremental publication was probably the best strategy for keeping the public's attention). Andrew, at the University of Toronto, had bravely stepped forward to set up a public archive of all of the published Snowden documents.[7] The university might have been a little nervous about this, but no one tried to stop him. No academic institution had yet stepped forward offering to set up a public archive of all of the documents, unpublished as well as published. Such an archive would require the institution to become involved in custodial decisions about which documents to release to news agencies and the public and when to do so. And in any case, maybe Greenwald and Poitras had not quite decided what to do with the whole archive. It was a complex question.

Andrew and I barely managed to get PGP and Enigmail installed on my laptop before I had to race for the four p.m. ferry. There wasn't time for Tor, for which he had given me only the most rudimentary instructions.

THE SAKHAROVS

Like some of Berlin's digital exiles, the Russian dissident Andrei Dmitrievich Sakharov used to carry his secrets around with him. In January 1980, Natalya Viktorovna Hesse, an old friend of Sakharov and his wife, was able to visit them in their apartment in Gorky just after their forced transportation there by the Soviet state. The Soviets had not yet decided what to do with them, so Hesse was able to stay with them for a month. The entire apartment was bugged, Hesse told a Russian journalist: "There isn't a corner where each sigh, each cough, each footstep, not to speak of conversations, can't be overheard. Only thoughts can remain secret, if they haven't been put down on paper, because if the Sakharovs go to the bakery or to the post office to mail a letter, the KGB agents will search the place. They will either photograph or steal the written thought."[8]

So what did Sakharov do?

> Andrei Dmitrievich [Sakharov], with his weak heart, his inability to walk up even five or seven steps without pausing for breath and trying to quiet his heartbeat, is forced to carry a bag that I, for example, can't lift. When once we went into a shop, he asked me to watch over this bag, but I wanted to see what was on a shelf, and I had to drag the bag after me. I just could not lift it. In this bag, Andrei Dmitrievich carries a radio receiver, because it would be damaged if left at home, all his manuscripts—both scientific and public ones—diaries, photos, personal notes. The bag must weigh no less than thirty pounds. He has to carry all this around with him. I think all this must weigh no less than thirty pounds. And this man with a bad heart—suffering from acute hypertension—is forced to carry this bag every time he leaves home, even if it is only for ten minutes.[9]

Sitting in the Berlin café, making preparations for my trip to the Chaos Communication Camp later that day and trying to decide whether I should attempt to install Tor, I, too, feel the burden of security. My own laptop and cell phone are like the listening devices in the Sakharov apartment. More than just listening devices, these objects emit my personal life into cyberspace. I have an indelible trail of data exhaust perpetually flowing behind me across the arc of my life. A trail that *does* have a mystifying quality because no ordinary person seems to know how to erase, edit, or dispose of it completely, and no one knows just who is reading and interpreting it. As Andrew has told me, many of the hackers, journalists, and activists bearing the burden of the WikiLeaks and Snowden documents have ended up in Berlin or had their paths cross there. I'm not sure who I might get to speak to in the city and at the Chaos Communication Camp over the next few days or whether I would or should want to hide anything. But it makes me uneasy, this worry of potentially exposing someone to risk or being exposed.

BERLIN: CITY OF FREEDOM, CITY OF EXILES

As much as people have fled Berlin, throughout its history they have also flocked to the city to be free. Berlin is a city of political exiles, free thinkers, reformers, and refugees.

As early as medieval times, serfs who came to the city and were able to stay for a year and a day were granted their freedom, generating the aphorism "City air makes you free." During Europe's Thirty Years War in the first half of the seventeenth century, Berlin was razed because of religious intolerance. When the chastened city emerged from the destruction, tolerance became a theme of the place. Twenty thousand Protestant Huguenot refugees were granted residence there in 1700 and an enlightened monarch, Frederick the Great, worked for decades on a constitution of tolerance that included early rights for religious freedom, equality of the sexes, equality before the law, freedom of speech, and universal education. Voltaire, in exile from France, was a guest at Frederick's court in Berlin and there developed many of his ideas for his best-selling tract "A Treatise on Toleration."[10] The Jewish Enlightenment began in Berlin in the mid-1700s. Led by Moses Mendelssohn, the movement strove for Jewish emancipation and assimilation. Frederick's grandson granted Jews in Berlin the rights of citizens and access to professions they previously had been excluded from. Hannah Arendt describes how the civil equality of Jews in Berlin was a product of the Prussian Enlightenment there.

By the 1800s, Berlin's reputation as a city of refuge, toleration, and freedom was well established, and emboldened political movements pushed for even greater reforms. The Young Germany movement called for radical democratic reform; Ferdinand Lasalle, from Breslau, mobilized Berlin factory workers; and Karl Marx and Friedrich Engels worked on *The Communist Manifesto* there. In 1848, popular revolt swept Europe with calls for universal suffrage, intellectual freedom, and democratic constitutions. When Berlin's poor went to the barricades in March that year, composer Richard Wagner joined them. In the 1870s, the first socialist party in Europe was formed in Berlin as leftists joined with labor unions to form the German Socialist Workers' Party, a forerunner of the Socialist Democratic Party. Berlin remained a place of ferment up to World War I. "The books, the writers, the actors! Berlin had been a great attraction for all of them. ... Everything was filled with a throbbing life," wrote one long-time resident, Heinrich Eduard Jacob, of the city in the summer of 1914.[11]

Granted, the city was also the center of the Prussian military and monarchy that ultimately led the country into the devastation of World War I. But when these institutions lay smashed, it was Berlin that became the center of resurgent democracy, emancipation, and reform. The king's own garrison in Berlin deserted. Some of the most trenchant critics of the old regime were artists working in Berlin—Bertolt Brecht, George Grosz, and Käthe Kollwitz. The Social Democrats took power soon after the war and announced the establishment of a new republic and constitution. The revolutionary communists known as the Spartacists, led by Rosa Luxemburg, would have taken things further still. Her words, engraved in Berlin's squares, still resonate in the city: "Freedom only for the supporters of the government … is no freedom at all. Freedom is always and exclusively freedom for the one who thinks differently."[12]

There was sexual freedom, too, and libertinism, with many voluntary exiles like Christopher Isherwood staying in the city to experience and write about it. When Adolf Hitler took over the chancellorship in 1933 and imposed his authoritarian regime, Berlin was still the heart of communist and anarchist Europe, of radical artistic movements, and of experiments in personal freedom. Berliners did not cheer his ascendance.[13] When Jean-Paul Sartre arrived in devastated postwar Berlin for a remount of his prewar antifascist play, *The Flies*, he famously said the place demanded no less than a commitment to "total freedom."[14]

The number of historical figures and thinkers who have come and gone through Berlin is striking, as is the way so many personal and political stories meet up there. The stories of contemporary digital rights exiles that weave themselves in and out of Berlin are only the latest installment of the city's long dance with freedom and repression.

When Julian Assange was under house arrest in the UK, many digital rights activists, hackers and journalists visited with him there. Among them were Jacob Appelbaum, Sarah Harrison (a WikiLeaks' editor and personal intimate of Julian Assange), and Laura Poitras, who was filming Assange and his entourage. The house, located on a spacious country estate, gave them a genteel environment in which to gather and work before events drove them and others into exile.

Assange was the first to go. On a lovely day in May 2012, when the UK Supreme Court rejected his appeal against extradition to Sweden, Assange donned a disguise and rode a motorcycle to asylum at the Ecuadorian embassy in London's Knightsbridge district.

Poitras was the second, although her exile was at first voluntary. She was known for her films about the Iraq War and had experienced increasing harassment at the US border whenever she traveled to or from her home country. She wanted to protect her film footage and materials, and Jacob Appelbaum suggested that she should move to Berlin. He, himself, had decided it would be wise to relocate there. Germany had very good privacy laws and a growing community of digital rights activists.

Poitras moved to the city in fall 2012 and set up a studio.[15] At the time of her move, she was making a film on surveillance, and it was not going well. Then in January 2013, she was contacted by someone claiming to work for the NSA. The person identified himself by a code name, Citizenfour.[16] Poitras was using encrypted communications for her projects, and she and Citizenfour communicated for a number of weeks that way before her correspondent asked to meet her. When she learned from Citizenfour the importance of the leaks he had to offer, she decided she needed a partner to help break the story and chose Glenn Greenwald, who at the time was writing for *The Guardian* newspaper.

Citizenfour was the thirty-year-old Edward Snowden. Poitras and Greenwald's interview with him in his hotel room in Hong Kong became the basis of the 2014 documentary *Citizenfour*, which won Poitras an Oscar and introduced Snowden as a sympathetic character to the world. At the time of the interview, Snowden was on the run. He had decided to identify himself to protect others but did not believe it would serve any social purpose to turn himself in and face the kind of long prison sentence and torture Chelsea Manning had by then been subjected to. Stranded in Hong Kong, Snowden needed to find a country that would offer him political asylum. And he needed help getting out of the city.

Poitras believed that she was already being followed, so it would not be easy for her to assist him. Julian Assange, whom Poitras knew well by this time, stepped forward. WikiLeaks canvassed its own diplomatic contacts to find a country that would offer Snowden asylum. It booked more than a dozen flights to different places in order to obscure his travel plans. And it dispatched Sarah Harrison, who was in Melbourne on WikiLeaks business, to meet Snowden in Hong Kong and accompany him on his journey.[17] Harrison and Snowden met for the first time in a taxi and made their way to the airport, where they boarded a plane. By the time the United States sent a warrant to Hong Kong for Snowden's extradition on June 14, 2013, charging him with high crimes under the Espionage Act, he had already departed.

The first leg of Snowden and Harrison's journey was to Moscow, where they hoped to take a second flight to Havana and go from there to South America. But by then, the United States had revoked Snowden's passport, and they found themselves stranded in the Sheremetyevo airport, where, for thirty-nine days, they evaded spies and the international press and survived in a building whose best amenity was four Burger Kings.[18]

At the end of it, they negotiated political asylum for Snowden in Russia, and he went into exile in Moscow, where he has remained since. Harrison accompanied him through this adventure and stayed with him in Moscow for three months, increasing the risk that she herself would be targeted when leaving the country. Her lawyers advised her not to return to the United Kingdom, and she went into exile in Berlin in late 2013, never returning to Melbourne to pick up the luggage she had left there.[19]

When Laura Poitras told Julian Assange that she had decided not to give WikiLeaks the Snowden archive to publish, he was furious. Assange was still yelling at her when she hung up the phone, she has said.[20] Poitras and Greenwald worked with *The Guardian* and a few other selected media outlets to publish the first Snowden disclosures and then went on to found *The Intercept*, the online media platform they intended would publish the Snowden leaks over time. Poitras and Greenwald are possibly the only people who have access to the whole Snowden archive, and because of the sensitivity of large swathes of its documents, it may never be fully published and mirrored on volunteer servers like the WikiLeaks archive has been.[21] Poitras and Greenwald (who lives in Brazil) almost never return to the United States now because it is potentially dangerous for them.[22]

The lives of the Berlin digital exiles would merge with those of a close-knit activist community in the city[23] connected with the Chaos Computer Club and with the long-flowing political life of the city. The club's contribution to their cause was to file a criminal complaint with the German Prosecutor in 2014 against the US, UK, and German governments, as well as the heads of their secret services, for their respective roles in the mass surveillance Edward Snowden revealed.[24] Harrison remained a WikiLeaks editor. When she started the Courage Foundation—an organization for whistleblower protection—Andy Müller-Maguhn joined its advisory board.[25] In 2016, Harrison and the rest of Berlin's digital rights community turned out in force to the Berlin premiere of Poitras's film *Citizenfour*.[26]

These exiles—Poitras, Harrison, and Appelbaum in Berlin; Greenwald in Brazil; Snowden in Moscow; Assange in the Ecuadorian embassy in London—have borne the burden of dealing with the Snowden and WikiLeaks archives for several years now, in one capacity or another, binding their lives inextricably together. In Poitras's 2017 film about Assange, *Risk*, Poitras would reveal that she was briefly involved with Appelbaum. She would disclose that Appelbaum, like Assange, had been accused of serious sexual misconduct and of bullying. The allegations had been swirling in the activist community for some time. The film would express the sadness of political exile, with its patina of melancholy similar to the bleak ambience of old spy movies set in divided Berlin.

The first arrow of exile, Dante Alighieri wrote, is that you "leave everything you love most."[27] The second, I think, must be the limbo of not knowing whether you will escape its confines and whether your personal sacrifice means enough. The third must be the betrayal, estrangement, or disappointment you might have to endure, because the lives of political exiles are often joined inextricably together. The last, surely, is whether you, yourself, might crack or fail in some way.

A CRYPTOPARTY

I make it back to the Chaos Communication Camp by train and later that night pitch a tent in the middle of a spectacular lightning storm. The electrical grid that snakes through every part of the camp withstands the deluge of water: there are no fires or electrocutions. Only the inside of my tent gets wet; there's a vent at the top I can't find the cover for.

I am not much further ahead in preparing my laptop's security. I have failed to install Tor and am still woefully ignorant of many basic aspects of security. I have a dilemma to face the next day, too. If I am not up to practicing high spycraft, if I have not mastered even a basic privacy tool like Tor, is it fair for me to try to interview some of these Berlin exiles and other activist hackers? How will we communicate, and where will I store my notes? What more can I glean about their stories that is worth putting them and myself at risk? And isn't the hacker story becoming too much about these high-profile individuals anyway, when there is the huge collective phenomenon of the progressive hacker scene to be reported on?

Dawn finds me hunched stiffly over a hot coffee served by one of the food kiosks that is, surprisingly, open at this hour. I look up when a slight, bearded young man, coffee in hand, sits down with a nod at the same picnic table. Minutes go by, and it occurs to me to ask him where I might charge my laptop. I ask also if he knows anything about the special internet access the CCC encourages campers to use. I'm a lawyer, not a tech person, I tell him apologetically. I'm trying to be more secure, I explain, but it's my professional ethic as a lawyer to act openly. When I try to act covertly, I get confused.

"Yes, well," he responds, "one gets confused in all kinds of political processes, not just technological ones."

He smiles warmly. He has a quiet, thoughtful demeanor.

"But," he says categorically, "in a place like this, you just don't go on the open internet."

He explains why: there are many hackers, and they love to hack into things. They can scan and see you anytime they like. Yes, they can get into your email. Yes, also your documents. Anything is possible. He smiles again. Yes, there are also security agencies that send people to this kind of conference, certainly.

He sees me blanching. Before coming here, I explain, I installed PGP, a nontracking browser, and an activist-run email service on my laptop, more for credibility's sake than from paranoia. But when I returned to the camp late yesterday, I needed to check in with my kids. I'd had to leave them on their own back in Canada, and they are only in their early teens. I joined the net using the camp's open WiFi connection. In my specific circumstances, how bad could that be? My brain churns ineffectually trying to sort through the implications.

If you have a free software system like Linux, he says (I notice he does not say GNU/Linux, as Richard Stallman would wish he had), you can see the source code and watch over it all the time. You can see if it has been infected. With free software for encryption, it is the same thing: you can check to see if it is doing what it is intended to do. You have to watch over this all the time. People are at risk because of social media and commercial websites. There are many ways of getting your computer infected with tracking technology.

We talk some more, and I learn that he is an artist. He gave a talk on "glitch art" at the camp yesterday. He explains that this involves working with technical representations and finding errors in code to display aesthetically. For example, in the presentation he gave yesterday, he produced errors in images to make visible the glitches in a sequence of code from a US drone system. He started this project three years ago, when he came across a leak by a group called DefenseSystems.com. The leak was that a drone operator did not know a video system for US drones had errors in it, which led him to kill civilians when directing a drone attack in Pakistan.[28]

Another thing he does are "PGPoems": he plays with code and network language to create partly encrypted poems. PGP, as I know, stands for Phil Zimmermann's public key encryption tool called Pretty Good Privacy. The reader of a PGPoem can see some words but has to do a public encryption key exchange with the artist in order to put together the whole thing.

It's still early. Most people in the camp have yet to emerge from their tents. I can hear mourning doves calling softly to each other in a stand of silver birch trees. We huddle over the picnic table, our cups of coffee steaming our fingers warm.

He pulls a small yellow book out of his backpack and hands it to me. Titled *Operational Glitches: How to Make Humans Machine Readable*, it is an artistic treatment of the computer as a control system over time, he says—say, by biometrics or metadata index. It is an essay on code.

I turn the booklet over in my hands, a small artefact of the interesting times we live in. The text is in German, with headings like "Die falschheit des glaubens an die richtigkeit technischer bilder" (the falsity of faith in the accuracy of technical images), "Frabe by frame by frame" (error by frame by frame), "predictive killing," "Produkttionsmittel" (means of production), and "das Codicht" (code). It is full of recognizable names like Heidegger and Marx. I look up into the artist's clear gray eyes and he reminds me also of Schiller and Goethe.

Who is this soulful German? His name, the booklet cover reveals, is Christian Heck.

Christian feels at risk as an artist not because he is disclosing secrets—that, he says, he does not do—but because he is making statements that authorities do not agree with. He knows they will monitor him. He also has a responsibility to friends, colleagues, and family. He never goes online unencrypted. Also, because pictures are full of metadata, revealing information such as time and place, he erases metadata so as not to leave traces: "Not just for me, but for all groups." There are many security methods for being anonymous online. He never uses Gmail, for example, because Google analyzes your email with that service: "Many people say, 'I don't want to be used as a product by a private company.'"

Christian describes his involvement in spreading privacy know-how. He participates in a peer-to-peer teaching collective called "CryptoParty," which is part of a grassroots internet privacy movement. When they organize a party, everyone can come, have a beer, and show one another how to encrypt a hard drive or email, use a Linux operating system, or work anonymously. (Later that day, I look up CryptoParty and find that the tech writer Cory Doctorow calls it "a Tupperware party for learning crypto." The *CryptoParty Handbook*—over four hundred pages, "to get you started"—was crowdsourced by activists from all over the world in less than twenty-four hours.)[29] Tactical Technology Collective is another interesting group, Christian says. It has a tent at the camp and does public education through animation. The group's kit is called "Security in a Box."

It may not be possible to make a whole system secure, "but you have to do your best," he says, looking at me kindly. "Just like a mother."

He explains all the various pieces you have to worry about in a security plan:

Your hardware or Mac address. This is your unique numeric computer identifier. If it is visible—as it is on an "open" network like the open WiFi connection at the Chaos Communication Camp—it identifies you like a fingerprint.

Your web browser. Popular web browsers include Firefox, Internet Explorer, and Safari. You need an alternative browser like Jondo or Whonix, and you must also think about the default settings you configure for them.

Your default search engine. Most people have Google as their default search engine. You need a search engine that does not track you and does not keep a history of your browsing, like the alternative search engine Duck Duck Go.

Your server. You need a network of proxy servers like Tor to hide your internet protocol address (from your router) and geographic location.

Your internet service provider. You need one like Frei Funk (Free Send) that does not keep log files and therefore cannot track you going into Tor.

Your operating system. You need one with free software like Linux (again, he says "Linux," not "GNU/Linux") so that you can see the source code and monitor whether it has been infected or not.

And there are two types of information to worry about:

Your content. You should encrypt all your messages and the documents you send (OTR for chats and PGP for email and attachments). You should encrypt your hard drive with Looks or Truecrypt.

Your metadata. You need a network of proxy servers like Tor to hide where you go and who you talk to. Tor does not encrypt the content of the message. Some people don't understand this and inadvertently leave their content exposed.

The Tor network, Christian explains, hides your original location. With Tor, Google has only the metadata for your web search from the last proxy server (in Romania, say). Your location and your IP address are hidden. You do not need to trust Tor because it does not know what route your message took or its original location. "Hide My Ass," another proxy server, does.

As Christian speaks, I am trying to square what he is telling me with what I already think I know about Tor. As I understand it, Tor is continually being improved. The way it currently works is that it uses two sets of PGP keys. Tor lays out a random path of multiple nodes every ten minutes, and one "temporary" key is sent to each node. The temporary key is for the substantive message that will be sent. If there are three nodes, a temporary key is sent to each of the three nodes. It is encrypted using each node's public key—that is, Tor uses each node's public key to scramble the temporary key's information. Only the node can unencrypt the temporary key it has just been sent using its private key. The node stores the temporary key for a short time, ready to use it on the next message it will receive. The next message will be the sender's substantive message with its content, encrypted or not, wrapped in three layers of encrypted addresses. The first node will open the first layer of the addresses with the temporary key it has in its possession. It will scrub the sender's metadata and then send the message on to its next destination. The second node will do the same thing with the next address, and so on.

But you really must have a clean computer before you go into Tor, Christian continues. If your computer is infected with malware, he says, someone spying on you could potentially see your whole route through Tor and all your correspondents. Instead of hiding yourself on the internet, you would be exposing your most sensitive networks. It would be like wearing an invisibility cloak you thought was working while it was not. It could expose your whole social network and put all of your correspondents at risk. A clean computer means a computer that has not been exposed to a possible hack through the internet before you start using Tor to hide yourself. Commercial sites are risky, and so are streaming videos and looking at PDFs online. This means you have to preconfigure your browser offline when you first get your computer and avoid using it for streaming, web surfing, and PDF downloads.

This is beginning to sound onerous to me.

But even with a clean computer, Christian says, if you are using the same browser (say, Safari) all the time and always configured the same way, security agencies can create a profile on you when you are using Tor based on the constant pattern of your browser and its particular configurations. (I struggle to translate this for my own understanding: even with Tor hiding your location and IP address, authorities can *still* profile you at the ends of the rabbit tunnel if you are using the same browser and configuration all the time? As if they can see you have a brown salt-and-pepper tail going into the rabbit warren and a brown salt-and-pepper tail coming out?)

Cryptoparties over beer and pizza, Christian says, start with what people are interested in. They are meant to teach normal people with normal computers, people who may have no clue about security when they start. Then they learn to be more adept through many little talks, he explains.

With his art, Christian says, he is searching for other ways to help people understand the dangers of "right now," other than through logical argument. Every week, there is a news story about surveillance, and this does not change people's behaviors online.

Christian himself learned to code because he wanted to make a movie using film cutting in real time. Adobe did not have that function, so he had to create it.

"But ordinary people have many things to do other than become technical experts," I say.

"Yeah, I know," he replies. "They have families and jobs from nine to five, et cetera, but it's just another way of behavior. You changed from using a Microsoft system to a Mac and learned how to work it, so you can change from Microsoft to Linux, for example." He smiles again, warmly.

Christian stands up, his coffee finished. We shake hands like friends, and I thank him for his lesson on the basic elements of user security. Combined with the primer Andrew Clement gave me before my trip, I feel much more knowledgeable about how things work.

As Christian walks away, a recent news story pops into my mind. I hesitate for a moment, then look it up, still using the open WiFi connection:

Kremlin Returns to Typewriters to Avoid Computer Leaks

The Kremlin is returning to typewriters in an attempt to avoid damaging leaks from computer hardware, it has been claimed.

A source at Russia's Federal Guard Service (FSO), which is in charge of safeguarding Kremlin communications and protecting President Vladimir Putin, claimed that the return to typewriters has been prompted by the publication of secret documents by WikiLeaks, the whistle-blowing website, as well as Edward Snowden, the fugitive US intelligence contractor.

The FSO is looking to spend 486,000 roubles—around £10,000—on a number of electric typewriters according to the site of state procurement agency, zakupki.gov.ru. The notice included ribbons for German-made Triumph Adlew TWEN 180 typewriters, although it was not clear if the typewriters themselves were this kind. ...

Documents leaked by Mr. Snowden appeared to show that Britain spied on foreign delegates including Dimitry Medvedev, then the president, at the 2009 London G20 meetings.

Russia was outraged by the revelations but said it had the means to protect itself.[30]

I will, it turns out, have the opportunity to talk with at least two of Berlin's digital exiles over the next few days at the Chaos Communication Camp. They are here, circulating, and it should be easy to approach them and perhaps set up interviews with other exiles, including Julian Assange in London, where I have arranged to go after Germany. But do I want to take on that burden?

For all of the reasons I have been mulling over, I decide not to. I cannot offer them security, and I do not want to become a target of surveillance myself. I have a regular job to hold down, a mortgage, and children. In any case, their stories are background to my main objective for this book—reporting on the collective movement I see emerging around the hacker scene and the direction that hacking is headed in this difficult political era. The technical problems I've been having with my tent will soon recede in importance: I will have so many people to talk to I will barely have time to sleep.

5

DEMOCRACY IN CYBERSPACE

First, the Governance Problems

HARRY

He is looking for a green tent in a sea of tents baking under the hot sun. As we walk through the Chaos Communication Camp and talk, he overshoots it several times.

Tall, with white teeth and the charming, natural manners of so many Americans I've met abroad, Harry Halpin works for the World Wide Web Consortium (W3C) on the standardization of cryptography and authentication.[1] He is also a research scientist at MIT. His boss is Tim Berners-Lee, the inventor of the World Wide Web.

At a panel discussion we had both attended on the second day of the camp, he had asked, "Why aren't countries other than the United States funding hackers' security projects?" He seemed to intend it as a provocation yet stopped short of offering his own views on the topic. At the end of the session, people had spilled out of the big-top tent into the inky summer night, avidly carrying on various debates. It was easy to approach Harry in the crowd and strike up a conversation but hard to finish it: people kept coming up to greet him. They were from Brazil, the United Kingdom, and other countries, male and female engineers and activists like Harry in their late twenties to thirties who had worked with him internationally in a multitude of ways.

We arranged to meet up midday and are now walking down one of the dusty roadways of the camp. Talking with Harry, it becomes apparent that the shortcomings of average users like me are not the only obstacle to building out democracy into cyberspace. There are daunting challenges to democratization in internet governance and design as well. I want to understand these, and that will require a level of knowledge beyond the primers that Andrew Clement and Christian Heck have given me.

Harry speaks fast, riffing out information and ideas, and I have to pay attention or I will miss something: "A lot of circumvention techniques are in fact funded by the US government, by the Open Technology Fund, but also by the navy, [which] was the primary founder of Tor.[2] I have to say, they have, by and large, funded the right stuff."[3]

Harry was a climate change activist in the US and the UK for the first decade of the millennium. He used to have long hair. Now he wears black button-down shirts, black pants, and a black satchel. He has been traveling and working internationally for a long time.

"But this is a short-term convergence of interests between the US and digital activists" he says. "A lot of these people at the CCC camp are anarchists, Marxists, or libertarians, while the US government is interested in overthrowing or countering the present regimes in Iran and China. Hillary Clinton has been one of the most enthusiastic proponents of open-source work, yet she is rabid when it comes to WikiLeaks. So you have this schizophrenic situation.

"For the activists, they should understand the convergence will end at some point, and they should be buffering themselves. The finances they are working with now will dry up, and then what will they use?

"But you have to ask yourself, why are there no other options for funding? Why aren't other governments, for example, funding this work? They have an interest to stop spying and the mass surveillance of their populations by the US, yet they're not cultivating a relationship with the activist technologists who can do this work."

At last, we seem to be headed for the green tent.

He jokes that he, a former hacker, is now part of the "standards industrial complex." At W3C, he puts companies like Google and Apple together with hackers to produce the standards that will allow interoperability on the internet. He recruited Apple to the W3C web cryptography working group at a Chaos Computer Club congress after noting in his talk that the company was not participating in the group.

Frankly, Harry says, the standards people and the companies he works with were "freaked out" by the Snowden revelations. He was freaked out by them: he had no idea how bad the surveillance had become. Right now, he is less interested in the technology and instead "obsessed with the social processes of getting this development into people's heads."

The law, he agrees, is inadequate to address the current challenges.

We duck into the green tent, and within seconds he is engaged in a deep-dive conversation with his copresenter for this evening's talk. I look for an electrical outlet to recharge my dead laptop, but outlets are an overtaxed resource at the camp. The many power bars are all bristling with other people's plugs. I balance my laptop on top of a dry gefilte fish that is some hacker's lunch on a long table crammed with computers. Gabriella Coleman, an anthropologist and academic who has written books on the free software movement and on the hacker/activist phenomenon Anonymous,[4] is in the tent, along with a bunch of French activists from La Quadrature du Net. I've reached the hub of the activist circle.

INTERNET GOVERNANCE: "LORAXES WHO SPEAK FOR THE TREES"

Harry Halpin has told me to look at Jonathan Zittrain's book *The Future of the Internet—and How to Stop It* if I want to understand better how the internet is governed. Zittrain is a professor at the Berkman Klein Center for Internet & Society at Harvard University. Later that afternoon, I get a cold beer at a bar nestled in a shady grove of trees and settle into a sofa under one of the many caravan tarps that cover groups of matching furniture, arranged like outdoor living rooms. Behind the sofa, someone is creating techno music at a console.

Techno penetrates the brain. The music, perpetually moving forward into an infinite space of shifting patterns, is strangely synergistic with the electrical pulses of thought. I noodle around on the web to find references to Jonathan Zittrain and stumble onto a video clip of his TED Talk called "The Web as Random Acts of Kindness."[5] Dandy.

In the video, Zittrain is down to earth and funny. He asks the audience to think about how the internet was first made—by geeks, he says, a bunch of guys who knew each other in high school, actually, who at the time of their invention had none of the capitalization you might think was needed to build a global infrastructure. "But they had an amazing freedom, which was they didn't *have* to make any money from it," Zittrain says. "The internet has no business plan, never did—no CEO, no firm responsible, singly, for building it. Instead, it was folks getting together to do something for fun, rather than because they were told to or because they expected to make a mint off of it. That ethos led to a network architecture, a structure, that was unlike other digital networks, then or since."[6] The internet, as Zittrain explains it, is basically a set of protocols. Anyone who wants to join the network can use those protocols to communicate, and anyone who wants to build an application on top of those protocols can do so. And it runs, more or less, by volunteerism, cooperation, and consensus. It has *stewards*, rather than bosses or overlords—Loraxes who "speak for the trees."[7] (The line from the Dr. Seuss children's book is, "I am the Lorax. I speak for the trees. I speak for the trees, for the trees have no tongues.")

I recall how Andrew Clement told me that the three main governance bodies of the internet—the Internet Engineering Task Force (IETF), the World Wide Web Consortium (W3C), and the Internet Corporation for Assigned Names and Numbers (ICANN)—run, to a large degree, by consensus. It seems an incredible proposition.

I skip along to find more details from Zittrain's book online. The IETF, a voluntary body, governs the architecture of the internet. It provides only the efficient packaging and routing of data between end nodes. First there was the ARPANET, the early wide-area network that linked university and research center computers. Then Vint Cerf and Bob Kahn figured out a code, or protocol, to allow any network, regardless of its features, to connect to this network. People say their protocol, known as TCP/IP (transmission control protocol/internet protocol), could run over "two tin cans and a string." (In his TED Talk, Zittrain shows a photo of them as gray-haired men, many years later, playing with strings and tin cans.)

By conception, then, the internet is a decentralized network of networks and a triumph of interoperable design. It uses a common protocol that creates a "connectivity commons"[8] everyone can share, as long as people do not enclose or sequester their part.

And with its neutral protocol that connects everyone to everyone, the internet has a marvelous generativity: anyone with an idea about what humans might do with this kind of connectivity can experiment and offer it to the world. Although the early internet might have looked like two tin cans connected by the string of Cerf and Kahn's protocol, the current internet has burgeoned into what looks more like a voluptuous hourglass. This is the common way of diagramming it, in any case.

At the bottom of the hourglass is the physical layer of the network—the part that Andrew Clement has been trying to chart with IXmaps, the wires and cables that convey data electronically. Then there is the applications layer, where anyone can develop software that will run on top of the physical layer. The narrow waist is the protocol layer, the simple TCP/IP code for connection. Above that is a content layer of language and images, and above that is a social layer—the behaviors of users (what they adopt, how they use the internet, and how they relate with each other). People can work on code and ideas at different layers of the net and know little or nothing about the other layers.[9] So there is both vertical decentralization (between layers) and horizontal decentralization (within layers) where anyone can plug in and experiment at any level.

The exception to the general decentralized pattern of the internet occurs when a company or government, say, builds a completely centralized system that does not allow interoperability at any layer of its sequestered network. Examples of completely centralized systems are China's national cybernetwork or AOL's early messaging service.

Today, it is more common to have closed, centralized services at only the applications layer of the internet, but these still threaten to balkanize the net and stifle its generative properties. This is a key insight of Zittrain and of others who study the internet: decentralization, free software, and open-source code that people can play with promote generativity (the proliferation of new ideas and experiments), while centralization and secret (or proprietary) code tend to kill it.

The IETF is concerned only with the connection layer, the waist of the hourglass. But this layer has implications for every other layer. The IETF maintains and improves the current internet protocol suite (the TCP/IP set of codes) that everyone uses voluntarily. It has no formal membership. Anyone can participate as a volunteer.

There is no voting process at the IETF. The work is often started by informal discussion groups known as "Birds of a Feather"[10] and gets done by working groups. They each have a mandate to tackle a problem that defines the scope of their work. Anyone can participate through an open mailing list or at IETF meetings. When the work is done, the groups disband.

TCP/IP provides end-to-end, or node-to-node, connectivity, so it covers how data is packeted, identified, transmitted, routed, and received. This is a neutral function, yet each of these steps is rife with privacy and security vulnerabilities, as Edward Snowden's leaks about NSA surveillance practices showed.

This is a lot of information to take in, and I need to absorb it to grasp the practical issues hackers are grappling with. But the heat and the scrolling are making me drowsy. I close my laptop and lean back into the sofa, surrendering for the moment to the protean patterns of the techno sound.

HARRY REDUX

That night, Harry Halpin delivers a talk about a lawsuit he and some fellow activists are filing against the United Kingdom. I learn he was on a terrorist list for his climate and antiglobalization activism. When he returned to the UK to finish his PhD, he says, his supervisor and friends were harassed by the police. He was forced to supply his DNA. When he went to France, the French police started a file on him. When he went to Copenhagen as an official delegate to the Climate Summit in 2009, he says, he was beaten so badly by Danish security agents that he couldn't see or walk.

At the time, he did not know that it was an undercover agent named Mark Kennedy, someone he knew in the UK and thought of as a friend, who was probably at the root of all this trouble. Kennedy was working for a domestic unit in the United Kingdom called the Association of Chief

Police Officers, which was sharing its intelligence with businesses being targeted by activists. Kennedy also carried on a two-year romantic relationship with Harry's copresenter on the panel, another climate activist, who was devastated when she found out her life had been hacked. Taking the microphone handed over to her by Harry, she tells the audience Kennedy had met her family. He was told by the command structure whether he would have dinner with her on any given evening. He was paid overtime for the nights he spent with her. Kennedy worked in over twenty countries. He worked for the private sector, as well, for the security company Stratfor, penetrating the animal rights movement, and for Densus, a private security firm in the United States.

East German Stasi agents had married dissidents during the Cold War and had children with them while spying on them, some for more than twenty years. But so, apparently, have the security agents of Western democracies. Ten women activists from the environmental movement sued Scotland Yard in 2011 for deception. Undercover police agents had lured them into long-term intimate relationships, and two of these men fathered children with the women they were spying on.[11]

I notice Harry is carrying his black satchel containing his laptop across his chest even when he is speaking on stage. Did Mark Kennedy have access to Harry's private email when he was spying on Harry and his copresenter? Most probably. Kennedy was mapping the social network of activists in order to identify the main "influencers." (His victims knew this because the security company Stratfor itself was hacked by a young American hacker named Jeremy Hammond. For that hack, Hammond is currently serving ten years in a US prison.)

Did Kennedy use the most intimate details of activists' online lives against them? Almost certainly. Harry's copresenter says her most debilitating thought is imagining Kennedy and his colleagues joking over her intimate correspondence with him.

Harry says he told his story about being put on a terrorist list to the Organisation for Economic Co-operation and Development (OECD) in Paris, where a US representative there took him to lunch and said he was sorry but could do nothing. Then several of Harry's friends were put on a terrorist list. When Harry's lawyer made a freedom-of-information request in the United States, he received 7,624 pages of information the US government had accumulated on his client. Harry still gets stopped when he goes to the UK under the Schengen (EU) border control and information-sharing system.

A New York district court recently held that damages for victims of improper police surveillance could flow from the knowledge alone of the surveillance, the harm of knowing it had happened. The harm of surveillance, Harry tells the Chaos Communication Camp audience, is that it destroys people's creativity and ability to organize. Do we destroy other public utilities, like the road system, in order to catch terrorists? If we destroy the internet, it will hurt our societies immensely. Data protection laws were put in place after World War II and the Cold War, he says, precisely because people understood how surveillance worked. "Today," he concludes, "the legal guarantees need tech guarantees to back them up."

I wander out of the big event tent into the night. Trying to reconcile the two Harrys I have come to know—the one who works for Tim Berners-Lee and the one who appears on terrorist lists—I walk down a dirt road that is flanked by a high embankment. Nineteenth- and twentieth-century machines stand like sentinels on its brow. A small railroad for transporting materials skirts its base. The machines have all been flood-lit with colored lights. Diggers, movers, balers, tractors, sifters—lovingly floodlit—the technology the object of hacker affection. Technology old and obsolete, crude or elegant, rudimentary or sophisticated, all fascinating to the hacker mind.

Around the end of the embankment, the road opens up into a large central field where the Chaos Computer Club icon, that fifty-foot-high laminate-clad model of a rocket ship—looking very much like the rocket in Antoine de Saint-Exupéry's *Le Petit Prince*—is pulsating with light and emiting vapors as if it is ready to take off. A few children are running around it or dancing with their parents close by.

A technically perfect sound system is playing impeccably cool music. The outdoor living rooms are full of reclining, amiable, conversing people. They float like illuminated islands in this large space of gathering darkness. In a stand of giant poplars at the edge of the camp, a thousand pinpoints of light shimmer like a thousand fireflies dancing in the trees on this fine summer night—magical, phosphorescent, digitally produced, fireflies.

OF TREES AND TONGUES

The next morning, Harry and I run into each other at breakfast. The sun is already blazing, and we find some shade under a tarp in the center field near the rocket. Sacha, an unassuming and somewhat frowzled Dutch hacker, joins us. The three of us are sweaty and thirsty, so I go and get us bottles of water to drink while we talk.

Thinking of Harry's talk the night before, I ask if his "standards" work dovetails at all with his activism. A lame question. He makes several attempts to respond with equivocal sounding sentence fragments before settling into the technical issues, which he has obviously decided are more to the point.

"The main problem with structural privacy," he explains, "is that our browsers assume the server should have complete control over our individual device—and we have to trust the server. The user is always transparent to the server. Also the user has no control over what the server sends her—what Google sends you, for example."

There is something almost impersonal about the way Harry speaks. He is friendly and kind, but like the internet, he transmits information as efficiently as possible from his node to mine. He speaks in paragraphs. He marshals and contextualizes what others are trying to say.

When the internet was invented, people didn't need to build secure protocols, he explains, because the internet was used primarily by an academic community for the purpose of sharing ideas in a cooperative manner. Cryptography, in any case, was mostly classified as secret information by the US government. On the early internet, everything was sent unencrypted with many identifiers. It was not until people realized the internet was going to be used for commerce and personal data that they recognized they needed to fix it. When the internet was being built, no one understood protocols. It was a messy job, with many security flaws.

"We're still trying to fix this infrastructural plumbing," says Harry. "At W3C, we are like the UN, talking to companies and trying to get their buy-in. The future is unclear. The model could become increasingly centralized. This is how it is going with Apple, Facebook, and Google as they create monopoly platforms and siloed services. The countervailing effort is toward decentralization and openness.

"It's in every big company's and in every country's interest to make passwords secure, for example," Harry says. "It's not in everyone's interest to make end-to-end encryption secure. And it's not in their interest to decentralize.

"And, in fact, it's very hard to build decentralized systems. That is, it's harder to build a privacy-secure decentralized system than it is to build a privacy-secure centralized system. Signal, for instance, from Open Whisper Systems in the hacker scene, is the best crypto package today, but it's a centralized product. Centralized is just easier to do. People may want decentralized products, but they forget the politics of scaling."

Many theorists of the internet do not understand protocols, Harry explains. They offer very naïve, flat solutions. "For example, they say, 'Why don't we create national internets for the public good?'" (I stop myself from confessing this has been my bright idea for the past month.) "Evgeny Morozov said this to me one time, and I responded, 'Well, the NSA is a national institution established for the public good.'" Morozov is the Malcolm Gladwell of tech writing, Harry says. Eastern European, he has lived in the United States for a long time and is in grad school now. He worked at the State Department for a time on a New American Foundation Fellowship in the internet policy unit and wrote a widely read article on the ways that repressive governments use the internet to track dissidents. "So he counters the tech utopia talk of Silicon Valley. That's good," Harry says.

"But he's a bit of a one-trick pony," Sacha chips in.[12]

"I do not understand how anyone can call themselves progressive and advocate national versus international communications," Harry says. "International communications, dialectically, opens up a space for change. It's a hacker concept: we should be able to communicate with anyone on the planet. China, Russia, Saudi Arabia: these are the states that support national internets. Lately, I'm seeing a big misunderstanding more and more in the press. Yes, Google as a monopoly is dangerous, but a government monopoly by the EU or US could be worse."

What about setting standards, I ask? People during the first Industrial Revolution managed to set standards for communications and other new technologies. So couldn't the International Organization for Standardization (ISO) and the UN's International Telecommunications Union (ITU) set standards that strike a balance between security and openness and between centralized services and a decentralized structure that allows experimentation and the generation of new ideas and products?

He grimaces slightly, head tilted. We are squinting at each other, even in the shade. The ISO has proposed the ITU as a potential governing body for the internet, says Harry, and every few years the ITU proposes itself at its annual general meeting. "The ISO stands out for its irrelevancy," he concludes. "They made a book of recommendations, but no one has followed it." In fact, in 1984, the ISO published a standard called "The Basic Reference Model for Open Systems Interconnection" (number 7498). The ISO model conceived of a networking system divided into seven layers, each one using a prescribed set of protocols to interact only with the layer immediately beneath it.

I tell him that my understanding is that the current governance structure is consensus based, but that the mechanisms for achieving consensus are imperfect. "The current governance structure isn't ideal," Harry says. "The IETF does standards for the internet. W3C does standards for the web and browser structure. Both are largely dominated by corporations and by white males. Theoretically, anyone can show up, but in fact it's the same old men who show up because when they were young, they invented the internet. They and the corporate representatives are the main attendees. It's expensive to attend, too, and it takes time—four meetings a year for the IETF and once a year for W3C. The mailing lists are pretty good, but a lot of the real decisions happen in the meetings."

"South America is now demanding a seat at the table and is a main player behind the NETmundial movement," he notes.

Most of the big internet companies are based in the United States, and most of the physical infrastructure of the internet is located there. US credibility as a neutral steward of the internet took a blow with the Snowden revelations.[13] Calls for a globally democratic net made headway when the IETF endorsed a call for all stakeholders, including all governments, to participate on an equal footing.[14] Two years later, in early 2015, the NETmundial Initiative convened in Brazil and declared a set of robust democratic principles for global internet governance. The governance process, it said, should be "democratic, multi-stakeholder, open, participative, consensus-driven, transparent, accountable, inclusive and equitable, distributed, collaborative and enabling of meaningful participation"[15]—a tall order.[16]

"One NETmundial idea," Harry continues, "is that if data is going to be really valuable, then companies that are collecting it are engaging in cybercolonialism. Hackers have been saying this for a while, and social movements are now taking this up, for example, at the Internet Social Forum, the Internet Governance Forum, and in the Pirate Party. NET-mundial is part of a large-scale, digital rights, social movement, but I don't think its advocates or supporters necessarily understand the revolutionary, anticapitalist implications of what they're saying. Because while you can't have the same companies and governments running the internet forever, this will have to be taken up politically at some point. The alternative is to just let Google run everything, but that's unpleasant at best. This is one possible future, however."

"Tim Berners-Lee, my boss, thinks of himself as a hacker. He writes code. He's pushing for a Magna Carta of the internet (he's British, so they say 'Magna Carta' not 'constitution')."

I think of John Perry Barlow's "Declaration of the Independence of Cyberspace" and many other declarations that have been written in recent years by NGOs, privacy commissioners, and international treaty bodies. The more frequently moral and legal rights are declaimed, it seems to me, the feebler they actually are in regulating the demons the tech is unleashing. "There are lots of declarations of rights," I say.

"Yes, there's a lot of declarations of rights," Harry replies, "but can we build these rights into the protocols and software?"

"At the 2015 meeting of IETF in Prague, Edward Snowden was one of the beamed-in speakers, and he got a standing ovation. Even programmers who might have come from the hacker scene and 'sold out' to work for large companies still believe in the hacker ethos. In fact, Richard Stallman and Julian Assange have an intellectual influence which is vast, certainly larger than Steve Jobs and Larry Page. Google and Microsoft have people from the hacker movement running their centralized cryptology programs. These hackers need *some* money, so they go to work for these companies. But their loyalty is with some concept of the internet, not with the companies."

"Decentralization, openness, human rights: most tech people generally believe in these things. Many companies donate money to the Electronic Frontier Foundation and to the Free Software Foundation, for example. It's a complex political space, but hackerdom is the conscience and consciousness of Silicon Valley."

"That said," he continues, "the biggest belief in the tech world is in the market. There's talk of the commons, but the market is the prevailing belief. Also, there's a lot of libertarianism. The Bitcoin community, especially, is almost postlibertarian, anarcholibertarian! Some projects, like Riseup, are anarchist. Some, like the Tor Project, are all over the map. Some, like HackingTeam, are just 'black hat' scumbags who will sell their services to anyone. But the common ground many tech people share is that they are rights-based: they believe in net rights, human rights. Decentralization is the overarching principle of the internet. The way the internet works is through decentralized protocol and free software. That's what most of the internet is built from. So these values have been deeply embedded in the internet for forty years."

Harry sums up his own work and the historical moment: "W3C? We are like the hacker intelligence agency. We want to avoid a Google *and* a state monopoly. Most people in the group are from the '70s and '80s era of the internet. A lot of the internet pioneers were part of the '60s student and social movements."

I stop to take stock of what Harry has just said. So the internet right now is governed by these hacker elders (Loraxes) speaking for ordinary users (for the trees)? What will happen when these pioneer elders are gone?

"Hacker politics will continue to develop organically over time in a way that is neither traditionally Marxist nor anarchist or any 'ist'," says Harry. "The hacker movement has been growing exponentially, especially since Snowden. The last CCC congress had ten thousand people attending! That's a crazy number."

"But movements take time. And right now, we have to address all the policy issues at once," he says. "Public intellectuals massively simplify the issues and don't understand the hacker scene." He looks into my eyes and says it out straight: "We need a book that can take a nuanced, intelligent position." I have been duly warned.

WHAT IS DEMOCRACY? OR HOW TO GOVERN DEMOCRATICALLY IN A WORLD THAT IS NO LONGER FLAT?

One of the most striking realizations for the layperson who wanders into this world is that, to begin to comprehend it, one must think multidimensionally. Apprehending the scope of the governance problems is similar to what it must have been like for people in the fifteenth century to apprehend the world is not flat. Everything potentially needs to be reconceived and recalculated, and new disciplines invented. Although forward thinkers are trying to map out the big picture, the multitude of discrete, knotty, technical, and policy questions that need to be fought over and settled in some way is daunting.

In this light, it is understandable that people allow themselves to indulge in simplifications of an exaggeratedly utopian or dystopian cast. As cybernetics scholar Thomas Rid has observed, "Myths work as conceptual aids, reducing complexity, condensing narratives, and making novel, yet unknown technologies approachable, either in a utopian or a dystopian way."[17]

Gabriella Coleman (the anthropologist and author of books about free software and Anonymous) has observed that hackers often work easily across political ideologies on discrete, practical problems they deem worthy, and that some eschew ideology altogether.[18] This may account for the fact that there are a lot of strange bedfellows and unlikely fellow travelers in the hacker space at the moment.

But what Harry Halpin seems to be getting at is that no one yet understands the political economy this new technological revolution is ushering in. Karl Marx's monumental analysis of the Industrial Revolution focused on the factory as the locus of production and political organization. His work still offers many insights into how capitalism works and why it is inherently unstable. But the digital revolution unfolding in the twenty-first century has yet to be fully theorized.[19]

What can a simple twentieth-century democrat offer in this context? Maybe the goal should be to remind people what a democracy is and why it remains a desirable form of governance, whatever complexity the twenty-first century brings.

What is a democracy?

Western liberal democrats might say it involves at least three things. The first is the idea of popular sovereignty, discussed in chapter 3. Democracy means government is answerable to the people. Politically sovereign people are free people. Governments that consistently fail to carry out the wishes of the people, either because they are captured by class or corporate interests or because their technocrats take important issues "off the table," are not democratic but tyrannical.

Liberal democrats might say the second thing a democracy involves is mitigating the domination of some over others. At the very least, this means that the majority rules but minorities are protected. Powerful interests are regulated and not allowed to run roughshod over the less powerful. In the same vein, a belief in the dignity and worth of each individual is central to the concept of liberal democracy. "Freedom" must be enjoyed by all, not just by the strongest, and this is achieved through institutional means such as a bill of rights, the separation of powers, regulation, tradition, and other social norms.

Finally, Western liberal democrats might say a democracy involves sharing a common wealth. John Perry Barlow called it the "commonweal" in his "Declaration of the Independence of Cyberspace." "The commonwealth" is actually a very old democratic idea dating back to the Latin concept of *res publica* ("public thing"), or republic. As US historian Gordon S. Wood has observed, republics demand more from their citizens than monarchies do. They are not held together by "trains of dependencies and inequalities, supported by standing armies, strong religious establishments and a dazzling array of titles, rituals and ceremonies."[20] Rather, as early American republicans stressed, democracies are ordered on the virtue of their people; they demand citizens place a moral value on social cohesion and the common weal.[21] A "commonwealth" is a political community founded for the common good.

These ideas correspond roughly to the great organizing principles of the Enlightenment—*liberté*, *egalité*, and *fraternité*. In these last two respects—*egalité*, or the concern for mitigating domination, and *fraternité*, or the concern for sharing a commonwealth—democracy is the opposite of libertarianism.[22] It is certainly the opposite of authoritarianism. It shares some ideals with anarchism.

But democracy traditionally has been based on the nation state, and in maps of the digitally networked world, the nation state is looking increasingly irrelevant. As John Perry Barlow declaimed, networks do not heed borders. But what he did not foresee, perhaps, was that they intensify complexity. They intensify concentrations of power and value extraction. And there seems to be little that nation states can do about these negative network dynamics. Indeed, the network utopianism and neoliberalism that have politically dominated the last few decades would have us surrender ourselves to the power of the networks, the tech, the innovation, and the creative destruction of it all.[23] After forty years of creative destruction, people have justifiably begun to question where surrender leads us.

For democrats, the current crisis in governance is profoundly dismaying. We know we need new theories of political economy and new social experiments to discover them. We know we need to invent new ways of democratic being.

HACKER GOVERNANCE: NOISY SQUARE

Even in the hacker world, governance is challenging. Sacha has been listening patiently while Harry and I talk to each other, cross-legged in our bit of shade. Sacha van Geffen is the managing director of Greenhost, a hosting company that focuses on environmental issues and digital rights internationally. It works a lot with nongovernmental organizations. He says it tries to support tech that promotes "an internet of human rights."

Harry has told me the Chaos Computer Club is very interesting but that the Dutch hackers are just as compelling and often overlooked. There is no long-standing, large-scale hacker organization in the Netherlands like the CCC, yet the Dutch have made some important contributions. Like Americans, they tend to put political emphasis on free speech, whereas the Germans have been consistently concerned with privacy.

Sacha tells me that Amsterdam was one of the first points in Europe that connected to ARPANET, the forerunner of the internet, which connected universities. A lot of Dutch universities were hooked up to this early version of the internet. The Dutch hacker group XS4ALL (Access for All) pushed a new idea that everyone, not just universities, should have access to the internet. The group set up a foundation and published a magazine called *Hactic*. Later, Amsterdam became the first municipality to attempt to create a digital city with free wireless access to the internet for everyone.

The World Wide Web was the first service that allowed ordinary people to use the internet. It took hypertext and put it on top of the internet around 1991 or 1992. The widespread use of the web took off around 1993 or 1994.

"When I first subscribed to XS4ALL," Sacha recalls fondly, "they would send a booklet of known websites on the internet. These might have 'web rings' for associated sites (you know, url addresses at the bottom of a web page) and the heading, 'Next Web Site.'"

"The point is," Harry summarizes, "the Netherlands was instrumental in getting ordinary people onto the internet."

"There is a space in the world for Dutch hackers," Sacha says mildly, "it just needs to be refilled! In the '90s, the Netherlands was very active in the hacker world. Since then, it's tailed off."

Dutch camps were first organized by the founder of XS4ALL. They happened every four years, in between the German Chaos Computer Club camps. At the last Dutch camp, in 2013, named "OHM" (for "Observe, hack, make" or the word *ohm*, the universal scientific measure for resistance, signified as Ω), there was a big fight over whether the company Fox IT should be a sponsor of the camp. The main organizer of the camp that year was an employee of the company.

"An anarchist from the hackerspace Puscii.nl, in Utrecht, wrote a piece titled 'What's Wrong with the Kids These Days?,'" Sacha continues. "Then the Chaos Computer Club said that if Fox IT was going to be a main sponsor, they were officially not going to be present at the event. This was a big political statement between hacker scenes. I said, 'Okay, we're not going to be there, but the kids are going to be there [meaning young hackers], and do we want them to be there with 'cool' techno companies teaching them how to spy and do bad things? Is that the only narrative we want to show them?'"

It was decided they could do one of two things—either organize a countercamp (but time was short, and that would take a lot of effort) or be at the camp.

Sacha told his fellow hackers, "Revolutions do not happen in silent circles. They happen in noisy squares, the embodiment of resistance." They would attend the camp. ("Silent circles" was a play on the name of a new security software company called Silent Circle, created by Phil Zimmermann, the inventor of Pretty Good Privacy, in which he partnered controversially with two former US Navy SEALs.) They registered the domain name "Noisy Square" and used it with the slogan "Putting the resistance back into OHM." They reached out to national and international organizations for donations and set up a large tent at the camp with its own politically based talks.

It was very tense at the OHM camp. Some incidents were blown out of proportion by the official organizers, Sacha says. For example, Sacha's group made a mock police hazard tape that said, "Police, do not cross."

Someone then wrapped the Fox IT tent with the tape. The organizers took it badly.

Noisy Square became highly influential. It socialized the creation of policy streams and the discussion of policy at hacker conferences. Every single hacker conference since OHM has had a space called Noisy Square, including the last Hackers on Planet Earth (HOPE) conference in the US. It is a safe place for politically aware hackers and technically aware activists to congregate. It reflects the growing pains of governance within the hacker scene itself as it struggles to maintain a politically informed purpose while its ranks are swelling with newcomers.

Still, there is the problem of finding funding for politically progressive hacking. "Private capital does not really fund freedom technologies or hackers, except Bitcoin," Harry says, returning to the issue that first sparked our extended conversation. "There isn't much of a business case for human rights. You have academic funding sometimes, but academic gatekeepers can affect how funding is used for progressive projects. To do a large software project is difficult, and you need big funding."

"Technology usually follows the path of least resistance. It makes the powerful more powerful and the unpowerful even less powerful—unless you pay attention."

6

CULTURE CLASH
Hermes and the Italian HackingTeam

It is nearly three o'clock in the morning on the fourth day of the camp. By this time, I've pretty much given up sleeping, there are so many people to talk to.

Under the glow of lanterns hung among the birch trees, several of us are eating a late dinner. Sitting at one communal table in the near dark, two men in their early thirties are speaking to each other in Italian. Italians! So they're here.

A big scandal involving Italian hackers broke only a few weeks ago. HackingTeam (whose members Harry Halpin called "scumbags") was a group of Milan-based hackers who allegedly sold their surveillance software to some of the worst authoritarian regimes on the planet. Numerous hacker, civil society, and university-based groups, including Reporters Without Borders, Privacy International,[1] Human Rights Watch,[2] and the Citizen Lab[3] at the University of Toronto, wrote reports or open letters denouncing them.

Then someone hacked HackingTeam and exfiltrated all its stuff through torrents, posting the 420 gigabyte file on HackingTeam's own Twitter feed with the file name "Hacked Team."[4]

The *colpo di grazia* in this *cause célèbre* had become the talk of the camp. Who had managed to pull off this admirable hack? The mystery was generating a lot of cheerful speculation.

Sacha van Geffen had told me a bit about the Italian hacker scene. Of the internet policy groups in Europe, at least two were Italian—the NEXA Center for Internet and Society in Turin and the European University Institute in Florence. German hacker meetings had good organization, but the Italian ones, apparently, had better food.

A friendly *"Siete Italiani?"* draws me immediately into a warm, familial conversation with these two men at the next table, one heavily bearded and looking like an early explorer and the other clean-shaven. There is a large Italian contingent at the camp, they tell me—forty-five citizens and tonight thirty or more hangers-on. It's a party.

This is Matteo's first time at the camp. He points at the dark-bearded Corrado—"He convinced me to come"—and they smile fraternally at each other. "It's amazing. In three days here, you learn so much. You realize that you learned more technical stuff than you did in a year. You learn that you can learn. That's why everyone talks about the hacker mindset—because it *is* a mindset."

"We study each other as well," Corrado chuckles. "You see a lot of people here who you think would not be party people, and then you see how they party!"

The two met each other in Chile as startup entrepreneurs. Harry has told me about the Latin Americans wanting to participate in internet governance and the digital economy, but a Chilean Silicon Valley? It seems unlikely.

"The Chilean government offers you money if you're willing to come to Chile and develop your stuff there," Corrado explains. "There's a review on the merit of your application, but you're not asked to bring funding. They want you to do something to build entrepreneurial culture, whether it's workshops or events. They had a dictatorship until the 1990s with Pinochet and a lack of entrepreneurial culture. So they started this program. At the beginning, they had mostly foreigners, but now they have more and more Chileans. They accept three hundred startups each year, and they take applications based on very early ideas."

How would he describe the experience in Chile?

"Awesome. You're working in a room with a hundred other people. They're great people. You can ask them questions, talk about ideas.

Corrado interjects, "But we feel more at home here."

"Because it was very business-oriented there." Matteo shrugs. "You had to think of a business plan and marketing and communication. Here, you can focus on tech only, and that's really more our skill set. I've been back for a year in my hometown. I miss the working environment in Chile, waking up and looking forward to that room with a hundred people. Then you come home to your parents' house. The great thing about Start-Up Chile was the community."

Corrado tells me three main hacker camps take place in Italy. The first and oldest is the Hack Meeting. It usually takes place in an abandoned or empty space, which the meeting occupies or squats in. People are told only a few weeks before the meeting takes place, which gives the organizers just long enough for the event to happen before the police catch on and get an eviction order. Generally, between two hundred to three hundred hackers attend, and these are "really, really left wing to the point that if you show empathy for someone who is not left wing, they'll say you're a fascist and you're out of there."

The second camp takes place near Venice and is called the End Summer Camp. There are workshops, but attendees spend a lot of time socializing.

Pescara, the third camp, is organized every four years, like the Dutch and Chaos Computer Club camps, by Oligrafix, a hacker group that has a "strong female presence," which is unusual. These hackers care about technology and society. This is the biggest event, it takes place in central Italy, but with all these events you never know if they are actually going to happen. Unlike in Germany, hacker culture in Italy is not well known or understood, so hackers can't just ask to use a big venue like the Chaos Computer Club does and expect to get it.

In Sicily, there is a strong hacker group called Freaknet. It does not organize events but operates the Museum of Working Computer Machines that has machines from years ago that have been kept in working order. Anyone can access and operate them, some of them online. In Sicily, one hacker meeting a few years back was held in a place that had been owned by the mafia and then confiscated by the police to become state property. The state tries to use these properties in useful ways, so the hackers were able to use it when they asked for it. As an organizer, to ask for a place like that is a little dangerous. "You expose yourself," Corrado says.

Do they consider themselves hackers or entrepreneurs?

"Neither," Corrado says without hesitation. "We're just enjoying the environment at the CCC camp."

"If I had to choose," Matteo says, "I'd say hacker, but in hacker culture you never define yourself as a hacker. Others do."

"You might call yourself an artist," Corrado offers.

"It's like being cool. It's lame if you *say* you're cool."

"Between 2005 and now, this event has changed," Corrado says. At the beginning, it was about how you use your computer. "Now, on the agenda you see stuff on making a rocket, on physics, on how to make cheese, which I don't care so much about. But so what? A few years ago, there was a proposal to work on having hackers in space because with the way things are going on earth, we may need to be in space."

Is this the origin of the distinctive Chaos Computer Club rocket mascot and logo, I wonder.

"The idea was, 'No one else is doing it, so let us do it, and in ten years we will be closer to the goal of having a rocket ship for travel in outer space.'"

I ask if they have heard about the HackingTeam scandal that broke a few weeks ago in the news.

Have they *heard* about the HackingTeam story?! "Usually, we call ourselves the Italian Hacker Embassy. This year we're calling ourselves the Italian Hackéd Embassy." He pronounces the "éd" in "Hacked" as an extra syllable and with a strong Italian accent. He shows me the T-shirt they had printed for that night. Their organizers have brought several kegs of special grappa all the way from Italy just to celebrate the event.

We head off cheerfully into the dark to go and drink some, and when we arrive at the large, brightly lit "Embassy" tent, a big, happy party is already well under way.

BLACK, WHITE, AND GRAY

Next afternoon at the "Italian Hacker Embassy," Gianluca Gilardi and Andrea Ghirardini greet me warmly and lead me across the recently jumping dance floor to grab some chairs and go outside. Corrado and Matteo set up this meeting and have brought me here to make the introduction.

Gianluca and Andrea are going to tell me the inside story of the HackingTeam hack—as much as they know, at any rate. But first, they are going to tell me about their own group, which was created three years ago. I want to learn more about how entrepreneurial culture both meshes and clashes with progressive hacker culture. (Our conversation will also lead me to an epiphany about computer security that tech insiders might find hard to believe, although many ordinary users will not.)

We sit in some dappled shade behind the big tent. Green windfall apples are everywhere underfoot. A nearby tree has been dropping its fruit onto campers, tents, and partygoers all week long. For the Italians, this does not seem to be a nuisance. They work around it.

Gianluca and Andrea tell me the decision to call their group "Hermes" was a collective one. Yes, the name is the same as that of a well-known luxury-goods company, but they wanted to call it Hermes anyway, after the Greek god of communication and intuition. Hermes is a center for research, digital rights, and online freedom. They, themselves, are not personally activists but support the organization's activities. Actually, they say, the group is really an umbrella for people who may not be able to claim that they are activists in their everyday jobs. Gianluca and Andrea have a way of revising their script as they go.

Gianluca is a lawyer, a large man who speaks with wry, tolerant amusement about the world. His curly, boyish hair is graying. Andrea, more intense, is a digital forensic expert. Their work for Hermes is their passion, if not currently their nine-to-five job.

One of Hermes's best-known projects is GlobaLeaks—software that allows people to make anonymous submissions. Unlike WikiLeaks, GlobaLeaks does not publish leaked information, and it does not sell a service or host a central platform. Instead, it gives clients software and knowledge about how to use it. On its website, Hermes has a list of all the entities using the GlobaLeaks technology and other leaker technologies. They are proud that several media outlets are now using the GlobaLeaks tools.

GlobaLeaks has an administrator who configures the software for the client but is not able to see the documents that are submitted. These are sent from the submitter to the receiver and encrypted on the server. Only the receiver, who is the owner of the private key, can decrypt them.

Fabio Pietrosanti and Matteo Flora are two of the founders of Hermes. The group consists of about twenty people, including civil and criminal

lawyers, programmers, entrepreneurs, hackers, and Unix system admin-
istrators. It was quite a feat in the beginning to get all this interdisciplinary talent to come together, Gianluca tells me. Hermes has other tech
projects, but GlobaLeaks is its best known. And many regard it as the
best leaking platform among the numerous leaking platforms inspired
by WikiLeaks that have proliferated over the last few years. These vary
wildly in quality. The list includes BaltiLeaks, BritiLeaks, BrusselsLeaks,
CrowdLeaks, GreenLeaks, JumboLeaks, Murdoch Leaks, QuebecLeaks,
and TradeLeaks. In 2011, the *Wall Street Journal* started a leak portal called
WSJ SafeHouse that used weak SSL encryption and was incompatible
with Tor, even though the site suggested that submitters should use Tor.
Some use PGP but not Tor and so fail to hide the identity of the leaker.
Some offer no encryption or onion router at all. *Al Jazeera*'s portal even
planted a tracking cookie on the leaker's browser.[5]

Gianluca and Andrea do not like the word "dominant." They expect
to be the "first" major player in the leak field—the first to balance privacy
and secrecy with ease of use. They are confident that GlobaLeaks is the
best software currently available. Other software may be more paranoid
and hypersecure, but it is not easy to use.

"For example," Gianluca says, describing the shortcomings of their
competitors, "just to get the information: you can't see it, so you have to
write it on a USB stick and take it to another computer that is air-gapped,
that's never been used, and then you have to decrypt it, and it's not easy
to get the key, and you can't manipulate or send it." He waves his hand
dismissively: "It's a mess."

One week before the hack of HackingTeam, Hermes was at an event
called "ePrivacy" at the Italian Parliament to advocate against government use of Trojan technology. HackingTeam had used Trojan technology to develop something called its "Remote Control System," which the
group sold to law enforcement and security agencies around the world.
It had recently been granted a global export authorization by the Italian
government in place of earlier export restrictions that had been placed
on it.[6]

Although HackingTeam repeatedly denied that its client list included
regimes that were known for repressing civil rights and that used its tools
to target citizens, journalists, human rights defenders, and pro-democracy
activists domestically and abroad, investigations by the Citizen Lab at

the University of Toronto suggested otherwise.[7] Reporters Without Borders called HackingTeam "a digital mercenary" and one of the "corporate enemies of the Internet."[8]

As soon as Trojan technology is inserted into a computer, Gianluca tells me, it allows the person who controls it to track and even control what happens on the computer. Hermes told the Italian Parliament that it was not a good idea for government to adopt it because buyers have to trust the private company that sells it to them.

Four days later, HackingTeam was hacked by an unknown entity, and the information that came out proved Hermes's point. Whoever hacked HackingTeam released everything—4 terabytes of data that included all of HackingTeam's source code, several years of emails, and all their documents. The material went out through torrents and was published in a searchable format by WikiLeaks. Now it is public, although only *cognoscenti* like members of the Hermes group might be able to understand it all, and they were currently working their way through it. The documents, if authentic, showed that HackingTeam's clients included Azerbaijan, Kazakhstan, Russia, and Uzbekistan; Bahrain, Egypt, Saudi Arabia, and the United Arab Emirates; Ethiopia and Sudan; as well as US agencies including the Federal Bureau of Investigation and the Drug Enforcement Administration.[9] The group received huge sums of money for its work.[10] Alarmingly, the documents confirmed that in 2014, HackingTeam developed a hack for the Linux "kernel."

Recall that the Linux kernel has been so widely adopted for its superior reliability and flexibility of use that it now runs most of the internet's servers, the New York Stock Exchange, nearly all of the world's supercomputers, medical equipment, sensitive databases, vehicles from cars to drones to warships, most of the Internet of Things, and most of the tech platforms that dominate the current US economy, including Amazon, Facebook, and Google.[11] But the kernel's superior performance qualities have been achieved, in part, by trading off security—a matter that has become a source of friction between some Linux contributors and its original developer, Linus Torvalds.[12] Ironically, HackingTeam targeted the Linux kernel in the only user-controlled phone system available on the market, Google's Android, turning it into a spying device that could track Android users, record their conversations, search their files, and even snap photographs of them.[13]

In a story that sounds like a Manichean struggle for the soul of free software, the security flaw had first been reported by a teenage hacker and contributor to Linux named Pinkie Pie, before being exploited by the "white-" or "gray-hat" hacker, Geohot. He created an app called Towelroot, which provided root access to the Verizon and AT&T versions of the Samsung Galaxy S5, allowing users of those phones to have "system administrator" control over their devices (Geohot was also the first person to "jailbreak" the iPhone).[14] Then, the definitely "black-hat" HackingTeam seems to have exploited this breach to develop a virtual "skeleton key"[15] for Android phones with the intent of selling their hack to clients—until HackingTeam itself was definitively "owned" by a mysterious "white-hat" hacker, and evidence of the group's perfidy was unmasked for everyone to see on WikiLeaks (widely viewed as "white hat" despite some of its questionable decisions). In one email about the key they were developing, a HackingTeam member smirks to another, "It works"). The reply comes back, "Good job, thanks!"[16]

But this is digression. Gianluca is explaining the point Hermes made to the Italian government: "If you are a law enforcement agency and you are using a black box [proprietary, nontransparent code], you have to trust that it works the way the maker says." HackingTeam claimed it did not have any back door in its products. But two days after being hacked, HackingTeam moved to shut down all the Trojan systems it had sold to governments around the world. The public rationale given by Hacking-Team and the governments involved was that now that the systems were hacked, others could see their source code and seize control of them.

Gianluca says, "This is off the record, but the suspicion is that Hack-ingTeam *did* have a back door to its products. How else could it have shut them down so fast without involving clients?"

I ask why it is off the record when anyone could infer it logically.[17]

Gianluca replies, "Well, there is logic, and then there is code. People are studying the code now and may find the back door, and that would be final evidence. But yes, one could suspect logically that HackingTeam had a back door that allowed them to shut down the systems and may also be the real reason they *wanted* to shut down the systems as soon as they were hacked."

Three companies have developed Trojan technology so far, Gianluca says: Gamma Group, from Germany, which was hacked last year;

HackingTeam, from Italy, which was hacked on July 6, 2015; and NSO Group Technologies, from Israel, which has not been hacked—yet.

The HackingTeam story is important because it was the first time the entrails of a private surveillance company have been exposed so thoroughly. This industry's growth in recent years, which has coincided with rapid advances in technology, has prompted gossip and speculation about its activities, but the industry has managed to keep much of its work in the shadows. There has been at least one attempt (in the United States) to ban trade in surveillance technology to repressive regimes, but it failed.[18]

"If one sells sandwiches to Sudan, he is not subject, as far as my knowledge goes, to the law," one HackingTeam lawyer wrote in a leaked internal email. "HackingTeam should be treated like a sandwich vendor."[19]

The Chaos Computer Club has challenged the use of Trojan technology in Germany. The German government's procurement of the technology was leaked by WikiLeaks early on, in 2008. The Federal Constitutional Court of Germany ruled that police could use this kind of "source wiretapping" technology only for internet telephony because internet telephony typically encrypts data as soon as it leaves the computer, making source wiretapping the only effective option. However, when the CCC did an analysis of the Staatstrojaner software being used by the German government, it found that its Trojan program had all kinds of extra functionality built into it: it could control a targeted computer, take screenshots, and fetch and run code. This was a violation of the constitutional court's ruling. CCC found numerous security problems with the software also. It could be controlled over the internet by German state agencies, but the commands were sent unencrypted and so were vulnerable to third-party attacks. The screenshots and data the software exfiltrated were encrypted by it, but so incompetently as to not be effective. And the data was sent through a proxy server in the United States and so potentially was subject to US surveillance.[20]

The Chaos Computer Club's findings, published in October 2011, were widely reported in the German press. CCC went on to testify several times before the German Parliament on legislation proposed to govern the technology's use.[21] The legislation that was ultimately passed ended up expanding the permissible use of the technology to searches of a computer's content in addition to "wiretapping" its communications.

On July 6, 2015 (by coincidence, the day HackingTeam was hacked), the Staatstrojaner technology was again challenged constitutionally, and the Chaos Computer Club was asked to give an advisory opinion to the court.[22]

A bicyclist pushing a slender-framed racing bike toward us through the fallen apples stops to join our group in the shade. I'm not sure who he is, but his simple dark biking suit, trim goatee, and round black-framed glasses are eccentrically nineteenth-century-looking.

Gianluca is saying Hermes does a lot of advocacy work with governments and international forums. Advocacy can involve installing platforms, he says, including on behalf of governments.

"Yes," the bicyclist quips, "we send Fabio to them. Fabio will fit in a normal envelope without a surcharge."

As he jokes with Gianluca and Andrea, I ask him if he has ever met the HackingTeam people. "It's very hard not to have met HackingTeam at some point if one is a hacker in Italy because it's a small scene," he replies. "In fact, I went to university with two of the HackingTeam members, so I know them."

He introduces himself as Matteo Flora, one of Hermes's founders, along with Fabio Pietrosanti and others. Ten years ago, Matteo Flora worked as a forensic computer expert for government. Now he is a hired gun.

How do Italian hackers view HackingTeam, aside from the fact they have become a national joke?

"I don't think any Italians feel they're a joke right now," Matteo says, suddenly serious. "It's an exorcism, in fact—like the Mexican ritual, Day of the Dead. By laughing at death itself, we exorcise darkness. Laughing at serious matters is something the internet has been doing since the beginning. 4chan has been doing this, laughing at dreadful things I'm sure they do not agree with, but you have to incorporate this stuff into your reality."

"We're laughing to try to understand what's happened," Andrea offers.

"To understand how a leak like this could happen," Matteo continues. "Losing so much information—4 terabytes—and so sensitive, in such a short time: it doesn't add up. I'm not saying you need a conspiracy theory, but it doesn't add up. HackingTeam knew they were the preferred target of activists around the world online. Activists even entered their offices. There's something that doesn't match up: you do security, but you are so losing control of security within yourself. The affair raises important questions. Can we really think a world without states using this kind of Trojan technology is possible? Can we enforce a world without it? Or at least limit the technology?"

Andrea adds, "Can a government develop this technology without a private company being involved?"

"There's no doubt that HackingTeam fuckéd up," says Matteo. He pronounces the "ed" as a second syllable, and we all giggle uncontrollably. "We can't answer these questions, but sometimes a good question is an answer in itself. "

"Now you're getting philosophical," Andrea teases.

"It's our responsibility to ask the right questions," Matteo says. "Yes, it is. I'm fairly sure it is."

Where will all this lead?

"Laughing is an exorcism," Matteo repeats. "But I don't think that people are yet fully ready to understand what's going on. Who is the bad guy—the guy creating the gun or shooting the gun? Right now, we're missing the bad guy. The one who's using the tool is also the bad guy. The complete lack of legislation on how the state behaves is a problem. *That* is what is enraging the community—the fact that you need to draw the line on what you do and governments and HackingTeam have crossed the line."

"Many times," Andrea says, emphatically.

Is HackingTeam finished?

Andrea lightens. "This is a very good question."

"I suppose the *company* is finished," offers Matteo.

"The Italian government dumped them," says Gianluca, "but the individuals are going to be in a HackingTeam business under a different brand."

"I don't know if all the people in HackingTeam knew of the bad things they were doing," Matteo says.

"Silence is also evil," says Andrea. "If you don't agree, you can resign. Many of us have done this."

Matteo shrugs. "It's hard."

"Yes, but many of us have done this," repeats Andrea. "One strange thing: a journalist from *The Verge* says in two different articles that he tried to contact the guy who stole HackingTeam's Twitter account. When he reached him, the guy said, 'I remember you,' and sent the journalist a Twitter message from Gamma [the German security company that was hacked earlier]. So the suspicion is the same guy hacked *both* Gamma and HackingTeam."

"The person who hacked HackingTeam knew a lot about Italian culture," adds Matteo. "On Twitter, he posted screen shots from a popular Italian TV show to shame HackingTeam's system administrator."

"The irony is that HackingTeam was likely hacked by a Trojan technology like the one it sells because the hackers gained control of the HackingTeam network. The information was supposedly exfiltrated through their system administrator's machine. If you compromise this, you have access to everything."

"A system administrator is the most similar thing to God," Andrea explains for my benefit.

"There was a text file on the desktop of Pozzi, the system administrator, that contained most of the HackingTeam passwords for their internal and *external client* machines … *in plain text*."

"That's so fucking wrong, you know!" says Matteo, wagging his hands in the prayer position, and we're all giggling uncontrollably again.

"You can look for 'Christian Pozzi sucks' on Twitter to see this," says Andrea. "It means, 'You are a fucking idiot.'"

Matteo twinkles: "No, it means you're being just a little bit naïve."

Gianluca shrugs with that bemused air he has, and Matteo leaves us for another appointment. Hermes has offered to help the Italian government, Gianluca tells me, "but government treats us as not reliable. They say, 'You don't have anything to gain.' It would be easier if Hermes *were* a private company."

I ask him how he manages his own computer security as a lawyer for Hermes. He tells me he took a week to prepare his own electronic security for the camp, longer than he took to pack. "This is a hostile environment," he says, looking around to indicate the entire camp.

When I admit I have used the open net connection at the camp, both he and Andrea shake their heads. Among the multitude of Italian gestures they've used that afternoon, this one clearly means, "Well, you're fucked."

"If they found you," Andrea tells me, "then they can see everything. If they put a Trojan on your computer, then they will see everything going forward, even if you change your passwords."

"You mean, put one on remotely?" Now I am getting worried, as the full meaning of Trojan begins to penetrate my denial.

Gianluca looks at me. "You should buy a new computer and start over."

If I import my old files to a new computer, will the Trojan be imported too?

Andrea shrugs. Yes, this is possible.

Wouldn't it be less expensive and time consuming to get a forensic expert to look for the Trojan?

Andrea replies, "Yes, possibly, if he's good." But he doesn't look too certain.

Brought down to earth by my own security problem, I feel more daunted than ever. Finally, I have grasped that security is a challenge shot through with uncertainty even at the most expert level. The "electronic frontier" that John Perry Barlow poeticized is as wild as it has ever been and more hostile than I ever imagined.

7

DEMOCRACY IN CYBERSPACE

Then the Design Problems

THE PROBLEM OF PROVABLE SECURITY

In fact, HackingTeam later told an investigative reporter it could "beam" its Remote Control System into a computer "over a Wi-Fi network."[1] This was in addition to more conventional methods of access used by the group, such as implanting malicious code with a USB stick or spear phishing (tricking a user to click on an infected link or attachment). For spear phishing, HackingTeam used authentic documents provided by its clients, including invitations to parties and election papers.[2]

Another method that critics of HackingTeam believe the group was using (and which the group referred to in its emails) is called "network injection."[3] This involves pinpointing where a target is browsing on the internet and sending a doctored version of a webpage the person has requested, so that while, say, a favorite Italian TV show is streaming as intended in the foreground, malicious code is burrowing its way into the target's computer in the background.

As Christian Heck, the artist, was trying to convey to me in our dawn Crypto Party the day before I met the Hermes group, as wonderful as the internet is, it is also the twenty-first century's ultimate weapon delivery system. It can deliver an anonymous attack on you or the Pentagon from anyone anywhere in the world. And you cannot protect yourself just by avoiding funny-looking emails and refusing to give your password to strangers. This is why people like the Berlin exiles go to such trouble to do their work on air-gapped computers (computers that have never been used to access the internet) and why Julian Assange, as a teenage hacker, kept his code hidden in a beehive.[4]

Ron Deibert, founder of the Citizen Lab at the University of Toronto, has said the easiest way for an attacker to install malware on your computer is to get you to download the apps and regular software updates you need because users will do this with little guarantee they are coming direct from a trusted source and are not infected with malicious code.[5] Indeed, automatic software updates may be precisely what HackingTeam used to "beam" into targeted computers.

The bottom line is that if the NSA wants access into your computer, it is in, Bruce Schneier, another well-known security expert, has said.[6] Even with free software or open-source software that you can study, watch over, or have checked out by a forensic expert, it may be difficult to detect the intrusion. Researchers at the French nonprofit Exodus Privacy, for example, have found that smartphones are infested with commercial tracking software from weather, flashlight, rideshare, and dating apps, collecting huge amounts of information from users. But to find the trackers, Exodus researchers had to build a custom auditing platform that searched through the apps for "digital signatures" distilled from *known* trackers: "A signature might be a telltale set of keywords or string of bytes found in an app file, or a mathematically derived 'hash' summary of the file itself."[7] The Yale Privacy Lab has tried to replicate Exodus Privacy's results with only limited success.[8] To find trackers, one has to know where to look and how to distinguish them.

Determining whether your computer has been infected with malware you have received through the internet is hard, but it is even harder to determine whether data you send over the internet is arriving securely at its destination. As Harry Halpin has pointed out, the internet was not designed to move information securely. It was built without any strong appreciation for provable security or advanced notion of how to achieve it. As a legacy technology, it has more pitfalls than a game of snakes and ladders.

THE PROBLEM OF DESIGNING PRIVACY-PRESERVING PROTOCOLS

My conversation with Hermes has prompted me to do more research into the problems hackers and users face in trying to achieve security or self-determination. These problems are fairly technical but are enlightening when you understand them.

To appreciate in broad terms the problem of designing "privacy for the weak"—that is, for the ordinary user—recall the hourglass metaphor used to depict the internet. This is the shape of the snakes and ladders board game you are playing. At the bottom is the physical layer—the wires and the routers that connect your computer to the server of your internet service provider (ISP) and the server to the continental routing exchanges and intercontinental cables that run along the ocean floors. Remember what Edward Snowden and others have said about the state surveillance operations at that physical layer of the internet and the cooperation between the "Five Eyes" states that make up the spying alliance Echelon (Australia, Canada, New Zealand, the United Kingdom, and the United States). This physical layer involves such a major infrastructure investment[9] that it probably can be fixed only at the state level, with national governments committing not to spy on their populations and preventing, where they can, the routing of communications through states that will spy on them.

On top of the physical layer of the internet is the applications layer, the layer of software applications that anyone can build to run on top of the physical layer. These include applications such as email services (Google's Gmail and Microsoft's Outlook, for example), web browsers (Apple's Safari, Google's Chrome, and Microsoft's Internet Explorer), search engines (Bing, Duck Duck Go, and Google), and the multitude of other apps that you sign up for or download (Bitcoin, Facebook, instant messaging, Lyft, Twitter, voice over internet protocol or VoIP, and Uber).

The Internet Engineering Task Force (IETF)—the body that develops and promotes voluntary internet standards—provided an initial set of protocols (coded rules) that covered the core functionalities of the early internet. These included protocols for functions like file transfer (file transfer protocol or FTP), electronic mail transport (simple mail transfer protocol or SMTP), remote login to hosts (telnet), host initialization

(Bootstrap protocol or BOOTP), and networking support (domain name system or DNS). Other well-known protocols include hypertext transfer protocol (HTTP) and early protocols for applying encryption, including secure socket layer (SSL) and transport layer security (TLS). These latter two protocols encrypt communications between a client's web browser and a server (say, the server used by Ashley Madison, the clandestine dating service). SSL is now considered so flawed it has been prohibited from use.

It is all snakes at the applications layer, for several reasons. First, all commercial applications today want to track you and gather as much information as they can about you. Second, there is a proliferation of protocols at this level, dating from all eras of the internet. They all remain out there "in the wild," and they have many flaws. The complexity of the terrain—the numerous predatory apps and the patchwork of inadequately secure protocols one might encounter, coupled with the amount of applications people now use—make security "forward planning" and "provability" a developer's nightmare.

The narrow waist, or transport layer, of the internet is the simple TCP/IP (transmission control protocol/internet protocol) protocol suite invented by Vint Cerf and Bob Kahn for connecting networks to networks, the layer that essentially establishes the internet. Unlike the telephone, which works by sending information over a dedicated open line between two parties, the internet sends information in spurts from computer to computer as capacity becomes available. The information is broken up into "packets," or chunks of digital data, that are reassembled when they reach their destination. This is called "packet switching." TCP/IP performs the task of delivering packets from the source host (the server of your email ISP, which might be Bell, Google, or Microsoft) across network boundaries to the destination host (the server of your best friend's email ISP, for example, or the server of one of your favorite websites), based on the IP addresses in the "packet headers." For this purpose, the IP protocol defines the packet structures that encapsulate the data to be delivered. It also defines addressing methods.

As Harry explained, the internet is designed so that the server (Bell's, Google's, Microsoft's, Ashley Madison's,[10] and for that matter your workplace's, your government's, or the server of another government) has complete control over your individual device, and you have to trust whatever server you are dealing with. If you are sending emails and you and your correspondent do not own and control email servers in each of your homes, this is a problem. The user is always transparent to the server. You might encrypt your email messages, but the server sees the metadata. Bell sees your IP address, the IP address of the person you are sending an email to, the time, the size of the message, the attachments, the subject line, the browser you are using, and the browser's configuration. And it logs all this information. This means that your commercial service provider can turn over your full records whenever a government agency requests them.

You have no control over what the server sends you, including the automatic updates for your apps, malware from your national security agency, ads, and proprietary code from commercial applications you can't see into (remember proprietary code is closed and nontransparent) and perhaps did not even ask to have in your device.

In the board game of snakes and ladders, there is one long, giant snake you want to avoid landing on because wherever you encounter it, it slides you all the way back down to the beginning of the game. This need-to-trust-the server problem is the giant snake in the game you are playing. Developers describe it as an authentication and web-of-trust problem.

Above the applications layer of the internet is a content layer of human language and images, and above that is a notional "social layer" of the behaviors of users—why they adopt a privacy-sucking app like Facebook, use the internet to stream movies, talk by text instead of email, or put up with a large corporate business model instead of adopting smaller, cooperative models.

The design problems are, broadly, how to build the ladders in this game of snakes and ladders. How to assist the user to move up toward the goal of privacy and self-determination? It is a question with many facets:

How to encrypt everything—the metadata as well as the content, the resting data as well as the moving data?

How to provide users with alternative apps, servers, and service providers so that they can avoid the worst privacy-destroying business models?

How to prevent third parties from tampering with data as it is being sent (man-in-the-middle attacks)?

How to allow recipients to authenticate senders so they know they are
  receiving only the data they want to receive from trusted sources (and
  not receiving trackers and other malware)?
How to route around the parts of the system that are not built with transparent code (free software) and therefore cannot be scrutinized or
  trusted?
How to ensure that protections like encryption and Tor work end-to-end
  so that there is nothing defeating them (malware, interception, profil-
  ing) along their journey?
How to keep things decentralized and interoperable so that, as with
  email, people can use their own versions and still talk to each other
  (so that everyone does not have to sign up to a centralized service like
  Messenger to be able to correspond)?
How to develop applications that are easy to use and will be widely
  adopted by users?
How to keep everything that gets designed updated without a Microsoft
  budget or any budget at all?

EMAIL: A CASE IN POINT

How much progress have hackers made on these design problems? I'm
watching an online privacy workshop for expert hackers from the second
day of the Chaos Communication Camp, and Harry Halpin is on the
panel.

"*Okay,*" says Harry. "*The moment you've all been waiting for. The ugliest
slide in the entire camp, and the ugly slide is about an ugly reality. Twenty-five
years after the deployment of OpenPGP on the internet, we still do not have virtually any messages encrypted end-to-end, and this is a massive failure of our
community. And basically, [we need] to understand how such a large failure
happened and what are the different angles for how we can fix it.*"

Harry clicks to change the PowerPoint slide on the large screen behind
him. It is a photo of the reality TV psychologist Dr. Phil, with the caption, "Oh, so you're using encrypted email? How's that working for you?"

Hackers won the cryptowars of the 1990s and created a cryptotool,
OpenPGP, that was stronger and more user friendly than anything that
went before. But twenty-five years after Phil Zimmermann invented
OpenPGP, apparently almost no one uses it. Hackers and hard-core

dissidents do, and the financial industry and the military have their own highly secure encrypted systems, but the vast majority of electronic communication is unencrypted.

Harry has told me that, in the world of security, two concepts have proven to be flawless—encryption and Tor. After more than twenty years in deployment, onion routing[11] and encryption have been proven to work. The unfortunate drawbacks are that they are not easy to use and can be defeated when used on the "legacy" internet.

Harry flips to his next PowerPoint slide, and the question "Why wasn't the net encrypted by default?" appears on the screen. Communications would be a lot more secure if the internet (content and metadata) were encrypted by default. Then add-on tools like OpenPGP and Tor would not be needed.

Vint Cerf has said that he worked with the NSA on designing a secured version of the internet, but the security technology they were using at the time was classified, and he could not share it with his colleagues. On the 1983 "Flag Day" for the launch of TCP/IP and what would become the public internet, there was no encryption. If Cerf could start over again, he would introduce strong cryptography and authentication into the system.[12]

"*What we've had to do,*" Harry is saying, "*we've basically had to bolt on the crypto after we've had massive deployment. A lot of people are trying to do this now, post-Snowden, but the fact of the matter is we've done it before. As you can see, every major protocol* [from the early days of the internet] *had some kind of crypto slapped on it in a roughshod manner after it was launched.*"

Harry goes to the next slide: "Designing protocols is hard."

A lot of the "bolt-on" encryption algorithms in protocols like RSA (Rivest-Shamir-Adleman), SSL (secure socket layer), and STMP (simple mail transfer protocol) have become weak and even obsolete as the computational power of computers has skyrocketed. As computers get strong enough to break older encryption algorithms, developers have realized that new encryption algorithms need to anticipate the future growth of computer power and not underestimate it. Ultimately, there may be quantum computers that will increase computational power beyond anything we have ever known.

"*Algorithm agility has been, of course, a mixed bag at best,*" Harry tells his audience. "*It essentially allows a lot of downgrade attacks, and we have a lot of legacy algorithms—RSA 1.1.5 and whatnot—still in the wild. And while now the standards community is trying to upgrade all these algorithms—trying to get off of RSA into elliptic curve crypto …—the fact of the matter is that we still need* [more] *algorithm agility because in ten, fifteen, maybe twenty years (twenty years, of course, being we don't know what the fuck we're talking about, but ten years being a clear and present danger), we do, of course, have quantum computation coming up, so we have to start thinking about getting postquantum algorithms into our core protocol.*

"*But it doesn't matter what* [crypto] *algorithms you put into your core protocol if your 'actual state' machine* [for example, your laptop with its vulnerable Linux kernel] *and your actual ability to prove the security of your protocol are flawed from the beginning.*" As an example, he points to a diagram of the "man-in-the-middle" attack made on the TLS encryption protocol: "*This is, of course, the TLS triple handshake attack, and it's a kind of miracle that TLS worked as well as it did, but when you really get down to it, when you bolt this crypto on after the protocols are released into the wild, you will, of course, open yourself, by sheer virtue of complexity, to all sorts of attacks.*"

If you look on Wikipedia, you can see the array of attacks made on the TLS and SSL protocols to date—renegotiation attacks, downgrade attacks (FREAK and Logjam attacks), cross-protocol attacks (DROWN attacks), BEAST attacks, CRIME and BREACH attacks, timing attacks on padding, POODLE attacks, RC4 attacks, truncation attacks, Unholy PAC attacks, Sweet32 attacks, and implementation errors (Heartbleed bug, BERserk attack, Cloudflare bug).

Harry flips the slide again: "Designing Privacy-Preserving Protocols Is Even Harder."

"*And while we at this point in the twenty-first century understand how to develop cryptographic protocols, what we don't understand, what to do at all, is designing privacy-preserving protocols.*"

"*So typically, if you look at the older protocol stacks on the internet, we were just sort of throwing identifiers around willy-nilly, and we're seeing more and more breaks* [from this flaw]. *Even in new pieces of software—for example, in TextSecure, probably one of the best postemail protocols out there—we're revealing people's phone numbers in multiuser chats.*"

"*The thing that all the* [old] *insecure protocols got right was that they were decentralized: that you could actually run your own* [email program], *and* [the connecting protocols] *were run through a standards body and we had some core agreement on them. … And the fact of the matter is that in the move to postemail … where we actually have some chance of getting end-to-end security right, decentralization is not being taken account of, so that you have end-to-end secure silos where you can't communicate with each other* [if both correspondents are not in the silo]."

As I am beginning to understand it, designing *decentralized* privacy-preserving protocols may be the ultimate design problem hackers now face. No one yet seems to have mastered it. Most postemail solutions to date are centralized because designing centralized systems is far easier. If you want to use the secure text app Signal, the people you are communicating with also have to be using it: it is a centralized system.

But true generativity and user self-determination cannot exist without decentralization. A decentralized system cannot be controlled by business or government.

Hackers agree they can't fix the decentralized legacy protocols for email, but the question is whether it is worth trying to improve them. *"Everybody's saying email is screwed, that we cannot fix it,"* a hacker named Meskio is saying on the video. *"I do agree email is screwed. But I'm concerned how much this actually is a problem with* OpenPGP *or just with the implementations for PGP that we have right now. There are lots of projects which are coming out that are trying to reinvent messaging. It's amazing that people are experimenting with that. We need it. But the reality is that the majority of people right now use email."*

Hackers are starting so many projects, in fact, that it bears remembering John Perry Barlow's caveat that "events are boiling up at such a frothy pace that anything I say about current occurrences surely will not obtain by the time you read this. The road from here is certain to fork many times."

Some are doing their best to ameliorate email. Others are chucking email and working on new kinds of communications. There is the Leap Access Project, trying to simplify key management; Mailpile, which is in a good state of beta; Pixelated; experimental Pond; Memory Hole; Coniks; Whiteout; and Signal/TextSecure, generally regarded as the most usable postemail solution to date.

But this plethora of projects raises another problem—the proliferation of standards. *"So what I'd like to ask for people to do,"* Harry says, *"before we go on to the hard-core problems: Everyone's producing their own protocols, people aren't cooperating properly. We'll go into this in more detail, but effectively there are some places where you can really make a difference in standardizing."*

Gus, a female hacker on the panel, takes over. She is from the group Simply Secure. There are too many tiny teams, she says. Please find existing projects and hook up with them. Then she outlines some common dilemmas hackers face in designing security. Support experts or newcomers? Educate users, or just make it work? Gather metrics, or respect your users' privacy? Create new apps, or work to fix existing apps in widespread use? (The existing app, WhatsApp, for example, was used widely by youth in developing countries including by many Arab Spring dissidents. Unfortunately, it was bought up by Facebook in 2014.) Ideal security or ease of use?

"There are really just a couple of threat models: either you're facing Mossad, or you're not facing Mossad," she tells the audience. *"So a scrambled keyboard might be over the top."*

Here, Gus really puts her finger on the most pressing design problem—usability. No tool, no matter how good, is going to be widely adopted by ordinary users if they don't find it easy to use.

Harry flashes another slide: "The net needs you!" It has a drawing of Edward Snowden with an Uncle Sam goatee (or is it day-old stubble?) blowing a whistle and pointing at the viewer. A list of current initiatives follows:

Modern Crypto
IETF Open PGP WG
W3C Security IG
Keys under Doormats

From his place of exile somewhere in Russia, Edward Snowden has been helpfully producing his own privacy-preserving tools for users and promoting some of the best ones made by other hackers. He has coinvented a cell phone case that monitors your cellular, GPS, WiFi, and Bluetooth connections and shows when your device leaks data.[13] And he is developing an open-source app for Android called Haven that turns a phone into a sentry for a laptop. Using the camera and other sensors in a mobile phone to log changes in a room (sound, light, and motion),

Haven can detect if your computer has been physically breached by an intruder in your absence.[14]

Harry picks up the mike again. *"Modern Crypto is where most of the good postemail discussions are happening. If you're interested in getting PGP working, the IETF OpenPGP working group chaired by the wonderful DKG has finally reopened. W3C is looking at how we could make Java Script not such a nightmare in the web security IG. And of course, there's a huge policy debate. You can say, 'This is just solutionism'—that we're trying to solve mass surveillance by just throwing out protocols that are secure and encrypted and privacy-preserving. But you know, if you want to try solving the laws on this, good fucking luck."* He holds up his palms to the audience with a big shrug and a good-natured smile.

REMAKING THE INTERNET FOR THE TWENTY-FIRST CENTURY

The alternative to all this retrofitting is to start fresh and build a new internet. But who will succeed in doing that?

DARPA (the Defense Advanced Research Projects Agency of the US Department of Defense) has spent over $100 million on a "Clean Slate" initiative to solve the technical issues "not fully appreciated" during the early development of the internet.[15]

But someone else is working on a new internet for the twenty-first century—the Chaos Computer Club. This is their take on the matter:

YOU BROKE THE INTERNET
We'll make ourselves a Gnu one

The summer of 2013 [the summer Edward Snowden made his first revelations] will remain the moment we finally realized how broken the Internet was, and how much this had been abused. At first #youbroketheeinternet was a cry of anger, but also a call to code the missing pieces for a new Internet architecture which doesn't fall to pieces like a house of cards.

If deployed on top of technologies that were not designed for it, end-to-end encryption has proven to be "damn near unusable," as Edward Snowden put it, let alone forward secure. But there are actually many new tools that have that feature at their foundation. Antiquated protocols like DNS, SMTP, XMPP and X.509 leak so-called metadata, that is the information of who is talking to whom. Also they put user data on servers out of the reach of their owners.

X.509, the certification system behind HTTPS and S/MIME, is broken and allows most governments and even many companies to run man in the middle attacks on you. The trust chain between the cryptography and the domain names is corrupt. Even if DNSSEC and DANE try to improve the security of DNS, they still expose your interest for certain resources. SMTP is so hopeless, you shouldn't even use it with PGP and XMPP fundamentally has the same problems: as long as all involved servers know all about who is talking to whom, it is already by far too much exposed knowledge—even if the mere encryption of the connection, which again depends on X.509, hasn't been undermined by a man in the middle, which is hard to find out if there is no human intervention and no reporting to the actual users when servers pass messages between each other.

This is not the way it has to be. We believe a completely new stack of Internet protocols is not only feasible, it already exists to a large extent. It merely needs better attention. Currently the majority of technology people are focused on improving the above mentioned protocols, even though they are broken by design ... and can only be improved in some partial aspects. Vastly insufficient compared to what humanity deserves.

Others focus on anarchic technologies designed to undermine democracy, as if it was democracy's fault that digital offences produce no evidence. They thereby foster platforms for bypassing social obligations like contributing taxes, but taxes are fundamental in order to produce infrastructure and social security for the weak. It is impressive how many people have been fooled into thinking negatively about taxes when they in fact depend on them for their own well-being. Only a tiny minority pays more taxes than it enjoys advantages from them.

This project is for those who want to look into a future of an Internet, which actually respects constitutional principles and returns democracy to a mostly functional condition.

Yet, nothing of this comes about if we don't provide incentives. Without incentives, Internet companies find no business model in protecting fundamental principles of democracy. Whereas universities have already delivered several decades of excellent research and working prototypes in this field, they aren't incentivized to produce an actually deployable product. Also standards organizations are powerless if the company that infringes civil rights the most is the one that will dominate the market. In practice, competition is at odds with philanthropy. Currently it takes enthusiasts to fill in the gaps between what researchers and companies have released and turn it into something that actually works for the population. We think we need incentives to polish the protocol stack of a GNU Internet, and by GNU we mean that the involved software needs to be free as in free speech, and that we need regulation to actually deploy an upgrade of the Internet to a version that protects its participants from eavesdropping and social correlation.[16]

When the #youbroketheinternet project first kicked off, some Chaos Computer Club members believed the EU might grasp its own geopolitical and commercial interests in supporting the creation of a new and secure civilian internet. In addition to countering US subversion of the original internet, the EU might want to support its own digital sector by challenging the dominance of US tech companies. Just as the future of energy might lie in clean tech, so might the digital environment's future lie in secure, civically enhancing tech. The visionary jurisdiction that seized the advantage of being first mover in this space might trigger the next tech revolution and reap its benefits.[17]

The CCC made a map of what a new internet might look like. You can see it online: http://youbroketheinternet.org/map. It is a riot of colored, overlapping rectangles running up and across a table that lists different problems to be solved: "Politics & Publicity, Interface & Usability, HTML-based Social App, Native Social Application, Many-to-Many Scalability, One-to-One Application, Hashable Routing, Transports and Mesh Networking, Operating System, Libre Hardware." There is an angry German bald guy in the middle and the logo "You Broke the Internet," and the color coding is described as follows:

Green: Projects that are available today.
Dark green: Projects that are available but aren't fully protective of metadata.
Blue: Projects in development.
Dark blue: Projects in development which will have little or no protection of metadata (but that doesn't mean they can't be an excellent piece in the general puzzle).
Yellow: Projects that may be okay but depend too much on the security of servers.
Orange: Products whose end-to-end encrypting client side has been open-sourced but whose server side remains proprietary (still the UIs may be very well worthwhile to re-use).
Red: Brands that currently occupy the respective layers with unsafe technology.
Dark red: Possibly cool but unsafe technologies that we need to replace.
Some projects appear on certain layers while leaving out others (in that case the beam passes under the grey box of the layer). The new Internet needs a complete GNU protocol stack equivalent to a connected light

green beam across all layers, and then some more aspects that the map does not show [18]

Studying the map, last updated in October 2015, induces in me a dull, aching feeling. Despite repeated efforts, I still don't understand it very well. It seems a monumental project. In fact, this CCC project seems more ambitious than the one to put a hacker on the moon.

But CCC's members' belief that the EU might eventually grasp its own geopolitical and commercial interests in shaping a new internet would turn out to be astute. In August 2016, the EU kicked off a major initiative called the "Next Generation Internet" (NGI). And the Europeans were saying a lot of encouraging things, like the NGI should be "user-" and "human-centric";[19] that it needed "to reflect European social and ethical values";[20] and that "trust at a global scale does not come for free: at the heart of sustainable trust lies actual *trustworthiness* that requires significant investment of time and resources. ... Transition at internet scale requires a systemic approach in addressing deep underlying technical issues, creating transition mechanism[s]—as well as (in some cases) changing legal and governance parameters."[21]

NGI appears to be a serious societal venture.

The Chaos Computer Club was invited to join the Expert Group at the first Next Generation Internet consultation, convened by the European Commission in late 2016, to discuss the group's ideas on NGI regulation.[22] We may not want Europe taking over the internet any more than Google or the United States, as Harry has observed. But some state investment in the infrastructure, social ideas, research, and projects that hackers would support might be essential to getting a "new internet" off the ground.

8

THE GATHERING STORM

The New Crypto—and Information and Net Neutrality
and Free Software and Trust-Busting—Wars

A NEW DIGITAL ERA CIVICS IS NECESSARY

A new, privacy-secure civilian internet might be built in this century,
yet even as one part of the European Union begins to look seriously
at the project, other parts of the EU are engaged in new efforts to curtail
the civilian use of cryptography. Hackers have not even begun to solve
the technical problems of "privacy for the weak" and a new crypto war
is brewing.

In truth, the pitched battles over digital issues critical to democracy
are intensifying and multiplying as I write this book. A new crypto war is
brewing—and so is a new transparency, or information, war—and a war
over net neutrality, and a war over free software, and a war over digital
monopolies. Privacy and transpency are at stake, but so are control over
the internet, ownership of the software in all of the systems and devices
we use in our societies, and even the sustainability of world economies.
Viewed soberly, the hacker quest to secure democracy for the citizen
seems almost quixotic.

Harry Halpin was not understanding the situation when he said that
despite the exponential growth of the hacker scene coalescing around
the Chaos Computer Club, the hacker worry is that "right now we have
to address *all* the policy issues at once." The challenge is monumental,
not just in its technical aspects but also in its political dimension. These

policy issues are not well understood or even known by most people, even by citizens who take a keen interest in the health of their democracies. "Privacy for the weak, transparency for the powerful" has been a good slogan around which hackers and digital rights activists have built some political awareness among the general population, but what people really need is a whole new civics education, a new civics discourse—*a digital era civics*.

Returning to my reasons for setting out on this journey into the world of hackers and hacking, I feel the urgency of my conviction that people need to see the world that is rapidly changing around them as clearly and comprehensively as hackers see it. Only then will they be able to move their societies and resources in directions that might preserve their democracies.

THE NEW CRYPTOWARS

Consider first what hackers are calling the new cryptowars. Since the terrorist attacks in Paris in 2015, many EU security officials and politicians have doubled down on their calls for laws that would ban encryption or would provide government agencies with the means to break it. In the United States, the same thing has been happening. In December 2015, a Muslim American couple attacked a holiday office party in San Bernardino, California, killing fourteen people.[1] After police found the iPhone the husband used for work, the Federal Bureau of Investigation (FBI) asked Apple engineers to create a back door to the phone and turn off its security features, including those that wipe the phone's stored content if someone enters the wrong passcode more than ten times.

In March 2016 I'm in San Francisco to interview cyberlawyer Cindy Cohn. She represented a Berkeley graduate student in the cryptowars of the 1990s, and since 2000, she has been working at the Electronic Frontier Foundation (EFF), the early digital civil liberties group based in the San Francisco Bay Area.[2] Apple has refused the FBI's request, and the case has turned into a public relations battle. On one side is FBI Director James Comey, claiming that law enforcement's vision is "going dark" because of the widespread availability of encryption and other security technologies in consumer products,[3] and on the other side is Apple, championing the privacy of users on pain of legal sanction. Apple has been saying that if it creates a back door for one user's iPhone, it will be inventing the means to break into all users' iPhones. The FBI has insisted under oath that only Apple has the ability to get inside the device. Meanwhile, hackers, Edward Snowden among them,[4] have highlighted the ironies in the standoff. They claim the FBI has the technical means to "break" into the iPhone—many hackers could do it. And Apple is hardly a hero of civil rights. The FBI likely recognizes the San Bernardino case is its best opportunity to "take on" encryption in the court of public opinion, and Apple recognizes that the commercial value of the iPhone might suffer if the company is publicly seen to provide a back door to the device.

Right now, EFF is representing many of the internet security experts participating as "friends of the court" in the Apple iPhone case. Cohn was to have appeared in court this week, but she is able to have lunch with me because the hearing was suddenly adjourned. The FBI backed down. After weeks of grandstanding in the media about the lack of back doors for law enforcement and the necessity of Apple's cooperation, the government stated in a last-minute court filing that it might have found other means to break into the phone.[5]

In Cohn's opinion, the cryptowars of the 1990s never really ended. Government agencies such as the FBI and the National Security Agency (NSA) have never stopped trying to shut down or circumvent civilian use of encryption. As Edward Snowden revealed, the NSA's Bullrun program has been battering at civilian encryption for years by getting tech companies to insert vulnerabilities into encryption systems and devices to make them exploitable, by obtaining details about commercial cryptographic tools through industry relationships, and by working through international bodies to push international encryption standards "it knows it can break."[6] The FBI has been campaigning against civilian encryption using the "going dark" metaphor since at least 2010.[7]

In the early 1990s, at the outbreak of the first cryptowars, Cohn was a young lawyer with an ordinary practice in a law firm in San Mateo, California.

I ask her how she got involved with EFF.

She laughs. "Actually, it was due to a gorgeous barista from France who worked in a local Palo Alto coffee shop and ended up becoming my roommate. In other words, quite by chance!"

They became friends. A lot of nerdy computer guys hung out at the place and had crushes on the barista. She and Cohn threw a housewarming party and invited some of the regulars from the coffee shop, EFF founder John Gilmore among them. Cohn ended up going out with one of Gilmore's friends. When the federal government went after Phil Zimmermann, EFF started looking for ways to challenge the government's cryptography regulations constitutionally. Gilmore asked Cohn if she would be willing to take on one of their constitutional challenges involving a Berkeley PhD student named Daniel Bernstein.[8]

Cohn asked Gilmore about the technology at the heart of the matter. "Does it blow things up?" He replied, "No, it keeps things secret." Four cases—the Bernstein case, two other constitutional challenges, and Zimmermann's case—were each litigated in different jurisdictions, but all of the parties kept in touch and loosely coordinated their strategies.

Cohn won the Bernstein case at two court levels. The lower court judge held Bernstein's code was constitutionally protected speech, establishing an important legal precedent. The court at the next level upheld the decision and elevated Bernstein's efforts even higher, declaring encryption a democratic boon: "Government attempts to control encryption ... may well implicate not only First Amendment rights of cryptographers," wrote Judge Betty Fletcher, "but also the constitutional rights of each of us as potential recipients of encryption's bounty."[9]

"It's an awesome decision," Cohn says, "but so frustrating because it can't be cited. At the second court level, the government asked for en banc review [that is, a review involving all the judges of the court], and while that was pending, it deregulated cryptography, so the decision became moot."[10] Today, the export of cryptography is no longer illegal. The regulations require people like Daniel Bernstein to email the government with an export request and a link to the code being exported. It is just an administrative notice process.

I ask Cohn what the next legal battle will be in the cryptowars. "There is a danger that cryptography could be outlawed again," she says. Or if not outlawed, the government could exert pressure that amounts to the same thing. "Right now, the situation is this. CALEA (the US Communications Assistance for Law Enforcement Act) remains the main piece of legislation on government access to our telecommunications. It used to apply only to telephone companies but was extended to internet companies after about a decade. It does not prohibit these companies from using or allowing cryptography. Indeed, it now specifically protects that. However, CALEA also says companies have to make their communications tappable. The reality is that the government pressures companies into setting up their security so that the companies always have access to the content of messages."

Cohn and I leave the local Vietnamese restaurant where we have had lunch and return to the EFF offices to drink tea on the rooftop patio. Earlier in the day, I walked here taking a route along Van Ness, a busy thoroughfare that cuts across San Francisco, routing traffic through the civic core of the city and past the grand City Hall, the Opera House, the Veterans' Building, the colossal Symphony Hall, and the Public Library— imposing edifices of state and culture from the previous two centuries. This civic heart of San Francisco reminded me of Berlin's Museum Island in the middle of the Spree River, which is crammed with buildings from the days of the German empire and the treasures it looted from other people. The San Francisco precinct is only an island in traffic, and the fortunes with which it was built were made in the Wild West out of a different history of primitive accumulation. Yet it is a similar demonstration of amassed wealth and power—a similar bulky, predigital sensibility imposing its will on the world and looking outdated in the twenty-first century.

Just up the road, a few blocks into the Tenderloin district where the EFF offices are located on Eddy Street, things got sketchy. I saw disturbed men roaming up and down the street, talking to themselves. Members of the Silicon Valley's new digital elite are rapidly taking over the city's real estate, pushing others out. The mentally ill and the destitute, always the most stubborn to displace, soil the edges of the central, Gilded Age city. The buildings around Eddy Street, I saw, were grand but mostly empty. Some were luxury car dealerships from the twentieth century, such as Rolls Royce and Cadillac, its splendid Moorish showroom empty except for a multiplex cinema stuffed inelegantly into one corridor. BMW was moving. Mini, a more recent comer, was hanging on. Construction lots and empty shops crowded the side streets.

EFF occupies a building, now painted an industrial gray, that looks like it was once a large house. The steps up to the entrance are fenced in. When I finally arrived at its door, I had to buzz up from the sidewalk to be allowed through a locked gate. Cohn tells me the security system is a vestige from when the building was owned by Planned Parenthood. EFF continues to use parts of it to fend off the regular break-in attempts in the neighborhood.

In yet another sign of the times, EFF has been expanding rapidly, from about thirty staff members to over eighty now, with new office space purchased across the street. Since the Snowden revelations, donations have been pouring in.

Hackers and concerned scientists have countered recent government attacks on encryption with an expert report titled "Keys under the Door-mat: Mandating Insecurity by Requiring Government Access to All Data and Communications," which argues there is no technical way to provide law enforcement "back door" access to encrypted content without under-mining the security of the internet as a whole.[11] The introduction to the report notes many of the signatories worked together on a response to the government's Clipper Chip proposal in the 1990s[12] (the same Clipper Chip the cypherpunks fought vigorously to defeat).

As these experts would be the first to admit, encryption and Tor are not unimpregnable. A 2012 document leaked by Snowden, titled "Tor Stinks," indicated the NSA was having trouble cracking it. However, more recently, Tor developers have warned that users who regularly use Tor to browse the internet can now be fairly easily identified: "Our analysis shows that 80% of all types of users may be deanonymized by a relatively moderate Tor-relay adversary within six months. ... Our results also show that against a single AS [autonomous system] adversary roughly 100% of users in some common locations are deanonymized within three months."[13] Reportedly, experts have also found a method for distinguish-ing Tor users by their style of typing.[14]

Nevertheless, if a critical mass of people started using encryption, Tor, and other privacy tools, everyone's security would be enhanced, because the larger the crowd, the harder it is to find someone in it. Widespread adoption would also bring more resources to developers, allowing them to keep one or two steps ahead of anyone who might try to crack the system.

To support mass adoption, EFF worked with the Tor Project[15] to develop versions of Tor that can run on Windows, Mac, and Linux.[16] EFF also ran a "Tor Challenge," which added over sixteen hundred volunteer nodes to the Tor network.[17] Users have also been expanding, with Tor adding 36 million users in 2010 alone.[18] As of 2014, it had over six thousand nodes.[19] Tor developers hope eventually to have hundreds of thousands of relay nodes[20] and are building a Tor home WiFi router that would sell for about a hundred bucks, so that one day all users might become nodes in the Tor network.[21]

Together, EFF and the Tor Project developed a web encryption tool for dissemination called "HTTPS everywhere." It encrypts users' browsing history when connecting to participating websites. In early 2017, EFF reported that half of browsing traffic was encrypted.[22]

The German-born political theorist Hannah Arendt believed "totalitarianism was not an all-powerful state, but the erasure of the difference between private and public life."[23] The civics lesson of the new cryptowars is that we are free only when we can control what people know about us and have some guarantee of autonomy and security in our thoughts and lives.[24] Draconian infringements on privacy that we institute in times of emergency to apply to some "other" almost inevitably end up metastasizing and applying to *us*.

It will be hard for governments and corporations to shut down privacy defaults and expectations if enough users adopt alternatives to the privacy-sucking funnels they are currently herded into. Librarians understand this. Facing warnings from federal agencies[25] and uncertain legal consequences in some countries,[26] these true champions of civil liberty have been actively running Tor nodes and training library users on encryption and Tor for some time now.

The hacker hope is that a critical mass of users asserting their privacy online with hacker-made tools could potentially establish what Jonathan Zittrain has called "code-backed norms"[27] strong enough to rival state and corporate-imposed norms; that is to say, social norms, which might not have any legal backing, which might even contravene existing law, but are enforced by code and the will of the people.

THE NEW INFORMATION WARS

While brewing political battles over cryptography threaten "privacy for the weak," even darker clouds are amassing to obscure the hope for "transparency for the powerful." Confounding new information wars are intensifying, with conflicting stories about Russian hacking of the

US election, accusations of "fake news," disturbing revelations about the political use of the Facebook platform, increasingly controversial information releases being made by WikiLeaks, and the threat of censorship by governments of Western democracies and "progressive" tech companies alike. How to make sense of it all?

Information wars are as old as politics. They involve the use of information and communication to gain competitive advantage over opponents. One might say they are endemic to democratic systems, in which various interests vie to win over the hearts and minds of individual voters. But in the digital age, information warfare has taken on properties both exhilarating and frightening. Although digital tech provides enormous scope for transparency, vigorous debate, and public understanding, it does the same for manipulation, censorship, and repression.

When WikiLeaks first hit the major media with the Manning leaks, cypherpunk fellow traveler John Perry Barlow tweeted, "The first serious info war is now engaged. The field of battle is WikiLeaks. You are the troops."[28]

PayPal moved to shut down WikiLeaks's accounts and strangle it financially. The loose affiliation of hackers and trolls acting under the name Anonymous picked up Barlow's quote. Brandishing it as part of their "Operation Avenge Assange" manifesto,[29] they swept down like the Furies of the internet, bombarding PayPal's website with a DDoS (distributed denial of service) cyberattack and posting their calling card:

Knowledge is free.
We are Anonymous.
We are Legion.
We do not forgive.
We do not forget.
Expect us.

When the security contractor HBGary proposed to deanonymize Anonymous, a small group calling itself LulzSec but operating under the broader banner of Anonymous[30] digitally eviscerated the company and its chief executive, Aaron Barr. They defaced the company's website, erased a terabyte of its data and research, stole its emails, and released Barr's home address and social security number through his Twitter account.[31] The emails revealed HBGary had a plan to leak fake documents to WikiLeaks in order to discredit the group.[32]

At the end of 2010, CBS pronounced, "WikiLeaks is winning the information war so far."[33] In 2012, *Time* magazine ranked Anonymous as one of the world's one hundred most influential "people."[34]

"Transparency for the powerful" seemed to be on the ascendant in the first part of the twenty-first century following the WikiLeaks disclosures of 2010, the Anonymous DDoS of PayPal and HBGary, Edward Snowden's game-changing revelations of 2013, and the Panama Papers leaks of 2015, which revealed widespread tax evasion and corruption among oligarchs and politicians.

Then the 2016 US presidential election happened.

Anyone looking for the civics lesson in the new information wars might find it helpful to review the sequence of events leading up to and after that election. In July 2016, a few months before the vote, WikiLeaks leaked nearly twenty thousand emails hacked from the Democratic National Committee (DNC).[35] The emails appeared to show that the DNC was trying to aid Hillary Clinton's campaign and sideline that of Bernie Sanders.[36]

There were allegations the source of the leak was Russian hackers working to get Donald Trump elected—assertions Assange denied.[37] Russian agencies were alleged to be running troll farms, computer-automated "bots" that flooded social media platforms, and fake news operations to manipulate American voters in payback for an election influence campaign Clinton had run against Putin when she was US Secretary of State.[38] The Russians were alleged to have used data analytics to target certain kinds of voters with fake stories, from cruder ones (Clinton had Parkinson's disease and ran a child-sex ring out of a DC pizza restaurant) to more subtle ones that mixed real facts with plausible distortions.[39] Russia was alleged to have targeted journalists and flooded their social media accounts with fake news to which they might be individually susceptible.[40] Russian sources paid for ads on Facebook. Many of these used the powerful psychological techniques of internet memes.[41] Researchers at the University of Southern California found that during a five-week period in fall 2016, nearly 20 percent of political tweets were generated by bots of unknown origin, a portion of which could well have been Russian.[42]

In April 2017, Facebook issued a report acknowledging that a lot of preelection disinformation had been spread via its platform and assured the public that it had increased its security. Google and Twitter tweaked their algorithms to counter bots and cyberpropaganda.[43]

"If there has ever been a clarion call for vigilance and action against a threat to the very foundation of our democratic political system, this episode is it," James Clapper, the former Director of National Intelligence testified before Congress on May 8, 2017.[44] But wasn't he the same James Clapper who had baldly lied to Congress in 2015, stating the NSA had not "wittingly" conducted mass surveillance on American citizens?[45]

Russia was also alleged to have interfered with electronic voting machines. NSA contractor Reality Leigh Winner leaked a classified document to *The Intercept* that suggested Russian military intelligence had hacked at least one supplier of voting software and sent phishing emails to over one hundred election officials just days before the November election.[46] The story was reported in June 2017, and Winner was swiftly arrested. The week before the story ran, Vladimir Putin had denied Russia interfered in foreign elections "on a state level," floating the idea that freelance Russian hackers with "patriotic leanings" may have done the hacking.[47] "Hackers are free-spirited people," Putin explained. "They are like artists. If they are in a good mood in the morning, they wake up and paint. It is the same for hackers. They wake up today, they read that something is happening in interstate relations, and if they are patriotically minded, they start to make their own contribution to what they believe is the good fight against those who speak badly about Russia."[48]

In November 2017, just days after the November 8 US election, *The Atlantic* magazine broke the story that WikiLeaks had been secretly communicating with the Trump campaign.[49] Julian Assange had been pushing Donald Trump Jr. to disseminate its leaks (which Donald Jr. did in at least one case), had been asking to publish Trump's tax records in order to undercut the perception that WikiLeaks had a pro-Trump bias, and had been urging the Trump campaign not to concede the election if Trump lost. At an October 10, 2016, political rally, Donald Sr. had effused, "I love WikiLeaks!" In December 2016, Assange had asked Donald Jr. to ask the president to suggest to Australia that it should make Assange its ambassador to the United States.[50] And the WikiLeaks Twitter account pushed the fake news story of a Clinton child-sex ring run from a pizza shop until as late as January 2017.[51]

Many supporters of WikiLeaks were dismayed to see it degenerate from a beacon of transparency into a vehicle used by Assange to advance his personal agenda. He was acting like a freelance political operative, not a publisher intent only on the accuracy of the material he was publishing.[52]

In February 2018, Robert Mueller, the special counsel investigating Russian interference in the 2016 election, announced the indictment of thirteen Russian trolls alleged to have been working out of a large Russian trolling operation in St. Petersburg known as the Internet Research Agency.[53] It was likely funded by an oligarch friend of Putin.[54] Reporter Adrian Chen, who had visited the place and done a thorough investigative story on it in 2015,[55] said descriptions of the troll farm and the effects of Russian hacking were exaggerated. In a 2018 tweet, Chen wrote, "Tried to tamp down the troll farm panic on @chrislhayes show last night. It's 90 people with a shaky grasp of English and a rudimentary understanding of US politics shitposting on Facebook."[56]

That may have accurately described the trolling complement assigned to the "American desk" at the Internet Research Agency when Chen investigated it, but hackers have said the Russians interfering in the US election were clearly more sophisticated adversaries than US agencies were prepared to counter and were adept at using the kinds of social media tactics and memes that hacker groups like Anonymous pioneered.[57] The United States was especially vulnerable to such an attack with its monopolized social media platforms that could be easily weaponized and its long-standing, polarizing "culture war" that had already debilitated its political system.

If this roller coaster weren't enough, in March 2018, the news that the Trump campaign had been using the sophisticated data analytics services of a company called Cambridge Analytica to target voters worsened with the awful confirmation that the data-harvesting firm it partnered with had been allowed to suck the whole social graph of Facebook users. Facebook threatened to sue *The Observer* to prevent the newspaper from breaking the story.[58] As described by *The Observer*, when a user downloaded an app that was supposed to pay them to take a personality survey for academic research, the app scraped all of the user's Facebook data and all of the data of the user's Facebook "friends" as well, without the latter's knowledge or consent.[59] The app was downloaded by 300,000 users, yielding a reported fifty million useable profiles.[60] According to an inside whistleblower, Cambridge Analytica then built a system to target users one by one with tailored posts, using psychometric parameters: it was individualized targeting on an industrial scale.[61] Alexander Nix, head of Cambridge Analytica, claimed the company possessed a massive database of four thousand to five thousand data points on every adult in America.[62] The company had also worked for the "Leave" campaign in the UK Brexit vote. No one had imagined political manipulation on a scale like this before.

Or had they? It soon became apparent that targeting its users was Facebook's business model. Facebook does not sell your data. It sells you. It serves you and other users up for targeting in the demographic slices required by advertisers and companies like Cambridge Analytica.[63] And the way that Facebook allowed apps to operate between 2010 and 2015 permitted third-party software developers like Cambridge Analytica's data-harvesting partner to covertly scrape and keep as much of Facebook's user data as they wanted.[64]

A 2011 Federal Trade Commission consent decree[65] obliged Facebook to prohibit third-party apps from scraping personal user data. Facebook was supposed to audit, but its approach was reportedly lax.[66] Potentially tens of thousands of apps did the same thing Cambridge Analytica's partner firm did.[67]

After damaging news reports began to be published, Facebook requested Cambridge Analytica's partner firm to erase the data it had collected from Facebook users. This was during the 2015 Republican primary, while Cambridge Analytica was working for candidate Ted Cruz and before it switched to working for the Trump campaign. Facebook said it believed the firm complied with its request, but it remained unclear whether the fruits of the data ever ended up being used in the Trump campaign.[68]

Then journalists began to connect the dots to conclude that Barack Obama's campaign team, lauded for its social media skills, had probably done a similar thing in the 2012 election—sucked out Facebook users' whole social graph without the consent of users' friends.[69] Tech bloggers pointed out that although Facebook, with over two billion users and a staggering amount of data, was the most worrying example of a company with an intensive data-harvesting business model, this was in fact the business model of most digital platforms.[70]

Between Russian hacking, WikiLeaks's meddling, and the possible use of Facebook for political ends by the Trump campaign, Americans had their cognitive ability to understand their own political environment seriously disrupted in the 2016 election cycle. And it looked a lot like Julian Assange's proposal for disrupting political elites in his early blog essays on the theory of leaking. Disruption and cognitive dysphoria were certainly the result in 2016 for the Democratic Party, the target of these three initiatives. A "conspiracy that cannot think is powerless to preserve itself against the opponents it induces," Assange had written in one of his earlier, prescient essays. "It falls, stupefied; unable to sufficiently comprehend and control the forces in its environment."[71]

It is uncertain whether these events actually affected the outcome of the 2016 election. Although the Democratic Party has seized on the idea of Russian and WikiLeaks interference as an excuse for its loss, the most immediately damaging effect of the hacking could be that the Democrats' preoccupation with it forestalls any serious reform of the party before the 2020 election.

Even so, Russian hacking should not be dismissed. Perhaps the most insightful take on the new information wars has come from a historian of the twentieth century, Timothy Snyder, the author of the best-selling primer *On Tyranny: Twenty Lessons from the Twentieth Century*, published shortly after the 2016 presidential election.[72] Snyder, who has studied Russia over a long period and reads Russian newspapers, has said the Russian government's tactic of inducing information dysphoria was honed on its own population. It is meant to support a certain kind of political equilibrium in which the Russian population is induced to tolerate as much as possible a state of oligarchy and radical inequality. These conditions are stabilized and institutionalized in Russia by way of "a very steady, efficiently and beautifully produced, diet of 'fake news' complimented by a series of … manufactured triumphs abroad."[73]

"This is a certain model," Snyder says. It is a model that Western democrats need to know is out there, and it is attractive to certain kinds of people—oligarchs and the far right in their own countries, for example. As a political model, it can stabilize a status quo of gross inequality, "but what it can't do is generate reform [because reform would mean the kleptocrats would have to go], and it can't generate wealth."[74]

Why would Russia want to use these methods on the populations of other countries? Snyder posits that in order to maintain power at home, Russian elites,

> came to understand ... that you have to remove the competition. You have to make the rest of the world more like Russia ... and to do so, partly by supporting the Far Right, but also partly by promoting this idea that there's no such thing as truth, that it's all relative, that there are no facts, because in that environment, political activity and political opposition become incoherent and impossible. They succeed at that at home and now they've been trying to bring that abroad and they've done so with some success, and one has to recognize their intelligence, and one has to be clear about their aims, because we are now in the middle of that.[75]

Snyder says propaganda "is not just a kind of muddling reality or meddling in reality." Rather, "You fill the public sphere with things that aren't true and you contradict yourself all the time."[76] Thinking of Donald Trump as a pathological liar is misguided in this context. Confusion and demobilization are regime policy.

Then, says Snyder, you blame the journalists—"the people responsible for factuality." You talk about having to crack down on them. Then nobody knows what truth is anymore, nobody trusts the media, and "you end up having a monopoly, or at least the strongest position, in the manufacture of the symbols of the day. That's clearly what they're up to. And it's probably more central and more important than we generally realize."[77]

According to Snyder, Americans need to understand that the Russians have not merely hacked the last US election. More insidiously, the authoritarian philosophy and methods of the Russian regime have migrated to the West and are being employed by Western politicians and their supporters, most prominently by the Trump regime. The civics lesson here is that democratic societies require a shared belief in factuality, a trust that we can at least agree on a methodology for ascertaining facts and a belief that facts matter. If you destroy that belief, then you destroy democracy. "That's the cheap and easy way to do it," Snyder says, "and that's what the twenty-first-century authoritarians have discovered. ... That's the process that is under way before our eyes."[78]

So are there technical fixes to this? Hackers would say monopoly corporations like Facebook, Google, and Twitter should not be acting as society's censors, with their secret algorithms for ranking and filtering information. But even when the problem is parsed carefully to look for better solutions, how can we expect technology to repair a weakened and imperiled civic space? The danger of putting too much emphasis on technical fixes is that we treat the computer as some kind of magic, oracular machine. In the digital era, the media has fractured into a few big outlets and thousands of smaller online ones, which has led to a situation where we are all living, to some extent, in our own bubbles, reading different messaging scripts. We are *all* vulnerable to believing the things we hear or read when they are repeated over and over again. The problem is not the plurality of information sources or even the trustworthiness of some of them. It is that we rely too heavily on computers for information, discourse, and connection.

Limit your exposure to the internet, Snyder recommends. Read books and long articles. Support investigative journalism. Take time to speak to other people, especially those you think you don't agree with. Make eye contact and small talk. Practice the kind of politics where you show up in person. Volunteer, and maybe run for office. Then you can react to propaganda according to the mental and social preparation you have made[79] and not just according to your click and network biases. A healthy civic space takes some sustained effort and physical presence on the part of citizens, some serious commitment to the value of social cohesion.

THE NEW NET NEUTRALITY WARS

Just as the fight over privacy (the cryptowars) and transparency and truth (the information wars) is getting dire, net neutrality is also being threatened with serious stakes for democracy.

Net neutrality is something ordinary users take almost for granted because it was built in when the internet was created. Conceived as a network of networks, the early internet gave people a basic code, or set of protocols, to connect computer servers all over the world for the purpose of sharing information. It was a network of interoperable networks. The net was decentralized in that the servers that made up the networks were numerous and diverse. Private and public, big and small, they were not controlled by any dominant player. The services people used, like email, were interoperable. You could use your own application and still be able to talk to someone using a different one. The net was open or generative of innovation in that anyone could use it, connect their server to it, and invent and offer new applications to add to the rich ecology of the whole. In sum, the net was "neutral" in that the basic protocol did not do anything but send information between servers. It did not monitor or discriminate against content or users. Anyone could participate, move around it freely, speak and associate freely, and use it for their own purposes. In short, there were no gatekeepers.

For years, internet service providers (ISPs)—the companies, such as AT&T, Comcast, and Verizon, that provide connections between one's home or business and the internet—had lobbied to become the gatekeepers of the internet so they could exploit that position for their profit. A typical "retail" ISP network connects anywhere from dozens to millions of homes, businesses, and cell phones to the rest of the internet. "Retail" ISPs, in turn, connect to "backbone" ISPs, which provide high-capacity, long-haul transmissions across the internet.[80]

ISPs planned to assume this gatekeeper role over individual users and other players in the internet by blocking the range of websites and services that users could access, either outright or through speed and data caps linked to content. In this way, they planned to force people to use the services and content they offered themselves and to increase charges. Hackers and digital rights activists recognized this would destroy the internet as a public good and turn it into the commercial property of monopolies. The ISP plans were largely beaten back. It took the Obama administration about six years to act in support of net neutrality, but in 2015 its Federal Communications Commission (FCC) reclassified broadband service (including internet) from an "information service" to a "telecommunications service" (a utility) subject to much greater regulation over neutrality and privacy.

One of the Trump administration's first moves was to reverse this. Trump appointed Ajit Pai, a former lawyer for Verizon, as chair of the FCC.

Once installed, Pai scheduled a December 14, 2017, vote at the FCC to reverse the statutory classification and gut net neutrality. Barely a week before the vote, he played a video of a comic skit at the Federal

Communications Bar Association dinner in which he and a Verizon executive played themselves:

> **VERIZON VP:** As you know, the FCC is captured by industry, but we
> think it's not captured enough.
>
> **AJIT PAI:** What plans do we have in mind?
>
> **VERIZON VP:** We want to brainwash and groom a Verizon puppet to
> install as FCC chair. Think *Manchurian Candidate*.
>
> **AJIT PAI:** That sounds awesome!
>
> **VERIZON VP:** I know, right?[81]

Internet pioneers Tim Berners-Lee, Vint Cerf, Steve Wozniak, and others wrote an open letter calling on senators to push the FCC to cancel
the December 14 vote: "We are the pioneers and technologists who
created and now operate the Internet, and some of the innovators
and business people who, like many others, depend on it for our livelihood. ... This proposed Order would repeal key network neutrality
protections."[82]

The signatories noted that the FCC had "not held a single open public
meeting to hear from citizens and experts about the proposed order" and
had seemingly ignored a forty-three-page technical comment submitted
earlier by over two hundred prominent internet pioneers and engineers.
The technical comment had stated, "the FCC (or at least Chairman Pai
and the authors of the [proposed order]) appears to lack a fundamental
understanding of what the Internet's technology promises to provide,
how the Internet actually works, which entities in the Internet ecosystem provide which services, and what the similarities and differences are
between the Internet and other telecommunications systems the FCC
regulates as telecommunications services."[83] The results of the Pai Order,
they said, "could be disastrous."[84]

More than twenty-three million comments were also filed at the FCC
in response to its rule-changing proposal. About a million of these were
bot-generated, falsely using the names of real people, and roughly half a
million were filed from Russian email addresses. Fifty thousand consumer
complaints went missing from the record, and the FCC's comment system
became the subject of a Government Accountability Office investigation
and an inquiry by the New York State attorney general.[85]

Despite the irregularities, the December vote went ahead, and the FCC voted in favor of gutting net neutrality.[86] As of January 2018, twenty-one state attorneys-general were suing to block the repeal, along with Mozilla, the NGO Free Press, and the Open Technology Institute.[87] On May 16, 2018, Senate Democrats got three Republicans to support them on a vote under the Congressional Review Act to block the repeal. The fight then moved to the House of Representatives. President Trump held veto power.[88]

The civics lesson people need to grasp in the net neutrality wars is that the fight for net neutrality is a fight for the future of free communication. As hackers would underline, in the digital era, if you expect to decide freely what you listen to and watch, receive, send, publish, create, and even think as a citizen, net neutrality is essential. Net neutrality is also about the future of media—which media outlets survive, what stories get told, and which are suppressed. It is a fight about innovation and free markets because an information economy depends on unfettered access to the internet. And it is a fight about political freedoms because political speech and organizing take place increasingly through the internet.

City councils have begun to take action to preserve net neutrality. They do not think it is a good idea to hand the internet and their local information economies over to a handful of monopoly ISPs. They are hacking this model. Seattle Council member Kshama Sawant has called on Seattle to invest in building its own municipal broadband infrastructure "so no internet corporation has the power to prioritize making money over our democratic rights." Public opinion, she said, was clear: "76% favor net neutrality, even including 73% of Republican voters."[89] It is an expensive infrastructure build, but around 185 other municipalities in the United States have done it.[90]

Chattanooga, Tennessee, is a model many look to. In a ten-year civic rebuild, the city's municipally owned electricity company built a physical fiber optic internet infrastructure with speeds as fast as one gigabit per second (about fifty times faster than the US average). They call it the Gig.[91] Danna Bailey, VP of the municipal electric board, has said, "We don't have to worry about stockholders, our customers are our stockholders. We don't have to worry about big salaries, about dividends. We get to wake up everyday and think about what, within business reason, is good for this community."[92]

There are other Gig cities, including Lafayette, Louisiana, and Bristol, Virginia, but none is as advanced as Chattanooga. Google has plans to roll out fast-speed fiber optic systems in selected cities, but most big telecoms do not see a profit incentive in what would be an expensive rebuild of their existing systems.[93]

They do see the profit in blocking cities from establishing their own broadband infrastructure. When Chattanooga lobbied the FCC to allow it to expand its broadband to neighboring communities, many of which get only a dial-up connection from the big telecoms, the industry moved swiftly, telling the FCC to block the city's plan, as well as a similar plan for Wilson, North Carolina.[94] A number of state legislatures (whose members receive big donations from Big Telecom) have passed state laws banning cities from building their own broadband networks. In Colorado, thirty-one counties have pushed back, voting to exempt themselves from the state law.[95]

THE NEW FREE SOFTWARE WARS

As privacy, transparency and truth, and net neutrality are under new attack, so too is free software. Richard Stallman's bedrock principle for freedom and democracy in the digital age—the idea that code should be free and in the control of citizen-users—is in danger of being overcome by "digital restrictions management" regimes (called "digital rights management"[96] regimes by the corporations that impose them) that deprive citizen-users of property rights and, hackers have argued, turn them into serfs of those corporations.

The recent struggles on the free software front are well known to hackers and people in the tech world, but for most ordinary users, the civics issues in these struggles need explaining.

I have heard hackers call the body of free software that forms the backbone of the internet and World Wide Web and that runs much of the digital world now (GNU/Linux) their *Mahabharata*. The *Mahabharata* was an epic Sanskrit poem. Composed between the fourth century BCE and the fourth century CE, its cumulative creation was part of the flowering of a civilization on the Indian subcontinent.

Like the authors of the *Mahabharata*, hackers have created their epic work over years of collective effort. They intend that their software, like the poem, will be widely studied, added onto, improved, and adapted. It is their contribution to Western civilization and to democratic society.

But copyright is ostensibly at odds with this aim. Since the 1970s, society has treated software as property subject to the law of copyright (and sometimes patents). Copyright laws give all control over a created work[97] to the copyright holder (initially, the creator of the work): a copyrighted work cannot be accessed, copied, distributed or modified without the consent of the holder. An exemption, known as "fair use," allows these uses, without permission, for limited purposes. In the United States, for example, the Copyright Act of 1976 (and its amendments) allows the "fair use" of copyrighted material without permission of the copyright holder for purposes "such as criticism, comment, news reporting, teaching ... scholarship, and research."[98] Other uses are evaluated as potentially "fair" on a four-factor test that balances the interests of the copyright holder with societal interests. Generally, courts have found that uses that do not undermine the commercial value of a work or are "transformative" of the original work—a parody of an original song or the use of a photo in a collage artwork, for example—are fair uses.

Copyright does not cover creators' ideas (in the way patents do) but, generally speaking, covers only creators' particular expression of ideas. The public policy behind copyright law is to enable creators to be paid for their works while still encouraging the generation and free dissemination of ideas, learning, knowledge creation, and innovation.

Recall that Richard Stallman was not against having users pay for a copy of a software program. He wanted to ensure that after users pay for or otherwise obtain an authorized copy of software, they will have "four freedoms"—(0) the freedom to run the software for any purpose, (1) the freedom to study how it works and to change it to do their computing as they wish, (2) the freedom to redistribute copies to help others, and (3) the freedom to distribute copies of their modified version to benefit the whole community.[99] "Hacking" the traditional law of copyright, Stallman invented the "copyleft license," called the GNU General Public License (GNU GPL, or GPL). The GNU GPL specified that the purchaser of software would have these four freedoms as a matter of contract. In short, "free software" is about giving users control over their own computing.

Stallman's struggle to "free" software from the repressive limits of traditional copyright "defaults"[100] were paralleled, in the same time period, by activists' struggles to "free" knowledge and artistic expression from them. The Creative Commons initiative, with which Harvard University law professor Larry Lessig ("Code is law") was closely engaged, invented the Creative Commons license, under which authors and artists can specify what the public can do with their works. Creators can choose among several versions of the Creative Commons license and set out different rights and responsibilities for users. Another related initiative, Open Access, sought to "free" public records and publicly funded research from enclosure by government agencies, for-profit academic journals, and search engines. Open access activists built new interfaces and sought reforms to the law.

In contrast to these careful legal approaches to the problem of traditional copyright defaults, other activists and users simply asserted a moral right (not to be confused with "moral rights" under copyright law)[101] to crack and modify, file share, "pirate,"[102] and remix the copyrighted works of others in potential violation of the copyright defaults attached to these works.

A host of treaties and legislation were written by states and corporate lobbyists to prevent and punish these latter activities, including the Anti-Counterfeiting Trade Agreement (ACTA), the Digital Millennium Copyright Act (DMCA), the Preventing Real Online Threats to Economic Creativity and Threat of Intellectual Property Act (the PROTECT IP Act or PIPA), the Stop Online Piracy Act (SOPA), and the Trans-Pacific Partnership (TPP). The 1998 US Digital Millennium Copyright Act (DMCA), which implements two 1996 World Intellectual Property Organization treaties, sanctioned the use of "digital rights management" (DRM) or coded access controls to copyrighted material and made it criminal to circumvent these and to create or share tools for circumvention.[103] In other words, the DMCA made it criminal to try to access DRM-shielded code without permission, which was a heavy-handed approach to punishing individuals for copyright infringement. Any attempt to do more than run an authorized copy of software—any attempt to share it or adapt it to make it work the way the user wanted it to—became a criminal act.

DMCA effectively made it criminal even to try to see, study, and criticize shielded code, essentially making an end-run around the "fair use" rights that copyright legislation provides. In short, DMCA locked code in a black box no one could open on pain of criminal punishment. More insidiously, it allowed copyright holders to impose whatever "terms of use" they wanted on users, such as restrictions on what platforms or devices they could use, a contractual right to unilaterally erase purchased material, the ability to turn off devices, and the installation of malicious functions on the users' computer (such as tracking and scraping functions to collect the user's personal information). Code that cannot be seen and studied might contain malicious functions that a company has not informed users about and might introduce security vulnerabilities that hurt users' computers and expose them to third-party attacks. DRM effectively allowed the copyright holder to take control of a user's computer to do the copyright holder's bidding instead of the user's and prohibited the user from even looking at what was being done.

On the other hand, the DMCA did provide that internet service providers and other intermediaries, such as owners of websites, were not responsible for the copyright infringements of their users,[104] a good thing from a digital rights perspective. The entertainment industry in the United States sought to reverse this. The Stop Online Piracy Act (SOPA) and its sister, the PROTECT IP Act (PIPA), which were pushed by the movie industry and other corporate interests, would have made ISPs and website owners responsible for the copyright infringements of their users. But in 2012, these legislative bills were put on hold indefinitely when the online community lit up in a week of protest so fierce it knocked legislators onto their heels.[105] EU states were just about to ratify an international treaty, the Anti-Counterfeiting Trade Agreement (ACTA), that committed them to pass domestic legislation along the lines of SOPA and PIPA when similar protests in Europe caused the EU Parliament to reject the agreement.[106] The United States sought to export digital restrictions management to other countries in the subsequent Trans-Pacific Partnership treaty (TPP), which were intended to benefit the already dominant American information sector (a sector that includes software, gaming, film, and music and that grossed over $1.5 trillion in 2014).[107] In early 2017, President Trump would pull the US out of TPP negotiations, but the "digital rights management" language remained in the text that other Pacific Rim countries were considering until the Canadian delegation insisted that the most problematic provisions—including copyright term extension, DRM rules, and intermediary liability—be suspended from the agreement that was finally signed.[108] As of April 2018, Trump was considering US reentry to the treaty.[109]

For the past two decades, corporations in the United States have been pushing the envelope of digital restrictions management under the DMCA legislation, arguing that consumers do not own the software inside the manufactured products they buy (products like phones, computers, coffeemakers, fridges, clothes washers, and vehicles). This goes far beyond the original purpose of copyright law, which was to ensure that creators (traditionally, artists, writers, performers, composers, and architects) receive reasonable remuneration for their work.

Digital rights organizations like EFF have been trying to push back. The implication of the corporate position is that as consumer goods increasingly become digitized and connected, consumers will not own, control, or have the ability to repair most of the things they buy and depend on. Like serfs, consumers will be merely tenants, and their overlords will be able to set and change the conditions of consumers' tenancies as they decide. The corporate position arguably amounts to a destruction of property rights for the ordinary consumer and an immense augmentation of property rights for big corporations—digital feudalism—or at least a new rentier type of economy (an economy in which one class holds title to finite property assets and passively profits by charging others for access to that property). While the business model for social media platforms sells its users' attention and its users' data or profiles, this second, pernicious business model devised by early twenty-first-century digital capitalism milks its users with rents, fees, and updates. Both models crush competition and monopolize markets through network effects and anticompetitive practices.

As described in chapter 1, even when a product is built around the free software kernel Linux, the manufacturer can thwart users' right to modify the kernel by designing the product's hardware to block or restrict any code that does not have the manufacturer's signature. Users are allowed to make their own versions of Linux, but they cannot sign those versions with the manufacturer's secret key, so they cannot make their versions run on the product. This practice ("tivoization") is named after the product TiVo, a digital video recorder where free software developers first came across it. With tivoization, the manufacturer can put malicious functionalities into the code and stop users from removing them. In 2005, Richard Stallman created the GPLv3 license with the help of lawyers working with him, notably Columbia University law professor Eben Moglen.[110] The GPLv3 license gave free software developers a way to contractually prohibit users (including companies) of their free software from "tivoing" it. Unfortunately, the original body of free software adopted by commercial interests was released under the earlier GPL or GPLv2 licenses. Added to this, Linus Torvalds has rejected the use of the GPLv3 for Linux software going forward.[111]

Potentially, someone could start building computers and smartphones that were made entirely of free software and free hardware and subject to GPLv3 licenses. But the capital investment required to go up against the existing monopoly manufacturers is daunting.[112]

For a glimpse of what the future with DRM could look like, consider what the digital restrictions management regime imposes on the early twenty-first-century farmer. In the Copyright Office's regular rule-making process under the DMCA, John Deere, the largest manufacturer of farm equipment, recently submitted that when farmers buy its tractors, they obtain not what most people would call ownership but rather "an implied license for the life of the vehicle to operate the vehicle."[113] A license agreement John Deere started to require farmers to sign in October 2016 "forbids nearly all repair and modification to farming equipment, and prevents farmers from suing for 'crop loss, lost profits, loss of goodwill, loss of use of equipment … arising from the performance or non-performance of any aspect of the software.'"[114]

"If a farmer bought the tractor, he should be able to do whatever he wants with it," one farmer told a *Motherboard* journalist. "You want to replace a transmission and you take it to an independent mechanic—he can put in the new transmission but the tractor can't drive out of the shop. Deere charges $230, plus $130 an hour for a technician to drive out and plug a connector into their USB port to authorize the part."[115]

Tractors and other pieces of farm equipment cost hundreds of thousands of dollars. Farmers' livelihoods depend on them. These machines regularly require repair, and farmers are used to being able to do it themselves to keep things running during planting and harvesting seasons. If they have to wait for a company technician and rely on company tools and updates to keep their tractor running, they are at the mercy of the company, its service department, its year-by-year planned profit margin, its decisions to make products obsolescent, and its continued existence. "What happens in 20 years when there's a new tractor out and John Deere doesn't want to fix these anymore?" one farmer asked. "Are we supposed to throw the tractor in the garbage, or what?"[116]

To avoid this oppressive business model, many farmers have begun hacking their tractors. A black market for John Deere firmware has grown out of the Ukraine and Poland, where its DRM controls are cracked and the "freed" software then made available to desperate farmers through invitation-only online forums.[117] Farmers risk being sued for breach of contract and prosecuted criminally under the DMCA for hacking their tractors, but it is a risk some feel they must take.

Consumers have rebelled against the DMCA-DRM regime and submitted over forty thousand comments to the US Copyright Office urging that consumers' property rights be restored.[118] Several pieces of legislation have been proposed to mitigate the effects of digital restrictions management, such as the Breaking Down Barriers to Innovation Act of 2015, a congressional bill that would improve the DMCA process, and "fair repair" legislation in the states of Minnesota and New York that would restore the right of owners to repair the electronic equipment they have purchased.[119] One piece of legislation that has been passed makes it legal for users to unlock their cell phones in order to change carriers.[120] There may be small concessions, but corporations are relying on this rentier economy based on leasing software the way earlier ruling classes relied on leasing land.

Think of this in light of the coming Internet of Things (IoT). Soon software will be ubiquitous in almost everything you use. There will be smart cars, smart homes, smart energy grids, smart health, smart cities, and smart government. If you and your democratically elected government cannot own and control the software you use, you will be at the mercy of the corporations that do. Governments use software, lots of it, and if they can't look into it, then who is really in charge in a democracy?[121] Jeremy Rifkin, a proponent of the Internet of Things and consultant to governments and businesses, has described the project in what could be its ultimate form: "The Internet of Things will connect everything with everyone in an integrated global network. People, machines, natural resources, production lines, logistics networks, consumption habits, recycling flows, and virtually every other aspect of economic and social life will be linked via sensors and software to the IoT platform, continually feeding Big Data to every node—businesses, homes, vehicles—moment to moment in real time."[122]

The stated goals of the IoT are to improve energy efficiencies, boost productivity, and reduce the costs of the production and delivery of goods and services dramatically. But it could lead also to corporate rent extraction, surveillance, and other abuses on an epic scale.[123]

Cisco Systems, a multinational tech conglomerate deeply invested in the IoT, predicts total profits over the coming decade will be more than $14 trillion.[124] In line with Rifkin, Cisco's CEO calls the project the "Internet of Everything."[125] And opting out will become more difficult as the IoT progresses.

The civics lesson in the new free software wars is that locked, proprietary code has the potential not only to destroy your privacy but also to reduce you to a condition of serfdom, without property, autonomy, or livelihood beyond your overmasters' control. As hackers have been warning, those who will not or cannot pay the rent in this neofeudal structure will become marginal, outlaw, or superfluous. It is a possible dystopia analogous to the one portrayed in the science fiction film *The Matrix*.[126]

THE NEW TRUST-BUSTING WARS AND THE UNSUSTAINABILITY OF CURRENT DIGITAL CAPITALISM

Consider, finally, the new trust-busting wars. In the first part of the twenty-first century, the future of privacy, transparency and truth, net neutrality, and free software hang in the balance, and so does the health of Western economies. Why is this so?

As hackers and people in the tech world would tell you, digital platforms, by their nature, tend to throw up large monopolies. Platform capitalism is a winner-take-all competition. First, users gravitate to the dominant platforms because they want to use the social media platform that everyone else is using, the software that is interoperable with other things they use, the platform with the widest coverage or selection, and the user interface they have become accustomed to. Then as more people use a platform, it becomes more valuable to users, and the platform controls more attention and data, allowing it to grow even larger. Finally, early advantages tend to become consolidated into market dominance. These are called "network effects" and are a powerful barrier that hackers seeking to offer alternative services have to contend with.

Monopolization does not mean the end of the struggle for dominance. To remain dominant, companies are driven to expand their exploitation of data and labor, to position themselves as a gatekeepers, to merge with other platforms and markets, and to enclose their ecosystems.[127]

Data extraction is part of the business model of every capitalist platform, whether it is a social media, a shopping, a service platform, or even a software platform that supports a physical product. Data confers competitive advantage, so the imperative is always to collect more. And finding and holding an as yet uncolonized human activity is like finding and conquering a previously undiscovered land or people. As Nick Srnicek, author of *Platform Capitalism*, has observed, "Whoever gets there first and holds them gets their resources—in this case, their data riches."[128]

Calls for platforms like Facebook to respect users' privacy miss the point that getting around privacy is at the core of the business model. These platforms will constantly push the envelope of what is socially and legally acceptable when it comes to data collection. It should be no surprise that their common pattern is to go ahead and collect data without consulting users, to apologize and equivocate where there are complaints, and to roll back collection only if there is very strong pushback.[129] As any Facebook user may have observed, the company has unilaterally and repeatedly changed its privacy settings since its inception, exploiting more intimate tranches of personal data each time.[130]

Extraction of users' free labor—creating "likes," reviews, and comments—is also part of many platforms' business model. Value is extracted from workers as well. "Crowd-sourcing" platforms like Uber and Airbnb commodify the time and possessions of workers while treating them as independent contractors instead of employees. Platforms like TaskRabbit allow workers to make a pittance fetching and delivering things, not unlike lackeys in earlier periods of historic inequality. Amazon's Mechanical Turk (MTurk) platform pays workers to complete microtasks that computers currently can't do perfectly, like identifying numbers or subject matter from images or transcribing sentences from audio. Most of Amazon's "click workers" make less than $2 per hour, yet the companies argue "click work" offers choice, autonomy, and equal opportunity.[131] By intention, there are no guaranteed hours, benefits, minimum wage levels, or employment standards for any of these workers unless they can successfully litigate under labor legislation to have these apply. The final indignity these workers will suffer will be when they are ultimately replaced by machines, as when Uber drivers are replaced by the driverless cars being developed by Uber investor Google.[132]

Platform capitalism leads to a convergence of markets. Tech insiders say that digital companies have little to leverage in terms of user data and share price unless their platform takes over the whole sector of, say, book selling, taxi service, online shopping, search, or mapping. Companies therefore aim to aggressively buy up, outpace, or crowd out competitors. The lack of diversity perpetuates itself. Alphabet (Google), Amazon, Apple, and Facebook dominate their respective markets. Figures from different sources vary, but in 2017, approximately 80 percent of the world's searches were done on Google, 77 percent percent of mobile social media occurred on Facebook, and Amazon had cornered the ebook market.[133] These companies are now competing to take over each other's sectors. Apple recently attempted to compete with Google's grip on mapping; Google is currently trying to use its search and mapping monopoly to expand into a shopping and smart car platform; Amazon is leveraging its monopoly in book selling to become the monopoly platform for retail and delivery of all consumer goods, as well as a dominant cloud service.[134]

Increasingly, as Harry Halpin described, digital platforms are enclosing their territory and centralizing the web experience. Business models known as "walled gardens" or "vertical integration" restrict users to a company's services, applications, and devices, preventing interoperability. The present goal of companies like Amazon, Apple, and Google is to become all-encompassing proprietary environments. Facebook, which serves the dependent user with social media, email, news, and shopping functions all from one platform, has already succeeded in convincing many people that it *is* the internet.[135]

Although digital platforms can attract huge amounts of equity investment if they look like they are going to dominate the attention of people in a new area of activity, a lot of these platforms are not very profitable in terms of producing income. As Douglas Rushkoff shows in his book *Throwing Rocks at the Google Bus: How Growth Became the Enemy of Prosperity*, "At the time of its billion-dollar purchase by Facebook, Instagram had raised $57.3 million, was valued at $500 million, and had generated $0 in revenue. ... Likewise, Tumblr netted negative $13 million the year it was purchased by Yahoo for $1.1 billion. ... Snapchat, a social media app, turned down a $3 billion offer from Facebook—all for its users' 400 million daily, dissolving pings."[136]

The endgame of this business model is an economy based largely on marketing and advertising. Yet the entire sector of advertising, marketing, public relations, and associated research accounts for less than 5 percent of the US gross domestic product (GDP)[137] and 0.7 percent of the gross world product (GWP).[138] Growing impediments to the sector are runaway "bot" activity and the rising use of ad blockers, which grew 41 percent in 2014 and 96 percent in 2015.[139]

Given that the income stream profit for all of these companies has come to out of the same 5 percent GDP that marketing and advertising make up, there seems to be no way they can justify their share prices.[140] In that light, every start-up sale is a pumped-up speculation on whether a new app will corner the most user attention and data. The developers walk away with most of the money.

This is a large problem for the economy. Much of the equity in digital platform companies' shares is essentially "dead," or noncirculating, capital. These companies and their founders have more money than they can usefully spend. Together, Alphabet, Amazon, Apple, and Facebook have a market value of approximately $3.5 trillion.[141] In 2015, *Bloomberg News* reported that "Apple Inc.'s cash topped $200 billion for the first time as the portion of money held abroad rose to almost 90%, putting more pressure on Chief Executive Officer Tim Cook to find a way to use the funds without incurring US taxes."[142]

Hackers know well that as monopoly platforms take over a sector, they make it hard for others to exchange value. They make it very difficult to introduce alternative business models and platforms.

Another large problem for the economy is that although digital technology creates new kinds of jobs, it is also killing jobs at a startling rate. New apps do not just tend to become monopolies when they dominate; they often collapse entire sectors of economic activity. The gutting of the music and media industries by digital platforms attests to this fact, as do the suicides of taxi drivers.[143] In many industries, digitized systems allow complex global supply chains to exploit the cheapest labor. Artificial intelligence is automating manual work and is making inroads on replacing higher-skilled work. Some experts estimate that job losses to technology over the next three decades could be as high as 70 percent and that unemployment could rise to about 50 percent.[144] Eric Schmidt, the CEO of Google, warned the Davos Economic Summit in 2014 that many professional, middle-class jobs that so far have been considered immune from automation will disappear.

In short, a dominant platform can collapse an industry with, as Douglas Rushkoff puts it, "nothing to show for it but shares of stock and no earnings. ... A couple of winners take it all while everyone else gets nothing. ... Total economic activity *decreases* as money is sucked up into share value."[145]

Some commentators believe that as profitability starts to become more of an issue, most of these digital platforms will end up charging some kind of rent or fee for service.[146] This might be a storage fee for every business that uses Amazon's cloud service, a cut of every financial transaction, a license fee for car makers using Google's driverless platforms, and a massive system of micropayments for social media, news, and other services. As the Internet of Things allows every physical thing (vehicles, roads, fridges, doors, trash bins, toilets) to be turned into a service, companies providing the software might charge micropayments per use, in addition to license and software update fees.[147]

As suggested earlier, not everyone will be able to afford these charges. Together with unemployment, underemployment, stagnant wages, and soaring costs of living (for housing, healthcare, education, and tech), these developments could create a gaping digital divide.[148]

What about charity? Aren't tech titans giving a lot back to the economy through charity? Even that is doubtful. "Good people of San Francisco, let's talk about the Google buses. Why do we hate them so?" began a 2013 opinion piece in the *San Francisco Chronicle* titled "Why We're Invisible to Google Bus Riders."[149] In the San Francisco Bay Area, the tech elite are a separate class, living in a separate reality from the rest of the population. In this region—where Facebook's founder Mark

Zuckerberg's overall wealth was $73.1 billion in 2017 and that of Amazon's founder, Jeff Bezos, was $85 billion;[150] where $100,000 Teslas are common; and where there is consumer demand for "raw water" at $37 a bottle[151]—the Silicon Valley Community Foundation is one example of the tech titans' brand of beneficence. With reportedly $13.5 billion of assets under management as of February 2018—surpassing the Ford Foundation as the third-largest philanthropy in the United States[152]—the foundation is a donor-advised fund. Local nonprofits call the foundation the "Death Star" and the "Black Hole" because, they say, "It is so hard to get money out of it."[153] Loopholes in the law allow donor-advised funds to avoid rules that make charities pay out a minimum percentage of their funds each year to support actual charitable work. "They got so drunk on the idea of growth that they lost track of anything smacking of mission," one nonprofit consultant told an *Atlantic* reporter, speaking of the foundation.[154]

The civics lesson in the new trust-busting wars is that digital capitalism, as it is currently practiced, does not serve the commonwealth. It is likely not even sustainable. Left unchecked, it will continue to generate monopolies, gross inequality, and economies that do not work for the majority of people. As any student of history knows, this is a dangerous prospect for democracy.

There is growing sentiment in Western democracies that these early twenty-first-century digital monopolies should be split up or regulated in the public interest—and some of them turned into publicly owned utilities. Because the advantages that network effects, access to data, and path dependency give to established platforms make it almost impossible for new entrants to take on a monopoly like Google,[155] breaking up these large corporations will have to be aided by the law. Hackers cannot take on the forces of monopolization alone.

During the late nineteenth century, hundreds of small railroads in the United States were being bought and consolidated by large companies. In answer to concerns about the concentration of power and anticompetitive practices in the railroad, banking, insurance, agriculture, and oil sectors, Congress passed the first antimonopoly (antitrust) legislation nearly unanimously in 1890. The Sherman Antitrust Act, named after Senator

John Sherman, is still the core antitrust statute in the United States today. Sherman argued, "If we will not endure a king as a political power, we should not endure a king over the production, transportation, and sale of any of the necessaries of life." The Sherman Act makes restraint of trade and the formation of a monopoly illegal and gives the US Department of Justice authority to obtain remedies in federal court. Later legislation set up the Federal Trade Commission, which allowed for the administrative enforcement of the act.[156]

During the Progressive Era, the administrations of Teddy Roosevelt and William Howard Taft used the Sherman Antitrust Act to sue forty-five and seventy-five companies, respectively. One of the best-known trusts busted up by Roosevelt was Standard Oil, which the US Supreme Court ordered broken into thirty-three separate companies.[157] Some monopolies, such as telephone systems, were allowed to survive because, by their nature, their size served the public interest, but these were then regulated as public utilities. Other infrastructure, like roads and bridges, was made fully public or state owned. There was a general consensus that competition in industry and public control or ownership of basic infrastructure were necessary for a healthy economy, even a capitalist one.

There have been some early moves in Europe to "trust bust" digital Goliaths. The European Commission has brought and won cases against Apple, IBM, and Microsoft, for example. In 2017, the EU fined Google €2.4 billion for its anticompetitive practice of ranking its own services higher than those of others in its search results.[158]

European laws generally make it easier to prove an antitrust violation than laws in the United States do, but Germany's antitrust legislation is cutting-edge. A coalition government agreement made in in Germany in 2018 included an update of antitrust laws, called "Competition 4.0." The update is designed for the digital economy: it recognizes that the measure of market dominance among most digital platforms is data rather than prices. Data dominance leads to lack of competition and abuse of consumers. Germany's Federal Cartel Office was the first to scrutinize Facebook's monopoly position from a data-gathering perspective. Its preliminary administrative finding was that Facebook was "abusing [its] dominant position by using its social network ... to limitlessly amass every kind of data." It noted that Facebook gathered its users' data from all of its products, including the messaging service WhatsApp and photo-sharing Instagram. It found Facebook gathered information through software on third-party websites, too, known as Facebook APIs (application programming interfaces). Any website that had a Facebook button reported user presence back to Facebook.[159]

European regulators have never gone after an American company to break it up, and that remains unlikely. But other trust-busting orders could be made. European regulators could block future acquisitions. Had Facebook been prohibited from buying WhatsApp and Instagram, those platforms would now be competitors of the company. At one time, Google was buying a startup every week. Regulators could categorize some of these companies as "essential services" and subject them to the same constraints as power companies and railways. That might mean requiring more public responsibility, more transparency, and caps on profits—and also telling social media companies like Facebook they must allow users to move their data over to competitors. Data portability could be key to cutting many platform monopolies down to a democratically acceptable size. Although it would likely change the social media business model to user-pay, it would certainly increase user self-determination and market competition. Finally, the EU and and European national regulators could prosecute Facebook under antitrust legislation. Remedies, short of breakup, could include an order requiring the company to change its terms of service and imposing fines of up to 10 percent of the company's global turnover.[160]

The EU General Data Protection Regulation (GDPR), which came into force on May 25, 2018, will also have a meaningful impact on platform monopoly power because it will restrict the circumstances under which, and the purposes for which, companies can collect personal data.[161]

In the United States, the Federal Trade Commission (FTC) could impose sanctions on monopoly platforms, challenge acquisition deals, and potentially impose privacy controls. It is the government agency that could break up an American transnational monopoly for anticompetitive conduct. But to date, it has not done so.[162] Silicon Valley has had close ties with the Democratic Party since Bill Clinton's presidency. Throughout the Obama administration and into Hillary Clinton's campaign for the presidency, the party kept insisting that tech was the economic engine that would move the country forward. Speaking of the scandal around Facebook's practices in the Cambridge Analytica affair, Chuck Schumer, the Senate leader for the Democratic Party, suggested self-regulation was the answer: "Facebook has an obligation to try and deal with it."[163] Not long after that, posters with the hashtag #ZuckSchumer, some of them mashing Schumer's face with that of Facebook CEO Mark Zuckerberg, began showing up in New York streets.[164]

THE GATHERING STORM

Winston Churchill called his book on the forces that led up to World War II *The Gathering Storm*. The metaphor and the history of that time are resonant now. In the decades preceding the war, the economic system seemed to be failing people. Despite the trust busting that took place around the turn of the century, privilege remained entrenched. Large concentrations of power, disparities of wealth, and fragile financial systems contributed to a disastrous stock market crash of 1929 that decimated world economies. The scourge of unemployment that followed fueled popular anger and nationalist sentiment. Propaganda stoked extremism. Governments were sclerotic, often class-bound, and incapable of responding effectively to crises they did not understand well.

Incapable of enacting the reforms needed to bring in a new order, democracies floundered. Some Western democracies faced authoritarianism as demagogues harnessed the rising popular unrest.[165] Historian Timothy Snyder has argued that fascism and communism were both responses to the globalization that took place in the second half of the nineteenth century with colonization and expansion of trade. Fascism and communism responded "to the real and perceived inequalities [globalization] created, and the apparent helplessness of the democracies in addressing them. They put a face on globalization, arguing that its complex challenges were the result of a conspiracy against the nation."[166] Fascists, in particular, embraced nostalgic myths of a glorious past "articulated by leaders who claimed to give voice to the people."[167] "Make Germany great again" was a stated aspiration of Hitler's and of the Nazi propaganda machine.[168]

The descent into authoritarianism in Germany was incremental. In Milton Mayer's recently republished classic *They Thought They Were Free: The Germans, 1933–45*, one of the first accounts of ordinary Germans' experiences living through Germany's descent into fascism,[169] a colleague of Mayer's, a philologist, observed, "We had no time to think about these dreadful things that were growing, little by little, all around us." The Nazi regime, he said, perfected its method of diverting people through "endless dramas" involving real or imagined enemies, and the people were gradually habituated "to being governed by surprise." "Each step was so small, so inconsequential, so well explained or, on occasion, 'regretted,'" he noted, that people were no more able to see it "developing from day to day than a farmer in his field sees the corn growing. One day it is over his head."[170]

Democracy failed in Europe in the 1930s, and it could fail in Europe and North America today.

Like the governments of the 1930s, Western governments today seem incapable of responding effectively to crises. Globalization in the late twentieth and early twenty-first centuries has created new winners and losers and new inequalities. The economic system that has been built over the last number of decades is extremely fragile. On top of this, the changes brought by digital technology have rapidly exacerbated inequality. In a few short years, the internet has become the infrastructure for our social, economic, cultural, and political interactions, yet few people inside government understand its emerging policy problems well.[171]

At the Chaos Computer Club's annual congress in Berlin, around Christmas 2010, not long after the 2008 financial crash and still in the dawn of the digital era, Dutch hacker Rop Gonggrijp summed up the evident paralysis: "Most of today's politicians realize that nobody in their ministries, or any of their expensive consultants, can tell them what is going on any more. They have a steering wheel in their hands without a clue what—if anything—it is connected to. Our leaders are reassuring us that the ship will certainly survive the growing storm. But on closer inspection they are either quietly pocketing the silverware or discreetly making their way to the lifeboats."[172]

9

HACKER OCCUPY

Bringing Occupy into Cyberspace and the Digital Era

THE OCCUPY MOVEMENT

In order to understand the proliferating hacker ethos at the beginning of the twenty-first century, you need to go back to the 2008 financial crisis, its fallout, and the ways it shaped the convictions of people who suffered from the crisis.

In 2008, the world's financial system collapsed. It started with the subprime mortgage market in the United States, and soon the whole shaky structure—built over the preceding three decades with deregulation, speculation, privatization, derivatization, globalization, predation, and downright fraud—was coming down. Major banks faced imminent shutdown, housing market bubbles burst, credit seized up. People lost their jobs, their houses, their retirement savings, their social security nets, and their dignity. Millennials came of age and joined a hard-scrabble labor market in which the workforce had been made intentionally precarious by capital.

Governments bailed out banks by distributing massive amounts of public money and by printing new money that went directly into the hands of financial elites to further their malefaction instead of into rebuilding the real economy. The worst economic downturn since the Great Depression ensued, and for most people it did not end. In Europe, governments reacted to a debt crisis by enacting austerity measures that punished their own populations instead of the bankers and speculators who had manufactured it or the corrupt elites who had made off with the cash. Financial institutions were allowed to turn whole nations, such as Greece, into debtor's prisons.

At the moment of collapse, Barack Obama had just been elected to office on a platform of transformative change. There was overwhelming support in the American electorate for radical financial reform and the prosecution of bankers. Even the bankers expected it. Yet Obama—the candidate borne into office on a wave of collective intelligence affirming "Yes, we can!"—hesitated. Uh, no, we can't, he demurred.

People were seized by the outrage of it all. Their eyes were opened to the growing evidence that democratic governments did not carry out the will of the people, no matter who was elected. Obama could have chosen, like Franklin Roosevelt before him, to save Main Street. He could have tried to reinstate the regulated capitalist system and productive economic base that created and sustained a large middle class in America in the mid-twentieth century. But instead, he chose to rescue Wall Street.

Within a few years, the perpetrators of the crisis were profiting from the disaster and piling up an even higher stack of derivatives, fraud, unpayable debt and financially engineered bubbles. There was no regulation of "moral hazard" for them. They were not shunned in the circles they moved in. They still had the support of the technocratic classes that had served and enabled them. To the predators and their enablers went the spoils. People hadn't even begun to understand how the large-platform monopolies that were forming at the time were further changing the power structures and social contract of the mid-twentieth century. But they had come to understand that although their Western democracies might be democratic in form, they were no longer so in substance.

In 2011, Occupy protests swept across the West. They were a spontaneous, visceral uprising by people against their governments' failure to pass effective financial reforms and bring bankers to justice. Hackers played important parts in Occupy and in the Arab Spring uprisings that immediately preceded and inspired it. And when Occupy stalled as a people's occupation of space in the physical world, hackers and the hacking ethos would carry it forward into the cybersphere and the digital era.

The Arab Spring was in some ways the result of the hacker scene going global. With the penetration of the internet globally (and despite companies imposing commercially walled access in developing countries), came the growth of the hacker. The core organizers of the Arab Spring revolutions came from the hacker scene.

The Arab Spring began in Tunisia in December 2010. Tunisia's local Pirate Party had been calling for internet rights, their members were arrested, and these arrests helped fuel protests. Tunisian activists like Slim Amamou credit WikiLeaks for what happened next. After its leaks revealed the US government no longer backed Tunisian president Ben Ali and would not help him if there was a revolution, the military and top members of Ben Ali's party refused to shoot at protesters. The protesters lost their fear that the US might push for international action to save Ben Ali.[1] Tunisian activists flying under the banner of Anonymous organized further protests, and Anonymous in Western countries jumped in to offer technical support. In the beginning, a small group of hackers made the protests happen, but the ability to use digital tools generalized rapidly. The number of digitally literate unemployed young people around the world was sky rocketing, and it was a demographic that had lots of energy, not much to lose, and time to spend on political life. The result was some very big protests. One of the largest took place in Tahrir Square in Cairo, Egypt.[2]

In early January 2011, Tunisian Anons and Anons from other countries launched Operation Tunisia. They made DDoS (distributed denial of service) attacks on government websites and got videos out to the world bypassing government censorship. Anons created a "care packet" for dissidents that provided advice on how to hide their identities on the internet and developed a "grease monkey" script (as an extension for Mozilla Firefox) to help them evade government phishing campaigns.[3]

As the protests spread to other Arab countries, Anonymous engagement spread, too. On January 25, 2011, Anons launched Operation Egypt, working in collaboration with an Egyptian group to restore mirrors and proxies that allowed Egyptians to access websites censored by the government. In Libya, they communicated with freedom fighters through AnonOps. Anons even pulled their signature stunt against Tunisian and Egyptian embassies, placing huge orders for pizza delivery to them, for the lulz. Before the Arab Spring, Anons had been based mainly in North

America, Europe, and Australia. After it, their banner spread a lot farther, particularly in the Muslim world.[4]

The protest camps that formed in Madrid and other Spanish cities in mid-May 2011 with the start of the Spanish Indignados movement took inspiration from the Arab Spring, and the Spanish occupations of city squares in turn inspired the Occupy movement in North America. The Vancouver-based group Adbusters Media Foundation (known for its anticonsumerist magazine, *Adbusters*) proposed a peaceful occupation of Wall Street. Adbusters cofounder Kalle Lasn registered the OccupyWall-Street.org web address on June 9, 2011. Adbusters sent an email to its seventy thousand subscribers stating, "America needs its own Tahrir."[5] Senior editor Micah White said, "[We] basically floated the idea ... and it was spontaneously taken up by all the people of the world; it just kind of snowballed from there."[6]

Anonymous encouraged its online community to take part in the physical protests, calling people to "flood lower Manhattan; set up tents, kitchens, peaceful barricades; and Occupy Wall Street."[7] A meme began to circulate of a ballerina dancing on top of the famous statue of the Wall Street bull.

Staged in New York City in Zuccotti Park, not far from the target of its name, the Occupy Wall Street protest began in September 2011, and by October it had swelled to an estimated fifteen thousand people as union members, students, and the unemployed converged on the spot with other citizens. By October 9, 2011, Occupy protests were taking place in 951 cities in eighty-two countries and in over six hundred communities in the United States.[8] A leader of the Indignados in Spain had called for a worldwide protest on October 15, 2011.[9] By the end of the month, there were Occupy camps in nearly two thousand cities worldwide.[10]

The movement's name came from earlier University of California protests held in 2009 and 2010, when students had occupied campus buildings to protest budget cuts, tuition hikes, and staff cutbacks flowing from the recession that followed the financial collapse of 2008. Their slogan was "Occupy everything, demand nothing."[11]

Occupy was described as a "democratic awakening."[12] But it was widely criticized for having no concrete program or demands. It seemed to be all over the place.[13] Yet there was a coherent constellation of concerns among protesters, centering around the economic system, its negative impact on the majority of people, and its deleterious effects on democratic governance. *The New Yorker* reported that the instigators of Occupy Wall Street were calling for specific reforms, such as tightening banking industry regulations, banning high-frequency trading, arresting the "financial fraudsters" responsible for the crash, and forming a presidential commission to investigate and prosecute corruption in politics.[14] *Bloomberg Businessweek* reported that protesters wanted employment and better jobs, more equal distribution of income, bank reform, and less influence by corporations on politics.[15]

Occupy had a lot in common, in fact, with the mass anti-Hoover protests of the Great Depression. The *Financial Times* found that people at the protests were concerned about "household debt, student debt, the unemployment rate, foreclosures, and the lack of prospects for people graduating from college."[16]

The movement had different focuses, but its overarching analysis was that large corporations and the global financial system had come to control the world in a way that disproportionately benefited a minority, undermined democracy, and was unstable. According to Wikipedia, Occupy's goal was to advance social and economic justice and new forms of democracy.[17] The movement's slogan was "We are the 99%." This was a reference to two facts: the top 1 percent of the population in the United States held disproportionate wealth compared to the rest of the population, and the after-tax income of the top 1 percent had nearly tripled over the last thirty years, according to a Congressional Budget Office report.[18]

At the time of Occupy's global mobilizations on October 15, 2011, occupywallst.org, the website for the New York protest, announced that "neoliberalism" was the cause of most of the wrongs Occupy sought to remedy.[19] The term *neoliberalism* has been criticized as having shifting and indeterminate meanings, but broadly it means a political and economic system that favors trade liberalization, inflows of foreign direct investment, privatization, and deregulation.

Neoliberalism encourages globalization and discourages government intervention. It holds that, in an increasingly complex world, the decisions faced by governments involve too many variables for governments to sort out effectively and are best left to the information-sorting forces of markets. In effect, neoliberalism has tended to give free rein to some of the most pernicious, extractive practices of capitalism.

In the last part of the twentieth century, neoliberalism ushered in a wave of globalization like the one experienced during the second half of the nineteenth century, with a new set of winners and losers. The winners, Occupy protesters held, were the global 1 percent, but they could have pointed to the top 10 percent and adopted the slogan "We are the 90%." Although the top 1 percent was making all its gains at the expense of the bottom 90 percent, the top 10 percent's share of American wealth was holding steady, and in the United States, this decentile holds the lion's share of wealth.[20] This 10 percent is the so-called meritocratic or technocratic class—the people earning six-figure salaries and more. In 2016, $1.2 million net worth would put you into the bottom of that class, with $2.4 million you would reach its median, and with $10 million net worth you were at its top.[21] This is the essential thing to grasp when thinking about neoliberalism: it is, above all, a class project. It is about consolidating the class power of the 1 percent and the 10 percent. Consider that after four decades of neoliberal policies, most Americans can't scrape together $500 for an emergency,[22] and a third of Americans can't pay the combined expenses of food, shelter, and healthcare, let alone the cost of a college education on top of these.[23] News reports are brimming with similar statistics about the declining conditions of the lower 90 percent in the United States and other Western democracies.

David Harvey—geographer, expert on Marx's theory of economics, and public intellectual who has written a book on the history of neoliberalism[24]—has acknowledged that the term has been used in so many ways it has come to seem incoherent. "And people say stop using it," he says. "Well, great, then. We don't have to talk about the concentration of class power anymore. Well, fuck you. That's exactly what we have to talk about. The class power that's been assembled is more concentrated than ever before, more than it ever has been."[25]

In 2011, Occupy was a global manifestation of people's growing conviction that representative democracy had betrayed them and that participatory democracy had become a necessity. It was a necessity, they realized, for people to be involved in the street, out of doors, as a presence, guiding and disciplining government if not determining matters directly.

Occupy was a movement that more than any other was intent on projecting a collective consciousness. Protesters created a democratic process of "working groups" (where protesters were able to have their say) and of "general assemblies" (where important decisions were taken by consensus).[26]

It is interesting to compare Occupy to the student uprisings that took place globally in 1968, beginning with the Prague Spring and US antiwar protests. These were a similar democratic awakening and, like Occupy, raised a constellation of related concerns and demands but no formulated political program. The philosopher Jean-Paul Sartre, from the World War II generation that resisted the Nazi invasion of France, interviewed a student leader of the May 1968 strikes in Paris, Daniel Cohn-Bendit, at the time and asked him why the students had not formulated a program:

J.-P. S.: What many people cannot understand is the fact that you have not tried to work out a programme, or to give your movement a structure. They attack you for trying to "smash everything" without knowing—or at any rate saying—what you would like to put in place of what you demolish.

D. C.-B.: Naturally! Everyone would be reassured, particularly Pompidou, if we set up a party and announced, "All these people here are ours now. Here are our aims and this is how we are going to attain them." They would know who they were dealing with and how to counter them. They would no longer have to face "anarchy," "disorder," "uncontrollable effervescence." Our movement's strength is precisely that it is based on an "uncontrollable" spontaneity, that it gives an impetus without trying to canalize it or use the action it has unleashed to its own profit.

There are clearly two solutions open to us today. The first would be to bring together half a dozen people with political experience, ask them to formulate some convincing immediate demands, and say, "Here is the student movement's position, do what you like with it!" That is the bad solution. The second is to try and give an understanding of the situation not to the totality of the students nor even to the totality of demonstrators, but to a large number of them. To do so we must avoid building an organization immediately, or defining a programme; that would inevitably paralyze us. The movement's only chance is the disorder that lets men speak freely, and that can result in a form of self-organization. For example, we should now give up mass-spectacular meetings and turn to the formation of work and action groups.

Cohn-Bendit spoke about how important it was for people to be able to come to a consensus about the nature of the problems they had to overcome:

It is essential first of all that people should express themselves. They say confused, vague things and they are often uninteresting things too, for they have been said a hundred times before, but when they have finished, this allows them to ask, "So what?" This is what matters, that the largest possible number of students say "So what?" Only then can a programme and a structure be discussed. ... We shall make proposals, but give us time. First we must discuss, reflect, seek new formulae. We shall find them. But not today.[27]

By December 2011, most of the major Occupy camps had been cleared by authorities, and the high-profile camps in London and Washington, DC, were dismantled in February 2012.[28]

Occupy protesters began to focus their energy on specific issues, forming new groups or joining established ones fighting on economic issues. For example, Occupy Homes formed to work with homeowners who had been victimized by predatory bank practices, with plans to occupy foreclosed homes, block evictions, and protest bank auctions.[29]

Following the 2008 financial crisis, Occupy was a first attempt to diagnose what was the matter with early twenty-first-century democracies. People were groping to understand what they were experiencing, how the world had been changing around them to dispossess them, and why they seemed to have so little power to protect their interests.

It's fair to say that Occupy largely failed as an attempt to assert democracy in real space, but like the '68 uprisings, it left an indelible mark on people's awareness of existing power structures. And the urgency people felt to assert their popular sovereignty continued to play out after the camps were shut down.

In 2011 and well into 2012 (after the shut down of the Zuccotti Park camp in fall 2011), the online actions taken in the name of Anonymous were frenetic. Anons DDoSed the website of the industrialist Koch brothers for the brothers' support of Wisconsin governor Scott Walker, who increased of the cost of benefits paid for by public-sector workers and limited their collective bargaining rights. Hackers operating under the Anonymous flag hacked Apple, defense contractor Booz Allen, the Democratic Party of Orange County, Florida, Monsanto, and NATO, among other targets.[30] A small group calling itself Lulz Security (LulzSec) emerged from Anonymous chat rooms. Over a short period, its members claimed responsibility for high-profile attacks on media companies (including Fox, News International, PBS, and Sony), games, pornography websites, and the CIA,

taunting rival hackers and the law enforcement units that tried to identify them.[31] LulzSec launched Operation Anti-Security and a multitude of
hacks ensued against law enforcement agencies and contractors in various
US states and other countries. Stolen credit cards were used to make donations to the American Civil Liberties Union, the Chelsea Manning Support
Network, and the Electronic Frontier Foundation.[32]

By 2013, many Anons were in jail after being apprehended in Austra-
lia, India, the Netherlands, Spain, Turkey, the United Kingdom, and the
United States,[33] but their efforts had been a kind of first attempt to bring
Occupy into cyberspace.

In Europe in 2011 and 2012, the urge to assert political agency led to
the rise of populist left-wing parties and sustained resistance to austerity
policies, particularly in Greece and Spain.

In 2016, people asserted their sovereignty in the seemingly reckless
rejection of the status quo in the Brexit vote in the United Kingdom
(in favour of the UK leaving the European Union) and in the election
of Donald Trump as president of the United States. The people's agency
was evident, too, in the unprecedented support shown for democratic
socialist candidates like Jeremy Corbyn in the UK and Bernie Sanders in
the US.

Large populations alienated from a system they feel is rigged against
them are unpredictable. They can swing to a radical progressive agenda
that actually redistributes power and does something for them personally
(as Americans did when they enthusiastically embraced Franklin Roosevelt's New Deal in the 1930s), or they can swing to nationalism and
"strong men" who manipulate their fear and anger (as Europeans and
British did when they fell in behind fascist leaders like Benito Mussolini, Adolf Hitler, and Oswald Mosley during roughly the same period).
Whichever way they swing, these populations share the same insecuri-
ties in, and frustrations with, the "democracies" they thought they were
living in. "Democracies" that don't seem to guarantee them rights, don't
provide them with the chance for a decent life, and congenitally do not
enact the policies they want, and at the same time, take important issues
like trade, labor, monetary policy, immigration, and culture right off the
table of public debate and hand them over to technocrats.[34]

This, then, is the larger political context in which one can understand the recent exponential growth of the hacking scene. It should be no surprise that people are turning to hacking in this era when reform seems out of sight. Since Occupy, hacking has become a practice and a metaphor for civic activism. The hacking ethos is inspiring a new way of thinking and acting as people begin the dogged work of dismantling the concentrations of power, mass surveillance and authoritarianism that have become the defining features of the new century.

A growing wave of citizen activists has developed an understanding that unless ordinary citizens seize the emancipatory potential of new digital technologies, class power will take these technologies over and turn them to the advantage of the upper 1 percent and 10 percent. "Of course, they are going to take this new technology, Artificial Intelligence, and turn it to their benefit," David Harvey has observed. "Labour lost the fight over automation of manufacturing and new organizational forms. Will they lose it in service also? The big question is, are we going to fight against AI coming in and lose, or are we going to find creative ways to use it and then push with it in certain kinds of ways?"[35]

As I will describe in the remainder of this chapter, hacking experiments are being tried all over now. These experiments are not only about privacy and transparency, as fundamental as these are to democracy. If you look around you with a little knowledge about what "hacking" is, you will find that people are hacking all kinds of things—not just privacy and transparency, but also monopolies, finance, corruption, censorship, law, electoral politics, and democratic decision making itself. Literally and metaphorically, they are striving to "code in" democratic values wherever they can.

You can see it in all kinds of human activity and at all levels. Yes, as described earlier, farmers are hacking tractors to "free" them from unfair digital restrictions management (DRM); computer programmers are "hacking" copyright to "free" software generally; academics are hacking commercial enclosures of knowledge; cities are hacking internet service providers (ISPs) to take their local economies back into their own hands—and much, much more.

The terms—*hackers, hacktivists, tech activists, Indignados, net citizens*—and the identities they represent, overlap. The goal they share is to distribute power to the people, to put the people's hands on matters as local, national, and global citizens. When power is distributed, they believe, many different experiments can be tried in different places at once, and the best solutions can be disseminated widely.

Karl Marx posited that transformative technology brings down the whole superstructure of a society—its social hierarchies, the role of labor, its distribution of wealth, the way it defines value, and the law that underpins it all. In the early part of the twenty-first century, we're in the midst of just such a transformation.

A MULTITUDE OF DIVERSE EXPERIMENTS

Daunting though it is, this is a moment of opportunity. Hacking experiments could potentially change the whole political economy.

Many stories could be told about the experiments taking place, but even a small selection demonstrates the "effervescence" of the historical moment. Taken together, these experiments might seem chaotic, and certainly they evince the "positive chaos" Wau Holland advocated in founding the Chaos Computer Club. One way to make sense of them is to understand they are riding a wave of rapid technological change and to categorize them according to the particular technological innovation they are relying on to create decentralized power.

Tech people will be familiar with recent breakthroughs that have been made in digital decentralized solutions, but laypeople may need a quick primer.[36] The first innovation in decentralized solutions was "federated technology," the basic structure of the current internet. In federated technology, multiple, central nodes connect other nodes, like the lines that can be drawn between solar systems in the night sky. Users are free to choose which nodes to interact with and, to some extent, which central "hub" nodes they want to play intermediary for them. Email is an example of an open, interoperable protocol that uses a federated architecture. More recent examples include XMPP for chatting, OStatus for microblogging (tweeting), and OAuth for authentication. Many of the hacking experiments discussed so far in this book utilize federated technology or the basic architecture of the existing internet to create decentralized solutions, often with a free software approach to development and dissemination.

The second innovation in decentralized solutions has been "distributed," or "peer-to-peer" (P2P), technology. Peer-to-peer networks do not use central servers, like federated networks. Instead, they use ordinary computers to process data and to deliver it to other computers without an intermediary. Most of the success with P2P networks so far has been in file-sharing solutions, like BitTorrent, although there have been numerous attempts to build P2P web services, such as Freenet, that would be resistant to spying and censorship because without a "middleman" server there is no central point to choke or capture data.

The third innovation in decentralized solutions has only recently been invented. It builds on P2P architecture but adds a permanent, tamper-proof, distributed ledger that relies on mathematical computation to record transactions. This is the "blockchain." Think of a chain that is being forged one link at a time, where each link is a mathematical equation that links to the next and so cannot be excised from the chain or modified after it is created. The blockchain is revolutionary in that it automates trust. You don't have to trust a central provider of a service, and you don't have to trust the people you are dealing with. You have to trust only the code, which allows your transaction to be processed using mathematical formulas that verify its authenticity and then to be recorded on a public ledger stored across many computers.

HACKING EXPERIMENTS USING FEDERATED TECHNOLOGY, OR THE BASIC INTERNET STRUCTURE

Trebor Scholz gets emails almost every day from all kinds of people—from Uber drivers in South Africa, programmers in India, and dog walkers in Los Angeles—saying, "Hey, how do we do this? What's next?"[37]

Recall that when monopoly platforms take over a sector, they make it hard for people to exchange value at their edges. When large incumbent players like Google or Uber enjoy the advantages of network effects, access to data, and path dependency, it is almost impossible for new entrants to take them on with competing business models and platforms. Some of the earliest hacking experiments around privacy in communications services have tried to break through this barrier, using the basic structure of the internet to offer alternative applications and platforms with the hope they might attract a critical mass of users and generate their own network effects. The same is happening with other services as people band together to create cooperative platforms.

You don't change platform capitalism by criticizing it, Trebor Scholz says, but by creating alternative models that show it up as a failure. Scholz is a professor of culture and media at the New School in New York City. He had been convening the Digital Labor conferences there since 2009, when he met Occupy activist and journalist Nathan Schneider at OuiShare Fest: The Age of Communities in Paris in 2014. They got talking, and later that year, Scholz published a paper, "Platform Cooperativism vs. the Sharing Economy," and Schneider wrote an article, "Owning Is the New Sharing," both of which mapped efforts underway to create cooperative platforms in various fields. After the Rosa Luxemburg Foundation published Scholz's primer "Platform Cooperativism," the term was "coined," and people started coalescing around it. Techies and luddites together—platform creators, platform workers, scholars, labor advocates, entrepreneurs, activists, investors, CEOs, New York City councilors—came to an event Scholz and Schneider organized at the New School in November 2015 called "Platform Cooperativism: The Internet, Ownership, Democracy."[38]

Platform cooperativism, Scholz and Schneider have written, is about "shared governance and shared ownership of the Internet's levers of power: its platforms and protocols. Democratic ownership and governance."[39] Yet it is about more than just providing a platform or killer app that is collectively owned by drivers or dog walkers. It is about building processes and ecosystems to support the development of democratic enterprises, not technological solutionism. In addition to the killer app (the technology), Scholz and Schneider emphasize, platform cooperativism requires appropriate forms of finance, law, policy, and culture to support it. "It's a radical horizon, to be sure," but not an absolute one, they have said.[40] If it flourishes, platform cooperativism will likely be only part of a mixed economy.[41]

Scholz recently founded the Platform Cooperativism Consortium,[42] which is made up of about forty organizations that support the use of cooperative business models with digital tech. It collaborates with the Inclusive Design Research Centre in Toronto, which has a team of about thirty full-time developers and seventy on standby. In January 2018, the Consortium started a legal clinic on platform cooperatives at Harvard Law School to find ways to make it easier to start these ventures legally.[43]

Currently, the law encourages the creation of capitalist corporations through all kinds of breaks and incentives without questioning whether these incentives would serve society better if they were given to cooperative enterprises.

Scholz maintains that the areas of economic activity for which platform cooperativism can offer practical solutions are endless. The Platform Cooperativism Consortium recently started working with three thousand childcare providers in Illinois, recyclers in Brazil, the only worker coop in the social care sector in Australia, and refugee women who want to start businesses in Germany. "It's basically grabbing onto the heart, the algorithmic heart of [platform] companies, ripping it out and putting in cooperative values," Scholz explains, which leads to fair pay, dignity on the job, and the ability to scale coops.[44]

Stocksy is a stock photo platform owned by about a thousand photographers in Canada that made approximately $11 million in 2017. Daemo, built at Stanford University, is a cooperative marketplace intended to make crowd-sourced work more equitable. Green Taxi is a Denver-based cooperative of more than eight hundred worker-owners that was set up with the help of their union, the Communications Workers of America. It is joining taxi drivers in New York and other cities to develop platform services that can begin to compete with Uber.[45] Banyon Project is a consumer cooperative that brings local news reporting to local news markets.[46]

As a form of economic organization, cooperatives are admittedly rare today. The United States currently has about three hundred to four hundred worker coops. France has 300,000.[47] But both Europe and North America have had ambitious economic cooperative movements in the past that innovators today might draw inspiration from. In the US, the National Farmers' Alliance and Industrial Union was a large network of purchasing and marketing cooperatives in the late nineteenth century that sought to advance both the economic independence and civic education of its members. It employed more than forty thousand lecturers with an urgent mission to increase political literacy among Americans and was organizing politically at the precinct level in forty-three states.[48] A similar rural, populist movement in Canada in the early to mid-twentieth century ushered in a stable economic system of producer cooperatives in the agricultural sector that served the country well for many decades. The Cooperative Commonwealth Federation (CCF), a Western-based political party of farmers and labor aimed to transform the capitalist economic system into a "cooperative commonwealth" by democratic means.[49] Calling for the socialization of banks and financial institutions and the public ownership of transportation, communication, and natural resources, it became the official opposition party in three Canadian provinces, eventually forming the government in Saskatchewan. The CCF was instrumental in establishing universal healthcare in Canada, which Canadians of all political persuasions would agree is now the bedrock of the country's social contract.

As of June 2018, Scholz could report the existence of some 240 digital cooperative platform businesses worldwide.[50] This tiny but growing sector of the economy could take off if, like the populist progressive movements of earlier times, it can seize people's political imaginations and get them organizing in earnest for their own economic interests.

Following in the tradition of farsighted, populist reforms proceeding from the rural parts of North America, farmers today are starting to organize digital cooperative platforms to free themselves from the economic oppression of digital monopolies. Farm Hack is a cooperative platform for creating farm equipment with the free software philosophy. "We are a worldwide community of farmers that build and modify our own tools. We share our hacks online and at meet ups because we become better farmers when we work together," the website states.[51] Some of the tools displayed on the site look fairly rudimentary, and there are no giant tractors yet, but there is a "Free Farm Manifesto" that advocates the free software movement's "four freedoms," adapted for the farmer—the right to know how a tool works, the right to modify a tool, the right to repair a tool, and the right to distribute both original and modified designs of tools.[52]

Scholz says he does not know what the odds are that platform cooperativism will win out over platform capitalism in this new digital era, but he knows what they are if people don't try.[53]

In addition to cooperative platforms where people are organizing labor and markets for economic purposes, there are many cooperative platform experiments organizing communities for social purposes. In Los Angeles, the Anarcho Tech Collective is hacking the police monopoly on 911 emergency services in light of the number of times police have used deadly force when responding to emergency calls.[54] The External Revenue Service is a cooperative platform that has set up an alternative "tax system," a new way of distributing charitable contributions. Enspiral is a growing collective that shares cooperative platform tools and strategies among social entrepreneurs.[55]

Important experiments are under way that aim to create cooperative "data commons." People are looking for ways to wrest control of their data back from governments and surveillance capitalists. The My Data coop in Switzerland, for example, experiments with patient-owned and controlled medical information.[56] Myuseragreement is a cooperative formed to provide users with terms and conditions on the use of their data that they can collectively dictate to the companies that interact with their devices.[57]

Many alternative social media platforms are being developed and offered to the public using the basic federated technology of the internet. Diaspora, an early clone of Facebook launched in 2010 with the help of the crowd-funding app Kickstarter, had some initial success but ran into trouble meeting users' expectations.[58] It was followed by Ello, which unlike Facebook allowed people to use pseudonyms. Ello also flamed out as a serious competitor to Facebook,[59] but developers continue to experiment with social network platforms that provide alternatives to the surveillance and datamining practices of the large commercial monopolies.[60] GNU MediaGoblin is a federated media publishing platform built with free software that is meant to provide an alternative to services like Flickr and SoundCloud.[61] RSS (Rich Site Summary or Real Simple Syndication) is a web feed that aggregates updates on websites and allows users to syndicate their online content across websites.[62]

Mastodon is an open-source alternative to Twitter. A modified version of GNU social,[63] it was released in 2016 by a young coder in Germany.[64] It is almost identical to the Twitter platform, except its messages can be up to 500 characters instead of 280, posts can be private, and there is no advertising. It has been more successful than App.net, an earlier attempt to replace Twitter. Mastodon grew rapidly after Twitter rolled out an update that irritated people in the way it presented "replies." Suddenly, hundreds of new users were joining Mastodon every hour. Any user can set up a server and host their own instance of Mastodon, which its developer encourages so that the costs of running it can be distributed among users.[65] Other federated, free software alternatives to Twitter include OStatus, mentioned earlier, a protocol stack that came out of StatusNet, which was eventually abandoned in favor of a group of standards developed by the W3C Social Web Working Group, started by Harry Halpin in 2014. Initially formed to produce a single, simple-to-use standard for federating the social web (for making it interoperable), it had the backing of IBM and interest from Google. Unfortunately, the working group ultimately failed to produce compatible standards because the hackers involved could not agree on which ones to employ. (The committee was composed mostly of semi-employed hackers rather than industry representatives, who more typically compose the working groups developing standards affecting industry interests.)[66]

Alternative cloud services are also making inroads on established, centralizing monopolies. OwnCloud, released in January 2010, is meant to provide a free software replacement to proprietary cloud storage. It has forked into NextCloud, which is more active now. These services are decentralizing in that they let you pick where you want to store your data, whether on your own private server or elsewhere.[67] Raspberry Pi Foundation has developed a kit called "Raspberry Pi" that lets users build their own small external computer out of a set of single-board computers. Many people are building these and using them as personal clouds or ad blockers,[68] although the Raspberry Pi single-board computer requires nonfree software to start up.[69] Other personal cloud projects include Cozy Cloud and Sandstorm.[70]

HACKING EXPERIMENTS USING P2P DISTRIBUTED TECHNOLOGY

Peer-to-peer (P2P) distributed technology and blockchain technology are still in their early stages of development, but they could offer radical solutions for distributed empowerment not thought possible just a few years ago. Recall that a P2P network cuts out the middleman server. In P2P networks, equal nodes function simultaneously as both "clients" and "servers" to the other nodes on the network. They make a portion of their resources (such as processing power, disk storage, and network bandwidth) directly available to each other. They become both suppliers and consumers of resources.

In the current state of P2P tech development, peer-to-peer networks usually implement some form of virtual "overlay network" on top of the physical topology of the existing internet, where the nodes in the overlay form a subset of the nodes in the physical network. Data is still exchanged directly over the internet's TCP/IP network and through the physical infrastructure of the internet, but at the applications layer peers are able to communicate with each other directly via the overlay links (each one corresponding to a path through the underlying physical network).[71]

It is possible to build a separate, physical infrastructure for a peer-to-peer network. The idea of every user having a personal server and acting as a Tor node is a step in this direction, although the data sent by these nodes would still go through the wires and cables of the existing internet and through its continental switching points. Theoretically, a completely new peer-to-peer global internet could be built that does not use any of the physical infrastructure of the existing internet, but as the hackers who are thinking about this would confirm, that is an enormous project that might be overtaken by quantum computing in any case.

The advantage of P2P networks is that they are both resilient and scalable. They are resilient because they have no one point of failure or shut down. They are scalable because as nodes join a P2P network and demand on it grows, capacity and resources also grow.

As mentioned earlier, P2P applications have been used most successfully to date to hack file sharing. Because of the lack of a central authority in P2P networks, governments and the entertainment industry cannot easily delete content on them or stop it from being shared. This has allowed the pirating of copyrighted material, but it also has potential for countering censorship.

Well-known peer-to-peer file-sharing networks include Gnutella, G2, and eDonkey. Freenet, the peer-to-peer web service for censorship-resistant communication and web browsing, uses distributed data storage to keep and deliver information.[72] Netsukuku is an experimental peer-to-peer routing system developed by the Italian FreakNet MediaLab around 2005.[73] FAROO is an early peer-to-peer web search engine released in 2008 with the plan of sharing up to 50 percent of its advertising revenue with its users. It uses a distributed crawler that stores search data on users' computers instead of on a central server. Whenever a user visits a website, the information is automatically indexed and distributed to the network. Search result ranking is done by comparing usage statistics.[74]

Osiris is a program that allows its users to create anonymous web portals via a P2P network that are resistant to denial of service attacks and censorship.[75] Peercasting experiments are also being tried by hackers where the P2P overlay network helps peers find a relay for a stream.[76] One new experiment from France, PeerTube, intends to become a competitor to YouTube. Supported by the nonprofit Framasoft and launched in 2015, PeerTube uses peer-to-peer technology and a federated group of servers and is being distributed under a GPLv3 free software license. The service is free.[77] Textile is a P2P alternative to Instagram for managing and sharing photos on the web.[78] Pinoccio is an Internet of Things platform that uses mesh networking,[79] and Beaker Browser is an experimental new browser for exploring the peer-to-peer web.[80]

P2P is best seen as a relational dynamic through which peers can freely collaborate with each other, create value in the form of shared resources, and transfer value without a central authority. It makes a "many-to-many" allocation of resources and determination of norms possible, outside the hierarchical decision making of governments and state-supported markets. In the past, the costs of scaling communication and coordination with predigital technologies made hierarchical decision making by states and markets necessary. P2P technology will not make the state and state-supported markets wither away, but it will make self-organization on a mass scale feasible.[81]

Theoretically, P2P networks can create virtual supercomputers that are powerful enough to run large ventures such as alternative stock exchanges, banks, central banks, interbank communications systems like the Society for Worldwide Interbank Financial Telecommunication (SWIFT) and international monetary institutions like the International Monetary Fund (IMF). In other words, P2P could lead to the formation of peer-to-peer institutions that could rival current economic institutions. Replacing key economic institutions, in fact, was the dream of populists in the Progressive Era. The National Farmers' Alliance and Industrial Union proposed public ownership of utilities as well as an alternative currency and banking system. Their Subtreasury Plan was meant to reengineer the country's monetary policy to reward labor over capital. Ironically, the plan became the rough blueprint for the creation of the US Federal Reserve in 1914, which, as the 2008 financial crisis demonstrated, serves the interests of bankers, speculators, and oligarchs over those of ordinary people.[82]

In the digital era, P2P technology could be used to transfer value peer-to-peer without a central clearing authority. P2P could create distributed storage systems where data can be stored across computers rather than on corporate clouds—the independent, reliable storage of vast amounts of transaction data being a necessary element of any financial institution. Distributed storage could give citizens control over all kinds of information, so that when hackers scrape government websites to save the climate change research discontinued by the Trump administration, say, P2P technology could be employed to store it in a resilient peer-to-peer network that cannot easily be shut down by authorities.

Granted, studies show that even with good peer-to-peer design there will always be tendencies to centralize. Indeed, in most peer-to-peer systems, the developers play a seemingly unavoidable centralizing role.[83] Another challenge for P2P networks is that with ongoing file transfers and swarm/network coordination packets, they use a lot of bandwidth compared to federated networks, where data is transferred only in relatively small quantities and for short intervals. Security is also a problem. Because every user on a P2P network is a server, a successful attack on one can potentially expose the whole network to routing attacks, malware, and corrupted data.

The biggest problem with P2P solutions is trust. You have to trust your peers not to cheat or abuse you, especially when transferring things of value, because there are no central authorities to guarantee, authenticate, or necessarily enforce your transaction.

HACKING EXPERIMENTS USING THE BLOCKCHAIN

This is where the blockchain comes in. The third and most recent innovation in decentralized solutions, the blockchain, builds on peer-to-peer technology and largely solves the problem of trust. As described earlier, it adds a permanent, tamper-proof distributed ledger that relies on mathematical computations to record transactions. Like a chain that is being forged one link at a time, each transaction is authenticated with a mathematical equation that links to the next and cannot be cut out from the chain or modified after its creation. The blockchain automates trust: it allows your transaction to be authenticated, recorded on a public ledger, and stored across many computers so that it cannot be erased or tampered with.

A growing number of applications are being found for blockchain technology by hackers and others, based on its capacities when deployed with P2P. These capacities include the secure transfer of value, secure distributed storage, and secure distributed computing.

Bitcoin, the cryptocurrency everyone was talking about at the end of 2017 when its market price soared to nearly $20,000 per "coin," is a leading proof-of-concept prototype of blockchain technology. It began as a "white paper" attributed to "Satoshi Nakamoto" (likely a fictional character but also the name of a real-life engineer and neighbor of some of the California cypherpunks).[84] Released as free software in 2009, Bitcoin has spurred the creation of hundreds of different kinds of "cryptocurrencies," "altcoins," or "tokens" since its creation.

The "tokens" transferred through a blockchain may hold monetary value (as in Bitcoin), or they can represent equity, decision-making power, property ownership, licensing power, and other things of value. So the blockchain, deployed with P2P technology, can potentially be used to create a relatively secure decentralized monetary regime, stock exchange, or banking system. And it can be used to create a relatively secure voting system, land transfer record, or credentialing system.

These larger systems would need to rely on the secure distributed storage and secure distributed computing capacities of the blockchain and P2P technologies. But they would also need some way of enforcing a set of rules between peers in each system.

Ethereum is a ground-breaking blockchain project created in 2013 by a nineteen-year-old coder, Vitalik Buterin. Building on earlier work by David Chaum (the cryptographer who inspired the cypherpunks), Buterin developed a new programming language for creating applications that can be executed across a large number of distributed nodes. "Distributed applications" (also known as "smart contracts") automatically enforce rules scripted in their code using the blockchain. They are like a self-executing contract.

Building on the idea of the "smart," or self-executing, contract, the blockchain can potentially be used to create decentralized autonomous organizations (DAOs), where many human beings or machines can have their interactions governed by a set of self-executing rules embedded in the code of the DAO's applications, enforced by the blockchain.

Theoretically, a decentralized, distributed stock exchange could be built one day with the blockchain automatically enforcing all of the rules governments failed to pass after the 2008 financial crisis: rules against derivatives and Libor fixing, against selling something (like physical gold) or loaning money against something (like real estate) many times over, and against high-frequency trading, and fraud. An alternative blockchain-based stock exchange could impose a microtax on transactions. To address the gross inequalities and concentrations of power that the existing financial system has helped to produce, what needs to be redistributed is not necessarily wealth but risk and bargaining power—a redistribution the blockchain could theoretically accomplish. All this might seem a long way off, but people are already experimenting with blockchain solutions for secure storage (Storg is one early prototype) and many more complicated things.

For example, the blockchain is being used to make sure people are paid for their work and to create systems of innovative micropayments. In Berlin, an equivalent of the commercial music streaming service Spotify uses the cooperative business model with the blockchain to pay creators twice as much as they get from Spotify.[85] Minds is a blockchain-based social media application similar to Facebook that pays its users.[86] SteemIT is an application that pays its users cryptocurrency to write content, and it works with third-party applications like dTube, an alternative to YouTube that uses the InterPlanetaryFileSystem (IPFS). DTube awards Steem currency when users upvote videos.[87] Twister is a blockchain-based distributed microblogging system using free software implementations of Bitcoin.[88] Filecoin, launched by Protocol Labs in 2017 with a stake of $205 million, is aiming to create a decentralized data storage network by allowing users to pay each other with its blockchain token, filecoin, for the use of spare storage capacity on their computers.[89] Brave is a privacy-enhanced anti-DRM browser, which works well and could replace Google Chrome and Mozilla Firefox. It pays its users a "basic attention token," giving them some reward for their clicks and time. When Brave held an "initial coin offering" (ICO) to raise funding, it brought in $36 million in thirty seconds.[90]

People are talking about creating low-cost distributed people's banks using blockchain, where individuals could get "frictionless" loans at low interest rates based on reputation and a wide distribution of risk. People could provide insurance for themselves using blockchain, collecting micropremium payments. Blockchain could furnish important solutions in developing countries, where people often lack credit and insurance, where property and identity records are often flawed, and where government corruption and war can destabilize regular ledger keeping. Ultimately, the blockchain could be used as a regulatory technology for many transactions.[91]

The blockchain and P2P could be used to create self-enforcing "data commons" in contexts like the city, patient populations, or national census databanks. Blockchain systems could give people some self-determination over their personal data and preempt corporations from gaining proprietary control over information that has important civic uses.

With the blockchain and P2P technology, distributed internet service providers (ISPs) could allow people to make small amounts of money whenever their computers were on, just for providing distributed computing power.[92] There could be a decentralized domain name system (Namecoin is one early experiment).

Theoretically, there could be a whole new peer-to-peer, blockchain-secure, (re)decentralized World Wide Web that would be made neutral, secure, and free of censorship by distributing data, processing, and hosting across millions of computers around the world with no centralized control[93] and by employing the blockchain to verify transactions and enforce rules automatically. This innovation would overtake (or gather together) earlier attempts to apply peer-to-peer technology to web functions. It would be the realization, in fact, of a new internet, at least at the applications level, built on top of the physical infrastructure of the existing internet.

SOLID?

Tim Berners-Lee, the inventor of the World Wide Web and Harry Halpin's boss at the World Wide Web Consortium (W3C), seems to be working on this project. But a pall hangs over the work because Berners-Lee, respected elder statesman and Lorax steward of the internet, recently greenlighted a standard for a mechanism that would implement digital rights management (DRM) on that very web.

In his role as executive director of W3C, Berners-Lee was final arbiter of what the standards council's recommendation on this would be, and he tipped in favor of industry wishes to have a standard. The Electronic Frontier Foundation, Richard Stallman, and many others in the hacker and digital rights community fought vigorously against it. There was a stark lack of consensus. In July 2017, a secret vote by members ran 108 for and 57 against, with 20 abstentions, among the 185 members who voted.[94] Nevertheless, one man decided the issue. So much for the Lorax style of "consensus" governance.

To appreciate what a big issue this now is in the technology world, recall the description of DRM and the Digital Millennium Copyright Act (DMCA) statutory regime provided in chapter 8. Hackers and others against the recommendation argued that the W3C would essentially be endorsing the DRM-DMCA model, making it harder to get the regime repealed. More immediately, it would be blessing the insertion by corporations of "black boxes" of code into everyone's computer through a standard mechanism, the encrypted media extension (EME), built into their web browsers. Black boxes into which corporations could include, in addition to the copyrighted materials that users' wished to access, all their usual malware to dictate terms of use, invade privacy, compromise security, and otherwise take control of users' computers. The EME mechanism was designed for video only, but W3C potentially could adopt standards for all kinds of DRM restricted material on the Web, including ebooks, documents, software updates, and pages for web services. Researchers and security experts were prevented from even looking into these black boxes to study what was there because the Digital Millennium Copyright Act made it a crime to do so. The DMCA ran over the rights of "fair use" people had to study what was in the black boxes and to use the copyrighted material itself for fair-use purposes. It effectively killed fair use, an essential element in any copyright regime that aims to promote innovation and knowledge.

According to hackers and digital rights proponents, DRM, DMCA, and EME broke the architecture of the free and open web, making it insecure and unfixable. If users could not monitor what their browser was admitting into their computer, they were hooped. Browsers are the door to everything on the web. DRM, DMCA, and EME injected the poison of black code into the system and made it criminal to clean up the pollutions it spread. It was a model that potentially encouraged a draconian lockdown of everything on the web—the gift to humankind that was supposed to be leading us all forward with its model of sharing and abundance.[95]

On Tim Berners-Lee's side was the argument that many browsers, including Chrome, were already shipping with the chosen mechanism, EME, inside them, so there might as well be a standard. Browser makers had decided that they wanted to include the capacity to access material restricted by DRM inside their browsers, and EME was a huge improvement over external "plug-in" mechanisms like Adobe Flash, which did not have open standards and were security nightmares. W3C did not invent DRM, and its role was not to advocate for any given policy position but to set technical standards. "Now [web-based] video is an open technology with common descriptions and APIs," Jeff Jaffe, the CEO of W3C told a journalist. "It's still encumbered underneath. We would still like to change that. It's on the list of things to get done someday."[96] Another argument on the Berners-Lee side was that if W3C created a standard for EME, the organization would have more influence to discourage abuses, and W3C did exhort industry to respect users' privacy and security.[97] Someone suggested this was like inviting a rabid dog into your backyard and hoping the rope you offered to tie it up with would restrain it. EFF asked that W3C at least get members to sign a covenant agreeing that they would not sue security researchers, but this did not happen. In January 2017, W3C offered optional guidelines instead.[98]

Others went further than just user security and fair-use arguments. They argued unapologetically that W3C should be standing up for the ideal of free software on the web. Ideally, all code on the web should have the "four freedoms." Nothing on the web should be in a black box. Stallman said that when he launched the free software movement in 1983, his mission had been to create free software alternatives for every piece of software people wanted to use.[99] Creators of software could be paid for releases and updates of their code, but people should have alternatives. They should be able to make copies and share their software, to study and modify it, and to offer their modifications to others. No software owner should have complete power over users, especially now that everyone needed software to live in the digital world. Under the free software model, you put out your software, you charge what you want or what the market will bear, and you make money again if you have useful updates and offer useful service, but you also live with the possibility of competing replacements and modifications for your software, so that ultimately software is not made a scarce resource in the hands of a few who forbid its replication or modification and sit on top of it for decades like feudal landlords with complete power over their dependants.

Jeff Jaffe's office at MIT is across the hall from Richard Stallman's, and Stallman put a sign on his door so that Jaffe and his visitors would see it daily: "MAKE DRM A FELONY: Those who make, lease or sell devices with DRM should go to prison."[100]

As for other creative material delivered over the web, such as music and films, people argued that it was not worth breaking the internet for the comfort of those industries. The music industry was changing rapidly, and Hollywood's losses to unauthorized copying and sharing on the internet might not even be that great because most people did not mind paying for films to receive ease of delivery and quality viewing.

Finally, some activists took an explicit "free culture" stance, arguing that cultural materials should be just as easily shared and modified as software and that there were emerging business models in music, in which creators gave away their recorded work and made money by other means, cutting out parasitic middlemen in the process. Copyright was not even practical for most things on the web, they argued, because it was impossible to find their creators, which meant that without the ability to obtain formal permissions easily, works under copyright would remain locked down and fall out of use.[101]

As the conflict revved up, Harry Halpin stated publicly that he would resign if EME were adopted as a W3C recommendation. "I myself believe that the web we want does not include DRM," he said, "and that this is a responsibility to our children, that the web that they inherit should allow and enable sharing."[102] He left the organization in late 2016, and EFF resigned its membership in W3C in fall 2017.[103]

Tim Berners-Lee has set up a small team at MIT's Computer Science and Artificial Intelligence Laboratory (CSAIL) to work on his decentralized web project. He calls it a "decentralized, linked data system," and its name is "Solid."[104] In late 2015, the project received a $1 million grant from Mastercard. It is open source.[105] Berners-Lee is hoping to get developers to work on this new *Mahabharata* (the epic poem with many authors) the way coders collectively worked on GNU/Linux and the Debian project.

"There are people working in the lab trying to imagine how the Web could be different. How society on the Web could look different. What could happen if we give people privacy and we give people control of their data," Berners-Lee has said.[106] "Right now we have the worst of both worlds, in which people not only cannot control their data, but also can't really use it, due to it being spread across a number of different siloed websites. Our goal is to develop a web architecture that gives users ownership over their data, including the freedom to switch to new applications in search of better features, pricing, and policies."[107] The Solid team also plans to offer a generic platform on top of which developers can build almost any kind of application.[108] It might also incorporate a built-in framework for micropayments, something that Berners-Lee worked on in the 1990s and W3C restarted in 2015.[109] "We are building a whole eco-system," Berners-Lee has said.[110]

The MIT webpage on the project does not mention blockchain, but the capabilities Solid is seeking to develop might suggest that blockchain tech would be involved. It turns out that is not the case—not as Berners-Lee currently conceives it, at any rate. Perhaps he is rejecting a P2P and blockchain design because he wants to build and scale Solid as quickly as possible.

Solid itself is a federated system, based on the central server-client model and on URLs for "linked data."[111] Yet if it is to provide an architecture for a newly decentralized web, it will have to accommodate blockchain and P2P elements in some way at some point because these are swiftly proliferating at the applications layer of the internet. For example, any new architecture will need to develop standards for interoperable distributed ledgers (and get these standards adopted by W3C) so that different blockchain apps can work interoperably on the web.[112]

The Solid project is immensely important because if it or some other privately funded, ambitious (re)decentralization project takes off, it could be the closest thing to a new civilian internet that we get, assuming it beats the Chaos Computer Club's "You Broke the Internet" effort and the European Union's "Next Generation Internet." It could decide a lot of the digital era "civics" issues now hanging in the balance just by how it is structured and coded. (Whether Solid or some other ambitious project will also beat the Defense Advanced Research Projects Agency's "Clean Slate" project to remake the internet is yet another question.)

If the race is informed by the hacker ethic, the goal will be an "open" web based as much as possible on the principles of user self-determination, net neutrality, free software, and decentralized power. There will be cooperation and synergies, as well as overlapping networks of participants. In 2016, Berners-Lee and Brewster Kahle, founder of the Internet Archive, organized the Decentralized Web Summit: Locking the Web Open in San Francisco. "With decentralized applications coming on stream and expanding every day," the first summit's website asked, "how might that momentum be harnessed to build something millions of people can actually use? What code is working and what is still missing? Can people work together to identify and tackle the roadblock issues?" Kahle told the developers and policy makers gathered at the event, "Let's use decentralized technologies to 'Lock the Web Open,' this time for good."[113] The 2016 summit was followed soon afterward by a high-profile workshop in Cambridge, Massachusetts, titled "Blockchain and the Web," organized by the MIT Media Lab and W3C.[114] A second summit, Decentralized Web Summit 2018: Global Visions/Working Code, took place in the summer of 2018, at which Berners-Lee presented Solid.[115]

THE BLOCKCHAIN REALITY CHECK

To sum up, in all of its applications, the blockchain, deployed with peer-to-peer (and other) technology, offers the potential of cutting out the middleman—whether it is the data miner, monopoly platform, financier, central bank, big record company, law enforcer, identity authenticator, or government records office. Blockchain offers the possibility that local and virtual communities can provide whole economies of value to each other, peer-to-peer, eliminating surveillance capitalism, government corruption, profiteering, and fraud. It offers communities the potential of expressing their own values in the way they design the blockchain. In "A Declaration of the Independence of Cyberspace," John Perry Barlow claimed that the legal order in cyberspace would reflect the ethical deliberations of the community instead of the coercive power that characterized real-space government, presciently foreshadowing what an innovation like the blockchain could do.[116]

Reality checks are in order, however. As the encrypted media extension debate shows, it may not be easy even for like-minded communities to agree on how to build things. Bitter divisions are possible, even within the hacker community. In addition to its idealistic applications, the blockchain offers the possibility for perfect surveillance and a stultifying enforcement of copyright. It could ensure that no transaction can be plausibly denied and no distribution of created material made without payment. If the values of the "old world" are encoded in the blockchain in any way (for example, centralization versus decentralization, scarcity versus abundance, surveillance versus privacy, and extraction versus fair distribution), the effects could be exponential because the code will execute them.

Hackers have been pioneers in the blockchain space, developing leading prototypes like Bitcoin. But although some of them might find ways, with little or no external funding, to pursue projects that are open source, free software licensed, ads- and surveillance-free, nonprofit, and commons-based, big money will be needed to develop large projects like Solid.

The corporate sector is quickly piling in behind hackers to take over start-ups or initiate their own blockchain experiments. By 2016, $1.4 billion was invested in blockchain technology,[117] and players like IBM, Microsoft,[118] Samsung,[119] and Deloitte[120] were entering the blockchain space, along with most of the major American, Canadian, and European banks.[121] By early 2018, Ethereum, the smart contract innovation of Vitalik Buterin, had a market capitalization of nearly $98 billion.[122]

Money can corrupt altruistic intentions. Things can go awry. Although Satoshi Nakamoto released Bitcoin's code into the wild as free software (and also "for free" as in "at no cost" or "free beer"), Bitcoin made its early adopters rich before it could even become a useful alternative currency. It has been reported that 97 percent of Bitcoin is held by 4 percent of Bitcoin addresses.[123] That concentration of wealth is worse than the concentrations amassed under the old monetary system of state fiat currencies (1 percent of the world's population owns about half of all wealth).[124]

The biggest reality check is understanding how limited the technology remains. The problem is scaling it. Currently, only a few blockchain transactions can be computed per second, and the energy costs for mathematical computation and for storing the blockchain on every participating node are significant.[125]

Another thing to understand is that as people use this technology to self-order, there is more pressure on them to become digitally adept because they are relying on the code to safeguard their interests and enforce behavior. For example, people who held Bitcoin in December 2017 were scrambling to find the USB keys they'd stored it on and the passwords they'd guarded it with when they had first acquired it for pennies. It is estimated that almost a fifth of the finite number of Bitcoins created have been lost.[126] To address the skills gap, intermediaries have inserted themselves everywhere in the cryptocurrency space, and there are many cautionary tales about their security and trustworthiness, and about price manipulation.[127]

"THE NEXT SYSTEM"

Despite the setbacks, the challenges, and the cold water that is being poured on many hacking experiments, people see their work as prefiguring a new model—as creating and living in a new model now rather than waiting for and relying on others to create it. Talk of a "next system" is spreading, along with debate about what its outlines might be.[128]

In February 2016, several months before the Brexit vote that would take the United Kingdom out of the European Union, Labour Party leader Jeremy Corbyn's shadow chancellor, John McDonnell, was talking about system change. For McDonnell, the task was bigger than creating a few more worker cooperatives. The project for Labour in the twenty-first century, he said, was to articulate "how we can change our economy to suit our society. ... We need to go much further than simply offering a defence of what we already have. Nor can we simply demand top-down nationalisation as a panacea. The old, Morrisonian model of nationalisation centralised too much power in a few hands in Whitehall. It had much in common with the new model of multinational corporations, in which power is centralised in a few hands in Silicon Valley, or the City of London. It won't work in a world in which technological change is providing opportunities to decentralise power."[129]

Leading up to the June 2016 Brexit vote and the general election a year later that would see Labour nearly sweep the Conservative Party out of power,[130] the Labour Party's political platform strongly supported a principle of public ownership adapted to the digital era. Yes, Labour had plans to renationalize Britain's abysmal privatized railway service, but for the most part the party's ideas about public ownership had more to do with Chattanooga's experiment in local broadband ownership than it did with nationalized railways.[131] Corbyn was emphasizing a local approach to public ownership that would encompass a plurality of means. He wanted local councils to become "public entrepreneurs" with greater freedom to choose how to deliver public services and kindle investment in their communities. He said he would give local levels of government more power to roll back the forced neoliberal privatization undertaken by earlier governments.

"Privatisation isn't just about who runs a service; it's about who services are accountable to," he said. "After a generation of forced privatisation and outsourcing of public services, the evidence has built up that handing services over to private companies routinely delivers poorer quality, higher cost, worse terms and conditions for the workforce, less transparency and less say for the public. ... It locks people out of decision-making."[132]

McDonnell highlighted the growing trend in the United States and the United Kingdom toward a model that uses the power of municipal government, together with the procurement resources of large nonprofit and public institutions, to build locally anchored economic development:

> Preston, inspired by the example of Cleveland, Ohio, has developed an extensive programme of work. ...
>
> They have got major local employers and buyers—so-called anchor institutions, like the University of Central Lancashire—to drive through a local programme of economic transformation. By changing their procurement policies, these anchor institutions were able to drive up spending locally.

They're looking to shift a proportion of the joint council's £5.5bn pension fund to focus on local businesses, keeping the money circulating in Preston.

And the council is actively seeking opportunities to create local co-operatives as a part of local business succession, working with the local Chamber of Commerce. The aim is to sustain high quality local employment, by giving the chance for workers to keep a business in local hands.[133]

It was clear in early 2016 that Labour was prepared to have a real conversation with the electorate about "system change" in the digital era that would rise above the usual rhetoric of the right and left. "Friedrich von Hayek, who taught for many years at the LSE [London School of Economics], is politically somewhat distant from myself, it's fair to say," McConnell said:

> But he raised a profound point about how information operates in a society, when he noted that centralised bureaucracies can be overwhelmed by the information processing demands of complex, modern societies. His preferred solution, of allowing the market to act as an information processor, was equally unviable.
>
> Markets can be crude information processors at best, as the crash of 2008 showed. ... We should look, instead, to how different forms of organisation can operate in the economy—not just the capitalist firm, or the nationalised industry, but many different ways of organising ownership and production. We need a far more sophisticated argument about ownership that does not just fall into the caricature of either pure privatisation, or pure state control.[134]

By 2016, the citizen energy of the Occupy movement was plainly flowing forward, beginning to formulate its alternative programs not just on the street but on regional and national political stages, too.

10

DISTRIBUTED DEMOCRACY
Experiments in Spain, Italy, and Canada

GETTING CONTROL OF DEMOCRATIC PROCESSES: THE INDIGNANT OF BARCELONA

The city of Barcelona—its squares still pockmarked from a desperate civil war between Fascists and a quickly thrown together coalition of Spanish and international units fighting for the democratically elected Republican government of Spain—was in the eye of a storm of historic forces that would remake Western democracies in the last century. And today, the city seems to be channeling forces that will remake them in the present century.

The Indignados, or indignant citizens of Spain, started the Occupy movement that swept the globe after the economic crash of 2008. In Spain, the financial crisis hit hard. The government of the day, the Socialist Workers' Party, had passed tough austerity measures in line with other European governments, but the measures deepened the crisis, and inequality and unemployment increased. Ordinary taxpayers were made to rescue financial elites while bearing the burden of wage and social cutbacks themselves. Popular anger grew as conditions deteriorated. By the fall of 2011, the unemployment rate had risen to 25 percent, and youth unemployment to 46 percent.[1] The financially engineered real estate bubble had burst, and the Spanish economy, like the US and other national economies, was reeling. The passage of a "Sinde" law—which, like the Stop Online Piracy Act (SOPA) tabled in the United States, allowed, without due process, any website that contained a copyright violation by users to be taken down—had angered people greatly because they understood that it would ruin the free internet.[2] They felt their democracy had been hollowed out.

People had started gathering in their neighborhood squares to discuss their situation. These assemblies grew. Banks were occupied, hospitals were occupied and saved from privatization, and vacant land and buildings were occupied and inhabited by squatters. Online protests denounced the Sinde law and unfair copyright enforcement. The student group Juventud Sin Futuro (Youth without Future) staged a large demonstration in Madrid. Demands multiplied for basic citizen rights to home, work, culture, health, and education.

In January 2011, users on Spanish social media networks had created a digital platform called Democracia Real YA! It invited "the unemployed, poorly paid, the subcontractors, the precarious, young people," and others to take to the streets on May 15, ahead of the next election cycle, in many towns and cities. The movement, which by this time was known as the Indignados movement or 15M movement (for the day the massive mobilization was to take place), rejected affiliation with political parties and trade unions and insisted on independence from institutionalized ideologies and agendas.

The occupations of the squares went on for weeks. By the following year, the movement was organizing itself into collectives and thematic groups formed to tackle specific goals.

Ada Colau was elected as mayor of Barcelona in May 2015. Before her election, Colau had been one of the activists helping people who were losing their homes because they could not pay their mortgages, and had cofounded Plataforma de Afectados por la Hipoteca (la PAH) (Platform for People Affected by Mortgages). Colau herself had held more than twenty jobs over her working life and lived as a squatter for a time.[3] Her election to municipal office was a victory for the Indignados movement and was accomplished quickly and with little money. One of the most tweeted photos in Spain that year showed Colau being dragged away by police from a people's occupation of a bank. The caption read, "Welcome, new mayor."[4]

Colau has spoken eloquently about the politics in Spain leading up to and following the 2008 financial crisis, and her statements are worth quoting at length because they tell much about the populist sentiment that took off in that country. "We have serious political problems here in Barcelona," she said in an interview shortly after her election. "There are problems related to the economic crisis, but this economic crisis is a consequence of a political crisis, of a profound democratic crisis. We've had a form of government where the political elites have a cozy relationship with the economic elites who have ruined the economy of the country, and the ultimate representation of this was the behavior of the financial institutions, of the banks. They defrauded thousands and thousands of people."[5]

Three years earlier, at a hearing on Spain's foreclosures crisis, Colau had spoken on a panel following a representative from Spain's banking industry. Famously, she turned to the banker who had just spoken and said,

> This man is a criminal. We've been negotiating for four years with the banks, with the public administration, with the courts, and we know exactly what we're talking about, and this leads me to question the voices of supposed experts, who precisely are the ones being given too much credit, pardon the irony, such as the representatives of financial institutions. We just had an example. I would say it was "paradoxical," to use a euphemism, if not outright cynical for the representative of financial institutions who just spoke, telling us that the Spanish legislation is great. To say that when people are taking their own lives because of this criminal law, I assure you, *I assure you,* that I did not throw a shoe at this man because I believed it was important to be here now to tell you what I'm telling you. But this man is a criminal, and you should treat him as such. He is not an expert. The representatives of financial institutions have caused this problem. They are the very same people who caused the problem which has ruined the whole economy of this country. And you are treating them as experts.[6]

Immediately after the event, Colau's Twitter following grew from eight thousand to a hundred thousand, and her name began to show up on political popularity polls. The need for an organization like la PAH to help people in financial distress was immediately obvious in the wake of the financial crisis, and by 2013 it had two hundred centers across Spain. "People came to us, and they couldn't even speak," she recalled. "They couldn't even explain what had happened to them. They thought that nothing good would ever happen to them again."[7]

Later she would say,

> When I encountered this banker who said there were no problems in Spain, when there are thousands of families in a dire situation, the least I could do is denounce these lies and talk about what was happening in reality. ... I think what surprised people more was that someone was talking about reality in Parliament, because, sadly, this had not happened in a long time. You have the paradox that while the corrupt politicians see the statute of limitations for their crimes lapse and they make off without going to jail, the families who got into debt for something as basic as accessing housing become indebted forever [under the law]. ... And it showed that if our institutions did not resolve this problem, it was because our institutions were accomplices in this fraud.[8]

Colau and others set up a citizen platform, Barcelona en Comú (Barcelona in Common), to gauge support for a united list of candidates to stand in the 2015 municipal election, and money was crowd-sourced to fund their run for office. She has said that city councils were key to a new way of making policy and to proving "there is another way to govern: more inclusive, working together with the people, more than just asking them to vote every four years."[9] She has talked about the democratic revolution all over southern Europe confronting neoliberal economic policies, which have become a problem around the world:

> In reality there's been a continuity in the past fifteen years at least. In the early 2000s, late 1990s, when they began the anti-globalization movement, there was a wide cycle of protest that began, that continues to this day. ... And all these mobilizations ... have had many things in common. First ... that we need to work as a network, because there's a single global and economic reality, and it's essential to work in alliances. Also, it's essential that there's real democracy, the awareness that even if we have formally democratic institutions, we have the sense that the decisions are not being made in Parliament but by the boards of directors or by international institutions such as the IMF, the World Bank, which are profoundly anti-democratic and which the people do not control, and that they also make decisions against their own people, generating misery around the world.
>
> This awareness of a kidnapped democracy has led to the rise of many grassroots mobilizations, propelled from the bottom, by the people, which are [working toward] direct representation. They've seen that formal democracy is not enough, that we need to find new ways of political

participation where everyone can be an actor and each person can directly contribute as much as each person can contribute.

So, I think that all of these mobilizations that have happened in the past fifteen years, that have also increasingly used new technologies, the Internet, social media, that have pursued new forms of innovation and direct communication, in some way, we are seeing an upgrade of democracy, an upgrade of the forms of political participation that have had many different expressions in different global movements, but there's clearly a nexus that unites them all.[10]

As the first female mayor of Barcelona, elected around the same time as the female mayor of Madrid, Colau talked about "feminizing" politics and demonstrating "that cooperation is more effective and more satisfactory than competitiveness, and that politics done collectively are better than those done individualistically."[11]

In Colau's first month in office, Barcelona's municipal government had a thirty-point plan that included doing away with the privileges of elected officials. The paid expenses, the cars, and the high salaries are "things that can seem simple," Colau said, "but are symbolically important because they send a message of ending impunity, of an end to a political class removed from the reality of the people."[12]

HACKING CORRUPTION: XNET'S 15MPARATO

At the Chaos Communication Camp in August 2015, not long after the election of Ada Colau as the mayor of Barcelona, I met Simona Levi, a founding member of the Barcelona-based group Xnet. Levi's group existed before the Indignados protests and was highly engaged in the politics that unfolded in the city following the 2008 financial crisis.

A gaggle of people had gathered in a tent at the camp for an impromptu meeting called by Gabriella Coleman, the anthropologist known for her seminal book on Anonymous. Coleman had wanted to bring together the academics, journalists, and activists who were increasingly becoming engaged with the camp and the Chaos Computer Club. The discussion circled around motives, methods, competency, and cultural appropriation, until a Dutch hacker piped up, "Sometimes I think academics are dissecting hackers like a strange species. But it should be about how to bring us all forward. Just describing hackers as diverse: that's fucking uninteresting. It has to be about how we come together and go forward."

Levi, a slim, dark-haired woman, interjected her view from the trenches:

Hacker philosophy is the last chance for real revolution to change the world. We *want* it to become "pop" so that our mothers also know about it.

Sometimes the study of hackers as a "tribe" puts them into a ghetto. It's better to think of it as an avant garde for a new way of thinking that will allow the revolution. It's a new philosophy of distribution, sharing, and diversity. With the Indignados movement, we are hacking everything now: the grid, the hospitals, the city. ... We have to take this academic idea of "hacker diversity" and open it up. We leak a lot of documents in Spain. In a small village, an old lady would hack and send us information on corrupt bankers, using GlobaLeaks. Newspapers say the source of the information is government, but this is not so. It's the hacker, including the old lady.

I found Levi that evening at the camp set up by La Quadrature du Net. The space was laid out elegantly, with low-slung tarps arranged like the silk tents of a nomadic caravan, Eastern carpets spread on the ground, and people sitting cross-legged around low tables. Andy Müller-Maguhn had referred to it as "the place where the French are serving tea," and in fact they were, around the clock.

Levi is an Italian who has been living in Barcelona since 1990. She is a well-known theater director in Spain and has a powerful presence. Forty-something, she trained as a dancer and then in physical theater at École Internationale de Théâtre Jacques Lecoq in Paris. I found out later that she is related to Primo Levi, the writer and Auschwitz survivor. Primo Levi had been a member of the Italian resistance and wrote about his experience in the Nazi camps and the loss of both guards' and prisoners' humanity there.

Xnet, Levi told me, had been active since 2008 and was probably one of the most important groups working in Europe on digital rights issues, including copyright, free software, net neutrality, privacy, the right to encryption, freedom of information, freedom of expression, free culture and information, and censorship on the internet. It was involved in the fight against the Anti-Counterfeiting Trade Agreement, an international digital-restrictions-management instrument along the lines of the American Stop Online Piracy Act (SOPA) legislation: both were successfully defeated by civil society groups. La Quadrature du Net in France had played a large role in that campaign, too.

Xnet had become widely known recently because it had succeeded in having many of the corrupt bankers and politicians responsible for Spain's financial crisis brought to trial. The first to be targeted by the group was Rodrigo Rato, Spain's minister of the economy from 1996 to 2004, managing director of the International Monetary Fund (IMF) from 2004 to 2007, partner of the prestigious financial firm Lazard, then briefly president of Caja Madrid before becoming president of Bankia, a large investment bank whose collapse triggered the Spanish financial crisis. Bankia received more bailout funds than any other institution in Spain. Levi estimated that one-seventh of the national debt could be attributed to it.

Wrapping one leg in front of the other, Levi leaned in to tell me the story.

Bankia was formed in 2010 through the efforts of Rato while he was director of Caja Madrid. In a restructuring of the financial system in Spain, Caja Madrid, the oldest savings bank in Spain, and six other Spanish savings banks (all of which operated like credit unions) were turned into privately owned banks and rolled into Bankia. Rato became its president. Bankia launched an initial public offering on the stock market in July 2011, but the price of its shares had been pumped up by the bank with fraudulent information. Risky preferred shares were also sold without proper disclosure. The bank's promotional material targeted families and small investors.

In 2011, Bankia reported profits of €300 billion, and a year later it had to be nationalized by the government[13] and then bailed out by taxpayers with losses in the billions.[14] Over 200,000 small investors, many of them pensioners, lost a total of €1.86 billion. Some lost their life savings.[15] When Levi first read the news, she was appalled, and she met with other activists to discuss what they could do. The group included a gardener, a chef, and a coder.[16]

On the first anniversary of the 15M occupations, Levi founded 15MpaRato (15M for Rato) with an anonymous call put out over social media networks: "A message for #12M15M from the internet quarter." She and the others collaborating on the project set a five-year plan for themselves in which they undertook to have Rato criminally convicted and sentenced by 2017. They encouraged people to submit any information that might help to imprison him.[17] "We were going for real, individual accountability for the bankruptcy of the Spanish economy," Levi told me. "Rato was a symbol of the collaboration between banking and government. He got rich as a banker on the laws he made. We said we'd start with him and through him get all the others."

At the start, Levi told me, nobody trusted them. But it did not take long to gather enough information for a legal case: "Then we did crowd funding that was famous. We received €20,000 in one day from citizens." They brought in 130 percent of their original goal and hired lawyers to assist in building and presenting the case. Under the "civil code" system in Spain, citizens can file complaints if they believe a law has been broken and have a judge decide whether to investigate. So much damning evidence was collected by 15MpaRato that the court was forced to take up the case, and in July 2012 it charged Rato and thirty-three board members of Bankia as well as Bankia's parent company.[18]

In 2013, after an anonymous leaker sent 15MpaRato eight thousand emails belonging to Rato's predecessor at Caja Madrid, Miguel Blesa, the group was inspired to set up an online leaking platform using the Italian hackers' system, GlobaLeaks. Xnet and others vetted the leaks received and then released information to journalists and posted it online so that people could work with it in an open-source fashion. Jokes and memes were a large part of the postings. The case against Bankia expanded its focus to include forgery and embezzlement when the leaks revealed a vast scam to siphon money from the bank, initiated by Miguel Blesa while he was president of Casa Madrid and continued by Rato, using "black" credit cards. Designed by Visa to be used by the ultra-rich, the credit cards were used by Bankia executives for their own enrichment and to buy off political parties and trade unions. Officials from every major political party and trade union benefitted from the scam. The court case became a criminal proceeding. All told, the trials would involve nearly a hundred bankers and officials.

It was very empowering, Levi told me, because it was the most impossible thing to do. Rodrigo Rato had been untouchable—a god, the architect of neoliberal policies in Spain. He had held the top post at the IMF in Washington, and after the prosecutor laid charges against him, he lost all his status. "Now he travels second class, and people shout at him when he goes through the airport," she said.

Simona Levi started Xnet in 2008 with a female coder and musician who goes by the handle Maddish. They both were artists and activists advocating for free culture and "copyleft" in Spain, and as a result they both were having problems with the Spanish copyright collection agency. The recently passed copyright legislation in Spain was predatory, and the collection agency was acting like the mafia, Levi told me, scamming artists and consumers and shaking down small businesses, aggressively demanding copyright royalties ("from bakeries, from hair dressers!" Levi exclaimed) and threatening them with high fines. Instead of giving money to artists, however, the agency was using money collected to speculate in the housing market. "And now," Levi told me, "they're all on trial, too." So this was Xnet's start before it expanded to other issues.

Xnet is a closed, guerrilla group, she said. "We launch projects, open them up, and then close them again, like the 15MpaRato Citizens against Corruption. The name is a pun: *pa rato* means 'for a long time.' Citizens against Corruption 'for the long haul.'"

"In Spain," she explained, "we have a tradition of the left and protest. The *doism* of hackers is different: we solve problems by doing. I think Spain is on the vanguard of change. Not because of Podemos [the leftist political party]; it is in fact a barrier. At the start of the Indignados movement, there were millions of very active people. In the first two months, eight million people were going every day to the squares. There was an 80 percent appreciation rate from the public. The fifteenth of May 2011 was called via Facebook. Podemos was not involved. They did not come on the scene until 2014. You don't need to impose your ideology like the left always wants to. It's not who you are, but what you can *do*. That is also hacker philosophy."

"Podemos will try to destroy what the people have created by coopting the movement in a Stalinist way. Like in the 1930s, when the Communists in Spain spent their time repressing the anarchists and lost the war." (Fighting on the same side as the anarchists, the Communists were supported by Stalin's regime in Russia and driven largely by its agenda. Some believe the brutal purges they carried out against the anarchists in the last days of the civil war in Catalonia may have contributed to the loss of the war and of the fledgling Republican democracy in Spain to the Fascists.) "Podemos," Levi continued, "instead of helping Xnet with the trial of a hundred bankers, said, 'You must be with us, or you must not exist.'"

"For me, the Indignados movement unfolded like the French Revolution. The very modern, innovative ideas of the Enlightenment were developed first in the 'republic of letters' and then moved to the Revolution in France. Today, the illustration is from the hackers. They started in the internet and are coming to the whole society."

The mass demonstrations in Spain, Levi told me, were different than the Occupy movement in the United States because in Spain "we had a successful system based on creating concrete solutions to problems. The movement in Spain was not a discussion, not just series of protests, but active and executed with skill. It is more transitive, active. Action is divided between health, housing, bankers, and the electoral process. And it's working in important cities. For example, they hacked the electoral system in Barcelona with the election of Barcelona's new mayor using technical tools, networks, self-organization, and crowd funding. In Madrid, a city with a population of nearly seven million, authorities wanted to privatize the health system, and the movement managed to stop it."

Xnet, Levi told me, was composed of only seven people. They worked passionately, she said, all day, every day, to achieve what they did. Each of them led in a particular skill field, which was a model of doing things that came from their open-source work.

What Levi was saying reminded me of the lack of a fixed leadership in the 1968 Paris student uprisings. I later found Daniel Cohn-Bendit's explanation to Sartre about why he thought that was a good thing:

> No vanguard, neither the UEC, the JCR nor the Marxists-Leninists, has been able to seize control of the movement. Their militants can participate decisively in the actions, but they have been drowned in the movement. They are to be found on the co-ordination committees, where their role is important, but there has never been any question of one of these vanguards taking a leading position.
>
> This is the essential point. It shows that we must abandon the theory of the "leading vanguard" and replace it by a much simpler and more honest one of the active minority functioning as a permanent leaven, pushing for action without ever leading it. ... In certain objective situations—with the help of an active minority—spontaneity can find its old place in the social movement. Spontaneity makes possible the forward drive, not the orders of a leading group.[19]

"We call it 'networked democracy,'" Levi told me: "Distributed power via a meritocracy, with skill and action." Not a vertical democracy. Not a horizontal democracy like Occupy's. "Obsession with process defeated Occupy," she said.

HAZTE BANQUERO (BECOME A BANKER)

It is the summer of 2016, and I'm on my way to Europe to visit Xnet in Spain and investigate another interesting citizen-hacker phenomenon, the Cinque Stelle movement, in Italy. As I leave North America, the campaign for the 2016 US presidential election is in full swing. Larry Lessig (author of "Code Is Law") is running for president, no less. Lessig has been writing about the need to carry the Occupy movement forward and the necessity, above all, for people to gain control of democratic processes. In America, Lessig believes, the first imperative is to get money out of politics,[20] and he is running on that program.

The people I'm traveling to talk to in Europe also see that citizens need to take control of democratic processes. These groups have already been successful at regional and national levels in bringing down politicians corrupted by money and in electing their own candidates to important posts. They, too, have formulated a program, and it is even more ambitious than Lessig's.

These citizens intend to hack the democratic process itself. They want to disintermediate governance, to move politicians who do not act in the interests "of the people" out of the way, and to enact a direct, distributed democracy. They are not using their votes as an anger-management tool, as the British have just done in the Brexit vote of June 2016 and the Americans will shortly do in November 2016.[21] They are using hacker-made platforms, hacker principles, and hacker humor to successfully marshal technology and achieve concrete goals, one thorny issue at a time. This is not "tech utopianism," but, I'm coming to believe, the hard work of democracy in the digital age.

After a sixteen-hour flight, I finally arrive in Barcelona so jet-lagged I barely make it to the theater in time to pick up the ticket Simona Levi has left for me at the box office. It is the opening night of *Hazte Banquero* (Become a Banker), a play that Levi and the Xnet collective have created and produced. The title is taken from a slogan that was used by Bankia in its promotional material targeting small investors.

Hazte Banquero is being performed in the historic Teatre Poliorama on La Rambla. George Orwell stood sentry on the roof of this building for several days during the Spanish Civil War and wrote about the experience in *Homage to Catalonia*. Orwell's book famously tried to tell the world about the Communists' betrayal of the anarchists in Catalonia during the civil war and its consequences, the history to which Levi referred when speaking about Podemos and the Indignados movement when I met her at the Chaos Communication Camp the year before.

It is a warm night, and a lively local crowd is pouring into the theater from the street.

As the lights come up on stage, an actor who is well-known in Catalonia strides out to set the scene. The story is complex, but it can be told and understood in plain language, she says. On a screen behind her, an image appears of an abstract painting: yellow astral strands of light connect what look like galaxies, and across it all are spatters of blue and purple paint. Hundreds of lightly written names appear on the screen within this network of connection, and then "15MpaRato" emerges in the center. The actor explains how networks work, how networked democracy can work. She charts how the "robbery" that was the Bankia scandal happened. There are many projections of financial information. She makes the audience laugh.

There is a shot from the Xnet website—a photo of a mouth speaking into an ear with the caption "Filtra contra corrupción" and "#crowdfundpaRato." So much information was leaked by the people that justice officials had to do something, the actor tells the audience. Their hand was forced.

"Our story tells how it happened," the actor says. "Are you ready?"

The play focusses largely on the "black" credit-card scam. Whenever a new character comes onstage, the real-life photo of the person involved in the scandal appears on the screen with key information and statistics, like a baseball card, including the amount they were implicated for in the scam. Crazy, freewheeling music plays while the characters describe how they used the money for themselves. Rodrigo Rato, the president of the bank, is shown in photograph after photograph posing with exotic hunting trophies—a gazelle, a lion, a bear—along with the cost of each shooting expedition ("elephant, €3,000 extra").

The damning evidence was in the emails. These appear on the screen as if they are being typed in real time. As the characters' thoughts become manifest, the audience guffaws at their audacity. When the bank's president and secretary sit at a desk and conspire, the camera of the president's laptop captures the conversation at close range from below and projects the intimate conversation onto the big screen behind them. It is an iconic image of collusion, like the swindlers in a Caravaggio painting.[22]

The play is sold out for its three-night run. People pack into the lobby, and some press around the box office hoping to obtain last minute tickets. Each night when the performance ends, a crowd streams out onto the street and people congregate in groups for a long time to smoke and talk.

The play is a targeted piece of strategic advocacy. It will tour the country for the next few months. The trials of Rodrigo Rato and nearly a hundred other bankers and officials will start in the fall, and the play informs people of their importance and keeps them in the public mind. Civil suits are also being contemplated.

On the second night, I follow the cast, the production team, and their entourage up the busy Rambla and down a long, narrow street to a tavern that spills out onto the cobblestones. I am absorbed in a conversation with Rubén Sáez, one of the Xnet collective. He has been collaborating with Xnet for the past five years and says that for two years he had no life and little sleep. His girlfriend almost left him because of the demands on his time. He has a day job as a chemist. He came to the collective through the Indignados movement. He went to the local meeting in his neighbourhood square one day and got involved. For so long, a culture of impunity has prevailed in Spain, where the wrongdoers were never held to account. The Indignados wanted to change that.

"Hacker philosophy is becoming more popular in Spain," Sáez says. "Distributed power, self-organization, independence and sharing: we want these things to become real in Spain."

First, he says, the Indignados were inspired by the Arab Spring. Then there was the May 15, 2011, demonstration of the Indignados, when the effects of the financial crisis were unfolding. The Indignados were in communication with Occupy in the United States. There was advice going back and forth. There were emails.

A friend of Sáez's leans over to comment on the show: "When I saw how those officials talked and thought: it was only about themselves, their own profit, what they could get, not about the institution or their public duty. It was disgusting."

MADDISH: PLATFORMS FOR THE PEOPLE

I am supposed to meet Maddalena Falzoni (Maddish) in the El Raval neighborhood of Barcelona, at La Monroe café next to the cinémathèque, but the square and the café are packed with people. *La Bohème* is being shown on a big screen outdoors. I find Maddish standing under a tree. She has to meet another friend later this evening, so she suggests we find another place as quickly as we can. She briskly heads deeper into the neighborhood. This Barcelona is diverse, bohemian, and teaming with people—laborers on their way home, local and itinerant youth, Muslims, gay men, artists, young and old mingling as in a village. Our trek ends in a small, dimly lit restaurant.

I ask Maddish about the usability of the platform Xnet built for 15MpaRato. She laughs. Usability! This is the most important thing. This is the biggest wall to climb over. You have to build your ideas out into cyberspace, and they have to be usable. You need to emulate the "big guys" because people are used to using their tools.

She is currently working on a platform called MaddiX that will allow people to create and use their own personal cloud, which is an essential tool for maintaining digital privacy these days. There is free software available now to do this, but it is difficult to install. She is creating an interface. It's not easy because she doesn't have funds for it, "but we have to make people understand what's necessary. This is a moment in which people know something is wrong, but we have to build an alternative."

Maddish came to this work as a musician who was interested in coding. She earned a high school degree in programming and learned to use the COBOL language. She was doing activist work and living in a squat. They did concerts. She was using computers for her music, for TV and film soundtracks, and for "social fighting." Then she discovered Linux and the philosophy of free software. "This is amazing!" she thought. "You can read all the code here. This is the future."

"I had a scientific mind, and I could do coding. So with all this background in art and social activism, it made no sense to work for a corporation and build a beautiful system for them. It was very easy to find a hacker community. It was possible to do the important things with no money."

When I ask how Xnet got so many leaks, she says that it has a large network of people working on these issues that it has built up over the years. "So we became the reference point on this very big leak. And there were really a lot of people who lost money in the scandal, too. We thought, 'If we wait for some politicians to do something about the corruption, it will never happen. Only citizens can do it.'"

Xnet used the Italians' GlobaLeaks system, Maddish says, because "the philosophy is don't reinvent the same code. We investigated different ones and thought GlobaLeaks was the easiest to use." She worked closely with Fabio Pietrosanti and his colleague Giovanni, who are based in Milan. They will be in Spain next week, she tells me. GlobaLeaks recently introduced a new level of support for their whistleblowing solution. It's not just a tool that they hand over. They have a new enterprise called Hermes. "They really give support to people who want to install whistleblowing."

She talks about some of the different collectives working in Europe. There is Linux France. There is a new group, Framasoft.org, in France, too, doing amazing work, she says. The nonprofit behind PeerTube, it has recently built all the tools you need to avoid central services, like corporate-controlled clouds. Framasoft contacted Xnet about a year ago and already had something like twenty-five tools, including a cloud, online. With one click, you can have a cloud account. Framasoft says that it does not want to have a lot of people using its cloud; it doesn't want to become Google. Instead, it wants want to disseminate its cloud as a demo for others to emulate. Maddish is working on a similar set of tools for users in Spain.

I ask her about the complexities of the way forward. Will these alternative tools ever pull ahead of the monopoly platforms?

"It makes no sense to find a solution for people who are fifty years and older now," Maddish says. "When I think of the future, I think of the next generation. The new generation has more facility with going from one service or app to another. I talk to my daughter about these issues, and she isn't interested. But she experiments. She will try this Snapchat app and then something different and something else again. So it's important that we build the tools now so that the next generation will live with alternatives and start using them. So that they have Quitter to try alongside Twitter. So that when they hit a wall—when the big company tells them, 'Your account has been suspended,' or tries to impose something they don't like—they can turn to try something else."

With tools like synchro, cloud, and email, the public is a little more aware about alternatives, she observes. But with social networks, we are behind. When Snapchat changes its privacy settings, no one cares. People need to know they can make an account with GNU social, a single platform from which other social media platforms can be used. It gives you more control over your data.

What is her experience as a female coder?

Her handle is Maddish, she tells me, so that people online don't know if she is male or female and are surprised when they realize she is female. Then she needs to demonstrate she knows as much as a man. Many women don't talk much on technical projects, but in the digital rights movement, there is no difference, and no distinctions are made.

I ask her how the different groups in Europe work together.

In internet advocacy, she says, they do lobbying all the time. When laws put our freedom in danger, all the organizations get involved.

Like Levi, Maddish is Italian. She came to Spain twenty years ago. In Spain, she says, there is a sense of community and sharing you don't feel in other places. Coders and hackers, they are just people with skills. What counts is how they use those skills in a community. Xnet is the most influential activist group for digital rights in Spain—not just with tools but also when it comes to hacking the system. It does more global hacking than tech. Xnet's approach is to seize the political moment. "We could do a great thing in three years or a very good thing that would be effective at the right political moment. We choose the latter."

PARTIDOX

I meet Alfa Sanchez, another member of the Xnet collective, at a café near La Munroe the next day. It is a sunny morning in the public square. A man with a dog helps me find the place and hands me over to Sanchez with a neighborly salutation.

Like Rubén Sáez, Sanchez is a chemist. He looks very young, but he is around thirty years old. He has a slight build and a bearded, open face. Sanchez had been working in his profession, and then, like many people, he becamc unemployed. At the time he was collaborating with PartidoX. When he lost his job, he started doing programming and webmaster jobs to survive. After the EU elections in 2014, Simona Levi asked if he'd like to work for Xnet while he was deciding what to do with his life. He's been working with them for the past two years, getting paid gigs when Xnet has funding to put on events. "This is my situation now," he says.

On the famous date of May 15, 2011, when the first mass Indignados rallies occurred, Spain was already deep in the financial crisis, Sanchez says. There was high unemployment. The bankers had been bailed out a second time, and the people were paying for the bankers' irresponsibility, for the housing bubble they had created, for their greed and bad legislation, for their very short-term decisions. The economy they had created was based entirely on buying and selling houses. People went to the streets, and the squares were full. Normally, the unions in Spain make the call for general strikes. "But in Spain the unions are very corrupt. This time it was just citizens—no left, no right. It was not about any political party. People were very skeptical about unions and political parties. We could see that a lot of what they were doing was trying to sell us the story that this crisis was like a storm, a force of nature that came upon us, and all we could do was work harder and earn less. They tried to make it seem like it was the citizens' fault. This, of course, was very enraging."

I ask him about the audiences at the play, and he says that they are people from the Indignados movement, sponsors of 15MpaRato, people who follow the cultural scene, and pensioners who were scammed. "You can see it in their faces. This is their story too." He feels glad to be reaching a lot of new people who are also getting involved.

PartidoX started as a joke, he says—"a freaky futurist party with advanced proposals around democracy and a concrete mechanism on how citizens could participate and control institutions. It got more serious the longer we worked on it. Xnet launched the project of PartidoX and gathered other people around it. PartidoX ran candidates for the EU elections using the hacker or programming ethic in politics."

"When hackers write code," Sanchez tells me, "they can work collaboratively, use open source, work on pieces, take existing ideas further. PartidoX had this philosophy in its bones. Our principles were (1) institutions had to be accountable and (2) you don't rewrite code but build upon others' work."

So PartidoX studied the most advanced ideas on democracy from around the world, he says: "For example, in Brazil, in Rio Grande do Sul, they elaborate the state budget with a wiki type application. It's called wiki governance and wiki legislation. PartidoX gathered all the examples together to show it's not a fantasy. These things have been done. We opened the discussion to the public and asked for amendments and comments. We got lots. It was *a lot* of work." He smiles and shakes his head.

PartidoX started as an anonymous group running for the EU elections. Its platform had been worked out with public participation, and it now was a legal party. The group launched its campaign with a video of two actors saying, "We come from the future."

"It's not acceptable to vote every four years for a face that you see on the TV and they give you a speech, and maybe they follow their agenda once they're elected and maybe not," he says.

Since the death of Francisco Franco, Spain's fascist dictator from 1939 to his death in 1975, the conservative People's Party and the Spanish Socialist Workers' Party had taken turns running the country. They had both played a role in creating corruption, the financial crisis, and its fallout.

PartidoX was on social media but received little coverage from the traditional media. Even so, the party received 100,000 votes in the election—short of the 250,000 votes that it needed to win, but Sanchez and others running the campaign learned a lot.

The party's main concerns were rethinking democracy, developing an economic program to address the financial crisis, and fighting corruption. No one knew who was behind the party, and still it went from zero to a hundred thousand votes. About four hundred people were working behind PartidoX, and of these about thirty to forty were very active. Thousands were following the group on social media and sharing information.

"For me," Sanchez says, "PartidoX was very revealing, very enriching. After the elections, we evaluated what we did. In Spain, we're a very advanced country in terms of freaky, futuristic politics—very open to using new tech in citizen organization. But basically, in politics nowadays, we learned, the TV is still very powerful. We have an internal joke now: Without TV, a hundred thousand votes!"

In fact, it was the leftist party Podemos that broadsided them very close to the election. "We were busy building our 2014 election platform," Sanchez says, "then three months before the election, Podemos came on the scene—just three months before."

Podemos had a lot of TV exposure. "Podemos really is a television product. The leader, Pablo Iglesias, has been working on a leftish TV program for many years. His face is very well known. He is on the air seven days a week for one and a half hours every evening. Everyone knows it's not ethical or even legal to have a political candidate on your TV channel all the time, so the guy asked his TV channel, 'If I run in the next EU elections, will I have to step out of my TV program?' They said, 'No, you can stay.'" On the voting ballot, instead of a traditional party logo, Podemos used a headshot of Iglesias with his signature ponytail.

PartidoX had been building from the social networks and the internet out to the citizens and the regular media and doing very well. Then Podemos expanded from TV onto the social networks and overtook PartidoX. It was not necessarily a question of a generational divide, Sanchez tells me. Politics are very intergenerational in Spain. Everyone has a mobile phone, so the generations are converging. It will become more and more so, he says.

Every fall since 2008, Xnet has hosted two important events—the Free Culture Forum and the OXcars (Oscars for the people or organizations that have taken the most notorious action for free culture that year). "We bring together people from all around the world who are working on digital rights, and we take stock of where we are, what victories we have had, what to do next," Sanchez says. Richard Stallman was there last year.

We leave the café and start walking down San Pau toward La Rambla so that he can show me the Xnet studio space. In Spain, he tells me, youth unemployment is close to 50 percent, and overall unemployment is at 25 percent. The distribution of work and wealth will be the defining challenge of the twenty-first century, and he is not sure legislators will be up to solving the problem. The owners of the robots will be like the slave owners of the cotton fields: all the wealth will go into their hands.

As we enter the studio, Sanchez points out the sign over the door from when the building was a canning factory. It is a useful-looking space with a kind of "green room" air about it. There are a couple of desks, tables with chairs, some couches, and in the back a high space that is big enough for rehearsals, workshops, and small theater performances. But the air is bad, and there is no source of natural light. "Sergio and I spend all our time here," he says, and I think of them there, in the prime of their lives, hunched over their laptops, sustained, if not by fresh air, then by their hope for a better world.

"Why the X?" I ask, referring to Xnet and PartidoX.

He smiles. "It is the unknown quantity. You know, the unknown quantity in the equation, right?"

When I arrive at the small, intimate square where Simona Levi and I have arranged to meet, she is seated already at the outdoor restaurant and calls out to me. She is wearing a kimono-style dress with small colored birds winging their way in flight across its black silk, the suggestion of agitated movement appropriate for the woman. Her hair is cut in a short dark bob. She broke her arm during the play's production but managed to work around the discomfort. Now, she takes her injured arm out of its sling. She shrugs. "It's mainly to flag to people not to bump into me."

We order wine, and she apologizes for having been so busy with the play's opening. The night before, while I was talking to Xnet members and their friends sitting around the taverna's tables in the street, she had been at the center of a big table of people inside. "I'm sorry I lost you," she says. "That was the new mayor of Barcelona sitting beside me," she explains, meaning Ada Colau. "I wanted to introduce you. She's a friend." She orders a regional specialty, cod omelette, and encourages me to have some.

"She [Colau] built a group called En Comú in Barcelona. They are taking the elections in several more cities now."

I ask if Xnet's politics have any links with the *horizontalidad* movement in South America.

Some of that movement's politics are like Xnet's, she says, and some are not. Xnet actually criticizes the horizontal democracy espoused by the Occupy movement, she reminds me.

"There is a misuse of horizontality and openness by the Left," she says. "Horizontality is not democratic because it doesn't take into account diversity, level of engagement, and competency. We are not all the same. When you give everybody the same authority to speak, you often have men dominating the discussion because they like to hear themselves talk. You get the biggest mouths and the most narcissistic dominating. Like Podemos. They might be completely incompetent, too.

"Xnet believes more in distributed and changeable leadership. I am a good theater director, so I lead in theater. But when it comes to code, I shut up; the leader is Maddish. In horizontality, the big mouth, the big fish, the male, the heterosexual, pushes forward. Xnet believes in distributed leadership, like the nodes in a network."

This is the networked democracy she told me about when we first met at the Chaos Communication Camp. My mind wanders for a second, thinking of the critiques I have read about John Perry Barlow's "Declaration of the Independence of Cyberspace,"[23] buoyed as it was by the frontiersman bravado and counterculture machismo of the early white, Western, male cypherpunks. Barlow has been criticized for being a white, Western, male of a prefeminist era; for making assertions of universalism that are belied by self-centric assumptions about the world; for pushing another one of those utopian projects that have never ended well for Western societies; and for valorizing cyberspace as some virtual, global polity divorced from local, embodied polities.

Listening to Levi, I can see the pitfalls in all of these things. I like the idea of networked democracy, of building a well-grounded politics based on pluralism, polycentrism, and rootedness in the real social relationships of local communities. Then again, I'm not entirely persuaded by the Barlow critiques. I still think there is value to be found in the "universal" organizing principles of the Western Enlightenment that Barlow espoused (*liberté*, *egalité*, *fraternité*) and in the contributions made by him and his (mostly white male) contemporaries to the genealogy of hacker ideas.

Levi is writing a book whose working title is "The Unbearable Stupidity of the Left," a play on Milan Kundera's 1984 novel *The Unbearable Lightness of Being*. "This new mistake of the left, horizontality, is like its earlier 'dictatorship of the proletariat.' You promise the base that they'll be the leaders, but you don't believe it. Now, in postmodernity, the left promises the base that it will have a say in everything, and they do these nonsense surveys online as if that is giving people a voice. When PartidoX asked the public for amendments to their draft election platform, they honoured 98 percent of the amendments they received. Podemos, on the other hand, did a survey, and you see in their final draft platform they have taken nothing from the people."

She reminds me again of the historical resonances: "During the civil war, and especially in Barcelona, while the Communists were busy suppressing the anarchists, they also lost the war. Today, Podemos, the traditional left, or communists, are repressing us and they are also trying to grab and coopt the movement. For example, the Communists adopted the slogan 'Freedom for women,' but they were in fact the last party to vote for women's suffrage in Spain. Conservatives voted for it earlier. Podemos is grabbing what the Indignados movement created, and then they lose the election. And they wouldn't carry the Indignados platform anyway. At least if they won the election, they would be the clear enemy. There's another analogy to the civil war. We choose the Communists as the lesser evil, and we get the Fascists in any case."

I mention that Alfa Sanchez has been telling me about the near success of PartidoX and its mystery candidates. Who were they?

She points to herself. "I founded and ran for PartidoX. *I* ran," she says. "It was hard work—hard because you were up against people who wanted to kill you, not physically but competitively. It's a competition for votes, and there is a finite number of them. It's different when you're just doing advocacy. You can do your thing, and they don't care so much. At first, we were using fake voices in the debates because we wanted to obscure our identities." She pinches her nose and speaks in a cartoon voice. "It was like this for the first ten months until we had to present the list with the names of real candidates."

Levi describes some of her earlier theater work. Her first two plays made her name in the European theater world. One was a feminist piece, *Femina ex Machina*, and the second was called *Non Lavoraremo Mai* (We Will Never Work Again).

I ask her about her use of humor in *Hazte Banquero*. Although I don't know Catalan, I found it very funny. I was laughing throughout the evening, and so was the rest of the audience.

"You know, Spinoza spoke about *la passione triste*. They, the bankers and politicians, have destroyed our lives, but I as an artist will give them zero help in making our lives sad. I don't want people going home feeling like they've been abused by history."

Who created all the multimedia effects with the split-second comic timing?

"Alfa is a monster, this boy," she exclaims. "He's a chemist. He's never been in a theater before. Yet he came to understand the comic timing perfectly."

She says that in the emails that make up most of the play's content, "the only thing the characters discuss all the time is how to get more money. The bank's constitution called for 'public control,' so the board was made up of political party members. The emails reveal them saying they will vote for this or that only if they can personally get what they want. The political party was just sucking money out of the bank. It was a mafia structure, that's what the people discover in the play. In the eight thousand emails that Xnet obtained, the word *crisis* (as in 'financial crisis') was mentioned only five times, while the word *remuneration* was mentioned fifty-three times." The players used coded language, too. For instance, the adviser to the king of Spain tells the bank president that he will give the money to a particular political party, "but instead of *party*, he uses the word *sensibilidad*."

At one point in the play, the three actors address who has been through the "revolving door" on the board of various banks, political parties, unions, government departments, or "arm's-length" agencies related to the scandal. They each open a computer printout that is so long it falls to the floor. The audience laughs. As they mention a name and an affiliation, the name appears on the big screen with a chart of all the organizations. And as a person is appointed to successive organizations, their printed name flutters like the wings of a butterfly up the chart to alight under the name of the second, third, and even fourth organization.

Levi, sitting on the side of the stage with the techies at the control board, jumps up to say, "I have a feeling this will take a long time, so I will change the scenography a bit, if you don't mind. Audience, if you would act as chorus and repeat the names in a sexy whisper as they are said. That would be good. And we will play some nice music. ..." The audience willingly complies, and the actors get into it too, swaying to the sexy bossa nova–style soundtrack and whispering the names suggestively. Soon, everyone is enjoying being silly.

Levi says she created this direction the day before the opening of the play, and the actors, who are professionals from the regular theater, "freaked out" about the late change. But then they got into it. And the second night, the actor playing Blesa, the first bank president, began to play with the audience, crooning "Cris-to-bal ..." and letting them answer, "Mon-to-ro!"[24] Levi smiles. "He did that for me."

HOMAGE TO CATALONIA

On my last day in Spain, I meet Sergio Salgado at the iconic Café Zurich in Plaça Catalunya just as it is opening. It is a place where people have been meeting for over a hundred years, one of the few cafés near the main transportation lines of the city that survived the Spanish Civil War. The day is *éblouissant*. Dazzling.

I imagine my own Canadian countrymen meeting here, part of the international effort to aid the democratic Republican government in Spain in its fight against Franco's Fascists, who were supported by Hitler's regime in Germany and Mussolini's in Italy. I recall how many in the Canadian contingent, known as the Mackenzie-Papineau Battalion, or Mac-Paps, were recruited in Vancouver's Stanley Park at a May Day picnic and smuggled to Europe on trains and ships in defiance of the government ban on their going.[25] An international movement had been a long-held dream of the left when these men left their democracy to help another. It seems also to be a dream of postleft, post-twentieth-century "progressive" politics, whatever these are. The 1930s was a time, like the current era, when people were organizing everywhere and at every level—unions, political parties, working men's clubs, farmers' cooperatives, civic organizations, the Labour and Socialist International ...

Salgado and I speak in French, as he doesn't speak English and I don't speak Spanish. We agree not to correct each other's grammar. He is from Galicia, an autonomous region in northwest Spain. He gives me a little more context about the financial scandal that was the subject of 15MpaRato. Savings banks had a social goal, he says. By their mandate, they could not seek profit and were supposed to help the community. The Caja Madrid was the biggest and oldest and in Spain, three hundred years old, and it held a lot of pensioners' savings. The government took this and other savings banks, which had a combined budget for social programs as big as that of the Gates Foundation in the United States, and transferred these social funds into the investment bank Bankia. They stole this money, too.

Part of the problem is that in Spain, as elsewhere, there has been less and less investigative journalism and more "click" journalism, Salgado tells me. The press searches for the scoop, dissects it, and publishes the story in uncontextualized bits. So the role Xnet played was necessary. When Rodrigo Rato and Miguel Blesa are criminally convicted, Salgado says, the message the press will convey will be "the system works." But the real story is that the citizenry has done it. And the citizenry needs to know this. This was the goal of *Hazte Banquero*.

Salgado wrote the play's script with Levi. He was good at searching out the right emails to include. Levi is the theater person. Salgado studied human behavioral ecology in Lisbon, went to the Science Po university in the capital of Galicia, and did a course in information technology at a college in Barcelona. He has worked with Xnet for five years. Politically, he has always been interested in digital rights.

Is he a hacker?

He replies, "Je ne touche pas le code." He doesn't do code. "Mais, politiquement, dans le sens important," he is a hacker. He is committed to the hacker ethic. The hacker ethic is a question of politics, not programming, he tells me. "C'est un question politique, ne pas un question de technique." It is an ethics of production; it is to produce results. "Dans la réalité," he says, people adhering to this ethic can create a capacity for massive production and effectiveness socially, politically, and culturally. Because the results of their efforts are digital. 3D printing, blockchain, protocols— lots of impactful technologies are at a tipping point at this moment. I notice he uses the same word Ada Colau used when talking about the bankers—"reality" rather than "in the real, physical world"—and wonder if this is just his French or a deliberate choice to juxtapose against the "unreality" Spanish elites have been living in.

Xnet wants to take the hacker ethic for the production of software and apply it politically, culturally, and socially, Salgado says. "C'est une methode pragmatique pour tous les activités humaines."

When I ask if Xnet considers itself a vanguard group or just a group of facilitators, he says the word they use is *catalyzers* because people are already thinking about these things. When the moment arrives to do something, Xnet is there.

Spain, he tells me, is a paradise of guerilla communication. There is a critical mass of people who know how to connect. Everyone, including Salgado's mother, uses social media tools for political communication, and as a society they are historically very political. The hacker principles are embraced by the population. La PAH (the movement against foreclosures), Xnet, and 15M do not put their faith in traditional parties. Between its first election cycle and the second, Podemos, the traditional leftist party, lost one million votes. "It is not a party of the twenty-first century but of the twentieth."

The new mayor of Barcelona, I have learned, has been working on a plan to achieve information self-determination for the city. Barcelona was already an early entrant into the "smart city" space when Colau came to office, with its municipal network of 500 kilometers of optical fiber, free WiFi routed through street lighting fixtures, and sensors to monitor parking, air quality, and garbage bins.[26] With its Barcelona Initiative for Technological Sovereignty (BITS), Colau's municipal government announced its intention to retain ownership of the network, the platforms, and the data; and to give citizens' some control over their own personal data,[27] while making information that belonged in the public realm accessible to citizens and companies.[28] It is a remarkably ambitious and risky effort, full of potential quagmires. The companies in this sector, apparently, "went crazy"[29] when they learned Colau's political platform might usurp their monopoly platforms.[30] The city has also taken on Airbnb, which it says has become a kind of welfare, something people have to do to get by. This is not popular with everyone in Colau's political base, but many see its wisdom.

The people of Spain are very intelligent, Salgado tells me, summing up our conversation. "They love complexity and diversity." They are politically sophisticated. "Les Indignados éclataient [burst] la réalité du société, politiquement."

We stand up and shake hands wordlessly, and I leave to catch my plane.

That fall, the case against Rodrigo Rato and nearly a hundred other officials would come to trial. Simona Levi would report that members of

Xnet were enjoying their time going to the trials in Madrid by day and performing their play by night.

The verdict would come down in February 2017.[31] Rato, president of Bankia from its formation in 2010 to when he abruptly resigned in 2012, was sentenced to four and a half years in jail for embezzlement related to his use of the corporate "black credit cards." The court found that Rato and other Bankia executives gave away credit cards to purchase political favors. The cards were used for expenditures lavish and petty. Miguel Blesa, the president of Caja Madrid from 1996 to 2010, before Rato took over and rolled it up into Bankia, was sentenced to six years. Rato was found to have replicated the "corrupt system" established by Blesa. Also in February, the former Bank of Spain governor was charged for allowing Bankia to float its initial public offering on the stock exchange while knowing its shares were overvalued.[32]

15MpaRato had sworn to see Rato sentenced by 2017. This mission accomplished, the group released a statement thanking everyone who made it happen. "The lawsuit is not over yet," they added. "15MpaRato and Xnet's fight against corruption goes on and more will fall. Expect us."

HACKING ELECTORAL POLITICS IN ITALY: "A NEW POLITICS IS POSSIBLE"

Leaving Spain, my next destination is Italy. I'm headed to Rome to investigate the rise of a controversial new force in Italian electoral politics—the citizens' movement known as Cinque Stelle (Five Stars) that calls itself an "antiparty." Danilo Toninelli and Riccardo Fraccaro are newly elected members to the Italian Parliament from the Cinque Stelle movement, and in late July 2016, I meet them at their parliamentary offices in the heart of Rome. Both are slim with dark hair, Fraccaro's gray at the temples. We sit down together in a small boardroom along with Silvia Virgulti, a Cinque Stelle communications staffer. Through an open window, a slight breeze wafts in with the sounds of the city as we talk.

Cinque Stelle is another manifestation of the populist sentiment that swept Western liberal democracies following the financial crisis of 2008. It was started by a comedian, Beppe Grillo, a popular, foul-mouthed performer known for his political rants. Grillo was channelling Italians' frustration with their politics after decades of entrenched patronage capped by the base vulgarities and corruption of Silvio Berlusconi's premiership. In 2004, Grillo was inspired when he read an article about the internet by tech consultant Gianroberto Casaleggio. Casaleggio (who died in 2016) was a counterculture figure from the same generation as Grillo. He was a European cypherpunk with long hair and granny glasses, a hippie technolibertarian who had worked as an executive for Italy's largest telecommunications company and ran his own Milan-based internet marketing consultancy.

Both Grillo and Casaleggio viewed Italian politics and the growing economic inequality in the world with disgust.[33] Casaleggio set up a website for Grillo, and he predicted that the blog Grillo would write for the platform and its interactive design would change Italian politics forever. In a country where people expect little from politics except graft and chronic dysfunction, the two wrote a book in 2011 titled *Siamo in Guerra: Per una nuova politica* (We Are at War: For a New Politics), in which they celebrated the internet for its anticapitalist and democratizing potential.[34] They also claimed it was "Franciscan," meaning perhaps that the internet as a phenomenon evinced an ethic of collective solidarity similar to that espoused by Franciscan monks, an observation meant to resonate in a Catholic society like Italy.

Grillo's blog became wildly popular in Italy and beyond, and his interactive webpages overflowed with, well, interaction, as people began to feel inspired, too. Oliviero Ponte di Pino, author of *Comico e Politico*, has written that Grillo spoke to the "stomach" of ordinary Italians.[35] Certainly, he resonated with a younger generation who were suffering through a 33 percent rate of youth unemployment. If they had jobs, they often earned so little that many had to forgo starting families or leave the country.[36] Emulating the Moveon.org practice of organizing local, in-person meetups, Grillo's nascent movement flourished. People came together to discuss their problems, and local cells multiplied to create a resilient political organism.[37] People began to feel they were participating in an important new phenomenon. At the start, it was aimed at giving ideas and advice to politicians, but their doors were closed and they did not listen.

In September 2007, Grillo organized a national day of protest, which he called V-Day, meant to cap off a "clean parliament" campaign started two years earlier. "V" stood not for victory but for *vaffanculo* ("go fuck yourself"). Two million people showed up to the "happening" in Bologna and the 220 other cities where it was live-streamed. Grillo led them all in a chant of "*Vaffanculo!*" directed at Italy's political elites.[38] They presented their manifesto. No one should stand for election who had been convicted of a crime. Politics should be a temporary service and not a career: anyone who had served two terms at any level (local or national) should go back to his or her original job. And last, voters should be able to choose individual representatives for parliament rather than voting for a slate of candidates composed by party leaders from a pool of party insiders who often had no ties to their local constituencies.[39]

Grillo and Casaleggio announced the launch of Cinque Stelle in 2009, and the group ran candidates in elections at various levels in 2010, 2011, and 2012, with modest results. But in 2013, in the national elections, it took a quarter of the country's votes, pushing Matteo Renzi's center-left Democratic Party (DP) into the difficult position of having to form a coalition with Berlusconi's party when Cinque Stelle, on principle, refused to make a deal.[40]

The Cinque Stelle movement is hard to categorize as either left or right, and as mentioned earlier, it even refuses to be called a political party (it claims to be an "antiparty").[41] In fact, it speaks to a restive mix of voters that in America might be either Bernie Sanders's "Our Revolution" supporters or Trump's working-class voters, although overall the movement seems to skew more to the left and to younger voters.[42] On the one hand, the movement has been anti-immigrant, virulently against the traditional press, and economically protectionist. On the other, it is environmentalist, distrustful of global capitalism, and fervently egalitarian. It is a "big tent" political organization, but it also is proving there has been a realignment of traditional political party views.

By consensus, Cinque Stelle is Euro-skeptic, suspicious of professional politicians, idealistic about cleaning up corruption in politics, and determined to use digital technology to make the Italian political system responsive to ordinary citizens. One of its signature policy recommendations has become the adoption of an annual basic income in Italy.[43] Other positions range right, left, and center on the traditional political spectrum. The five stars in its name stand for the five policy areas the movement initially decided to prioritize—public water, sustainable transport, sustainable development, a right to internet access, and the environment.

I ask Fraccaro and Toninelli how they became involved with Cinque Stelle.

"Most of us came to it through Grillo's blog, one of the top ten most influential blogs in the world," Fraccaro replies. "Each one was about a different issue. I was inspired by an event called the Cinque Stelle Woodstock, held in 2008. We talked about 'solutions to the problems,' we heard music, there was open discussion with people from all over Italy, all ages and classes. I came to agree. A new politics is possible. A politics that does not divide but unifies." Fraccaro organized a meetup in his locality and eventually ran for the general election.

Toninelli says that, for him, he had "arrived at a point where I did not want to vote anymore because I did not feel respected by any of the political parties. I was already working politically on issues relating to food and education. Those issues were essential but not covered by political parties. When I had the opportunity to become involved, I became a registered member of Cinque Stelle, and I set up local events in town halls. And what I realized, what struck me as extraordinary, was that we actually had a white canvas to paint what we wanted, other than the basic principles of equality and direct democracy that the movement was based on. What's new is the power pyramid is upside down. Before, if you wanted to be a politician, you had to enter a party like it was a company. With Cinque Stelle, the citizen can decide to become a politician and they're directly involved in choosing candidates."

Direct democracy, Fraccaro explains, is an institutional tool for citizens to legislate or block legislation. This is real democracy because the citizens can use their power directly. "E-democracy is a tech tool to use in the simplest way possible. One must not underestimate this tech tool because we know revolutions in history are based on tech innovations. The two main revolutions we had in Europe previously, in the fifteenth and nineteenth centuries, were based on the printing press and the steam engine. An information and an energy revolution. Today, we are facing two bigger revolutions at once, based on the internet and on sustainable energy, and these are changing society. We have the possibility to change democracy."

Casaleggio, the creator of Cinque Stelle's "operating system," they tell me, believed it was essential to break through the barriers between citizens and politics. He felt that ridding intermediation allowed people to create a "global intelligence" that would let citizens make better decisions.

I ask Toninelli and Fraccaro how the "operating system" works. Is the platform "transparent," or does it give the coders undue influence with how the algorithms are designed?

It is transparent, they say, with majority voting.

The critique of direct democracy is that in its purest form it can amount to "mob rule," in which there is no protection for individual rights and minorities. In this pure form, it is not a consistent social contract. And it lacks expertise. Ordinary people do not have time to research or even to vote on every question.

But Cinque Stelle practices both direct and representative democracy. Toninelli says that so far they have had a political process that includes open discussions; election of councillors; an online voting system that allows all members to vote and decide, by majority, who runs for office; and elected officials putting legislative proposals online with an invitation to members for their input, comments, and revisions.

"This is not wiki legislation," says Toninelli, "but we have added more functions to the platform. Now, every registered member can make their own legislative proposal, and the elected members will review them and choose one per month to work on. Two elected officials are assigned as 'mentors' to the member making the proposal to help them refine it, and he can count on the two MPs to present the proposal as a bill in Parliament."

Last week this happened for the first time, and Toninelli acted as tutor for the citizens to help them present the proposal. They have received fifteen hundred proposals since they began accepting them from members a month and a half ago.

Silvia Virgulti has been translating our conversation up until now, and she makes an expression to mirror my own: fifteen hundred is a lot of proposals.

"Our victory is to see that citizens are happy to be making these proposals," Toninelli says. "Cinque Stelle is currently in opposition, not the government, so we cannot pass the proposals by ourselves. Not yet. The most important part of direct democracy is how spokespersons are chosen. In Cinque Stelle, anyone can run, and the whole membership votes on who the candidates should be. Second, all the proposals must be discussed for a minimum of a month on the internet platform before they are adopted as a Cinque Stelle position."

They have about 400,000 registered members now, who can vote on party positions. Cinque Stelle belongs, at the supranational level, to the Europe of Freedom and Direct Democracy (EFDD) group. All members of EFDD espouse some form of direct democracy, but their similarities do not necessarily go any further. Toninelli and Fraccaro say that you need to join a coalition to have any influence at the EU level, so Cinque Stelle joined EFDD to be free from decisions that might be imposed on them from other parties. A minimum of seven groups is needed to form a coalition under EU rules.

When I ask them how Cinque Stelle is a "new" politics, Fraccaro says that "Cinque Stelle was born because of a political crisis. Citizens don't feel like they live in a democracy, and the economic crisis demonstrates it. What we have had is a wealth transfer from the lower classes to the upper classes. How can one say we live in a democracy when that is happening?

"Cinque Stelle has actually established ourselves as the major political force in Italy right now. What we advocate is neither left nor right: that's not the point. The point is, 'What is the solution to the problem? Is it right, or is it wrong?' Political parties divide people with left and right, but they do the same thing in the end and blame each other. Neither the right nor the left listened to the people.

"According to some polls, Cinque Stelle is the top political force in Italy, and we made it there because we are trustworthy for the citizens. It was simple: we kept our promises. The left and right never kept their promises, and so they demonstrated that they're not good politicians."

What they have come to understand in their short time in political office, they say, is that although politics is complex, complexity often is used as an excuse. "If we need to accomplish big things, citizens understand that it can take a long time, but the path must be trustworthy day by day," Toninelli says. "To get rid of poverty in a month is not enough, but to cut our own wages [as elected officials], we did it in a day. Our movement is bound to grow because direct democracy is the right method. The horizontal organization is the right one, not the vertical."

Was there an Occupy or Indignados movement in Italy?, I ask.

Toninelli replies that in Italy the movement was called Forconi but lasted only a short time "because we were able to listen to it. Cinque Stelle is not the parallel to the Indignados because we are over the division between the left and right."

But many of the Indignados dislike the traditional left, I offer. They say that Podemos came from traditional party politics and used the momentum of the grassroots movement to coopt it.

Yes, Toninelli says. Podemos was born criticizing the old left parties but then they're actually the same thing. It was formed by professional politicians, not by the citizens.

What is the role of humor for Cinque Stelle?

"I think our power is that we're citizens," Toninelli says, "and by using humor and irony, we're remaining citizens. Is it black humour? I think at first it was more rage. Not anymore though. The humor now consists in not taking oneself seriously and doing one's best. Grillo makes fun of us, and we make fun of him."

And Beppe Grillo's role, is it not a little anomalous?, I ask.

"Beppe Grillo has created the values, principles, and ethos of Cinque Stelle. His role is in keeping the rules of legality and transparency. And Casaleggio helped Grillo transform the vision of a better world into a citizen's party."

There seem to be historic resonances between Cinque Stelle and earlier anarchist movements in Italy and some overlap in principles, too, such as "self-organization," "local solutions," a "rejection of coercion," and "collaboration." "Of course, the past influences the present," Fraccaro says. "Casaleggio studied the anarchist movements a lot. That allowed him to create a vision and solutions for the present. Some principles are shared. The idea of decentralizing every power is one of the main themes of the Pirate Party, too. Today, governments are subject to capitalism, not the other way around. This will lead to two possible results. You will either have countries governed by a few people in an authoritarian way or political movements that will try to transform the country into a system of direct democracy and citizens' choices, based on citizens' needs. That's what Italy is facing today."

Toninelli excuses himself. He has to leave for another meeting. "I would just like to add the idea of financialized capitalism," he says, pulling on his jacket. As he goes out the door, Virgulti calls out in Italian, "Don't forget to put your collar down." Her job as a communications officer is also to mentor new members of Parliament (MPs).

"We are aware we are not perfect," Fraccaro concludes. "We are not better than the people who elected us. But if we want to grow as a community, we must trust this community. We may face wrong decisions, but if they are shared, we will grow together, and we will walk the path together without leaving anyone behind. That is our slogan: 'No one can be left behind' ('Nessuna deve rimanere in dietro')."

Silvia Virgulti takes me to see the rest of the offices for the MPs, which seem newly renovated while being housed in an old stone building. We pass into a long room lined with large tables where about eight male MPs work side by side, their computers aligned across the tops of the tables. The energy in the place feels like an old-style news room. The men range in age from their late twenties to their early forties and, like Fraccaro and Toninelli, are dark and slim, some with tinges of gray. In an inner office, separated from the larger room by wood-paneled walls with glazing halfway up, four more men stand around the desks, discussing something animatedly. "Che cazzo!" (What a dick!) one exclaims, then stops abruptly as I enter.

In a country where the political system has been described as a gerontocracy, Cinque Stelle has allowed younger people to break in. The youngest Cinque Stelle deputy was twenty-four years old when elected in 2013, and the oldest is sixty-something. Registered members are from all walks of life, Virgulti tells me—carpenters, engineers, teachers, and lawyers. "These people didn't know what they were facing when they came in, but they learned. It took them some time, it was not easy, but they learned."

Virgulti opens the door to the next inner office and asks something of the four young men there, who are grouped together working out something in an informal meeting. They are very busy.

Their Cinque Stelle colleague Virginia Raggi must be even busier. She was elected mayor of Rome a month ago. Virgulti says it is a challenge when people have not held office because the learning curve is steep, but Parliamentary staff are trying to help them over at the municipal office.

At around 6 o'clock, I go back out through security to the street, Via degli Uffici del Vicario. A stone's throw away is the Parliament building in Piazza Montecitorio. Across the narrow street of black cobblestones is the venerable gelato shop Giolitti, its windows glistening in the evening sun. Its trade is still busy with tourists and office workers emerging from its doors, gelato cups in hand. The air is still warm, and the light is golden.

There are criticisms of the Cinque Stelle movement. Beppe Grillo has retained ownership of the Cinque Stelle copyright and denied political adversaries the right to use it. He remains the "guarantor" of the movement's direction. In many rounds of purges, members have been voted out of the party and off its platform for dissident views or violating the party's tenets. More than a quarter of the Cinque Stelle representatives across both houses of parliament were expelled between February 2013 and January 2015[44] for errors such as appearing on talk shows against Cinque Stelle rules and suggesting that Cinque Stelle might negotiate with the Democratic Party.[45] These expulsions have been justified by Grillo and others as being necessary to maintain the movement's integrity.

In his comic performances, Grillo has expressed some fairly wacky ideas (one was that HIV was a conspiracy of pharmaceutical companies), and he has stirred up feelings against illegal immigrants.[46] This might be a concern if he unduly affects Cinque Stelle's policy positions on health or immigration. But it might be a good sign that diverse views can coexist in a polity without splitting it—the hope being that if people keep talking to each other, they might temper and inform each other's views, or at least find compromises they can all live with. When Cinque Stelle representatives in the Senate proposed decriminalizing illegal immigration in 2013, Grillo and Casaleggio attacked the idea in their blog. Yet when it was put to a vote on the Cinque Stelle platform, the members went against the founders and backed the proposal.[47] Since then, one commentator has observed, the party has "criticized the left for what they consider its lax policies toward illegal immigration, but stop[ed] well short of the right's full-throated call to deport 600,000 illegal immigrants."[48]

Concerns were also raised within the movement about the transparency of the movement's operating system, which was run on a website owned by Casaleggio Associates, a consulting firm that served corporate interests that were potentially at odds with the movement. The platform was subsequently transferred to an ostensibly arm's-length nonprofit entity named the Rousseau Foundation[49] (after the Enlightenment's "most radical theorist of democracy").[50] However, a document was leaked that showed the nonprofit was essentially being run by Casaleggio's son.[51] Meanwhile, Grillo has refused to use a third-party monitor or open-source software like the "LiquidFeedback" software developed by the German Pirate Party.[52]

Of course, all of these things could be addressed by the Cinque Stelle membership at some point. As it would turn out, the most concerning thing about Cinque Stelle is its small and falling participation rates. Months after my journey to Italy, I would check on those rates and find that from 2012 to 2017, online participation fell from an average of 36,000 to 19,000 participants. Although the number of registered members eventually grew, that increase made the decline in active participation steeper—a drop from 68 percent to 13 percent over the same time period.[53] By 2018, less than 5 percent of the 10.7 million people who voted for its candidates were registered with the website. Both the online discussions and the choice of candidates, which are open to every registered member to participate in, would be shaped, in fact, by a small, active minority. The Parliament leader, Luigi Di Maio, would receive only 490 votes in his online primary for the 2018 election.

   Still, Italians seem to want to have the option of direct participation that Cinque Stelle's operating system provides, and they seem to place confidence in their fellow citizens who do participate. Votes for Cinque Stelle have not just remained strong since the 2013 election but risen. The movement has gotten the voices of ordinary Italians back onto the political map and opened up a chance for them to renew their democracy. Even if they do not succeed this time around, politics will not go on as before in Italy.

   Indeed, in March 2018, Cinque Stelle would become the leading party in the national elections, winning 33 percent of the votes and allowing it to form a coalition with the far right La Lega party[54] to govern the country.[55]

HACKING DEMOCRATIC DECISION MAKING ITSELF:
A CANADIAN ALGORITHM FOR GLOBAL DEMOCRACY

John Richardson was once thrown into jail with some of his clients, and he appealed his arrest all the way up to the British Columbia Court of Appeal. This was in 2002, the year of the Woodward's Building protest in Vancouver's Downtown Eastside, the part of the city known for its disabled, mentally ill, homeless, and drug-addicted and its community activism. The former department store building had been empty for more than a decade, and the government had promised to build more affordable housing in the area. Homeless people grew frustrated and occupied it, and Richardson became their lawyer. After the police threw them out, people camped on the sidewalk. Richardson was arrested on a day when police started hitting people with batons and throwing their belongings into garbage trucks. The stuff was going into the crushers, and the police were harassing people into leaving. When the police told Richardson he could not cross the police line to reach his clients, he crossed anyway. He said later, "It was kind of like you make a call. It was a split-second decision."

The events were filmed and provoked public anger. Union representatives arrived on the site the next day and handed out tents and mattresses so people could continue to camp there. Because a municipal election was going on at the time, the city wanted to avoid a repeat of the earlier scene, so it made a deal that led to the creation of public housing as part of the redevelopment of the Woodward's Building.

I know Richardson through the civil liberties community in British Columbia. I'm meeting with him in Vancouver, not long after my trip to Italy, to learn about his new enterprise that, as I understand it, is a hack on democratic decision making itself. We sit at a table looking out over Coal Harbor toward the dark green mass of Stanley Park and the snow-dusted coastal mountains beyond. Small sea planes fuel up and take off, engines whirring. A large percentage of the high-end condos looming behind us are owned by wealthy foreigners (the global 10 percent), who leave them vacant most of the year and pay risibly small property taxes and often no income tax to support the local economy.[56] This is no longer a city where working people can afford to live and go to May Day picnics, although the union movement in the province is still one of the strongest in the country.

I tell Richardson about the Spanish collective Xnet, its actions in Barcelona and Spain, and its ideas about distributed action and distributed political power. I tell him how Xnet has differentiated itself from the traditional left, which it says relies on ideology and protests, while members of Xnet, as social hackers, act and use their own skills to take things in hand and make actual changes. It is a revolutionary way of doing things.

He asks how they make decisions, and I compare Xnet's process to the old communist idea of a vanguard or central committee. Xnet members have a small guerrilla group that initiates things, but they are more like anarchists. Anarchists don't believe in democracy in any case, I add a little flippantly, realizing as I do that these old labels are getting me into trouble. They don't map satisfactorily onto how hackers engage in politics and I'm making a hash of what Simona Levi has told me about the role Xnet has played within the broader Indignados movement. (Xnet's manifesto is, in fact, "Democracy, period." Its members are not anarchists.)

"A central committee is not revolutionary!" Richardson says. The Occupy movement embraced the anarchist rejection of democracy, that is, the idea that minority votes should lose. So it tried to run meetings and make decisions by consensus. People were supposed to make a certain hand gesture to indicate their support for something, and later they tried using hand-held voting machines. He knows this because he traveled down to Zuccotti Park in New York City to talk to people during the Occupy Wall Street protests.

"But it's a limited paradigm," he says, "because you have limited options presented, and they're expressed in a certain way, and the group ultimately votes in the old way. It's amazing to think how much our society is actually determined by the optimal size of group decision making. Beyond optimal size, we do delegated authority: the board will appoint a CEO, Parliament will appoint a cabinet, a group size that can actually manage it. This creates hierarchy. Hierarchy is ultimately related to optimal group size for decision making."

Large groups, he tells me, can be very smart—smarter than the smartest experts. There is the famous jellybean example. Statistically, the average of the guesses of large groups of people will be the most accurate determination of the number of jellybeans in a jar. But this works only for groups of twenty to thirty and for simple decisions. The question is how do we scale up to increase intelligence by adding more people to decision making and examining more complex questions.

"All of society's problems are solvable—war, poverty, global warming. It's the group decisions that wear us down," he says. "When you talk to people on the ground, they have solutions. They're just paralyzed by the systems. People on the ground know what to do but can effect change only through group decision."

I ask him if he's ignoring the political dimension, the question of political will.

He's not ignoring it at all, he says. In fact, his new start-up is all about how to distribute power and influence fairly across a group or population.

Richardson studied math and philosophy before he went to law school. He created a legal clinic for Vancouver's Downtown Eastside and then went on to start Ethelo, a small, nonprofit, digital tech company that is inventing new ways of making decisions. As a mathematician, he studied group decision theory and was interested in what the legal philosopher John Rawls had to say about the conditions needed for making a good decision and a good social contract. Richardson asked himself, How can you quantify fairness in a group decision? Is there a way you can quantify it mathematically? That's the genesis of it.

He grabs a napkin and scrawls something on it. This is the formula he started with and he's been been refining it ever since: Decision strength = [Average support] – [Variance in support].

Each person's support for a decision will fall on a spectrum from total opposition to total support. The variance in that support across a group indicates the polarization of the group. Decisions that polarize groups are weaker than decisions that unify groups. Calculating this strength score across all possible decision scenarios, Richardson explains, is how the Ethelo algorithm identifies optimal outcomes. It is more sophisticated than the hand signals of Occupy.

People will support outcomes they do not like if they think the process is fair, Richardson says. And they will resist ones they like and will benefit from if they feel the process is unfair. Many social animals insist on fairness in social relations.

What is Ethelo? Take a problem, apply collective analysis, and Ethelo will generate a ranked list of possible decisions in order of their likelihood of being supported by a group. It can fine-tune the level of fairness, too.

The scores are crowd-sourced, produced by algorithms that capture collective analysis. The Canadian government's Department of Public Works is one of Ethelo's major clients, and its online endorsement calls the software program, "An exceptional advance on the state of the art that is clearly ahead of competitors."

There's a host of companies offering services for crowd-sourcing and group decision making right now. They all use computer technology but lack a model of group decision making, Richardson claims. They use a model that pulls together information and gives it to a single decision maker. That approach is not as sophisticated as Ethelo in terms of incorporating social factors like fairness, distributed influence, minimization of resistance, and optimization of buy-in. Another client, Lead Now, the largest online political organization in Canada, led a campaign in the last election on strategic voting. It was an "anything but Harper" campaign (the Conservative government of Stephen Harper was seeking reelection), and it used Ethelo.

Right now, Ethelo is a managed service company, but when Ethelo 2.0 is released, the goal is to enter the mass market with a turnkey platform that any group can use on its own.

Richardson sees this kind of decision making as revolutionary in our democracies. "What would happen to human society if we could make smarter decisions instead of dumber decisions?," he asks. "But how do existing social conditions/political frameworks affect the development of this kind of technology? This is a question that should not be underestimated. It comes down to money. People who have money right now aren't visionaries."

"If you were to corner the market for the 'decision-making' platform," I ask, "what would you do with it? What would your goal be?"

"Global democracy," he says without hesitation. "A single world government. Every person gets their input—one humanity. We have to have a common operating system for democracy—global democracy."

One platform controlling the decision making of the entire world? Isn't that a little scary?

"There could be a pluralism of smaller systems—as long as they were compatible with each other, as long as they could plug into the one operating system. Think, for example, about Linux. It is the dominant, most stable operating system in the world now. It achieved its stability by opening up its code and letting lots of minds peck away at it. Google is based on Linux. Linux is the go-to operating system. That's what we would do at a certain point: open up our code and see where that takes us."

NO MORE WRECKING BALLS

Many more groups are conducting experiments in hacking democratic processes along the lines of what Cinque Stelle, Ethelo, and PartidoX have done. They include the Democracy Earth Blockchain, Loomio's algorithm for collaborative decision making, Madrid's CONSUL, the Pirate Party's Liquid Democracy, the P2P Foundation, and the P2P blockchain political parties in Argentina and Australia, which vote only the way citizens want them to.

Direct democracy is not a new idea, and neither is participatory democracy, self-organization, shared leadership, or direct action. The difference is what can be achieved to upgrade the quality of Western liberal democracies with these and related ideas, employing digital tech, networks, and a hacking ethic.

The citizens who used their votes for Brexit and Donald Trump in the last half of 2016 felt they did not have much more than these wrecking balls to change the status quo. If Western liberal democracies can be upgraded in the twenty-first century, these citizens might have more to work with than mere votes next time. Both technological and philosophical innovations will be needed. As suggested earlier, the new political economy has yet to be fully theorized. What you see in the experiments of Xnet, Cinque Stelle, and Ethelo is a first cut at the project.[57]

11

THE VALUE AND RISK OF TRANSGRESSIVE ACTS

Corrective Feedback

BERLIN'S GRAFFITI

People started writing graffiti on Berlin's walls just as the final months of the Nazi regime were closing in. Some of it was meant to shore up Germans' morale while the city was being obliterated by Allied bombs. Film footage from the time shows Berliners scurrying along devastated streets past messages that assert they will never surrender.[1]

In the spring of 1945, as Germans faced their final defeat, a few resolute souls vented their bitterness on the walls of the Chancellery itself,[2] the seat of Nazi power. Around the corner, the crushed pit of Hitler's bunker lay smoldering.

When Russian troops stormed into Berlin, they mistakenly assumed the Reichstag was the symbol of power in the city and made a point of desecrating its walls with the chalk they had used to draw their campaign maps and the charcoal they took from its rubble. Germans made the decision some time ago not to erase most of this graffiti. For a time, it was covered up by plasterboard. People were sick of the war.[3] But after 1990, when the Reichstag was reconstructed following German reunification, and the plasterboard was removed, the graffiti was not all sandblasted away. Today, German parliamentarians walk to their duties past its excoriations. One message in Cyrillic taunts, "You got what was coming to you, you sons of dogs." Another outside Chancellor Angela Merkel's parliamentary office warns, "You reap what you sow."[4]

Indeed, from the end of World War II on, graffiti became an abiding feature of Berlin.

After the war, Germany was divided into four occupation zones—an eastern zone under Soviet control and a western zone under the control of France, the UK, and the US. The city of Berlin was in the eastern zone, and it also was divided into four occupation zones, so that West Berlin, which was occupied by the Allies, was like a tiny island of democracy inside the communist zone. By 1961, a fifth of the population of the Soviet-controlled German Democratic Republic (GDR) had escaped to the West,[5] many through West Berlin.[6]

Nikita Khrushchev, premier of the Union of Soviet Socialist Republics (USSR), told GDR leaders they should build an "iron ring"[7] around West Berlin to keep East Germans from escaping. Walter Ulbricht, chairman of the State Council of the GDR, was in favor of walling in the East Germans because, he said, "There are many issues that cannot be resolved with an open border."[8]

In June 1961, at an international press conference in East Berlin, Ulbricht said that "No one has the intention of building a wall,"[9] but on the night of August 12 to 13, East German soldiers laid more than thirty miles of barbed wire along the border with West Berlin.[10] By morning, the wall had become a fact.

On either side of the rising barricade, people stood watching, stunned. To prevent any rebellion on that first night, more than ten thousand armed soldiers and Combat Group members were deployed, along with several hundred tanks.[11] Within a few weeks, trenches were dug, and construction was complete. One East German doctor who managed to flee during this period (there were still escape routes through the buildings that straddled the divide) said, "On August 13, I saw tears in the eyes of men whom I had never seen cry before. The blow was hard and terrible. The reaction was not an immediate awakening of any immediate will to resist but sheer depression."[12]

The wall on the east side was blank and bordered by a no man's land. The west side of the wall was also dangerous, but a few brave individuals managed to scrawl graffiti on its cinder blocks even though they risked being shot by the East German guards who kept watch from towers.

By the early 1980s, much of the 156 kilometer wall was covered with graffiti. It was especially dense in the Kreuzberg neighborhood within the US-occupied sector, an area surrounded on three sides by the wall.

The first graffiti writers had been influenced by the New York City graffiti and squatting scene of the 1970s (New York was another city suffering from the poor decisions of its governing classes). Over time, the west side of the wall came to express the cumulative sentiments of a divided people. Love, sorrow, anger, hope, and horror transmogrified the brutal barrier into a vivid testament of social imagination.

One well-known graffiti painting from the period, titled *Mein Gott, hilf mir, diese tödliche Liebe zu überleben* (My God, help me to survive this deadly love), depicts a fraternal kiss between USSR premier Leonid Brezhnev and GDR leader Erich Honecker, head of the country's Socialist Unity Party. The image, painted in 1979, was based on a photograph of the two men taken on the occasion of the thirtieth anniversary of the founding of the German Democratic Republic. The USSR and the GDR had just signed a ten-year agreement of mutual support under which East Germany would provide ships, machinery, and chemical equipment to the Soviet Union, and the Soviet Union would provide nuclear power and fuel to East Germany.[13]

In 1989, when Germans tore down the wall with their bare hands and surged both ways across the divide, graffiti surged with them into East Berlin.

Large neighborhoods in East Berlin (such as Mitte, Friedrichshain, and Prenzlauer Berg) were vacant except for the poor pensioners, mostly widows, who had been left behind, too frail or impoverished to compete for more comfortable housing elsewhere. The riot of graffiti that ensued expressed a range of motives and meanings. Where the state had held iron control it signified the state had lost control. The graffiti reclaimed public space. The people took the city as their own and used it as their canvas. The West German newcomers brought their paint, and the East Germans, who had not had their say in a long time, joined in. For the East Germans, graffiti was a literal performance of freedom. A punk-anarchist, technosaturated youth culture flowered, evincing chaotic disobedience in the face of any kind of authority. As one techno DJ from the time put it, "We played in clubs that belonged to no one, in parts of town for which no one was responsible, in buildings that according to the land register didn't even exist. We lived predominantly during hours of the day when all normal people were sleeping."[14]

Throughout the 1990s, it was punks and old ladies in the stately apartments of the Friedrichshain district (stately but for their cold and disrepair) until the old ladies began to die off in the new century. Although many squatters remained, the neighborhood started to be gentrified. Even with gentrification, the elaborate graffiti on the wall of the Kino Cinema still changes every month. More desultory scrawls deface the beautiful classical statues from the time of the Prussian Enlightenment, like a lingering reservation on the right to complain. The member of Parliament for Friedrichshain, who zooms around the neighborhood with a punk haircut, on a motorbike, went to Russia recently to visit Edward Snowden and tried (unsuccessfully) to convince the German government to grant him asylum.[15]

THE VALUE OF TRANSGRESSIVE ACTS

Freedom is a transgression against power, a physical, mental, social, or political space we claim: it is the spirit in us to resist. Freedom is a gesture, a joke, a word, a sign. Sometimes it is violence against the violence of property or against violence itself. Sometimes it is love, an example we give one another, an encouragement, an affirmation of our humanity. Free things like graffiti and speech, thought and ideas, language and code, humor and love are irrepressible, and so it is that they can transform power relationships.

Before the fall of the Berlin Wall, during the last, restless days of life under the Communist regimes of Eastern Europe, the British playwright Tom Stoppard wrote a play about the performance of Shakespeare in Czech living rooms. In the country where the Velvet Revolution issued from the green room of a theater, it was incubated in people's homes, where Czechs put on amateur and semiprofessional performances of classic plays that expressed coded dissidence to the totalitarian regime. In Stoppard's *Dogg's Hamlet, Cahoot's Macbeth*, a nonsense language called "Dogg" is spread by a workman like a virus from the performance of a fifteen-minute comical production of *Hamlet* to a serious performance of *Macbeth* taking place in a dissident Czech's living room under the surveillance of secret police. With what the audience has gleaned about the nonsense language from the comic production of *Hamlet*, it can understand the powerful, subversive meaning the language takes on in the production of *Macbeth*.

Stoppard's message is that if language and ideas are infectious like viruses, their transmission cannot be controlled, even by authoritarian states. The same could be said for code, and hackers have said it many times. "Our code is free for all to use, worldwide," states Eric Hughes's "A Cypherpunk's Manifesto": "We don't much care if you don't approve of the software we write. We know that software can't be destroyed and that a widely dispersed system can't be shut down."[16] In "A Declaration of the Independence of Cyberspace," John Perry Barlow declares, "In China, Germany, France, Russia, Singapore, Italy and the United States, you are trying to ward off the virus of liberty by erecting guard posts at the frontiers of Cyberspace. These may keep out the contagion for a small time, but they will not work in a world that will soon be blanketed in bit-bearing media."[17]

In his classic 1968 essay "The Tragedy of the Commons," the American philosopher Garret Hardin argues that the social arrangements that produce responsibility are arrangements that create coercion of some sort.[18] Hardin was writing about the problem of an exponentially expanding population in a finite world, but he applies his argument to any finite resource that can be used freely by human beings. Indeed, the argument could be applied to any shared resource in a democratic commonwealth, including the internet or cyberspace. The inexorable and therefore tragic result of freedom in any commons, Hardin says, is the ruin of the commons. In a commonly held pasture, for example, the result is overgrazing, as herd owners seek to maximize their own immediate interest at the expense of the collective and the long-term welfare of the resource.

How might this be regulated? According to Hardin, prohibition is easy to legislate (although not necessarily easy to enforce). But how, he asks, do we legislate temperance? Hardin puts stock in administrative law, a type of legal regulation in which custodians have the flexible rule-making and discretionary powers to "evaluate the morality of acts [taking account of] … the total system." Morality, he points out, "is system-sensitive:"[19] "the morality of an act is a function of the state of the system at the time it is performed."[20] For example, dumping waste into a river in an unpopulated frontier, where nature can purify or dilute it, might be moral, where dumping it in a metropolis and creating a cesspool is not.

But as Hardin observes, giving custodians this kind of flexible, discretionary power makes them susceptible to corruption: "The great [governance] challenge facing us now is to invent the corrective feedbacks that are needed to keep the custodians honest," Hardin suggests. "We must find ways to legitimate the needed authority of both the custodians and the corrective feedbacks."[21]

In the early days of the American republic, politics were rowdy. The people "out of doors" provided corrective feedbacks to officials, petty and great. They pushed back against the restraints on populism that the patrician "founding fathers" wanted to write into the Constitution. The American people's innovation was a new kind of social compact—a constitutional democracy based on popular sovereignty. The ingenuity of this form of governance was that it worked something like mutually agreed-on mutual coercion. It was a democracy which, in addition to institutional checks and balances, had high citizen participation, diverse civil groups, and a foundational tradition of civil disobedience (the Boston Tea Party and the Underground Railroad being just two examples of this tradition). As American democracy evolved, it was distinguished by large social movements, including the antislavery movement, the woman suffrage movement, the Progressive movement, the civil rights movement, and the antiwar movement during the Vietnam War years, which changed power relationships in the country profoundly.

Coercion, or corrective feedback, from the less powerful can come in many forms: civil disobedience to unjust laws, certainly, but also strike, boycott, work-to-rule, and sabotage; the occupation of space and shows of solidarity; the defiling of values and flaunting of alternative ones; witness, moral suasion, shaming, shows of contempt; dignified comportment; the testing of limits, displayed prowess, intellectual influence; the living of an alternative way of life, virtuous example; persistence, and yes, humor and love. All of these can transgress the status quo, the complacency of power.

Today, Berlin's antigraffiti task force processes about fifteen arrests a week, with offenders fined between €100 and €1,000. "We know we'll never be able to completely eliminate graffiti," says Marko Mortitz, who heads the task force. He estimates the property damage from graffiti at about €35 million to €50 million a year.[22] It is a rough equilibrium the city has arrived at over time.

The potency of, and need for, graffiti in Berlin may be gradually receding. In the digital age, the new graffiti is arguably memes. If graffiti is an irrepressible expression of people's dissidence from the status quo, memes are even more so. Take the recent meme based on the 1979 graffiti painting *My God, Help Me to Survive This Deadly Love*, mentioned earlier. In 2016, on the wall of a barbeque restaurant in the old town of Vilnius in Lithuania, two artists painted a mural of Russian president Vladimir Putin and United States president Donald Trump in a similar embrace. "Make Everything Great Again," reads the caption next to it.[23] In Bristol, another wall sprouted an image of Donald Trump and pro-Brexit campaigner Boris Johnson kissing during the run-up to the 2016 Brexit referendum.[24] The images, and the conceit, have since gone viral online.[25]

At the end of the World War I, the poet T. S. Eliot wrote, "This is the way the world ends. Not with a bang but a whimper,"[26] possibly describing the eerie whine before an aerial bomb blast. In the twenty-first century, the world could well end with a tweet and a very big bomb blast. Yet there is hope that the collective wisdom of people, expressed through a plurality of transgressive, freedom-asserting, transformative acts, might incrementally push and pull us toward temperance and away from catastrophe. Corrective feedback.

THE RISK OF TRANSGRESSIVE ACTS

> 3.4.22. "Is the Cypherpunks group an illegal or seditious organization?"
> - Well, there are those "Cypherpunk Criminal" t-shirts a lot of us have …
> - Depends on what country you're in.
> - Probably in a couple of dozen countries, membership would be frowned on
> - the material may be illegal in other countries
> - and many of us advocate things like using strong crypto to avoid and evade tzxes [sic], to bypass laws we dislike, etc.
>
> 3.5—Self-organizing Nature of Cypherpunks

3.5.1. Contrary to what people sometimes claim, there is no
ruling clique of Cypherpunks. Anybody is free to do nearly
anything, just not free to commit others to course of action,
or control the machine resources the list now runs on, or
claim to speak for the "Cypherpunks" as a group (and this last
point is unenforceable except through reptutation and social
repercussions).
3.5.2. Another reason to be glad there is no formal Cypherpunks structure, ruling body, etc., is that there is then no
direct target for lawsuits, ITAR vioalation (sic) charges,
defamation or copyright infringement claims, etc.[27]

As people begin to hack more concertedly at the structures of the status quo, the reactions of those who benefit from things as they are will
become more fierce and more punitive, at least until the "hackers" succeed in shifting the relevant power relationships. We know this from the
history of social movements. At the dawning of the digital age, farmers
who hack tractors will be ruthlessly punished.

Of course, it must be acknowledged that hackers are engaged in a
whole range of acts, from the altruistic to the plainly nihilistic and dangerous. On the altruistic side of the continuum, they are creating free
software (GNU/Linux and other software under GPL licenses), Creative
Commons (Creative Commons licensing), and Open Access (designing
digital interfaces to make public records and publicly funded research
accessible). They are hacking surveillance and monopoly power (creating privacy tools, alternative services, cooperative platforms, and a
new decentralized internet) and electoral politics and decision making
(Cinque Stelle, En Comú, Ethelo, Liquid Democracy, and PartidoX). They
have engaged in stunts to expose the technical flaws in voting, communications, and security systems widely used by, or imposed on, the public
(by playing chess with Germany's election voting machines, hacking the
German Bildschirmtext system, and stealing ministers' biometric identifiers). They have punished shady contractors like HackingTeam, HBGary,
and Stratfor, spilling their corporate dealings and personal information
across the internet. They have exposed the corruption of oligarchs, politicians, and hegemons (through the Panama Papers, WikiLeaks, and Xnet).

More notoriously, they have coordinated distributed denial of service (DDoS) attacks to retaliate against corporate and government

conduct (such as the Anonymous DDoS that protested PayPal's boycott of WikiLeaks; the ingenious use of the Internet of Things to DDoS Amazon; and the shutdown of US and Canadian government IT systems). They have hacked into databases (Manning and Snowden), leaked state secrets (Manning, Snowden, and WikiLeaks), and, in doing so, betrayed their own governments (Manning betrayed US war secrets, and Snowden betrayed US security secrets). They have interfered with elections (such as the hack and leak of the Democratic National Committee in the middle of the 2016 US election) and sown disinformation (the Russian hacking of US social media). They have interfered with property rights in order to assert user ownership, self-determination, and free software's four freedoms (farmers have hacked DRM code to repair their tractors, and Geohot unlocked the iPhone and hacked the Samsung phone to allow users administrator-level access to their devices) and to assert open access to publicly funded research. They have created black markets to evade state justice systems (such as Silk Road on the dark web) and cryptocurrencies that could undermine state-regulated monetary systems. They have meddled in geopolitics as free agents (Anonymous and the Arab Spring, and Julian Assange and his conduct with the Trump campaign). They have mucked around in and could potentially impair or shut down critical infrastructure. (The notorious "WANK worm" attack on NASA is an early, notorious, example, but hackers could potentially target banking systems, stock exchanges, electrical grids, telecommunications systems, air traffic control, chemical plants, nuclear plants, and even military "doomsday machines.")[28]

It is impossible to calculate where these acts nudge us as a species. Some uses of hacking—such as the malicious, nihilistic hacking that harms critical infrastructure and threatens lives, and the hacking in cyberwarfare that injures the critical interests of other countries and undermines their democratic processes—are abhorrent and cannot be defended. The unfolding digital era looks very grim when one considers the threat this kind of hacking poses to peace and democracy *combined* with the dystopian direction states and corporations are going with digital tech.

But somewhere on the continuum of altruism and transgression is the kind of hacking that might lead the world toward more accountable government and informed citizenries, less corrupt and unfair economic systems, wiser public uses of digital tech, more self-determination for the ordinary user, fairer commercial contracts, better conditions for innovation and creativity, more decentralized and robust infrastructure systems, and an abolition of doomsday machines. In short, some hacking might move us toward a digital world in which there are more rather than fewer democratic, humanist outcomes.

It is not clear where the line between "good" and "bad" hacking should be drawn or how to regulate it wisely in every instance. Citizens should inform themselves and begin to consider this line-drawing seriously, however, since we will be grappling intensely with it for the next century or more. My personal view is that digital tech should not be used for everything. I think we should go back to simpler ways of running electrical grids and elections, for example. Systems are more resilient when they are not wholly digital and when they are smaller, more local, and modular. Consumers should have analogue options for things like fridges and cars, and design priorities for household goods should be durability and clean energy use, not interconnectedness.

In setting legal standards, prohibiting something and enforcing the prohibition are two different things. Sometimes a desired social norm can be struck by prohibiting a thing and not enforcing it strenuously. And the law can also recognize the constructive role that civil disobedience plays in the evolution of social norms, through prosecutorial discretion and judicial discretion in sentencing.

Wau Holland told the young hackers at the Paradiso that the Chaos Computer Club was "not just a bunch of techno freaks: we've been thinking about the social consequences of technology from the very beginning." Societies themselves, however, are generally just beginning to grapple with the social consequences of digital technology and with how to characterize the various acts performed by hackers, morally and legally. Each act raises a set of complex questions. Societies' responses will be part of the dialectic that determines where we end up. Should these various hacker acts be treated as incidents of public service, free speech, free association, legitimate protest, civil disobedience, and harmless pranksterism? Or should they be treated as trespass, tortious interference, intellectual property infringement, theft, fraud, conspiracy, extortion, espionage, terrorism, and treason? I invite you to think about this as you consider how hacking has been treated by societies to date.

HACKER CRACKDOWN 3.0

Bruce Sterling wrote about the alarmed response to hackers in the 1980s and 1990s in his vivid account *The Hacker Crackdown: Law and Disorder on the Electronic Frontier.*[29] Many of these early hackers were precocious teenagers without any (or any well-thought-out) ideas about the political impact of their acts. State and law enforcement hysteria at the time was justified, perhaps, by their realization as "custodians" that as computerized systems became ubiquitous, important infrastructure could be at risk. Authorities were playing security catch-up. Some of that period's hysteria was calmed down by the efforts of more responsible groups such as the Electronic Frontier Foundation and the Chaos Computer Club, which worked to educate authorities and the public about the civil liberties aspects of digital tech.

The second wave of hacker crackdowns came when hackers challenged US restrictions on cryptography in the cryptowars of the early 1990s. At that time, Phil Zimmermann managed to thwart prosecution with the help of strong institutional allies, including the MIT Press and the newly formed EFF. During that period, too, Daniel Bernstein established that encryption code was not only constitutionally protected speech but also a democratic "bounty."

In contrast to these two periods of hacker activity and custodial crackdown, hackers in the early twenty-first century have often been politically motivated and articulate about their aims, and they have not escaped punishment. They have been jailed and faced long prison sentences, been exiled, and faced torture. Hacker crackdown 3.0 started with the Obama administration, which seems to have understood very well the threat that hackers, whistleblowers, and digital rights activists posed to the US establishment.

As mentioned earlier, the Democratic Party has always had a close relationship with Silicon Valley and has invested a lot in it politically. Since the Clinton administration, Democrats have insistently championed the tech industry as the new driver of the American economy, ignoring the economic emiseration spreading in much of the rest of the country as their economic policies sent American manufacturing abroad.[30] The revolving door between Obama administration officials and Silicon Valley corporations is notorious,[31] and there was seldom an important political event or "blue ribbon" government panel during Obama's time where Eric Schmidt, the executive chairman of Google, did not appear to pontificate.[32] Obama referred to Google in half of his State of the Union speeches.[33]

More generally, as the cybersphere has increasingly become a space for commercial and financial markets on the one hand and for state surveillance and cyberwar on the other, states and corporations have treated the security and stability of the internet as overriding concerns. They have become increasingly allied in their responses to hacking, and their separate justifications for harshly repressing it have begun to elide.[34] Governments everywhere are partnering with digital tech companies as they move to secure ever greater levels of social control over populations, whether through border controls, law enforcement, entitlement regimes, or electoral systems.

The first hackers to be harshly punished during the Obama era were Anonymous. As described earlier, Anonymous emerged as an amorphous collective phenomenon, without central organization or leadership, from a loose online community coalescing around participation in 4chan's scabrous, unmoderated image board. Initially, Anons were engaged in creating memes and pranks, performing hacks on targets they considered worthy of contempt for the "lulz" (a riff on the texting abbreviation "lol," for "laugh out loud"), usually meaning finding laughs at others' expense or finding amusement in trolling.

But after 2007, Anonymous actions became increasingly political. After the Anons tasted their first "blood" in a rowdy tangle with the Church of Scientology over the latter's attempt to force the removal of a video from the internet, Anonymous grew in strength and by 2010 had morphed into something like the avenging spirit of the free internet. They cultivated an aesthetic of sulfuric righteousness. Their catchphrase "We are legion" was taken from the New Testament story where Jesus exorcises a demon from a man into a herd of swine. Asked its name, the demon replies, "I am Legion, for we are many." In their online declarations, Anons wore a mask representing Guy Fawkes, the rebel who tried to blow up the House of Lords in London in 1605. The disguise was inspired by the futurist movie *V for Vendetta*, in which citizens wear masks in a

show of collective action and dissent as they march on the British Parliament. Even though most Anonymous participants had low levels of
technical ability (usually just enough to follow instructions to engage
in DDoS attacks),[35] many Anons reveled in playing up to the media's
negative stereotype of the hacker as the technically dangerous, antisocial
pubescent, nihilistically wreaking havoc from his parents' basement—
the "hacker-as-folk-devil,"[36] the trickster.

In reality, Anonymous had a "prismatic" set of political beliefs and
aims[37] but one strongly shared allegiance to the idea of a free internet.
Anons were against censorship or control of the internet of any kind.

As described earlier in chapter 8, Anons jumped in to stand up for
WikiLeaks in late 2010 with Operation Payback and Operation Avenge
Assange, which retaliated against PayPal and other entities for actions
they took against WikiLeaks after the Manning leaks. Postings made by
Anons at the time included a call-to-action video titled "Operation Payback #Anonymous Message RE: ACTA, SOPA, PIPA, Internet Censorship
and Copyright,"[38] demonstrating their engagement in a wide set of digital rights issues.

As described in chapter 9, their political engagement and their participants broadened further with the Arab Spring. Tunisians identifying
as Anonymous launched Operation Tunisia with Anons in other countries in early January 2011.[39] As the protests spread to other Arab countries, Anonymous engagement spread too. On January 25, 2011, Anons
launched Operation Egypt.[40]

Later in 2011, members of Anonymous participated in the physical
protests of Occupy wearing their Guy Fawkes masks,[41] and in the last half
of 2011 the online actions taken in the name of Anonymous were frenetic. Anons hacked the websites of the Koch brothers,[42] Apple, defense
contractor Booz Allen, the Democratic Party, Monsanto, and NATO,
among other targets.[43] A small group of people calling themselves Lulz-
Sec emerged in May 2011 from Anonymous IRC chat rooms, and over a
short period, they claimed responsibility for high-profile attacks on the
CIA and media companies such as Fox, the News International, PBS, and
Sony, taunting rival hackers and members of law enforcement units who
tried to identify them.[44]

In June 2011, LulzSec launched Operation Anti-Security with Anonymous and other hackers. A multitude of hacks against law enforcement

agencies and contractors in various US states and other countries ensued over the remaining months of 2011.[45] Stolen credit cards were used to make donations to the ACLU, the Chelsea Manning Support Network, and EFF.[46]

LulzSec members were fairly quickly arrested, starting in early June 2011 with one of the founders of the group based in New York, who went by the handle Sabu. Facing more than 124 years in prison, he became an FBI informant and helped identify his associates as part of a plea deal.[47] Teenage members of LulzSec were arrested in the UK.[48] More members were arrested in March 2012, one of whom was Jeremy Hammond, who went by the handle Anarchaos.[49] Hammond was charged for his hack of Strategic Forecasting Inc. (Stratfor) in December 2011 (the hack that informed Harry Halpin about Mark Kennedy, the private security contractor who infiltrated Harry's climate change group).[50] Later, Hammond admitted to hacking other private security firms, law enforcement agencies, and military and police equipment suppliers.[51]

In all, dozens of people were arrested in Australia, India, the Netherlands, Spain, Turkey, and the United Kingdom for their involvement in various Anonymous hacking exploits.[52] In the United States, two were arrested for their participation in Operation Chanology against the Church of Scientology. One Anon, a truck driver who was arrested for the DDoS of the Koch brothers, had run the Anonymous DDoS tool (the low-tech Low Orbit Ion Cannon) for only about sixty seconds. Fourteen Anonymous were arrested in relation to the PayPal DDoS.[53]

Vague computer fraud laws became the legal instrument of choice to deal with them. In the United States, Anons were charged under the Computer Fraud and Abuse Act (CFAA),[54] a statute passed in 1986 (amending an older piece of legislation) during the first hacker crackdown of the 1980s.[55] The CFAA carries penalties for hacktivist activities that are far more severe than what would be meted out to activists in real space. For a sit-in, arguably the physical parallel to a DDoS action, the charge, if any, might be trespass, a misdemeanor carrying a fine of a few hundred dollars or a short prison stay.[56] Under the CFAA, Anons were charged with felonies, and the sentences they faced were increased under US Sentencing Commission guidelines according to the number of victims, the scale of financial loss involved, and the "special skill" or "sophisticated means" used in their actions.

In addition to the increased fines and jail sentences, US fraud laws make perpetrators liable to pay restitution to their targets.[57] The Koch brothers argued that their loss was not only the direct loss of the Anonymous DDoS attack (less than $5,000) but also the cost they incurred hiring consultants to strengthen their online security, a figure of $183,000.[58] So the truck driver who felt good about his sixty-second contribution as a worker in the fight against billionaire oligarchs[59] was facing personal ruin for his action. Not surprisingly, most hackers charged under the CFAA have agreed to plea bargains. (Although even with a plea bargain, the truck driver was sentenced to pay the Kochs $183,000. In the DDoS he participated in, the Koch Industries website had been down for about 15 minutes.)[60]

The chilling effect on online protest is intentional in the legal framework. It effectively encloses cyberspace for state and commercial interests and excludes it from the public realm. It makes the exercise of constitutional free speech and civil disobedience online prohibitively costly for citizens. In most US states, everyone taking part in a DDoS protest can be held jointly and severally liable for the action.[61]

Contrast this to the approach taken by a higher court in Germany in an early DDoS case from 2001. An activist, Andreas-Thomas Vogel, coordinated a DDoS protest against Lufthansa and was charged with "coercion." The higher court voided Vogel's conviction, holding that "the online protest did not constitute a show of force, but was intended to influence public opinion." Vogel's group, Libertad, applauded the ruling, stating, "Although it is virtual in nature, the Internet is still a real public space. Wherever dirty deals go down, protests also have to be possible."[62]

In many ways, Anonymous and LulzSec made themselves easy targets with their trollish, chaotic embrace of the antisocial hacker identity. But the debate about how online political protests ought to be treated has been percolating since the early days of the internet, when groups such as the Critical Art Ensemble, the electrohippies, the Electronic Disturbance Theatre, and the Strano Network were using DDoS as a tactic.[63]

During the Obama era, the treatment of whistleblowers and leakers, and the journalists working with them, was also revived as a societal debate, and the administration decided to come down on this kind of hacking with equal severity.

Under US law, anyone leaking classified information can be prosecuted under the Espionage Act. However, the legal situation of people who report and publish such leaks is less certain. In its seminal decision in *New York Times Co. v. United States*, 403 US 713 (1971)—the case in which the Nixon administration sought an injunction against the *New York Times* to stop it from publishing stories based on Daniel Ellsberg's leaks of the Pentagon Papers—the US Supreme Court held that "any system of prior restraints of expression comes to this court bearing a heavy presumption against its constitutional validity." The government, it said, "carries a heavy burden of showing justification for the imposition of such a restraint." In the Pentagon Papers case, the Court held that the government had not met the test, and the *New York Times* was able to go ahead with publication. (Daniel Ellsberg, on the other hand, could easily have been convicted under the Espionage Act. When all the major newspapers published his leaks, the government made a political decision not to follow through with his prosecution.)

After the Pentagon Papers affair, successive governments respected the tacit social compact that had existed before Nixon's assault on freedom of the press and did not go after reporters and publishers of classified secrets. They investigated leakers, but not too strenuously. Publishers generally gave the government notice if they intended to publish or broadcast sensitive stories, providing the White House with an opportunity to convince them to kill or delay a story on national security grounds. After 9/11, the Bush administration managed to kill a lot of stories this way, and for over a year it delayed publication by the *New York Times* of its explosive leak concerning the NSA's secret mass surveillance operations.[64]

Then in 2003, the Bush administration set a very bad precedent. The leak by Bush Republicans of information that outed undercover CIA agent Valerie Plame prompted the Bush administration, with the support of many Democrats, to appoint special counsel Patrick Fitzgerald to investigate the affair. He subpoenaed numerous Washington, DC, reporters and made them testify before a grand jury. Reporter Judith Miller went to jail for contempt of court for refusing to cooperate. As journalist James Risen (who would later be prosecuted in another case) has observed, Fitzgerald "became a role model for career prosecutors, who saw that you could rise to the top of the Justice Department by going after reporters and their sources."[65] Government officials saw that they themselves suffered little blowback from the affair. "The political, social, and legal constraints that previously made government officials reluctant to go after journalists and their sources" had been seriously compromised.[66]

In May 2006, Attorney General Alberto Gonzalez told an ABC interviewer the government had the legal authority to prosecute journalists for publishing classified information.[67] In January 2008, Risen, who as a *New York Times* reporter had won a Pulitzer Prize for the NSA mass surveillance story, was subpoenaed. The Bush administration wanted to force him to reveal his source.[68]

On assuming power in November 2008, the Obama administration, rather than reversing this damaging trend against press freedom, doubled down on prosecutions against whistleblowers and leakers, and on the journalists working with them. It aggressively surveiled the communications between journalists and sources and brought more prosecutions against leakers than all previous administrations combined.[69] James Risen had successfully had his subpoena quashed just as the Obama administration was coming into power and assumed it would drop the case. But the Obama administration appealed the decision and won, setting the damaging legal precedent that there is no reporter privilege in a criminal investigation. (Risen appealed the 4th Circuit Appeal Court's decision to the US Supreme Court, which declined to hear the case, thus leaving the precedent standing in Virginia and Maryland, where the NSA, Pentagon, and CIA are all located.)[70]

Public opinion was finally aroused by the litigation, and the Obama administration drew back. In 2014, Attorney General Eric Holder said that as long as he was in office, "no reporter who is doing his job is going to go to jail."[71] The prosecutors in the case ultimately did not force Risen to reveal his source.[72] The Department of Justice issued an ambiguous set of guidelines stating that it would not treat "ordinary news-gathering activities" as criminal conduct. A year later, it dropped the word "ordinary," still without defining what "news-gathering activities" might be.[73]

During these years when the Obama administration was attempting to lay down this legal framework in the context of the Risen subpoena, it was no doubt planning how it would deal with hacker whistleblowers, leakers, and publishers, and the journalists who work with them.

WikiLeaks published the "Collateral Murder" video of the US military helicopter attack on Iraqi civilians in April 2010, and by May 2010 Chelsea Manning had been arrested. She was held for three years before her 2013 court martial hearing, for a long period in solitary confinement, stripped naked at night, and sometimes left naked.[74] Manning was charged with twenty-two offenses, including communicating national defense information to an unauthorized source, violations of the Espionage Act, stealing US government property, disobeying orders under article 92 of the Uniform Code of Military Justice, computer fraud crimes under the Computer Fraud and Abuse Act, and the most serious charge, aiding the enemy, a capital offense, although the prosecutors were not seeking the death penalty. Manning was acquitted of aiding the enemy and convicted of nineteen of the other charges.[75]

The military judge held that providing classified information for mass distribution is treason if the government can prove the defendant knew she was giving intelligence to the enemy by direct or indirect means. Although the prosecutors failed to prove this intent in Manning's case, the ruling is troubling because, as one commentator said, "it blurs the distinction between leakers and spies."[76] The thirty-five-year sentence the judge imposed on Manning was the longest ever in a leak case.[77]

Julian Assange was not arrested until December 2010, and the arrest was not for publishing leaks but for the sexual crimes he was alleged to have committed in Sweden.[78] As described earlier, he was imprisoned in Wandsworth Prison in London for a short time in January 2012 as he faced extradition to Sweden, and then he was held in a long house arrest while lawyers fought over his legal rights. But it was widely believed that he was the subject of a "sealed" grand jury indictment in the United States. Hillary Clinton, who was US Secretary of State at the time WikiLeaks released its trove of confidential State Department cables in November 2010, became a harsh critic of Assange. (Some news outlets reported her saying to staff at one point, "Can't we just drone this guy?," although Clinton, when asked, said it would have been a joke had she said it.)[79] Assange believed that if he agreed to be extradited to Sweden, he would subsequently be extradited to the United States. At the end of May 2012, just as the UK Supreme Court was reaffirming its decision to allow his extradition to Sweden, Assange sought asylum from the Ecuadorian embassy.[80]

In September 2012, journalist Barret Brown was arrested. Brown, a young freelancer from Texas, has been called the Hunter S. Thompson of his generation by some admirers of his work (others think him more of a throwback to Ambrose Bierce).[81] In early 2010, he became fascinated by the Anonymous phenomenon, calling it one of "the most important and under-reported social developments to have occurred in decades."[82] When the hack of security contractor HBGary occurred, it provided Brown with a windfall of material for his investigative journalism. Brown was the first to discover HBGary's plot to discredit WikiLeaks and Glenn Greenwald (one of the journalists who broke the Snowden story) with disinformation. But the HBGary information dump was too large for Brown to sift through alone. He repurposed an earlier journalism platform he had started called ProjectPM[83] and created a wiki page where he asked others to delve into the material. Gradually, they exposed a web of links between government agencies, companies, law firms, lobbyists, and shady security and intelligence contractors—what Brown called the "cyber-industrial complex."

When Jeremy Hammond (the Anonymous/LulzSec hacker) hacked private security firm Stratfor in 2011, the data trove was even more disturbing. It showed a Stratfor executive chatting casually about renditions and assassinations.[84] Brown pasted a link to the hacked Stratfor material (which he had found on an Anonymous chat channel) onto the private chat channel for ProjectPM.[85] The hacked documents had already been published by WikiLeaks.[86]

The HBGary documents showed that in November 2010, the law firm Hunton and Williams had brought together a number of private contractors (including Berico, Endgame, HBGary, and Palantir) to form a team that would work on discrediting critics of the Chamber of Commerce.[87] Brown had begun digging to find out more about Endgame, a little known outfit that *Businessweek* had reported on in 2011. "Endgame executives will bring up maps of airports, parliament buildings, and corporate offices. The executives then create a list of the computers running inside the facilities, including what software the computers run, and a menu of attacks that could work against those particular systems," *Businessweek* claimed.[88] As a journalist, Brown had begun to wonder whether foreign actors could buy this information to use against systems in the United States.

Then the FBI raided him.[89] The agents had a warrant to seize Brown's laptop for any information relating to Anonymous, Endgame, and HBGary and any kind of correspondence that might reveal his sources. To pressure him further, they charged his mother (he had been at her house when they made the raid) with obstructing the execution of a warrant.[90]

As mentioned earlier, Jeremy Hammond was quickly arrested, in March 2012, following the hack. Potentially facing thirty years in prison, he took a plea deal and was sentenced to ten years. Arguably, he had been entrapped by the FBI.[91] Brown, the journalist, was facing a sentence of 105 years. Initially, he was charged for pasting the link to the hacked Stratfor material and for credit card fraud (because a few pieces of unencrypted credit card information were found in that large body of material).[92] These charges were later dropped, but the FBI's treatment of Brown, the journalist, sent a strong message to the press from the Obama administration, which had been frustrated in its attempt to extradite WikiLeaks publisher Julian Assange and to shut down his online platform. It also seemed to show that private security contractors could act with impunity to attack citizens and journalists by illegal and nefarious means, whereas the journalists who tried to expose them would face the full force of the law. In early 2015, Brown was sentenced to more than five years in prison for being an accessory after the fact, obstructing justice, and threatening a federal officer, all stemming from the FBI's investigation of the Stratfor leak. He was also sentenced to pay nearly $900,000 in fines and restitution to Stratfor.[93]

In March 2013, Obama's Department of Justice subpoenaed all records on Barret Brown's ProjectPM website from its domain host, CloudFlare. The subpoena asked for the IP addresses of everyone who had accessed or contributed to ProjectPM and described it as a forum through which Brown and others had engaged in, encouraged, or facilitated "the commission of criminal conduct online." Not surprisingly, journalists are afraid to go anywhere near the Stratfor files now.[94]

These successive prosecutions and legal maneuvers by the Obama administration were sobering to the hacker, activist, and journalist communities. But the emotional "high-water mark" of the Obama era crackdown probably came with the prosecution of digital rights activist Aaron Swartz from 2011 to 2013.

Swartz was a whiz kid who at age fourteen was already affiliated with MIT and Harvard. A brilliant programmer and innovator, he was involved in the development of the web feed RSS, the organization Creative Commons, the social news site Reddit, and DeadDrop, an early version of Secure Drop, a now widely used leaking platform.[95] A deeply altruistic individual, he left his lucrative career in tech start-ups to pursue digital rights projects around "open access," the idea that public documents and publicly funded research should be publicly accessible and not sequestered in government or for-profit databases. One of Swartz's first projects was to create a free interface for the public to access court records that had previously been available only through a clunky, pay-for-use platform called Pacer. Then, as part of the academic community at MIT, Swartz used his guest-user access to the academic journals stored in the proprietary database and digital search platform JSTOR to download its entire contents. The FBI obtained a surveillance video that showed Swartz as he connected a computer to the MIT network in an unmarked and unlocked closet and set it to download JSTOR's articles systematically. It was not clear if Swartz intended to use the database for his own research and analysis (as he had used the Pacer court database) or to release it publicly, which would have been illegal.[96]

In July 2011, Swartz was indicted on charges of wire fraud and—under the Computer Fraud and Abuse Act—charges of computer fraud, unlawfully obtaining information from a "protected computer," and recklessly damaging a "protected computer." He faced thirty-five years in prison, $1 million in fines, asset forfeiture, and possible restitution to JSTOR,[97] although the FBI had no proof of intent other than the surveillance video and a political manifesto Swartz had written, titled "Guerilla Open Access Manifesto":[98]

> Information is power. But like all power, there are those who want to keep it for themselves. The world's entire scientific and cultural heritage, published over centuries in books and journals, is increasingly being digitized and locked up by a handful of private corporations. Want to read the papers featuring the most famous results of the sciences? You'll need to send enormous amounts to publishers like Reed Elsevier. …
>
> There is no justice in following unjust laws. It's time to come into the light and, in the grand tradition of civil disobedience, declare our opposition to this private theft of public culture.[99]

Eloquence was not a crime when John Perry Barlow wrote "A Declaration of the Independence of Cyberspace," but in this new period of clampdowns, the FBI took Swartz's manifesto very seriously.

While charges were looming over him, Swartz coordinated the inspired advocacy campaign that successfully challenged the Stop Online Piracy Act (SOPA), the draconian piece of legislation that would have shut down websites without due process for any commission of copyright violation by their users. Swartz and his fellow activists argued SOPA would wreck the internet and allow large monopolies to crush smaller competitors.

Swartz developed software that helped people write to their democratic representatives, and internet users joined his campaign in massive numbers. Four million emails were sent, ten million signatures were collected by Google, eight million phone calls were made, and three million tweets were tweeted. Then, on January 18, 2012, the internet went dark. Wikipedia, Google, Craig's List, websites big and small, hung their "offline" notices on their home pages to show their protest. Using creative images and cutting humor, over 115,000 websites and blogs participated. Like the Danish theaters that protested the Nazi occupation of Denmark by canceling their performances in 1943 and the Czech theaters that passed messages critical of the Communist regime from the stage in 1989, the blackout showed what civil society could withhold from the powerful when it set itself to resist.[100] Legislators quailed and withdrew the SOPA and related Protect IP Act (PIPA) legislation. It was an unprecedented defeat of legislation that had been strongly backed by corporate interests.

In September 2012, federal prosecutors added more felony counts against Aaron Swartz, increasing his potential sentence to fifty years of imprisonment.[101] Swartz rejected a deal that would have given him six months in jail for pleading guilty. Then, in January 2013, after two years of prosecution, Swartz took his own life.[102]

After Swartz's death, prosecutors dropped the charges. JSTOR had withdrawn sometime earlier from the position that charges should be pressed. Swartz's family and supporters criticized MIT as an institution for not using its clout to try to persuade prosecutors to take a less heavy-handed approach.[103] Hackers flying under the name Anonymous hacked two MIT websites and replaced them with tributes to Swartz, and a number of other hacks were made against MIT and a large Swiss academic publisher.[104]

Speaking in the wake of Swartz's death, journalist David Sirota speculated on the Obama administration's agenda in prosecuting someone like Aaron Swartz so aggressively:

> The prosecution of Aaron Swartz in my opinion was about sending a particular, laser-like message to a group of people that the Obama administration sees as politically threatening, and that is, essentially, the hacker, the information and the democracy activist community. And the message that the Obama administration wanted to send to that particular community was in my estimation, "We know you have the ability to make trouble for the Establishment, so we are going to try to make an example out of Aaron Swartz, to scare as many of you as possible into not making that trouble."[105]

The prosecution and subsequent death of Aaron Swartz shocked many in the hacker community. "Hackers for right, we are one down," Tim Berners-Lee wrote. "We've lost one of our own," lamented Larry Lessig, who had been an early mentor of Swartz at Harvard: "We are standing in the middle of a time when great injustice is not touched. Architects of the financial meltdown have dinner with the president regularly. In the middle of that time, the idea that *this* was what the government had to prosecute just seems absurd, if it weren't tragic."[106]

"He was the Internet's own boy. And the old world killed him," Swartz's former girlfriend said simply.[107]

The digital rights movement had its first martyr.

WHERE POWER MEETS ITS LIMITS: THE MAKING OF MARTYRS

The making of martyrs is a story, repeated throughout history, about the limits of power, and social movements that persist and prevail usually have martyrs. By whatever accident or act of stupidity it is done, when power pushes people too far, it strikes the flint of their humanity. Power meets an implacable collective sentiment to which it must, sooner or later, concede.

The US Justice Department made a martyr out of Aaron Swartz and galvanized the digital rights community, including a new generation of millennial activists.

At the end of his term in January 2017, Barack Obama drew back a little from his course and commuted Chelsea Manning's sentence, saving her a possible twenty-eight more years in a federal prison or the more likely fate that she would succeed in killing herself.[108] He was taking a long view of his presidential legacy.

In the Trump era, signs are that the crackdown on hacker transgressions might get even more severe. Although Trump said he loved WikiLeaks during his election campaign and his son Donald Jr. was in contact with the group (tweeting out one of its links[109] in the run-up to the 2016 election), Trump has repeatedly threatened the press and said he is going to "stop the leaks." Building on Obama era precedents, legal prosecution of hacker leakers, hacker whistleblowers, and the journalists who work with them, will be much easier for the Trump administration to carry out. And there are ominous signs that the administration intends to pursue more brutal tactics, too:

> **PRESIDENT DONALD J. TRUMP:** I think he's a total traitor and I would deal with him harshly. ... This guy's a bad guy. And, you know, there is still a thing called execution.
> **JOHN BOLTON [APPOINTED NATIONAL SECURITY ADVISOR IN APRIL 2018]:** My view is that [he] committed treason, he ought to be convicted of that and then he ought to swing from a tall oak tree.
> **SECRETARY OF STATE MIKE POMPEO [FORMER DIRECTOR OF THE CIA]:** He should be brought back from Russia and given due process. And I think the proper outcome would be that he would be given a death sentence.[110]

Trump and his officials are speaking here, of course, about Edward Snowden.

Snowden would become the Nelson Mandela of the digital era, an internationally recognized cultural hero, but as of 2017 and 2018, his fate remained unknown. What might be done to whistleblowing hackers, publisher hackers, and the individual journalists who worked with them remained a pressing question. The Trump administration seemed to be laying the legal groundwork to go after Snowden and, more explicitly, after Julian Assange and his WikiLeaks associates in the furthest degree possible, when it began framing framing WikiLeaks as "a non-state, hostile intelligence service."

The words were first used by CIA Director Mike Pompeo in an April 2017 address at a think tank event.[111] Four months later, it popped up in the reauthorization bill for the 2018 intelligence budget, raising concerns that the term had become government policy: "It is the sense of Congress that WikiLeaks and the senior leadership of WikiLeaks resemble a non-state hostile intelligence service often abetted by state actors and should be treated as such a service by the United States."[112]

The term, "non-state hostile intelligence service" has no legal meaning or precedent, but it seems to portend the use of deadly force against WikiLeaks personnel. Senator Ron Wyden voted against the authorization bill, objecting to the use of the ambiguous label, which, he said, "may have legal, constitutional, and policy implications, particularly should it be applied to journalists inquiring about secrets." The notion that the "US government has some unstated course of action against 'non-state hostile intelligence services' is equally troubling," he emphasized.[113]

In June 2018, Julian Assange would be rotting in the confines of his tiny sanctuary at the Ecuadorian embassy in London for a sixth year, the tragedy of his character being that he would likely never be a Nelson Mandela figure, despite his sacrifices and influential contributions to democratic freedom in the digital age. He had pushed the edges of transgression very far with his leaks during the US election and later with leaks of CIA hacking tools and methods,[114] leading even those who were grateful for his contributions to question his judgment.[115] More damaging to his legacy, perhaps, was that he had offended the morality of a moral movement both in his treatment of women and in his questionable dealings with the Trump campaign.

In 2018, Assange's situation deteriorated. Sweden dropped its charges against him, but the UK confirmed it would arrest him if he stepped outside the embassy on a warrant for illegally skipping bail. A court upheld that warrant in February 2018.[116]

The newly elected Ecuadorian president, Lenin Moreno, was not as sympathetic as Rafael Correa had been toward Assange and referred to Assange's situation as "a stone in his shoe."[117] His government made it a condition of Assange's sanctuary that he refrain from making statements that might interfere in state relations. In addition to meddling in the US election, Assange had become obsessed with the Catalonian independence referendum (in the two weeks leading up to the vote, he sent out over a hundred tweets about it).[118] Under pressure from other governments or for its own reasons, the Ecuadorian government cut off Assange's internet access in March 2018.[119] In May 2018, Moreno ordered the Ecuadorian embassy in London to withdraw the additional security added to protect Assange,[120] even though many threats had been made against Assange's life over his time there and in 2016 a man seen scaling the wall of the embassy had been chased away by the security detail.[121]

In 2018, it seemed only a matter of time before Julian Assange would meet either harsh justice or a more tragic end. And yet one could not help feeling that he might always exist in limbo to prick the ire of the great and the powerful. His resilience, to many, had become comfortingly folkloric.

And what of the social hacking experiments under way? Whether these too are subject to crackdowns will depend on how threatening they are to existing power structures and how hard they fight back.

In Spain, after a surge of suicides related to evictions, the PAH organization had gathered 1.4 million signatures to force the government of Prime Minister Mariano Rajoy to change the mortgage laws, and it went to politicians' homes to protest. The government began attacking Ada Colau and calling members of the PAH "Nazis" and "terrorist sympathizers." When Colau was awarded a European Citizens' Prize, Rajoy's party called it a scandal and demanded the prize be withdrawn. The government tabled draconian new laws that many believed were aimed at Colau and her movement. It proposed stiff fines for those taking part in unauthorized protests or disrupting public events, with fines up to €600,000 for protests near Parliament.[122]

In September 2017, at the time of Catalonia's unilateral referendum on independence, the violence the Rajoy government would use against peaceful protesters was strikingly gratuitous.[123]

However, in the push and pull between the "custodians" and the "corrective feedback" of tech savvy populists, the tables would definitively

turn in favour of the populists. In the May 2018 elections, the Rajoy government fell, brought down by corruption scandals that were, by then,
piled high as the trash in a summer garbage workers' strike. The National
Court judges who sent Rodrigo Rato to prison said they did not believe
Rajoy's testimony in which he denied any knowledge of a secret party
slush fund racket that sent former party treasurer Luis Barcenas to jail for
thirty-three years.[124] The Podemos party, for its part, failed to win enough
seats to form a government or even to force a coalition government. The
leader and the spokesperson of Podemos, Pablo Iglesias and his wife,
respectively, were embroiled in their own scandal, facing criticism about
their acquisition of an expensive villa outside of Madrid. Submitting to
the populist example, the couple would call a plebiscite on whether they
should remain in office.[125]

DEMOCRATIC CONSTITUTIONALISM AS CONVERSATION
LEADING TO ROUGH CONSENSUS

One might argue that the best-functioning constitutional democracies
manage to enact their constitutionalism as a kind of ongoing conversation
between their constituent parts, which allows them to arrive over time
at successive states of rough consensus. Corrective feedback. Rough
consensus. Running code.

Canada is not the paragon democracy some Americans like to
think it is, and yet its history provides at least one good case study of
a well-concluded constitutional conversation. The problem of Quebec
separatism has been a difficult and drawn-out conversation in Canada,
in which Canadians have had to consider what would have to be done
if everyone's needs were to be included in a vision of the country. In the
1970s, members of the separatist Front de Libération du Québec (FLQ)
were blowing up mail boxes. They kidnapped a foreign diplomat and
killed a government minister. The federal government's reaction was
fairly harsh, and separatist sentiment in the province of Quebec grew.

In the early 1990s, a unilateral referendum for separation nearly succeeded. Canada decided to allow a political party that explicitly sought
the break-up of Canada, le Bloc Québecois, to sit as "Her Majesty's loyal
opposition" in Parliament, even though the group's agenda was arguably
treasonous. In 1998, the sitting government asked Canada's Supreme

Court to rule on what a fair referendum question for separation might be so that if another referendum were held, it could be done lawfully.[126]

In the current decade, the country seems finally to have arrived at a peaceful equilibrium with an official acknowledgment of Quebec's nationhood within Canada and numerous policies (old and new) that try to accommodate Quebec's special status in the country. Some collective vision of who Canadians wanted to be as a people evolved and guided the country through these travails. It helped Canadians to listen to each other and finally assimilate corrective feedback constructively.

Entertaining this notion of constitutionalism, it is interesting to reflect on how the Chaos Computer Club has navigated the constitutional conversation in Germany over the last three decades.

As described in the first chapter of this book, the response to computer hackers in Germany hardened in the mid-1980s, as it did in the United States. Sentiment turned against the Chaos Computer Club, and hacking came to be viewed as criminal and a major threat to the economy and infrastructure. The US Counterfeit Access Device and Computer Fraud and Abuse Act was adopted by the Senate in the summer of 1984, and it was held up as a model in German legislative debates.[127] The German Parliament eventually followed the American approach and passed detailed legislation treating hacking as fraud. The preexisting law against fraud in Germany had been deemed inapplicable because it required an interpretation that a hacked computer had been made to err, and it was considered impossible for computers to err.[128] The new legislation spelled out that people were acting illegally if they entered wrong information, manipulated the work flow of programs, changed or blocked accurate data from being processed, and did numerous other specified acts.[129]

But the Chaos Computer Club continued to work to influence expert and public opinion, playing with ideas of ownership, public space, private property, equal access, and shared use in the digital sphere. With the fall of the Berlin Wall in 1989, the group came in step with the cultural moment and began to establish itself as an important civil society fixture in the newly unified Germany and in the freedom culture of Berlin.

In 2008, when members of the CCC stole the fingerprints of the German minister of the interior and distributed them as plastic imprints that could trick biometric readers, they may have been breaching EU personal data protection laws, but one had to admit it was funny. The minister responsible for security had no security. The CCC hackers came off as competent and clever, and the minister was made to look foolish. The prank evinced the Wau Holland ethos of fighting bad uses of technology with technology, humor, and ethics. It was a strategy of "positive," not negative, "chaos."[130]

CCC's hack on Germany's digital voting machines around the same time, in 2006, was a real service to the democratic process in the country and, as noted earlier, led Germany and other European countries to return to paper voting systems. The stunt started when Hamburg-based club members boasted they could make the voting machines play chess. The makers of the machine issued a challenge to prove them wrong, and when the CCC hackers showed that they could, the evidence helped Germany's Federal Constitutional Court decide to strike down the country's use of electronic voting.[131]

"The CCC has greatly contributed to having an informed discussion on cybersecurity and internet governance in Germany," Jan Philipp Albrecht, the German member of the European Parliament and vice chairman of the committee for civil liberties, justice, and home affairs, said in 2017. "Their work on the security issues of voting machines has saved German elections."[132]

Over time, the Chaos Computer Club's serious analysis, tech prowess, and international working relationships positioned its members as go-to experts.

As mentioned earlier, when the German government's procurement of Trojan technology was leaked by WikiLeaks in 2008, the Chaos Computer Club mounted a legal challenge against it. The Federal Constitutional Court of Germany ruled that police could use this kind of "source wiretapping" technology only for internet telephony. Not long after the ruling, the CCC did an analysis of the Staatstrojaner software being used by the German government and found the program had all kinds of extra functionality built into it: it could control a targeted computer, take screenshots, and fetch and run code. This was a violation of the constitutional court's order. CCC found numerous security problems with the software also.[133]

The CCC's findings, published in October 2011, were widely reported in the German press. CCC testified several times before the German Parliament on legislation proposed to govern the technology's use,[134] and when the Staatstrojaner technology was constitutionally challenged again, the Chaos Computer Club was asked to give an advisory opinion to the court.[135]

Over the long history of its engagement, CCC showed it was willing to disobey the law in the spirit of peaceful, nondestructive civil disobedience (the 1984 Bildschirmtext hack, for example), but the group has generally evinced a strong respect for democratic values, distinguishing its members from libertarian or nihilistic hackers. This has included explicit advocacy for the payment of government taxes in order to realize a shared commonwealth and for liberal constitutionalism. Recall the discussion on the "You Broke the Internet" website.[136]

Following the Snowden leaks, as mentioned earlier, CCC made German complicity in spying done by the US's National Security Agency (NSA) a "rule of law" issue, filing a criminal complaint in 2014 against the German government for aiding foreign spying by the NSA and its British counterpart, the Government Communications Headquarters (GCHQ). Without fear or apology, the club invited Edward Snowden, by then a fugitive from US law, to give testimony as a witness.

Whether or not Germans agree with the Chaos Computer Club on every issue, the group commands respect for the long conversation it has sustained with government, the media, and the public since the 1980s about the social consequences of technology, especially when it would have been easy for them to sell out and cash in on their technical prowess. To the extent there is a thoughtful conversation going on in Germany and Europe today about society and technology, it owes a lot to the contributions the CCC has made over the years in the way of corrective feedback.

The authority of CCC's "feedback" was proven most recently when the German digital rights community was able to quickly check the misguided investigation and potential prosecution of two journalists for the crime of "treason" in the Netzpolitik affair. The affair was still swirling at the time of the 2015 Chaos Communication Camp.

The two journalists were contributors to a policy blog called Netzpolitik and had leaked information and documents about the German government's planned expansion of state surveillance. The prosecutor, Harald Range, was looking into whether they had betrayed "state secrets" when they reported that the government had new plans to monitor Twitter and Facebook chats, as well as a €2.75 million project "to process massive online data sets."[137]

There is, of course, no more serious crime in the legal lexicon than "treason." The last time a journalist had been accused of treason in Germany had been in 1962, when the Minister of Defense accused journalists at *Der Spiegel* of publishing state secrets.[138]

The digital rights community responded vigorously. More than two thousand people marched in support of the journalists, and Netzpolitik received €100,000 in donations within a few days. CCC and others organized an open letter of support for the journalists, signed by Julian Assange, Glenn Greenwald, Andy Müller-Maguhn, and dozens of other journalists from around the world.[139]

The Minister of Justice intervened and told the prosecutor that the legal opinion he had solicited from an academic consultant was incorrect: the information leaked did not constitute a state secret.[140] But the digital rights community and the Green Party questioned why the Minister of Justice and Chancellor Angela Merkel had been so tardy: they had allowed the prosecutor to proceed for two and a half months before stopping him, and therefore they must also answer for this anti-democratic attack on press freedom.[141] The minister sacked the prosecutor.[142] The public uproar continued; the minister was accused of having scapegoated the prosecutor on political grounds.[143] Then, on August 10, the federal prosecution service dropped the charges against the journalists.[144]

Markus Beckedahl, founder of Netzpolitik and one of the journalists involved in the scandal, wrote that

> The attention and the public debate have protected us. We hope that the attempted intimidation against us and all other journalists who report on the surveillance complex and the NSA [National Security Agency] scandal has failed on a grand scale. If that is so, this confrontation has strengthened journalism in Germany. ...

"Now would also be the right time to discuss improved whistleblower protection. Germany is still a developing country in this area," he added.[145]

This occurred just days before the start of the 2015 Chaos Communication Camp, where Beckedahl and his colleague came to celebrate the victory, dissect the case, and plan how to continue the national conversation. They were part of a keynote presentation kicking off the first day of the camp, held in a big top tent bursting at the seams with people.

12

MAINSTREAMING HACKERDOM
A New Condition of Freedom

A CITY UPON A HILL

The Boston-Cambridge area in Massachusetts, where the hacker story began, has been a high tech hub longer than Silicon Valley.[1] It is also a hub for higher learning—Boston College, Brandeis, Harvard, MIT, Northeastern, Suffolk, Tufts—the list is long. The area is densely populated. From an airplane at night, the lights of the Eastern seaboard stretch like jeweled tissue an immense distance along the coast. This is the brain center of the American continent.

It is also the birthplace of the American creation myth, Massachusetts being the place where the first Congregationalists landed to settle in the New World—a landscape that prompts one to ruminate on the ardor with which Americans have historically regarded their democracy. Even as their ships carried them to these shores, these early migrants gathered on deck to pledge themselves to a new way of being. On the *Mayflower*, they pledged themselves to the principle of rule under law by the consent of the governed.[2] On the *Arbella*, they prayed to build a new society that would set an example of communal affection and unity. Their settlement in New England would be like "a city upon a hill," watched by all humankind. They would show the world that through God's grace the wicked could be restrained "so that the rich and mighty should not eat up the poor" and "the poor and despised" should not be compelled "to rise up against and shake off their yoke." They, "the regenerate," would model the interdependence of men and show that "every man might have need of others." Indeed, theirs would be a society built on the "bond of love."[3]

And if they failed? Their city upon a hill, their leader John Winthrop warned, would "be made a story and a by-word through the world" of God's judgment.[4]

Congregationalism was named for its innovation in governance. Congregationalists disintermediated bishops and presbyteries and emphasized the right and responsibility of each congregation to decide its own affairs without having to submit to any higher earthly authority.[5] The Congregationalists believed democracy was a form of government required by God. Having started their movement of democratization in the Church, they went on to have a profound influence on early American democracy. The democratic tradition begun in the first Plymouth Colony was soon followed by the Massachusetts Bay Colony, Connecticut, Rhode Island, New Jersey, and Pennsylvania.[6]

Boston and Cambridge would become the cradle of American democracy, fomenting the American Revolution against the British monarchy. American tourists still flock here to follow the "Freedom Trail" of the Revolution and marvel at the daring men and women who created their nation.

This part of North America is and always has been in earnest. Throughout the 1800s, early abolitionists and reformers of all kinds lectured, met, and organized here. Walking through the streets of Beacon Hill, one can't help thinking of Henry James's descriptions of these early do-gooders after the Civil War, picture them bustling down the modest brick sidewalks by gas lamplight, off to the African Meeting House, the Baptist church, and the Athenaeum. Meeting in each other's homes. Striving to manifest morality in politics.

The past is never far from mind in this geography, but it is the opportunities and conundrums of digital society that are the bleeding edge focus of every elite institution in Boston and Cambridge now. Every one of them has a program, an angle, and hacker-themed projects. Just look at their websites.

The Harvard Business School's website states that its Digital Initiative

> studies the digital transformation of the economy, and seeks to shape it by equipping leaders and engaging our community with cutting-edge research.

As a think/do start-up at Harvard Business School, D/I brings together leading scholars and practitioners to explore the re-invention of business in a digital, networked, and media-rich environment. We traverse disciplines, methods, sectors, and communities to develop and share novel insights, approaches, and values in this evolving space.

As a statement of purpose, it is a bit "everywhere and nowhere," as John Perry Barlow might say:

We think about the changes spurred and facilitated by the digital transformation in three key layers: economics and strategy, organizations and culture, and individual skills and capabilities.

In fact, reading it to the end is a little like chewing dry meal, but it is an excellent specimen of the genre:

Our expansive view of "Digital" encompasses technologically-based phenomena such networks, media, mobile, data, cloud services, as well as the associated strategies, gatekeepers, leaders, crowds, creators, designers, platforms, and property rights that are every bit as important. The interactions among them are what excites us most.

D/I is informed by the values and practices from the Internet ecosystem, embracing the potential of networks and platforms, embodying the virtues of user-centered design and agile development, and knowing the power of design-thinking, collaboration, openness, and interoperability. We revel in our service as an HBS innovation test-bed. We endeavor to experiment, to create and facilitate new conversation and co-creation, ultimately fostering exploration of the intersections among disciplines, methods, sectors, and geographies.

To be fair, there are so many directions this new digital world could go that the number of research projects, academic careers, and business applications that could be generated over the rest of the century is boggling.

Since the 2016 presidential election, the Kennedy School for Public Administration at Harvard has changed its webpages' emphasis from stressing the importance of centralized global governance structures to highlighting issues such as citizen participation, transparency, collaborative solutions, elite capture of democratic processes, and the democratic potential of cities. "Millions are disappointed with their elected leaders, frustrated about an economy that does not work for them, and angry at elites they view as self-serving," the website paraphrases the dean as saying. "There is no greater public problem today than the lack of trust in our political and economic systems, and there is no more important challenge than restoring that confidence."[7] The Kennedy School has "Technology and Democracy" fellowships, and it has run a #Hack4Congress project:

> While the founders of the American republic may have conceived Congress as the linchpin of our democracy—the branch of government closest and most responsible to the people—few would argue that our contemporary Congress shares much in common with this early republican ideal. ...
> ... Congress needs "fixes"—but where will these new tools and solutions come from? By bringing together political scientists, technologists, designers, lawyers, and lawmakers under the banner of #Hack4Congress, the Ash Center hopes to foster new digital tools, policy innovations, and other technology innovations to address the growing dysfunction in Congress.[8]

MIT's Media Lab has some of the more thoughtful webpages. In one video, Joi Ito, then director of the Lab, explains,

> AI's rapid development brings along a lot of tough challenges. For example, one of the most critical challenges is how do we make sure that the machines we "train" don't perpetuate and amplify the same human biases that plague society? How can we best initiate a broader, in-depth discussion about how society will co-evolve with this technology, and connect computer science and social sciences to develop intelligent machines that are not only "smart," but also socially responsible?

LIBRE PLANET, THE HEART OF FREE SOFTWARE

I have finally arrived in Boston. I want to see what's going on at these institutions. It seems that a mainstreaming of hacker experiments has begun within academia and is gaining momentum especially within the Boston-Cambridge hub. What does this augur for hacking? What are the prevailing ideas about where we are headed? And how do academics think progressive hackers and citizens might succeed or fail in building democracy out into cyberspace?

It is March 2017, and the number of hacker-themed events taking place here in this month alone is dizzying. It's a schedule that would challenge the stamina of the most fervent Boston reformer. Among other things, the 2017 Libre Planet conference is happening this week. This is the annual conference put on by Richard Stallman's Free Software Foundation. I plan to go there first, to see Stallman in the flesh and walk the halls of MIT where the first hackers lived and breathed code around the early mainframe computers of the late 1950s.

The Libre Planet conference kicks off with a party at the Free Software Foundation offices in Boston and a Chinese dinner hosted by FSF for female participants. I arrive at their location in Franklin Street on a crisp, black night, and jostle up the stairs to the second floor. *Wired* writer Steven Levy once depicted Richard Stallman as a beleaguered survivor of a dying hacker culture,[9] but happily, that is no longer the case. The place is packed, with people squeezing down hallways, draped across the boardroom table, and busily attending the beer table. And there is a surprising number of women, and older hackers, a real mixture of types, some looking like clean-cut Washington aides and others more alternative. I talk for a while with a young hacker from Seattle sporting a large beard and a kilt, then briefly with someone who worked for the Clinton campaign, or was it the Democratic National Committee, and says the United States is no match for the sophistication of Russian hackers. Then I trickle out with about twenty other women and we go off to enjoy copious amounts of Chinese food at a favorite hacker restaurant, where I end up arguing amiably with a virulent libertarian all night. After swearing she (herself a single mother) would gladly let me and my kids die in the street if I were unlucky enough to find myself unemployed like so many others these days, she kindly buys my train ticket at the end of the evening when I'm caught short of US cash, saving me a late-night walk across the Boston Common.

The next morning, I take the train from Boston over the Charles River to Cambridge: first stop MIT, Kendall Square. As I climb the stairs of the station to street level, the campus architecture seems to float above me, light and slightly futuristic. There are vast, quiet spaces to walk between buildings, with none of the hubbub of the Harvard quadrangle. Many MIT buildings have names but tend to be known by their assigned numbers, including the one where I am headed—the architecturally adventurous Stata Building, number 32.

I register for the Libre Planet conference and pick up the schedule. Marvin Minsky's AI Group, the academic home that harbored the "golden age" of hacking at MIT in the 1960s and 70s (becoming the AI Lab in 1970), merged in 2003 with the Laboratory for Computer Science to form CSAIL, short for the Computer Science and Artificial Intelligence

Laboratory. CSAIL has been located in the Stata Building since 2004. I ought to be visiting its offices, but for now I imagine the group like a recent release of an original program I will download later.[10]

One of the conference sessions I want to attend is located in an older building next door. As I wander across a side passage to scope it out, I look again at the schedule, realizing with a tingle that this is Building 26. Building 26, where the earliest hackers tinkered and the object of their desire, the TX-0, was housed on the second floor.[11] The hallway has the polished linoleum, metal doors, and retro feel of a 1950s high school. The posters on the bulletin board outside the Games Lab reveal the current millennial cohort's political preoccupations:

> Noam Chomsky
> Racing to the Precipice: Global Climate, Political Climate
> March 23, 2017
> 5–6 pm

> Voices of Resistance
> Dario Fo
> Accidental Death of an Anarchist
> March 21, 2017
> Free

> Isn't God a Moral Monster?
> March 7, 2017
> Free dinner served

> Change the World
> Major or Minor in Political Science
> MIT Poli Sci

The Libre Planet conference agenda shows that the free software community is hard at work with a multitude of hacking projects. One session is optimistically named "The Cloud Is Dead." But the talk I'm most looking forward to is Eben Moglen's, near the end of the day. As a young constitutional attorney and Columbia University law professor, Moglen volunteered to defend Phil Zimmermann for exporting PGP (Pretty Good Privacy) cryptography in the 1990s.[12] Then, as Moglen relates the story, Richard Stallman called him up and said he had a few legal issues he needed help on. Moglen replied that he had been using Stallman's GNU Emacs program[13] every day for years, so it would be a long while before he got to the limit of the free legal advice he could offer Stallman.

And so began a long friendship and collaboration between the two. Moglen worked out the legal wording for Stallman's Copyleft license. He started the Software Freedom Law Center at Columbia University, which provides pro-bono legal services to developers of free, Libre, and open-source software. His Freedom Box project aims to put a personal server into everyone's home so that users can avoid the privacy-gouging business models of commercial internet service providers (ISPs). Moglen himself was a hacker when very young. More recently, he led the legal side of drafting Stallman's new GPLv3 license and organized a public comments process for people to critique it.

Moglen has likened the current mass surveillance engaged in by governments and businesses to an environmental disaster, like air or water pollution. He sees it as the environmental destruction of people's freedom, and in his opinion, a few laws or even hacker tools are not going to solve it. It will take a number of major governments and big companies rejecting the whole model of "surveillance capitalism" to turn things around.

He begins his talk at the Libre Planet conference with a recitation of recent dystopian events, including the election of Donald Trump,[14] and addresses the members of the audience as if they were his old friends: "We are at the place, I would say, for which the free software movement exists. This is really what it was that motivated a bunch of young people to take a fairly abrupt view of how technology ought to be designed and operated—because of this. Because of the possibility of this."

He suggests that the free software movement has done a great deal among governments and industry to mainstream the idea that users of technology have rights. It is the one basic public-policy point, he says, that you can make around the world today to almost everybody to good effect:

> And we have positioned ourselves as the experts on what it means for users to have rights. We have a whole bunch of answers to real practical questions on what would it mean for users to have rights.
>
> Copyleft is part of those answers, and GNU, and a series of philosophical and political positions about technology are part of those answers. [But] those answers are still way more than most of the rest of the world wants to receive. A drink from a fire hose, in two senses: too geeky for most of the world's decision-makers and most of the world's users and too uncompromising for a whole bunch of people who are

within organizations or social structures which make it hard for them to agree with us as completely as they would like to because there are real impediments to doing that—the interests of their businesses, the natures of their livelihoods, the dependencies that they themselves have on the things that we would urge them not to be dependent upon, and so on.

Which has meant that all my life doing this, most of us did fit in this room, where it was always a pleasure to see people and it's a pleasure to see you now, and it's wonderful to see so many old friends. But here we are.

And in a conversational tone we can say that for the last couple of years we have been watching the world come to a crisis about which we know an awful lot. Which doesn't mean we can do an awful lot. We have, after all, got a really serious problem at the moment because even though the thing we're dealing with feels exactly like what we have grown up to be to deal with it, the scale of it has escaped our ability to believe that we're going to be effective very quickly.

And the question "What can we really do?" is the one that's resounding within our crania. We can *do*, but what can we *really* do about a mess this big? Which in truth is where we are.

Moglen hardly breathes between sentences, and his talk is such an intimate reveal of a veteran hacker's thoughts in conversation with other hackers that I feel compelled to write down every word in order to capture the urgency of it. He continues:

We have now before us the greatest teachable moment in our history as a movement with respect to everybody else. There are more people out there in the world who would be receptive to a message about why users of technology have rights and why those users' rights are so crucially important to the survival of political liberty. There are more people out there who want that message than have ever wanted it in all our time.

It began with Snowden, to be sure. But even that is now comparatively small in scale to the global anxiety felt largely by young, relatively technologically adept people, who feel two things happening—societies slipping out of control around them to their own immediate disservice and a whole bunch of things going on that they themselves are a part of but that they know are not quite right.

They feel it about Facebook. They feel it about Twitter. They understand why the deliberative quality of the world around them seems to be falling apart, but they don't exactly know how their own social media habits contribute to that falling apart.

They do understand that they're being watched all the time. ... They do know that there is something wrong with it. ... And they would love to hear something can be done that isn't as desperate as "the red pill." ...

They would really like to hear that you don't have to give up everything you've ever done in order to get behind the Matrix and save the world.

The audience chuckles.

"So, what can we really do? Actually, I need to rephrase the question," Moglen says, leaving us hanging for a beat in suspense:

> What can we *really* do before otherwise we *do* get wiped out? I do need to point that out. We really *are* in the world we always thought we would be. When Richard called it slavery, it wasn't a metaphor. It was simply an archaic political term for what it is like living in a world in which machines that you can't understand and you can't modify and you can't do anything about control you and everybody else.

"What if Google does replace the Linux kernel in Android with a non-free kernel?" he asks the audience. "Users would have no rights at the bottom of the only mobile computing stack in which they have any rights." Or what if we lived in cashless societies and "citizen rating" determined what you pay and when you get it or if you get it at all?

> Let me tell you what the result is. It's called slavery. But it doesn't feel like that because it feels like inconvenience. It feels like friction in life, and if only you would be subconsciously adjusting to be a more compliant person, it would get more convenient. I hope you do understand that that's a much better way to run a despotism than running a gulag. … So what can we *do*?

He says (and I'm paraphrasing here) that we can save Copyleft—the idea that users have rights that can be vindicated in law and by broad consensus—because governments and other crucial research funders are beginning to discriminate against projects that want to use Copyleft. We can get tools into the hands of ordinary people who want to be free. They have to be built for purpose, and they have to be usable and ready to go.

This is no time for us to be in one of our purist or perfectionist moods, he says. We have to deliver the bits right now to people we want to be our allies. We need to get into the schools. We need to start teaching people how to think about the technology now and let the technology catch up to their educated expectations. We need to pass on our ideas to eight- and twelve- and sixteen-year-old people.

We do have a Snowden generation of people who were eleven, twelve, and thirteen when Edward Snowden came along. They were born at the beginning of the twenty-first century, and psychographically they look quite different from the people around them. According to Moglen, "They were very affected by Mr. Snowden—as I said, I think because he looks so much like Harry Potter, but perhaps for other reasons too—and what they learned there is going to provide an important opportunity for us when they grow up in another five years." If we have bits to offer them then, "in sort of shiny packages"—code that offers real freedom and real privacy—they will take them up in a heartbeat. "And I know manufacturers around the world who know that, too."

So we have to educate the consumers of the near future. We are two product cycles out on the guys building stuff. He does think that Android will be an enclosed system by then, he says, and "should that be true, we'll have had to do a lot of consumer education for things that don't quite exist yet but that we *must* have."

RICHARD STALLMAN AND THE FREE SOFTWARE FOUNDATION AWARDS

Eben Moglen leaves the stage to great applause, and a little later Richard Stallman—the man himself—shuffles to the table beside the lectern and sits down. I've seen him more than once that day, striding off with others and looking too busy to interrupt. And now he is here to give out the annual Free Software Foundation awards.

The first part of his talk is aimed at sorting out a few doctrinal points. He speaks to the audience in an avuncular manner that reminds me of how Wau Holland used to address younger members of the Chaos Computer Club.

> Now I want to criticize a couple of the talks today which labeled things with the name of a despicable person. ... [This is] one of those details where I occasionally disagree with Eben. Our "age" is not the age of Trump. No, there's a lot more going on in our age than him. What makes these more than a slight mistake is that they assign to him a bigger victory than he really had, essentially declaring us defeated when we're still fighting [he says, his inflection rising in an encouraging tone].
>
> So don't say that he trumps anything. In fact, I suggest usually not using his name. I typically call him the troll or the cheater or the liar or the loser because he actually lost the election. ...[15]
>
> Now, we face a fight that's gone on for decades, and we're nowhere near complete victory. It may go on for more decades, so the most important

point is to remind people what we're fighting for. ... We're fighting for freedom, and we want complete success for freedom. We want to free everyone. We want to escape from nonfree software. ...

Even when we compromise and tolerate something that's intolerable, we have to remember and tell each other that it is intolerable and that that's a battle that we're going to have to fight and win someday. ...

When it comes to big data, often we see the wrong approach by mainstream human rights organizations. Their first thought is to put limits on its permissible use. ... But when a hero is designated as a spy or a traitor, the government will always give itself permission to use that data to catch the hero.

I'm talking about people like Edward Snowden. Let's have three cheers for Edward Snowden!

Without a moment's hesitation, he leads the crowded amphitheatre in a spontaneous cheer:

Hip hip.

"HOORAY!" [everyone yells enthusiastically].

Hip hip.

"HOORAY!!"

Hip hip.

"HOOORAY!!!"

"For a democracy, we have to forbid that data from ever being collected. ... Data, once collected, will be misused."

Now, one of the vital things that we need to do is reverse engineering, so we've decided to do more to encourage people to do it. It's very hard to do, but if you're clever, you can find a way to do it. We have some priorities, which you'll find on the GNU website.

And to recognize people who do this hard job, we plan to give out a reverse engineering medal from time to time. We don't have one now, but when someone does a heroic job, we'll give one out.

People chuckle, and Stallman goes on to cover some of the technical problems the Free Software Foundation is looking at now, including tools for buying digital books anonymously and free software security patches for the internet of "stings" (he's a punster) and for sites that can be run only with nonfree Javascript.

When the time for the awards arrives, Stallman stands to give them out: "The 2016 award for the advancement of free software goes to a true champion of free software—Alexandre Oliva!" Stallman describes how Oliva has contributed to GNU and even liberated the Brazilian taxpayer by creating a free software program to replace the government's proprietary one.

A lovely, big, shambling guy with a head of black curly hair tinged with gray comes up to receive the award, chuffing with emotion and possibly crying:

> Thank you, this is such a wonderful dream. Please do not wake me up. Are you sure it's not moonlight or Miss Columbia or Philippines? This is too good to be true!
>
> I first met GNU in 1991. That was just before Linux was published. So I really met GNU, and I fell in love at first sight.
>
> But five years later, I met Richard, and that defined the rest of my life. It was so inspiring to hear that technology was not just "nology." There was an ethical aspect, and there were social aspects. They were a lot more important than everything I learned before. So I sort of didn't have a choice.

He pauses here, looking down at the floor to gather his words. "I learned that I would have to work on it from that point on. And I did. But I was never sure what I was doing was right because—here he sighs heavily, not once but twice—"I'm so insecure, I'm so … ," he trails off. "This award means a lot to me because it tells me that something I was doing was *right*."

He pronounces the last word in such a mild yet emotional tone that the crowd stands up in an extended ovation that is so warm it makes my heart feel three times bigger.

When the awards are over and everyone is chatting and gathering their stuff to leave, Stallman calls out, "Look at GNU.org/help to see a list of various kinds of work we need people to do! … There will be something there for everyone's capacity."

PROS, CONS, AND DISOBEDIENCE AWARDS

Richard Stallman's Free Software Foundation is one moderately sized nonprofit organization struggling to promote the cause of free software and develop hacker tools. It is closely connected to the hacker scene and has loose affiliations with academia. As larger academic institutions like Harvard and MIT jump into the mix, embracing the hacker ethos and setting up programs for hacker-themed work, three things become apparent.

First, these institutions underscore the rising significance of hacking with their interest in the phenomenon.

Second, these institutions are mainstreaming hacking by raising elite and popular awareness of it and by leveraging new resources and respectability for hacker experiments. You know cultural mainstreaming is going on when the Chaos Computer Club is lauded in Bloomberg News as a new hero that the US Democratic Party might wish it had on its block:

> The Hackers Russia-Proofing Germany's Elections: The Chaos Computer Club, a multigenerational army of activists, has made the country's democracy a lot tougher to undermine.
> ... The loose confederation of about 5,500 hackers isn't a bunch of bored teens in it for the lulz. Its 29 local chapters are stocked with professionals who run security for banks, head encryption startups, and advise policymakers. The group publishes an occasional magazine, produces a monthly talk radio show, and throws the occasional party, too.
> All this has made CCC into something that sounds alien to American ears: a popular, powerful, tech-focused watchdog group.[16]

And you know there is mainstreaming going on when MIT's Media Lab creates a Disobedience Award. This was one of Joi Ito's innovations a number of years after taking over the job of director there. Carrying a cash prize of $250,000 and funded by Reid Hoffman, cofounder of LinkedIn, the Disobedience Award is being offered for the first time in 2017. It will be handed out for "responsible disobedience" across any discipline, including scientific research, civil rights, freedom of speech, human rights, and the freedom to innovate.[17] In a promotional video for the award, Reid Hoffman says, "My hope is that the prize helps us understand the way that we make progress as a society and as humanity is by recognizing the right heroes who take personal risks, and sometimes that risk is a form of disobedience to help us evolve as humanity." Martha Minow, dean of Harvard Law School,[18] says in the video, "Social movements, political movements, legislation, art, education, all contribute to changes in human consciousness. That's what produces the conception of rights, and it's in the light of demand for rights that rights become real." Martin Luther King Jr. is quoted. Even Malala Yousafzai says something. Joi Ito summarizes, "Questioning authority and thinking for yourself is an essential component of science, of civil rights, of society. At some level, civil disobedience is at the root of a lot of ... creativity."

Ito himself has the cherished identity of a "creative" and an "innovator" in the tech world, and he is in many ways the ultimate mainstreaming and crossover figure between the various tech subcultures, hacking included. He was an early investor in Flickr, Kickstarter, Twitter, and a host of other start-ups, which made him wealthy. He obtained his education in unorthodox ways, pursuing undergraduate degrees in computing and physics but finishing neither[19] and taking online courses instead from the New School for Social Research.[20] As a young man, he worked as a disc jockey in the alternative scene in Chicago and started a nightclub in Japan, where he helped to introduce rave culture. Timothy Leary "adopted" him as a godson. He worked for a time in traditional media before pivoting to start the first commercial internet service provider in Japan. He became a tech blogger and was on the early editorial mastheads of both *Mondo 2000* and *Wired* magazine.

Associated with the "free culture movement," which advocates against strict copyright laws and for the free exchange and remixing of created material, he became chairman of Creative Commons, where he served for more than five years. He has sat on the boards of ICANN, Mozilla's Open Source Initiative, and Sony and more recently the Knight Foundation, the MacArthur Foundation, and the The New York Times Company.[21] He has spoken at the World Economic Forum, lunched privately with President Obama, visited Tunisia weeks after the Arab Spring revolution, and gone to the Vatican to talk with Catholic clergy about ethics. He is like the Forrest Gump of tech in that he seems to show up everywhere. *Foreign Policy* magazine named him one of the top global thinkers: he told them the "best idea" was "users controlling their own data."[22] Soon after coming to MIT, he introduced mindfulness meditation training to the Media Lab.[23] He may be hacking the institution itself.

Not to get carried away, I remind myself that over the last few decades universities have for the most part become, and resiliently remain, corporate-style enterprises. When I call Ito's office to make an appointment to speak to him, I am told that he is booked up for March and April before he leaves for paternity leave. He might be willing to answer some questions by email, but his (very nice) assistant has to speak with the Communications Department first. In the twenty-first-century university, this is not surprising. Even regional universities have

Communications Departments that intercede to protect the corporate reputation, enforce the branding, reassure the sponsors, and vet communications products.[24]

There may be a Media Lab Disobedience Award, but no university has yet stepped forward to become the public custodian for the complete (published and unpublished) Snowden archive. Some academics have looked into it, but they have not taken on the responsibility: it's hard enough to get their institutions to confer an honorary doctorate on Snowden. Snowden himself has suggested that a certain unnamed public university with a center that has the technical capability to protect the archive (perhaps the University of Toronto's Citizen Lab?) had been asked by a certain unnamed news organization (perhaps Laura Poitras and Glenn Greenwald's *The Intercept*?) to become the repository for the documents. "And," said Snowden, "they said, 'Whoa!! That is too hot for us!'"[25] In a similar vein, the Harvard Kennedy School granted Chelsea Manning a fellowship when she was released from prison but rescinded it when CIA director Mike Pompeo canceled an appearance there and sent a scathing letter to the administration stating it was "shameful of Harvard to put its stamp of approval on her actions."[26]

And here is the third thing that is apparent in the increasing institutional embrace of hacking: universities' agendas do not always align with hackers'. Harry Halpin has said a problem arises when academics become the gatekeepers of what gets pursued. Large project funding is usually funneled through universities if it is not purely commercial, and only academics are eligible to receive it. Other hacker concerns are that academia itself has an increasingly extractive business model. Corporate sponsors may exploit the university as a public institution, and well-paid professors may exploit hackers as employees and contributors. Conflicts of interest may arise when ideas are commercialized. The very platform billionaires who have skimmed the wealth out of the digital economy are often the ones giving money to universities to fix the system. Large, philanthropic funding depends on the whims and biases of the donor class and is not a deliberative and systemic response by society. Given the profound impact that digital technology and platforms will have on all of our futures, do we want to continue with such an approach?

Take one complicated example. Reid Hoffman, Pierre Omidyar, the Knight Foundation, and the Hewlett Foundation have recently donated

$27 million to set up the Ethics and Governance of Artificial Intelligence Initiative with the MIT Media Lab and the Harvard Berkman Klein Center for Internet & Society. It is "a global initiative to advance AI research for the public good." Part of its purpose is to put money into the hands of universities so that they can look at these problems in a more disinterested way than the tech industry can itself, which is running a similar but private initiative called OpenAI.[27]

This is another partnership between Hoffman and Ito, and it is interesting to watch the many videos that the two fellow venture capitalists, friends, and "thought partners" have done separately and together. They talk about steering toward a digital utopia instead of a dystopia. And yet there are contradictions, even a certain tone deafness.

In one 2016 video, they agree that to adapt to the accelerating change and unpredictability of the digital age, individuals, organizations, and businesses need to embrace "risk over safety." To illustrate, they launch into an enthusiastic discussion of their venture capitalist approach in which they make "a set of bets" with a fixed downside (a fraction of your capital—say, $5 to $10 million you can afford to lose), and "the game" is to find one of those "unicorns" like Uber or Airbnb that with network effects will take off in a "superlinear" curve and make you "a massive winner."[28]

In the video, they don't talk about the social distribution of risk in this kind of job-killing, monopoly-platform, casino economy. They do not talk about the risk of systemic collapse. They seem not to grasp that, for the listener, it is not the least edifying to hear that cocky traders in unicorns have taken over the economy and *they* are comfortable embracing risk over safety.

Toward the end of this video, Ito does say, "We have growth in nature," and it is usually controlled, but if it gets out of balance, we call it a tumor. We have certain "capitalist-DNA based tumors," he says, that need to be addressed but without eliminating capitalism itself.[29]

His own biases as a venture capitalist aside, how could Ito talk about the risk of systemic collapse or eliminating capitalism when the Media Lab is primarily funded by a consortium of ninety capitalist corporations?[30] Corporations that pay membership fees of $250,000 a year that entitle them to share in any commercialization of Media Lab research?[31]

MIT'S MEDIA LAB

On a dreary day, I walk into the place itself. The Media Lab's silver-skinned atrium is six stories high, and inside it looks like an early iPod, with the kind of white, minimalist design Steve Jobs perfected for Apple. Covering one wall is a large triptych. It's a panoramic photograph of Marvin Minsky's home. A founder of MIT's Artificial Intelligence Lab (not to be confused with the Media Lab, which opened a decade and a half later, in 1985), Minsky was known for fostering hackerism at MIT in any way he could.[32] There has been a recent memorial celebration of his life and career at the institution and the triptych is a temporary exhibit. In stark contrast to the minimalism of the Media Lab building, his living space, displayed here, is a riot of color and curious objects.

Wired writer Steven Levy once described the MIT Media Lab as "the smarty pants citadel of digital creativity."[33] The names of the Media Lab "groups"—Affective Computing, Civic Media, Human Dynamics, Lifelong Kindergarten, Scalable Cooperation, Social Machines, and Viral Communications—are displayed on a touch-screen directory beside curvy, branding symbols, each of which is meant to represent the letters "ML" in a distinctive way. As I ride a glass-walled elevator up to the top floor, I catch glimpses of creative behavior on passing floors. The word *media* in Media Lab's name stands for "stuff," and *lab* stands for the interdisciplinary approach the place takes toward engineering problems. Its website states: "We are an antidisciplinary research lab working to invent the future of #" with a rotating stream of words that float into the space following the hashtag and decorously disappear—"engineering," "hacking," "extended intelligence," "trust," "wellbeing," "crypto currency," "consumer electronics," "3d printing," "privacy," "open source," "perception," "art," "space," "agriculture."[34]

I've come to observe an event hosted by the director of the Media Lab's Human Dynamics Group and an eminent name in engineering, Sandy Pentland.[35] One of his collaborations, with John Clippinger, is called the Institute for Innovation & Data Driven Design (ID3). ID3 is a nonprofit organization and its website states it was "formed to develop and field test legal and software trust frameworks for distributed, self-signing digital assets, currencies, and data-driven services, infrastructures, and enterprises."[36] Clippinger, a research scientist at the MIT Media Lab and former senior fellow at Harvard's Berkman Center for Internet & Society (now called the Berkman Klein Center for Internet & Society), is also a veteran of the AI Lab (he was a graduate student there in the early 1970s) and of the student movement of the 1960s and 1970s.

Clippinger's online descriptions of the ID3 project sound very twenty-first-century hackerish and quite similar to Tim Berners-Lee's "Solid" project over at CSAIL. Like Solid, ID3 aims to build a new "redecentralized" internet at the applications layer, on top of the physical infrastructure of the existing internet. Clippinger has some intriguing things to say about the way law and governance will change in this new ecosystem. Conventional law and policy-making, Clippinger says, are

> too ham-fisted, slow moving, impractical, and unenforceable to address the robust needs of commerce and social life on open networks. In a sense, law itself must be re-conceptualized if it is to function well in networked environments. Now is the time to engineer a great leap forward to digital, network-native forms of law, where rule of law derives from the collective sentiments of a given community or network of users and functions in a more algorithmic, and self-executing way.[37]

Clippinger suggests that the ID3 platform will be able to handle the smallest of user ambitions to the largest—say, from neighborhood carpooling to social media apps to creating job markets, distributing basic necessities, starting commercial enterprises, and even establishing new kinds of financial institutions. It will "enable sustainable, bottom-up forms of governance to take root and grow." Clippinger posits that

> Ever since Hobbes proposed the State as the only viable alternative to the dread state of nature, citizens have entered into a notional "social contract" with "the Leviathan" to protect their safety and basic rights. But what if networked technologies using the Social Stack could enable individuals to negotiate a very different sort of social contract (or contracts)? What if digital systems enabled people to band together into quasi-autonomous governance units for mutual protection and provisioning without resorting to government while reaping superior forms of services and protection?[38]

Elsewhere, John Clippinger has enthusiastically embraced the writing of the great American jurist Oliver Wendell Holmes Jr. for his description of the evolutionary nature of the common law. "So it didn't have a fixed, logical form," Clippinger has reflected, "but it was really a form of how you create social cohesion, expression, and ordering. ... This notion of a living law ... decentralized, distributed, reinventing itself, adapting to its local terms ... how do you design systems like that?"[39] Clippinger is aware, no doubt, that the common law, like computer technology, is not a magical medium transforming human inputs. The value of cross-disciplinary work, perhaps, is that the poetry of one discipline inspires another.

Today's event at the Media Lab is not about a vision of digital common law and distributed governance, however. It is touting a vision of neoliberal governance that is still being proselytized in academic circles. The speaker, Parag Khanna, is a senior research fellow in the Centre on Asia and Globalisation at the Lee Kuan Yew School of Public Policy at the National University of Singapore. In his new book, *Connectography: Mapping the Future of Global Civilization*, he argues that globalized supply-chain networks define the current world order. "Connectivity, not geography, is our destiny," the book's blurb states. The current race between countries is to see who can connect to the most markets, the blurb continues, and the United States can "regain ground" by "fusing with its neighbors into a super-continental North American Union of shared resources." "The world's ballooning financial assets are being wisely invested into building an inclusive global society. Beneath the chaos of a world that appears to be falling apart is a new foundation of connectivity pulling it together."

In the publicity material for the event, Khanna comes across as a neoliberal apologist, a young man making his career by doubling down on prescriptions for creative destruction wrought by globalized, deregulated networks, even as populist opposition to this agenda surges around the world.

The *Wall Street Journal* has called his book "a well-researched account of how companies are weaving ever more complicated supply chains that pull the world together even as they squeeze out inefficiencies." According to the *Journal*, Khanna "has succeeded in demonstrating that the forces of globalization are winning."

"How to organize or self-organize the world?," he asks his audience of young MIT students. We are moving, he says, from the Westphalian world of nation states begun in 1648 to the supply-chain world begun in

1989. Countries are building so much infrastructure across borders that they have extended their sovereignty.

He advances his PowerPoint presentation to the next slide. First, he says, we had "End of Cold War + expansion of capital markets + infrastructure build out + communication revolution = total globalization."

He clicks to the next slide: And now, in the supply-chain world, we have "Free markets + competitive advantage + division of labor + lots of Big Data = perfect capitalism."

Perfect capitalism, he says, means (he clicks to the final slide, and here he abandons the math signs) "perpetual optimization of land, labor, capital; inefficiency is the enemy; relentless competition."

But in neither his talk nor his book, which I read later, does Khanna probe deeply into whether globalized, digitized capitalism has actually yielded "extended sovereignty" for nations or resulted in competition, prosperity, fair distribution of rewards, or well-being.

He concedes that development will not be even. It will adhere to the strands of networks, and the parts in between are becoming or will remain hinterlands. In the wealthier countries of the supply-chain world, more people are employed in the most lucrative digital tech and finance sectors, for example. But it is hard to quantify the wealth that is being created, Khanna admits. For example, the $6 trillion to $7 trillion of trade in services is difficult to attribute to specific countries because organizations are constantly changing their structure (and their tax strategies, he might have added). Spotify payments by Swedes do not show up in Sweden's GDP, he says. He has an economist friend who joked that the amount of trade in services is so hard to quantify, you might be better off studying quantum physics.

Brushing that aside, and summing up his talk, he asks, "How do we leapfrog to a better way of governance?" We need to move beyond democratic populism to technocratic governance, he argues—beyond antiglobalization, anticapitalism, and antitech to a global utilitarianism. From "bad inequality to good inequality."

To me, the maps of global networks Khanna is showing us look like the apogee of neoliberal complexity, with measurements of success abstracted from people's actual well-being—a global engine of extractive capitalism and an intensifier of concentrations of power. I'm with the populists who think that while technocrats like Obama and the Clintons were telling us to surrender to the creative destruction of global networks (the global investment treaties, deregulated finance, privatization, unaccountable supra national governance structures, and platform monopolies they were imposing on us), they were actually executing a massive redistribution of risk and wealth. Since the 2008 economic meltdown, I want to tell Khanna, the trajectories of inequality have continued. In the United States in 2017, the top 10 percent of Americans own 77 percent of the country's wealth—a higher percentage than they owned in the Gilded Age. The twenty richest Americans own more than the bottom half of the population (some 152 million people).[40] Meanwhile, the US is innovating a new kind of poverty in which the costs of housing, education, and healthcare have risen so astronomically that they are now beyond the means of most Americans, who live constantly on the brink of ruin.[41]

I feel my anger rising as Khanna omits talking about the interstices in the beautiful, networked, technocratic world he is describing—the blighted towns destroyed by deindustrialization, the real unemployment and precarious employment figures, the lack of a living wage, the evictions, the rising homelessness, the 76 percent of Americans who in 2014 had no savings whatsoever,[42] and the 42.5 percent of Americans who in 2016 lived on less than double the poverty line.[43] During the 2016 presidential election campaign, there was talk of rising mortality rates due to suicide and alcohol and drug abuse, the "diseases of despair." Yes, there is despair, but there is also rage.

Is Khanna ignoring the fact that after forty years of globalization, centralization, deregulation, and technocratic governance—the neoliberal agenda he seems to be promoting—people have realized they're getting screwed, and they are withdrawing their consent?

When I pose this question to him immediately after his talk, he concedes, "There is cynicism about the positive power of tech and connectivity because it is undermining local, rooted community. But if there had been a federal jobs retraining program in the US, we would not have ended up with Trump."

As I listened to Khanna, I was reminded of what Wau Holland once told his young audience at the international hackers' meeting at the Paradiso: "Everybody must face the question 'What am I doing?'"

Months after leaving Boston, I would think of this Wauism again when I came across a new blog post by Joi Ito. Either his thoughts about the digital economy had evolved since his earlier video talks, or he had decided to be more frank about them. In this blog, he was beginning to sound downright disobedient to the corporate culture in which he and the Media Lab were embedded. He sounded like a hacker taking on the Khannas and Silicon Valley unicorn hunters of the world:

> We live in a civilization in which the primary currencies are money and power where, more often than not, the goal is to accumulate both at the expense of society at large. This is a very simple and fragile system compared to the Earth's ecosystems, where myriads of "currencies" are exchanged among processes to create hugely complex systems of inputs and outputs with feedback systems that adapt and regulate stocks, flows, and connections. ... [Today] values and complexity are focused more and more on prioritizing exponential financial growth, led by for-profit corporate entities that have gained autonomy, rights, power, and nearly unregulated societal influence.
>
> The new species of Silicon Valley mega companies ... are developed and run in great part by people who believe in a new religion, Singularity. ... The notion of Singularity—that AI will supersede humans with its exponential growth[44] ... is a religion created by people who have the experience of using computation to solve problems heretofore considered impossibly complex for machines. They have found a perfect partner in digital computation, a ... system of thinking and creating that is rapidly increasing in its ability to harness and process complexity, bestowing wealth and power on those who have mastered it. In Silicon Valley, the combination of groupthink and the financial success of this cult of technology has created a positive feedback system that has very little capacity for regulating through negative feedback.[45]

Those who think that "given enough power, the system will somehow figure out how to regulate itself, [that] the final outcome [will] be so complex that while we humans couldn't understand it now, 'it' would understand and 'solve' itself," are naïve, Ito concludes, since the more likely scenario is not a limitless ascending Bell curve but an ascending, and then diving "S" curve. "Most people outside the singularity bubble believe in S-curves," Ito writes: "namely, that nature adapts and self-regulates and that even pandemics will run their course. Pandemics may cause an extinction event, but growth will slow and things will adapt."[46]

HARVARD AND THE BERKMAN KLEIN CENTER FOR INTERNET & SOCIETY

Harvard, like MIT, lies across the Charles River from Boston but further afield. It is the site where the Congregationalists set up Newtowne, their first settlement in the Massachusetts Bay colony. Not long afterward, they set up the University with the goal of educating their future leaders. The Education for Leadership Act of the General Court of Massachusetts appropriated funds for that purpose in 1636.

Harvard. Stolid and prim, its brick buildings replete with white dentilled cornices and multipaned windows, its freshman dormitories bearing names such as Wigglesworth and Pennypacker Hall, its signs telling the public to stay out of its buildings. Although there could be no more "establishment" a place (Harvard still turns out a ruling class), specters of insurrection waft close by in Cambridge Common, where George Washington once gathered his Revolutionary army.

Many young people want to get into Harvard because of the networks it can open up for their careers. (Parag Khanna spoke of global networks of professional and technocratic belonging, too, and of the professional "circuit" as a means of concentrating privilege and power.) Groups of college-age kids and their parents trail by and knot in the campus squares; groups from many different countries, including the Chinese parents, grandparents and kids who file by in the some of the longer trails of hopeful applicants. Over the last few decades, many universities have become globally competing research and credentialing businesses, and Harvard is one of the biggest.

Set against this background, the Berkman Center for Internet & Society at Harvard ("Klein" was added to the name in 2016) began in 1998 as something countercultural to the rest of the institution. In the best academic tradition, its founders wished it to be an importer of new, radical ideas already circulating outside the institution.

In 1999, a strategic planning committee met to consolidate the initiatives that the recently formed center wanted to pursue. The cofounders were Charles Nesson and a bright young law student, Jonathan Zittrain. Others involved included Larry Lessig, who came to take the Berkman chair and was planning his book *Code and Other Laws of Cyberspace*, and the ubiquitous John Perry Barlow, cypherpunk *cum* Berkman fellow traveler, and the Center's first official fellow. Nesson recorded their aspirations to set up an open knowledge domain that would share with, rather than compete with, other universities. He also recorded the administration's response. As a document that throws light on a seminal moment at the institution, it bears reading in its entirety:

Open Code / Open Content / Open Law: Building a Digital Commons in Cyberspace

Dear Colleagues,

The most important message I took from the May 20 [1999] strategic planning meeting was that the case has to be made for the importance of open code to a wide audience. [Richard Stallman might have preferred Nesson to have said "free software."][48]

I want to share the story of the Berkman Center's own case to make within Harvard, and I hope others of you will share stories of your own.

Earlier this spring, the Berkman Center proposed the formation of a legally independent nonprofit entity—a consortium of educational centers to foster the development of open software, open research, and open content (<http://www.opencode.org>). The Provost of Harvard responded to this announcement with a note stating that the permission of Harvard's President and Fellows would be required for the Berkman Center to sponsor the formation of such an entity "outside Harvard" (<http://www.open code.org/faq/>).

This is, I believe, a request from the hierarchy of Harvard to be persuaded of the wisdom of the path we at the Berkman Center espouse. It is an opportunity for us to present our case for open code in an open way to the leadership of a great educational institution—an institution with a glorious past, a glowing present, and an uncertain future.

Even more important, it is an opportunity to explain, not only to the administrative hierarchy of Harvard, but also to others in similarly situated institutions and to the world at large, why openness in code, content, and law is essential to the future. It is an opportunity for us, in conjunction with other institutions, to attract and engage an international audience to consider the argument for openness, to deliberate in structured and moderated discussion, and to form rough consensus. ...

Unlike the frontier Columbus opened when he discovered America, there are no pre-existing purple mountains and fruited plains in cyberspace. Cyberspace exists only as we build it, and how we build it is up to us.

So, the key strategic insights for me from our May 20 meeting relate to who we are and what we can do. We represent the integration of three important communities: coders, teachers, and lawyers. We have the capacity to challenge the boundaries of our separate cultures in service of an open cyber environment. We can combine our talents to design open architecture. We can, as coders, build it. We can, as teachers, fill it with open content. We can, as lawyers, defend it. ...

We are making an argument for open information technology. We need to understand, articulate and project our argument. We need to explain the relationship of open code to freedom, justice, security, and education. We intend to initiate and foster a campaign for open IT that makes the issues of openness central to the institutional, local, national, and international politics of the future. We are building the environment in which we intend this argument to develop (<http://opencode.org/courseware>).

The Internet was born of public spirit out of government and education. It grew in the eighties as an open domain. In the nineties it was discovered by capital investors, who realized that investment in Internet produced exponential return. So began a still-growing rush of capital into the Internet that has produced an unprecedented growth of the proprietary domain. But there has been no balancing growth of the open domain. Rather, we must organize and build it. We need to convince our institutions—government, academic, philanthropic—that the creation of a substantial open domain serves their missions. ...

Harvard, like other similarly situated institutions, faces three broad options: (1) Do nothing. Just keep going as we are, with pens and yellow pads; (2) Invest in helping teachers reach new audiences and teach in new ways; (3) Set up Harvard.com—commit to the commercial online education business. ...

The model of university as producer of knowledge-as-product-for-sale is a closed one. Knowledge is treated as property to be copyrighted, patented, classified, licensed, and litigated. Under this closed model, creative work cannot progress without negotiations about license fees. ... As faculty become work-for-hire, money becomes the currency of the campus, and legality the dominant feature of relationship.

Under this model, the nature of Harvard will change fundamentally—for the worse, I think. ... The Berkman Center aspires to demonstrate a different model—open IT, we call it. We encourage cooperative work dedicated to the open domain ... [and] in the public interest. Intellectual community and creative process is our product, knowledge the by-product. This approach galvanizes spirit and produces educational works of great distinction and wide public utility. ...

But there are questions. In particular, can such a model be sustained by tuition and endowment?

Who will support IT?

Who will join our list?(<http://eon.law.harvard.edu/cgi-bin/opencode/join_in.cgi>)

Who will participate in our next lecture and discussion series? (<http://cyber.law.harvard.edu/online>)

Who will contribute talent? (<http://cyber.law.harvard.edu/people>)

Who will contribute funds? (http://cyber.law.harvard.edu/sponsors.html>)

Who will work with me in a patent group to advance the open genome and defend open code? (<http://www.opencode.org>)

Who will work with Larry Lessig to found the Berkman Press?

Who will work with John Perry Barlow to develop open MP3?

Who will work with Eric Eldred to build a Copyright Commons?(<http://cyber.law.harvard.edu/cc>) …

Who will tell friends we need help?

We think we have a working business model. We service an open knowledge domain to an audience of customers we judge best able to contribute to it. That is and always has been Harvard's mission and the mission of educational institutions in general. Open IT is a mission we hold in common with other great institutions, so let us join to build a magnificent common resource for us all.

Charles Nesson

aka eon[49]

Nesson and his colleagues succeeded in persuading their administration to let them set up an open educational software project they called H2O with other universities that might otherwise have been viewed as competitors. And the Berkman Center went on to become involved in almost every cutting-edge policy issue related to digital technology over the succeeding three decades. Ultimately, Nesson and his colleagues would lead the way to mainstreaming a "cutting-edge approach" to all things digital throughout Harvard.

The Berkman Center has always focused on technical as much as on legal solutions. The Center's stated mission is "to explore and understand cyberspace; to study its development, dynamics, norms, and standards," and its stated method is "to build out into cyberspace."[50] Today there are many internet and society-themed research centers around the world. These include centers at Berkeley, Cambridge, the Indian Institute for Technology, Oxford, Stanford (set up by Lessig in 2000), St. Galen (Switzerland), University of Toronto, and Yale. Recently, the Berkman Klein Center set up a global Network of Internet & Society Centers with other institutions.[51]

One Berkmanite has referred to the difficulty of keeping track of the "Berkmaniacal collection" of projects and activities the center undertakes each year.[52] These have included projects on Creative Commons licensing, cyber security, democratic debate, digital finance, digital health, harmful speech online, identity management, internet filtering and tampering, internet governance, internet robustness, media law, and stopping malware, as well as court cases.[53] And increasingly, there has been a focus on social science research.

EMERGENCE

There is a dizzying number of interesting people to speak with at the Berkman Klein Center. However, the two I most want to see are Samer Hassan and Yochai Benkler. They have been thinking for a long time about how something like a hacking movement might succeed despite the odds against it. Maybe they can tell me how hackers and citizens might build democracy out into cyberspace despite the formidable obstacles arrayed against them.

Samer Hassan is from Spain. I arrange to meet him at the student cafeteria at around two o'clock, just as the crowds are thinning out. He arrives at the top of the escalator, forty-something, bearded, and with a straightforward manner about him. We sit at a long table in the dining hall and settle into a conversation that outlasts the waning afternoon light. Since coming to Berkman in September 2015, Hassan has been traveling back and forth between Cambridge and Madrid, where he is an associate professor in computer science. He comes to the work from a human rights and sociology background, having done his PhD thesis in social theory and complex systems. He works on decentralized collaboration, social movements, and collaborative communities. These are communities like Wikipedia (a much studied subject at Harvard), but he says that collaborative communities also encompass Hack Labs, which have been around for more than thirty years, and Fab Labs (fabrication labs that are open to nongeeks), a newer phenomenon that grew out of MIT.[54] These networks, Hassan says, are huge. They are typical grassroots movements—open communities of people who are collaborating to create common goods, whether an encyclopedia or a community center, with an open-license approach (like Free Software's GPL licenses or Creative Commons's licenses). These initiatives can be online or offline.

The Madrid social center called Tabacalera, which opened in 2010,[55] is one example. Spain has always had a tradition of social centers squatting in (as opposed to renting) their spaces. The name for this type of center is Centro Social Occupado Autogestionado (CSOA), meaning "occupied, self-managed social center." The tradition has existed for decades in Barcelona, but squatting social centers have been established in every big city in Spain. Madrid's Tabacalera is a huge municipal initiative of 9,000 square meters of space for community groups and social activity. It is autonomous and self-managed by people who live in the neighborhood and by contributors, not by the state. A lot of people from the Indignados, or 15M, movement helped set it up.

The tradition of these social centers connects directly to the anarchist movement in Spain. The Spanish, Hassan says, have much more affinity to social movements than they do to the idea of trying to reform the state. Until very recently, in fact, these social groups would not participate in electoral politics; they would not deal with the state but would organize outside the state.

When I ask Hassan what hacking means in this context, he says that hacking is between reform and revolution. Hacking is a disruptive reform that is revolutionary. It makes reformers happy because it does reform but does not break the system. Revolutionaries are happy because it is not complying with the values of the system and is triggering emergent effects that might ultimately break down the system. In complex systems analysis, a small change can trigger huge changes and emergent properties, so that the whole macro structure changes. So, Hassan observes, you are actually hacking a "reform" with the hope that its emergent properties change the whole.

I ask him what emergent properties are. He replies with a phrase that sounds like a riddle: it's when you have a property that is not in the macro but emerges from the interaction of the micro. The beautiful shapes that a flock of starlings makes when the birds are on the wing are emergent patterns. The birds do not want to form this pattern or have this pattern in their minds, Hassan explains. When they fly together, they know only the micro interactions between them. You could take three rules—don't get too close, don't cross paths, and proceed forward—and the flock pattern will emerge but not as a preplanned, predestined, or imposed thing. It is completely bottom up. Emergence is always bottom up, he says.

I am reminded that Chaos Computer Club member Rop Gonggrijp once said that Wau Holland "felt chaos theory offered the best explanation for how the world actually worked." The club, Gonggrijp said, was about "adapting to a world which is (and always has been) much more chaotic and non-deterministic than is often believed."[56]

Hassan asks me if I know the book *The Cathedral and the Bazaar: Musings on Linux and Open Source by an Accidental Revolutionary*. I do. Eric Raymond wrote the book to advocate a free software approach for corporations, recommending that they leave out the ethics of free software and adopt it as a self-interested process of open-source software. Hassan's point, I suppose, is that social systems can shift rapidly to new means of production with no one planning or predicting it. It is more complicated than just the political question of rallying a critical mass of people to a certain way of doing things. The process by which free and open-source software became the bones of much of the present digital world was an emergent process, not a purely political one.

At the Complutense University of Madrid, where Hassan is an associate professor in the Computer Science Department, his favorite course to teach is cyberethics. In it, he engages student engineers in a participatory way about the social implications of tech—privacy, censorship, free software, and the commons. "It's actually revelatory for many," he says. At many universities, including MIT, this kind of course is optional, but his is compulsory. "If you want a computer science degree, then you have to take this course. When you program an app, you have to think about its social implications."

After nearly three hours, Hassan looks at his cell phone for an important message. "Aargh! Yochai was supposed to get back to me, and now it's been three days."

I ask him what Yochai Benkler is like to work with.

"I think he's adorable," he says.

ENLIVENING A MORAL IMAGINATION

The entrance to Hauser Hall on the campus of Harvard Law School is a beautiful update on Craftsman functionality and design. A single full-length portrait of US Supreme Court justice Oliver Wendell Holmes Jr., proponent of the common law, hangs at the end of the passage to the classrooms. Yochai Benkler has his office in this building on the third floor, where I have a scheduled meeting with him in half an hour.

Through the power of the free internet, I've watched several important lectures Benkler has given. I've also ordered his books and waited for them to arrive at the Harvard bookstore (although I later discovered they could be freely accessed at http://www.benkler.org).

Benkler's first book, *The Wealth of Networks: How Social Production Transforms Markets and Freedom*, published in 2006, made his reputation in academic, business, and governance circles, and now he is a busy Harvard professor. *The Wealth of Networks* argued that "large-scale cooperation, such as free and open-source software or Wikipedia, was not a bizarre side story of the Net, but a core vector through which the transition to a networked society and economy was happening. ... Online cooperation was happening ... it was a stable feature of this new environment ... and it was central to the future of networked society."[57] These days, Benkler might be the first to agree that business followed his insights but not in the way he envisioned. It took up his idea of large-scale, peer-based collaborative production in a big way—as a new engine of value extraction. No doubt business was delighted to learn that people will work collaboratively for free. It realized it could base whole business models on the premise, profiting both from people's labor and their personal information. *The Wealth of Networks* garnered awards and a lot of recognition for Benkler, but his hope that society would embrace the full promise of commons-based peer production (a term he coined) to achieve democratic and humane ends was not realized.

Benkler's next book, *The Penguin and the Leviathan: How Cooperation Triumphs over Self-Interest*, which I read last night in preparation for our meeting today, was published in 2011. It reads like a popular business book and seems to be an attempt to convince the business community that adopting his moral propositions along with the rest of his message would be in their self-interest, too.

What seems to reveal most about Benkler's thinking, however, is a talk I found online titled "The Idea of the Commons and the Future of Capitalism," which he gave for the Creative Commons Global Summit in 2015.[58] In the video recording of the talk, he speaks of labor and a sharply growing income inequality. He tells his audience that today there is an increasing technological embodiment of contingent work, now sometimes called "the sharing economy." But this is not sharing, he says: this is extraction, and we need to insist that sharing is sharing and contingent work under extractive conditions is contingent work under extractive conditions. "And don't use us to legitimate you."

Records, Benkler says, show that income inequality in the United States was flat during the 1950s, 1960s, and 1970s under both the Democrats and Republicans and then shot up after that regardless of who was in power. By the mid-1970s, the word *solidarity*, which had been ubiquitous from World War I to the late 1960s, lost its hold on people's imaginations, and the neoliberal ideas of incentives and rationality took hold. In a world that was uncertain and complex, neoliberalism told us there was no way to plan. The most rational way to view the world was as a collection of individuals—strangers acting on each other in their own self-interest. Collective models had failed. We needed to free markets from collective impositions. Property was the core economic engine.

It is rare to hear a law professor talk about economic history in such an expansive way and even rarer to hear one speak about the state of the social imagination at different times in history. As I sit in the entrance of Hauser Hall watching parts of the video again, I find myself looking forward to asking him more about this.

In the video, Benkler continues: "Then the theoretically impossible started to happen," he says—free and open-source software, the Creative Commons, and Firefox began to appear. They showed that people *could* govern themselves with collective models and *could* reach a rough consensus. It was not the state agencies that broke the Microsoft monopoly; it was free software. "Whoever would have predicted that a bunch of free software developers would beat Microsoft in its core web server function?" Benkler asks. And yet free and open-source software "moves"; it grows through boom and bust. It happens not at the periphery but at the very core of innovation and growth.

According to Benkler, the 1980s and 1990s saw the implementation of neoliberal policies pushing everything into market- and price-based approaches, even inside companies and in nonprofit organizations. "What we are seeing now," he says, "is a re-emergence of a networked information society where, for the first time since the Industrial Revolution, the most important inputs into the core economic activities of the most advanced economies are widely distributed in the population." Yes, there are new efforts to harness these inputs for more market-oriented and extractive ends, but "a solution space" is emerging for an entire range of problems—the opportunity to build social production into the general system.

One result is that "the commons" has started to emerge as an organizing principle in place of the older concept of the "public good." Why? Benkler says the commons is appealing because it is a reimagining, not a complete rejection, of the property model. You keep your "self"— your individual integrity, your sense of being able to be both part of and apart from the collective—and at the same time you recognize that creativity, freedom of speech, and thought all depend on a robust public domain. It is not that there is property and the little bit that is left over is the commons. Rather, the commons are integral to all market societies, whether the roads, the navigable waters, or the basis of knowledge (or the internet, I think Benkler might have added—the "connectivity commons").

Benkler's message is that we cannot exist in complex society without commons because uncertainty and complexity mean that property, like central planning, also fails. And individual incentives also are imperfect because when you have to standardize every little bit so that you can price it, you lose a lot of information. By contrast, the public domain and commons-based exploration have allowed diverse people to use diverse resources to apply diverse knowledge and to experiment. They show that our innovation, growth, and creativity are an evolutionary process, not something that can be managed from the start, and a process that requires enormous experimentation. Without the commons, modern market society would atrophy. The work can be done individually or collaboratively, commercially or noncommercially. A diversity of vehicles (coops, markets, or purpose built) can be used, but what is critical is that the commons locates the authority to act where we can actually act—in our own bodies with our own social relations. Where the law locates it elsewhere, Benkler says, the commons claims authority back:

> So we're moving to a concept of cooperative human systems ... [not only in theory] but also in terms of just building systems. We're seeing the emergence of a science of cooperation which has both basic science characteristics and design characteristics to build functioning cooperative systems. We are at the very early part of this moment. It's just the moment

when the paradigm shift can even be conceived, but that is the science of the future, and that is the organization design and platform design of the future. That's where we're going … the recreation of future market society.

Capping this bold assertion, Benkler summarizes his argument. The binary pair of property and markets versus state planning does not exhaust the means of achieving growth and material well-being. Cooperative social action in the commons can also support growth and be more efficient and sustainable. We can turn away from a governance of pure delegation *to* citizenship exercised as peer governance and a progressivism aware of the fallibility of the state. "We're … part of an intellectual moment in the history of early twenty-first-century capitalism," Benkler tells his audience. "We're standing at the end of forty years of the dominance of an idea that has underwritten … an extractive model of capitalism. It's not the only model. There is another model, and we [the Creative Commons movement] represent its very core."

As I climb the stairs of Hauser Hall to the third floor, I wonder what the man himself will be like and how he views his own work now. Yochai Benkler's assistant ushers me into his office with a glass of water she has poured for me. Benkler shakes my hand. He has a full salt-and-pepper beard, wears gold wire glasses, and is dressed as I have seen him in his videos in jeans and a white shirt with the cuffs rolled up. He is fit in his early fifties, a person whose most immediately striking trait is that he is comfortable in his skin. He has a gentle kind of gravitas.

I have sent him some questions in advance of this meeting and asked him to talk to me about what interests him most. He is taking a chance on whether meeting me will be time wasted, and therein lies his kindness. We have half an hour scheduled, so once he has greeted me warmly, he starts right in. His desk (it's not clear to me whether this is where he actually works) is a table with chairs around it for others to sit. There are piles of papers.

He says that of all the issues I've flagged, the biggest is whether people can make a living from collaborative production and how you get them to come together to do so. It was one thing to suggest they could in 2006 when he wrote his first book, another thing to write what he did in *The Penguin and the Leviathan* in 2010, and another thing again in 2017 now that things are much changed. He is pessimistic. A decade ago, there were over a million free software developers. They made their stuff, they sold and serviced it, and they had some success. If there was one place where worker-owned coops could take off, it should be in free software services and development. But there is not one—not even a partnership. Consultancy firms, law firms, and accountancy firms operate as partnerships, and even partnerships are absent in the digital sector.

The starkest disappointment for Benkler over the past decades has been the failure of community networks—the failure of the people who built or intended to build the physical infrastructure of the internet and make it publicly owned and available to everyone. This was in 2001 and 2002, even before WiFi was established as the standard means to connect to the internet. It was not a technical issue that prevented the physical infrastructure of the internet from being free and public. It was people's habits of mind: they had unfounded fears about privacy and security, and so they let the private sector take it over. When people have the tech and the will to do it and yet don't, it's sobering. Guifi in Catalonia is one example of a free public infrastructure, but these are rare now.

I mention that I was speaking with Samer Hassan the day before and that, knowing what he did about complex systems theory, Hassan was optimistic there might be certain innovations that could trigger rapid, major change.

Benkler says he is not optimistic. He laughs. He has a more dour view, he says. Have I looked at the history of real-world coops? Benkler has studied this history, he tells me, and he cannot find any reason why some succeed and others do not. It seems that whether coops are formed and sustained or not depends on locally and culturally rooted factors. If there was a coop of dairy farmers in Wisconsin in the 1940s, then that is still the way farmers produce milk there now. If you take the same coop and try to move it to New Hampshire, then it falls apart. It is a question of socializing people's habits of mind around the idea.

Yes, social systems are complex, and things can shift very quickly. We saw it with free software and Wikipedia. Benkler has been around this block for a long time, he says. He remembers when economists mocked him for asserting that unlicensed wireless was as important as licensed wireless, and yet now it is the primary carrier of data. When you have commons-based peer production yielding substantial pieces of infrastructure and informational goods, he says, first it is laughable, then it is a threat (they said it was Marxist or would destroy learning), and then it just becomes normal. He firmly believes you can move through this cycle, at least with discrete innovations.

But he says he does not believe in magic, in the sense that systemic change could take place suddenly at any time. Histories have their own dynamics. What he sees now is more centralization, more appropriation, and the state back in full force in surveillance and social control. He sees Uber and Airbnb turning collaborative potential into a system for extracting value from labor and for regulatory avoidance. It will require some external shock or strong act of will to push us back in a liberatory direction.

But if some universal platform arose to replace Google and Uber, wouldn't that be revolutionary?, I ask. (I don't mention Tim Berners-Lee's "Solid" project or John Clippinger's ID3 project, but this is the kind of thing I have in mind.)

That is something that Samer Hassan is working on right now, Benkler says, and he agrees it could change things a lot if it were adopted. It is a general-purpose, blockchain-enabled system to allow people to share their labor and work flow—the components of a system that would allow people to use it to make a living.[59] "There is a difference between despair, what you can imagine, and what you can predict absent some major disruption," he says, smiling a little ruefully.

I ask him if the future will depend on the idea of a guaranteed basic annual income.

Yes, he replies, but the devil is in the details when dealing with an idea advocated both by those on the left and by followers of Milton Friedman (the father of neoliberal economics). It would have to be large enough to do away with capitalism. Where would the budget come from? The poverty line in the United States is about $11,000; multiply that by about 330 million people and you are looking at $3.5 to $4 trillion a year. Eliminating all entitlement and defense spending still would not be enough to pay for it. The fiscal side is genuinely challenging. You might ask whether you're better off with much more targeted policies. But it is the biggest idea right now and bears some careful work.

(I reflect that even a Marxist like David Harvey is skeptical of guaranteed annual income schemes that are not accompanied by a change in social and political relations on a deeper level. That is what Silicon Valley wants, Harvey has said—death by Netflix![60] Other commentators, such as political scientist Sheldon Wolin, have observed that without some controls over the cost of basic goods like housing, education, and healthcare, capitalists will always find a way to capture the public money put into guaranteed income schemes by hiking up prices.)[61]

Benkler is an Israeli American who worked on a kibbutz in Israel in his youth. When I ask him whether the experience has influenced any of his views, he says that he tries to base his work not on his anecdotal knowledge but on proper research sources.

It strikes me that one must have a better idea of human nature after working in a commune, but I leave it at that. One of his book acknowledgments ends with a note to his partner: "Finally, to my best friend and tag-team partner in this tussle we call life … with whom I have shared nicely more or less everything since we were barely adults."[62]

Many kibbutzim today, Benkler says, are just group ownership in a classical capitalist mode. They employ various kinds of labor and lead a nice capitalist life in what you might call a club, if you wanted to be uncharitable. His father was in Israel's bus drivers' coop, he says. For many years, the only way to become a member was to be a son. Membership was inherited. Otherwise, you were a wage employee. There are people who say that the famous Mondragon cooperative in Spain has different classes of membership, he tells me. Then you have consumer coops and credit unions, and these are not so different from a customer loyalty club. So these organizational forms relieve you from some of the worst extractive practices of the oligarchic capitalism that we have lived through for the past forty years, but they are not true cooperatives. In Detroit, he says, with the near total collapse of the local economy, they seem to be doing some genuinely innovative things.[63]

Have I read Cory Doctorow's book? Benkler asks me. "He has written a beautiful science fiction novel that has just come out, called *Walkaway*. He writes about a world where a utopia and a dystopia exist side by side. The dystopia is fully extractive surveillance capitalism. In the utopia, people have just walked away from that to create a postownership, collaborative society with 3D printing and networks. What's beautiful about the book is that it imagines a world that takes the economics of free software … and transfers it to the economics of shelter, food, and the necessities of human life."

Your work is really about changing social norms, isn't it?, I ask. As Benkler has said in *The Wealth of Networks*, the value of discussing these possibilities is not really to predict what will happen but rather to enliven people's moral imaginations as to what is possible. (In the book, his exact words are "The object of a discussion of the institutional ecology of the networked environment is, in any event, not prognostication. It is to provide a moral framework within which to understand the many and diverse policy battles we have seen over the past decade and which undoubtedly will continue into the coming decade.")

He sits forward.

"Yes, a critical part of this discussion is about shaping a moral imagination—people's sense of the feasible, the plausible. I've been studying oligarchic capitalism, and in the span of fifteen years during the 1970s and 80s—only fifteen years—I saw the mindset of the regular captain of industry change radically. He used to see himself as a steward of the stakeholder." He was promoted from within, Benkler says, to be a competent and loyal servant of the company. He was not after money but status, and it did not enhance status to be seen going after money. "Now, everyone sees money as the only way to status. There's been a fundamental shift in what a well-socialized person can and should do in the world. A decade ago, Wikipedia, MyBarackObama, was what cool people did. Ten years ago, what I predicted in my first book looked real; today, it looks like a utopia."

I ask him if he has a theory about how and why revolutions succeed.

He has a general approach, he responds, based on the belief that there are integrated systems in human relations. These are the technical, institutional, cultural, social norm and knowledge frameworks that more or less structure most human behavior and the degree of room people have at any given time to change behavior. Then, he says, you get a shock. It could be Admiral Perry arriving on your shore, the Great Depression, or the internet. And that is the moment when a lot is up for grabs. With the shock comes change, adjustment, and then stabilization. When things are stable, it is harder to make change.

The point is to be ready, to know what a transformative moment looks like, so that when a moment of perturbation arrives, you can diagnose which of the integrated systems is the most likely place where you can effect change. That is where he thought we were ten years ago, he says. He is not sure anymore if we are still there because the rate of technological change is moving very fast.

Right now, he says, we see the rise of economic nationalism and illiberal majoritarianism in countries like Hungary, Russia, Turkey, and the United States. "I guess it's essential," he says, "to still believe that we are in the middle of a transformative moment and there is still opportunity to identify which systems are most susceptible to redesign, and to work out how to interface with the other systems so they can adapt together and not pull us back."

Much more than half an hour has gone by. Benkler has been generous, given the premium every Harvard professor puts on his or her time. I close my notebook and thank him.

Walking back across campus to the train station in Harvard Square, I pass piles of hard snow and long lines of prospective students and their parents, willing to pay large tuition fees if only they can get onto the admissions list.[64]

THE EPICENTER OF A CIVILIZATION

Boston is a city where the abolitionist and former slave Frederick Douglass spoke many times. The African Baptist Church of Boston, also known as the African Meeting House, was one of his venues. Built in 1806, it has recently been refurbished and opened as part of the Museum of African American History. I go there one snowy afternoon toward the end of my stay in Boston.

When I enter the church through a door that connects it with the rest of the museum, I'm alone in the company of a young docent. She tells me the history of the place, then pauses to let me take in its neatly painted pews and second-floor gallery. It is a perfectly proportioned speaking hall. The silence resonates with all the speeches ever made from its plain wooden pulpit.

The docent invites me to climb up into the pulpit, and I comply, feeling a little foolish. I'm not prepared for the emotion that seizes me when I stand there. It feels as if I've entered a magnetic field between two giant opposing forces. It is overwhelming to stand where great orators like Douglass stood and looked out and spoke of freedom—to come upon this spot as an accidental tourist and suddenly recognize it as the epicenter of a city, a people, a civilization that loves freedom.

In his autobiography, Frederick Douglass tells the story of how his white master took a newspaper away from him one day when he realized his wife had been teaching Douglass how to read. As the man seized it, he told his wife that one could not teach slaves to read because it would make them uneasy in their slavery. Douglass used to observe that this was the best argument he had heard in favor of abolition. And learning to read was in fact his pathway to freedom.

Eben Moglen, the constitutional litigator, law professor, and old ally of Richard Stallman, relates this story in one of his own speeches, given at Columbia University not long after the Snowden revelations. Moglen himself is a great orator, with a sense of both history and tragedy that makes him sound premodern. In his Snowden speech, which can be found online, he introduces the idea that we live in slavery when we do not have control over the code in our devices. If we want to recover our condition of freedom,[65] we need to work together. It takes a union, he says, to end slavery.

And if we do not recover that condition of freedom in the digital age? In his Snowden speech, Moglen quotes the eighteenth-century historian of the Roman empire Edward Gibbon:

> In the third chapter of his *History of the Decline and Fall of the Roman Empire*, Edward Gibbon gives two reasons why the slavery into which the Romans tumbled under Augustus and his successors left them more wretched than any previous human slavery.
>
> In the first place, Gibbon said, the Romans had carried with them into slavery the culture of a free people—their language and their conception of themselves as human beings presupposed freedom. And thus, Gibbons says, oppressed as they were by the weight of their corruption and military violence, the Romans yet preserved for a long time the sentiments, or at least the ideas, of a freeborn people.
>
> In the second place, the empire of the Romans filled all the world, and when that empire fell into the hands of a single person, the world was a safe and dreary prison for his enemies. … To resist was fatal, and it was impossible to fly.[66]

These are tragic thoughts. But I recall also what Moglen declaimed at the Libre Planet conference. He said—and I believe it, too—that people feel something is wrong. They feel a whole bunch of things are going on that they themselves are a part of but that they know are not quite right. They feel it about Facebook, they feel it about Twitter, and Google, and Uber, and electronic voting machines. They fear what this century could hold. Millions of people are waiting to hear the message, millions want to hear the message—that users of technology have rights, that technology must serve and not subject humankind, that it is citizens who must ultimately control code, that we can and must code for democracy.

The job before us, really, is to build a new condition of freedom.

Historically, technology tends to develop in a nonlinear, haphazard manner. How innovations come about, catch on, and succeed in different places and circumstances is a process not wholly determined by the nature of the technology. It also hangs on human agency, culture, and to some degree, chance.

We can't be sure how digital technology is going to develop next. But if it is possible that the shift will come through some emergent pattern, some "positive chaos," then it is all the more crucial for people who care about democracy to be alert and actively experimenting. We are many. There will be something to do for everyone's capacity.

CODA

In the fall of 2018, as the seventh anniversary of Occupy Wall Street approached, a new mass mobilization was being organized with a new political target in mind. Kalle Lasn and his team at Adbusters put out another call to their now huge international listserv. It was time, they said, to occupy Silicon Valley.

They posted their memes for the battle.

The first: on a pink background, a ballerina dancing on a cracked iPhone, the screen of which screen displays a Facebook "like" icon. The accompanying text reads,

17TH SEPTEMBER 2018
#OCCUPY SILICON VALLEY
AN ONLINE OCCUPATION:
WE SHUT BIG TECH DOWN FOR A DAY

The second: a Nazi flag, red, with a white circle in the middle, and inside that, a black swastika formed from four Facebook "f" logos.

The third: on a blue background, a cackling "happy face" emoji. And its message?

OPEN THE CODE
MOTHERFUCKERS
WE HAVE THE RIGHT TO KNOW

NOTES

CHAPTER 1

1. See "Reichstag, New German Parliament," Foster + Partners, Berlin, Germany, 1999, http://www.fosterandpartners.com/projects/reichstag-new-german-parliament.

2. In 2016, the number grew to twelve thousand people. Darko Janjevic, "Chaos Computer Club: Europe's Biggest Hacking Conference Underway in Hamburg," *DW*, December 28, 2015, http://www.dw.com/en/chaos-computer-club-europes-biggest-hackers-congress-underway-in-hamburg/a-18944610.

3. Steven Levy, *Hackers: Heroes of the Computer Revolution* (Sebastopol: O'Reilly, [1984] 2010). Some hackers do not ascribe to the ethic as articulated by Levy, and there are many academic studies on the diversity of hackers. Some of the academics working in this field include Goetz Bachmann, David Berry, Jessica Beyer, Paula Bialski, Finn Brunton, Anita Say Chan, Gabriella Coleman, Laura DeNardis, Marco Deseriis, Ricardo Dominguez, Joan Donovan, Tor Ekeland, Virginia Eubanks, Karl Fogel, Felipe Fonseca, Volker Grassmuck, Christina Dunbar Hester, Benjamin Mako Hill, Matthew Hull, Matthew Jones, Tim Jordan, Christopher Kelty, Beth Kolko, Sebastian Kubitschko, Lawrence Liang, Sylvia Lindtner, Geert Lovink, Fenwick McKelvey, Colin Milburn, Luis Felipe Murillo, Lily Nguyen, Whitney Phillips, Matt Ratto, Thomas Rid, Renee Ridgway, Andrew Russell, Molly Sauter, Rebecca Slayton, Johann Soderberg, Felix Stalder, Ravi Sundaram, Yuri Tahkteyev, Douglas Thomas, Fred Turner, MacKenzie Wark, Sarah Meyers West, and David Murakami Wood.

4. Levy, *Hackers*, 16–17.

5. Levy, *Hackers*, 28–34.

6. Levy, *Hackers*, 57.

7. Levy, *Hackers*, 48.

8. Joseph Weizenbaum, *Computer Power and Human Reason: From Judgment to Calculation* (San Francisco: W. H. Freeman, 1976).

9. Weizenbaum, *Computer Power and Human Reason*.

10. The Cyberpunk Project, http://project.cyberpunk.ru/idb/hacker_ethics.html: "The Cyberpunk Project (TCP) is a remotely available data-well net of files about cyberpunk subculture, cyberpunk science-fiction and general cyber culture in the form of collected information. It is the result of years of gathering data and sorting it, to compile a host of cyberpunk-information related documents and work. The TCP started in 1996 and was actively supported until late 2002."

11. Levy, *Hackers*, 451.

12. Levy, *Hackers*, 169–170.

13. Levy, *Hackers*, 164–165.

14. Levy, *Hackers*, 222.

15. Levy, *Hackers*, 276, 458–459.

16. Levy, *Hackers*, 437–450; Richard Stallman, correspondence with the author, December 17, 2017.

17. Levy, *Hackers*, 448.

18. Levy, *Hackers*, 450. In his book, Levy divides hackers by generation into "true hackers" (the MIT hackers), "microcomputer hackers" and "game hackers". So the statement he assigns to Stallman means that Stallman believed he was the last of his generation of hackers at MIT, not that no other hackers existed at the time.

19. Levy, *Hackers*, 447, 450.

20. Attributed to the early Jewish leader Hillel.

21. Initially, Stallman stipulated only the last, three freedoms, and numbered them 1 to 3. Then he realized it was necessary to articulate a fourth freedom, which he wanted to state first, so he numbered it 0, which was apt because computers count from 0 and not 1. Author's communication with Richard Stallman, March 4, 2019.

22. Richard Stallman, "The Initial Announcement of the GNU Operating System," in *Free Software, Free Society: Selected Essays of Richard M. Stallman* (Boston: Free Software Foundation, 2002), 26–27. It is interesting that in his initial announcement Stallman said he planned to give his software away for free, however, it is important to remember that "gratis" or "given away at no cost" is *not* part of the definition of free software.

23. Richard Stallman, "Releasing Free Software If You Work at a University," in *Free Software, Free Society*, 63.

24. Gerard Alberto and Ruth Oldenzeil, eds., *Hacking Europe: From Computer Cultures to Demoscenses* (London: Springer-Verlag, 2014), 8–9.

25. Alberto and Oldenzeil, *Hacking Europe*, 17.

26. Kai Denker, "Heroes Yet Criminals of the German Computer Revolution," in Alberto and Oldenzeil, *Hacking Europe*, 171, citing a biography on the Chaos Computer Club's cofounder Wau Holland written by Daniel Kulla, *Der Phrasenprüfer. Szenen aus dem Leben von Wau Holland* (Löhrbach: Pieper and the Grüne Kraft, 2003),16.

27. Denker, "Heroes Yet Criminals," 171, citing Kulla, *Der Phrasenprüfer*, 20.

28. Denker, "Heroes Yet Criminals," 170.

29. Denker, "Heroes Yet Criminals," 172.

30. Denker, "Heroes Yet Criminals," 168.

31. Caroline Nevejan and Alexander Badenoch, "How Amsterdam Invented the Internet: European Networks of Significance, 1980–1995," in Alberto and Oldenzeil, *Hacking Europe*, 199.

32. For extended details about this KGB hack story, see the collection of contemporary news articles in *Phrack World News*, part 2, no. 25 (March 29, 1989), http://phrack.org/issues/25/10.html.

33. Reenactment of the Wau-Pengo debate (1989) at the 31st Congress of the Chaos Computer Club (31C3), Wau Holland Foundation, https://www.wauland.de/en/index.php. The reenactors in this video use a transcript. I transcribed the interview from this video to make my own transcript and have used excerpts from the transcript without showing the gaps to make reading the conversation easier. The excerpts are in the order they were spoken.

34. The early Dutch entrepreneur and tech journalist Luc Sala described the after party and the kind of cross-fertilization that was going on between the European and California scenes around this time in a "personal perspective" on the early hacker/New Age magazine *Mondo 2000*. He stayed for some time in the communal Mondo house in Berkeley and ended up driving across the country in winter with John Perry Barlow to the latter's ranch in Wyoming. He wrote about the California scene in "New Age & Mondo: A Personal Perspective—Part 1," Mondo 2000 History Project Entry #8, Acceler8or, March 28, 2012, https://www.acceler8or.com/tags/chaos-computer-club:

> Psychedelics were the not so secret but illicit link between the various subworlds of art, literature, music, new age and technology. … convergence … was the hallmark of Mondo. They covered the whole gamut of alternativity. …
>
> As this was the Bay Area and Silicon Valley was close, the link with the computer industry was easy and logical. There was the money and the excitement. In those days everybody looked at the new possibilities, whether it was in music with synthesizers; in broadcasting with digital media; in entertainment with the emerging computer games. And virtual reality was definitely the magic potion that would free us from the limitations of space and time, the ultimate trip, the electronic drug. Most of the people involved had a sixties background, although there were also the catch-up hippies like myself, who missed out on but were fascinated by the likes of Leary and the Zeitgeist of the sixties.

35. Re-enactment of the Wau-Pengo debate.

36. In German, an *eingetragener verein*.

37. Katie Krause and Ole Schultz, "Our Own Private Germany," *Matter*, November 7, 2014, https://medium.com/matter/our-own-private-germany-6ce44ac93a7b.

38. Krause and Schultz, "Our Own Private Germany."

39. Gerard Alberto and Ruth Oldenziel, "Introduction: How European Players Captured the Computer and Created Scenes," in Alberto and Oldenzeil, *Hacking Europe*, 1–2.

40. Academics have done a lot of work pointing this out. See the important work of Gabriella Coleman, Alex Golub, Chris Kelty, and Molly Sauter on this subject. Journalist Bruce Sterling has also acknowledged the story is more complicated than Levy has told it. Although I have distinguished the cultural origins of hacking in different European countries, there is not space in this book to cover in any detail other groups like the early phone phreakers or the hacker underground (Julian Assange's habitat as a young hacker) that emerged out of the phreakers, except briefly where the latter intersects with Assange's story. Nor do I cover in detail some of the early groups that used distributed denial of service (DDoS) tactics for political protest, although I do mention some of these in chapter 11.

41. Read the Wau-Pengo debate transcribed at some length in this chapter. Wau Holland cites the hacker ethic as Levy summarized it.

42. As is mentioned in chapters 2 and 11, both Assange and Anonymous have explicitly espoused free software principles at various times.

43. Stallman received the award in 1990. The World Wide Web was invented in 1991.

44. Levy, *Hackers: Heroes of the Computer Revolution*, 271.

45. It is estimated that contributors to Torvalds's Linux project number in the hundreds of thousands and that its code is now more than 19 million lines long. Craig Timberg, "Net of Insecurity: The Kernel of the Argument," *Washington Post*, November 3, 2015.

46. Stallman, "Releasing Free Software If You Work at a University," 64–66.

47. Timberg, "Net of Insecurity."

48. Sebastian Anthony, "International Space Station Switches from Windows to Linux, for Improved Reliability," *Extreme Tech*, May 9, 2013, https://www.extre metech.com/extreme/155392-international-space-station-switches-from-windows -to-linux-for-improved-reliability.

49. Aaron Pressman, "The iPhone Decade: One of the Tech Industry's Biggest Innovations Celebrates Its Tenth Anniversary," *Fortune*, June 1, 2015, 25.

50. Timberg, "Net of Insecurity." According to Richard Stallman, GNU/Linux is used in internet servers, the New York stock exchange, the platforms of Google, Facebook and Amazon, and in many other places. Author's correspondence with Richard Stallman, March 4, 2019.

51. Richard Stallman, correspondence with the author, September 17, 2018. See also https://www.gnu.org/philosophy/open-source-misses-the-point.en.html.

52. Author's communication with Richard Stallman, March 4, 2019.

53. Unless a new free software smart phone comes onto the market in the meantime. One currently in development by Purism is the Librem phone. It is made entirely with free software, including its kernel. Richard Stallman, communication with author, July 6, 2019.

54. Pressman, "The iPhone Decade."

55. Leon Trotsky, *My Life: An Attempt at an Autobiography* (New York: Dover, 2017), 215.

56. General Keith Alexander was the director of the US National Security Agency from 2005 to 2013. He famously advocated that security agencies should "collect the whole haystack" of personal digital information available, rather than bothering with legal warrants to look for "needles" or specific information.

57. "The 2600 crowd" refers to the name of a publication, *2600: The Hacker Quarterly*, and an associated conference that grew out of a culture of early telephone hackers in the United States known as *phreakers*. In the 1960s, these early hackers discovered that a 2600 hertz tone (which could be reproduced with a toy whistle from a Cap'n Crunch cereal box), would allow them "operator" access to phone systems. "*2600: The Hacker Quarterly*," Wikipedia, https://en.wikipedia.org/wiki/2600:_The_Hacker_ Quarterly (accessed January 1, 2019).

58. Although he has never openly admitted it, Assange has hinted that he was responsible for the notorious WANK worm attack on NASA, too. See Robert Manne, "The Cypherpunk Revolutionary," *The Monthly*, March 2011, https://www. themonthly.com.au/issue/2011/february/1324596189/robert-manne/cypherpunk- revolutionary: "By October 1989 an attack was mounted from Australia on the NASA computer system via the introduction of what was called the WANK worm in

an attempt to sabotage the Jupiter launch of the *Galileo* rocket as part of an action of anti-nuclear activists. No one claimed responsibility for this attack, which is outlined in the first chapter of *Underground*. In an article he later published in the left-wing magazine *CounterPunch*, Assange would claim the WANK worm attack was 'the origin of hacktivism.' In a Swedish television documentary, *WikiRebels*, made with Assange's co-operation, there are hints he was responsible."

59. Manne, "The Cypherpunk Revolutionary."

60. Andrew Greenberg, *This Machine Kills Secrets: Julian Assange, the Cypherpunks, and Their Fight to Empower Whistleblowers* (New York: Plume, 2012), 96.

61. And the start of a brave new world. Aldous Huxley's 1932 novel, *Brave New World*, about a technological dystopia, takes its title from Miranda's speech in William Shakespeare's play, *The Tempest* (act 5, scene 1): "Oh, wonder! / How many goodly creatures are there here! / How beauteous mankind is! O brave new world, / That has such people in't."

CHAPTER 2

1. The "Collateral Murder" video was leaked by Bradley Manning to WikiLeaks. Taken from a US military helicopter, it shows gunsight footage of Iraqi civilians being killed. Crew members can be heard chatting as if they are playing a game. Assange decided that this was the leak to edit and package for the press, and it made WikiLeaks a household name.

2. Bruce Sterling, "The Blast Shack," *Webstock*, December 22, 2010, http://www .webstock.org.nz/the-blast-shack. In fact, Sterling thought the cablegate affair was a "dismal saga" and a "melancholy business": "it's going to take me a while to explain why this highly newsworthy event fills me with such a chilly, deadening sense of Edgar Allan Poe melancholia. But it sure does. Part of this dull, icy feeling, I think, must be the agonizing slowness with which this has happened. At last—at long last—the homemade nitroglycerin in the old cypherpunks blast shack has gone off."

3. Andrew Greenberg, *This Machine Kills Secrets: Julian Assange, the Cypherpunks, and Their Fight to Empower Whistleblowers* (New York: Plume, 2012), 58.

4. See "Cypherpunk," Activism.net, https://activsm.net/cypherpunk/crypto-anarchy .html (accessed June 20, 2018).

5. Greenberg, *This Machine Kills Secrets*, 52.

6. Greenberg, *This Machine Kills Secrets*, 78–79.

7. Timothy C. May, "The Cyphernomicon," version 0.666, September 10, 1994, http://www.kreps.org/hackers/overheads/11cyphernervs.pdf.

8. Greenberg, *This Machine Kills Secrets,* 81.

9. May, "The Cyphernomicon."

10. May, "The Cyphernomicon."

11. Robert Manne, "The Cypherpunk Revolutionary," *The Monthly*, March 2011, https://www.themonthly.com.au/issue/2011/february/1324596189/robert-manne/ cypherpunk-revolutionary.

12. May, "The Cyphernomicon."

13. May, "The Cyphernomicon."

14. May, "The Cyphernomicon."

15. Eric Hughes, "A Cypherpunk's Manfesto," 1993, https://www.digitalmanifesto .net/manifestos/16.

16. Steven Levy, "Crypto Rebels," *Wired*, February 1, 1993.

17. "The *Whole Earth Catalog* (WEC) was an American counterculture magazine and product catalog published by Stewart Brand several times a year between 1968 and 1972, and occasionally thereafter, until 1998. The magazine featured essays and articles, but was primarily focused on product reviews. The editorial focus was on self-sufficiency, ecology, alternative education, 'do it yourself' (DIY), and holism, and featured the slogan 'access to tools.'" *Whole Earth Catalog*, Wikipedia, https://en.wikipedia.org/wiki/Whole_Earth_Catalog (accessed January 1, 2019).

18. May, "The Cyphernomicon." As Thomas Rid has pointed out, this was a bit of an exaggeration: not everyone on the cypherpunk mailing list wrote code. Only about 10 percent of them did, and 5 percent worked on encryption projects. Thomas Rid, *Rise of the Machine: A Cybernetic History* (New York: Norton, 2016), 264–265, Kindle.

19. Greenberg, *This Machine Kills Secrets*, 110.

20. Greenberg, *This Machine Kills Secrets*, 123.

21. Greenberg, *This Machine Kills Secrets*, 100–101, 129–130; Manne, "The Cypherpunk Revolutionary."

22. John Perry Barlow, "A Declaration of the Independence of Cyberspace," https://www.eff.org/cyberspace-independence (accessed December 30, 2018).

23. Bruce Sterling, *The Hacker Crackdown: Law and Disorder on the Electronic Frontier* (Project Gutenberg ebook, 2008), Kindle, 3590.

24. John Perry Barlow, Keynote Address, Stanford Blockchain Workshops, video, November 6, 2015, https://www.youtube.com/watch?v=ExKt1BNsX0s.

25. Sterling, *Hacker Crackdown*, 3410–3415.

26. See "John Perry Barlow," Dead.net, http://www.dead.net/band/john-perry-barlow.

27. Sterling, *Hacker Crackdown*, 3408.

28. Barlow, Keynote Address.

29. Sterling, *Hacker Crackdown*, 3360–3376.

30. Sterling, *Hacker Crackdown*, 3601.

31. "Pinedale Wyoming Population History 1990–2015," https://www.biggestuscities.com/city/pinedale-wyoming (accessed January 1, 2019).

32. Sterling, *Hacker Crackdown*, 3610.

33. John Perry Barlow, "Crime and Puzzlement: Desperadoes of the DataSphere," Electronic Frontier Foundation, June 8, 1990, https://w2.eff.org/Misc/Publications/John_Perry_Barlow/HTML/crime_and_puzzlement_1.html.

34. Sterling, *Hacker Crackdown*, 3619.

35. Sterling, *Hacker Crackdown*, 3619.

36. Sterling, *Hacker Crackdown*, 3623.

37. John Perry Barlow speaking at the Stanford Blockchain Workshops with John Clippinger, "Blockchain: Law, Regulation, Policy, the Law of the Horse," video, November 6, 2015, https://www.youtube.com/watch?v=wtMezbrA3gw.

38. Sterling, *Hacker Crackdown*, 3387.

39. Sterling, *Hacker Crackdown*, 3387–3400.

40. Sterling, *Hacker Crackdown*, 3395.

41. Sterling, *Hacker Crackdown*, 3389.

42. Sterling, *Hacker Crackdown*, 4172–4177.

43. Sterling, *Hacker Crackdown*, 4182–4191.

44. MIT researchers may have invented a public key encryption system, but cybernetics scholar Thomas Rid claims that the idea originated with the British signal intelligence agency GCHQ, which kept it secret for many years. Rid, *Rise of the Machine*, 241.

45. Steven Levy, *Crypto: How the Code Rebels Beat the Government, Saving Privacy in the Digital Age* (New York: Penguin, 2001), 190.

46. R. W. Apple Jr., "Twenty-five Years Later: Lessons from the Pentagon Papers," *New York Times*, June 23, 1996, https://www.nytimes.com/1996/06/23/weekinreview/25 -years-later-lessons-from-the-pentagon-papers.html.

47. David W. Dunlap, "1971: Supreme Court Allows Publication of Pentagon Papers," *New York Times*, June 30, 2016.

48. In its decision *New York Times Co. v. United States,* 403 US 713 (1971), the US Supreme Court held that "Any system of prior restraints of expression comes to this court bearing a heavy presumption against its constitutional validity" and that the government "carries a heavy burden of showing justification for the imposition of such a restraint." Although there was and is still no law on the books that says the government cannot prosecute journalists for seeking out and publishing leaks of classified information as accessories after the fact, successive US governments have never done so, tacitly respecting this practice as part of the larger principle of "freedom of the press" guaranteed by the US Constitution. However, the line is increasingly thinning. The Obama administration brought an unprecedented number of prosecutions against leakers, including Chelsea Manning, and it went after journalist James Rosen for his emails and James Risen for his sources. After these cases caused a public uproar, it dropped its cases, and the Department of Justice issued a set of guidelines stating that it would not treat "ordinary news-gathering activities" as criminal conduct, without defining those activities.

49. Levy, *Crypto*, 190–191.

50. Levy, *Crypto*, 194.

51. Levy, "Crypto Rebels."

52. Levy, "Crypto Rebels."

53. Greenberg, *This Machine Kills Secrets*, 75.

54. Levy, *Crypto*, 252.

55. Rid, *Rise of the Machine*, 268.

56. Greenberg, *This Machine Kills Secrets*, 85.

57. Greenberg, *This Machine Kills Secrets*, 85.

58. Greenberg, *This Machine Kills Secrets*, 86.

59. Greenberg, *This Machine Kills Secrets*, 83–84.

60. Levy, *Crypto*, 288–289.

61. Levy, *Crypto*, 290; Greenberg, *This Machine Kills Secrets*, 87.

62. Levy, *Crypto*, 266–267.

63. Levy, *Crypto*, 256–260.

64. Levy, *Crypto*, 296.

65. Barlow, Keynote Address.

66. David Hershkovits, "John Perry Barlow Talks Acid, Cyber-independence and His Friendship with JFK Jr.," *Paper*, April 2015, http://www.papermag.com/john-perry

-barlow-talks-acid-cyber-independence-and-his-friendship-wit-1427554020.html: "It was described as techno-utopian," he says. "There was a certain calculation to that. The best way to invent the future is to predict it. I felt that if I were persuasive enough in giving a vision of the future in which the Internet was inherently free and could not be controlled, we had a better shot at it."

67. Hershkovits, "John Perry Barlow."

68. See "John Perry Barlow," Dead.net, http://www.dead.net/band/john-perry -barlow.

69. NetBSD is a free and open-source Unix-like operating system that descends from Berkeley Software Distribution, a Research Unix derivative developed at the University of California, Berkeley. See The NetBSD Project, netbsd.org.

70. Greenberg, *This Machine Kills Secrets*, 113.

71. Manne, "The Cypherpunk Revolutionary."

72. Manne, "The Cypherpunk Revolutionary."

73. Manne, "The Cypherpunk Revolutionary."

74. Greenberg, *This Machine Kills Secrets*, 127.

75. R. U. Sirius, "Cypherpunk Rising: Wikileaks, Encryption, and the Coming Surveillance Dystopia," *The Verge*, March 7, 2013, https://www.theverge.com/2013/ 3/7/4036040/cypherpunks-julian-assange-wikileaks-encryption-surveillance -dystopia.

76. Manne, "The Cypherpunk Revolutionary."

77. May, "The Cyphernomicon."

78. Manne, "The Cypherpunk Revolutionary."

CHAPTER 3

1. Steven Levy, "Lawrence Lessig's Supreme Showdown," *Wired*, October 1, 2002.

2. Lawrence Lessig, *Code and Other Laws of Cyberspace* (Cambridge: Basic Books, 1999).

3. Lawrence Lessig, "Code Is Law: On Liberty in Cyberspace," *Harvard Magazine*, January–February 2000.

4. Lessig, "Code Is Law."

5. Cited in Thomas Rid, *Rise of the Machine: A Cybernetic History* (New York: Norton, 2016), 285, Kindle.

6. That is "democrat" with a small "d." In American party politics, Lessig has been both a Republican and a Democrat. See "Lawrence Lessig," Wikipedia, https://en .wikipedia.org/wiki/Lawrence_Lessig#Political_background.

7. Lessig, "Code Is Law."

8. Andrew Greenberg, *This Machine Kills Secrets: Julian Assange, the Cypherpunks, and Their Fight to Empower Whistleblowers* (New York: Plume, 2012), 148.

9. Julian Assange, "State and Terrorist Conspiracies," November 10, 2006, originally posted at me@iq.org, reposted at https://cryptome.org/0002/ja-conspiracies.pdf.

10. Julian Assange, "Conspiracy as Governance," December 3, 2006, originally posted at me@iq,org; reposted at https://cryptome.org/0002/ja-conspiracies.pdf.

11. Assange, "Conspiracy as Governance."

12. Assange, "Conspiracy as Governance."

13. Greenberg, *This Machine Kills Secrets*, 130.

14. Robert Manne, "The Cypherpunk Revolutionary," *The Monthly*, March 2011, https://www.themonthly.com.au/issue/2011/february/1324596189/robert-manne/cypherpunk-revolutionary. Ellsberg later became an ally of Assange and attended the Chelsea Manning trial with Assange's lawyers.

15. Greenberg, *This Machine Kills Secrets*, 160.

16. Greenberg, *This Machine Kills Secrets*, 159–160. See the original source that Greenberg cites: Raffi Khatchadourian, "No Secrets: Julian Assange's Mission for Total Transparency," *The New Yorker*, June 7, 2010. Assange later denied this, but see also the 2006 email from Assange to John Young (presumably in the batch Young released on Cryptome) that Greenberg quotes at 159: "Hackers monitor Chinese and other intel as they burrow into their targets. When they pull, so do we."

17. Greenberg, *This Machine Kills Secrets*, 131–132.

18. Manne, "The Cypherpunk Revolutionary."

19. Manne, "The Cypherpunk Revolutionary."

20. Manne, "The Cypherpunk Revolutionary."

21. After sending Assange some cables relating to the US ambassador in Iceland, Manning downloaded 93,000 logs from the Afghan war, 400,000 incident reports from the war in Iraq, and 250,000 State Department cables. Manne, "The Cypherpunk Revolutionary."

22. *We Steal Secrets: The Story of Wikileaks*, directed by Alex Gibney, Jigsaw Productions, 2013.

23. Heather Brooke, "Inside the Secret World of Hackers," *The Guardian*, August 24, 2011; Vernon Silver, "The Hackers Russia-Proofing Germany's Elections," *Bloomberg Businessweek*, June 26, 2017.

24. "Chaos Computer Club," Wikipedia, citing "CCC Publishes Fingerprints of Wolfgang Schauble, the German Home Secretary," *Heise Online*, March 3, 2008, link no longer available. The event happened in 2008.

25. See "Welcome to Project Blinkenlights," Blinkenlights.net, http://blinkenlights.net/project.

26. Julian Assange, Jacob Appelbaum, Andy Müller-Maguhn, and Jérémie Zimmermann, *Cypherpunks: Freedom and the Future of the Internet* (New York: OR Books, 2012), 8–9.

27. Khatchadourian, "No Secrets."

28. Manne, "The Cypherpunk Revolutionary."

29. Khatchadourian, "No Secrets."

30. "Assange: WikiLeaks Is the Intelligence Agency of the People," *New Statesman*, April 5, 2011. Since CIA director Mike Pompeo accused WikiLeaks of being a nonstate intelligence agency, however, Assange has backpedaled on the characterization.

31. Greenberg, *This Machine Kills Secrets*, 298, 300.

32. Greenberg, *This Machine Kills Secrets*, 302.

33. Marcel Rosenbach, "Top German Hacker Slams OpenLeaks Founder," *der Spiegel*, August 15, 2011; Greenberg, *This Machine Kills Secrets*, 302–303.

34. Greenberg, *This Machine Kills Secrets*, 303.

35. Rosenbach, "Top German Hacker."

36. Greenberg, *This Machine Kills Secrets*, 299.

37. Greenberg, *This Machine Kills Secrets*, 301–302. For Domscheit-Berg's side of the story, see Janek Schmidt, "Daniel Domscheit-Berg about WikiLeaks: 'The Dispute Became So Absurd,'" *Scribd*, November 6, 2011, https://www.scribd.com/document/71853929/Daniel-Domscheit-About-WikiLeaks.

38. See "Chaos Computer Club," Wikipedia, https://en.wikipedia.org/wiki/Chaos_Computer_Club.

39. Mike Butcher, "WikiLeaks Watch: Julian Assange to Be Freed on Bail (Plus Bonus Downfall Parody)," *Tech Crunch*, December 16, 2010.

40. Esther Addley, "Q&A: Julian Assange Allegations," *The Guardian*, December 17, 2010.

41. Butcher, "WikiLeaks Watch"; Michael Hastings, "Julian Assange: The *Rolling Stone* Interview," *Rolling Stone*, January 18, 2012.

42. Manne, "The Cypherpunk Revolutionary": "In July the first of the Manning tranche, the Afghan War Diary, was published. Assange held back only 15,000 of the 93,000 reports. Unforgivably, those released included the names of perhaps 300 Afghans who had assisted western forces. A Taliban spokesperson, Zabiullah Mujahid, claimed that a nine-member commission had been created after the documents were released 'to find out about people who were spying.' Assange was unrepentant. Both in private and in public, he argued that if they were collaborators they deserved to die."

By contrast, it seems that the unredacted leak of the State Department cables was not wholly deliberate on Assange's part. One version of the story is that when Andy Müller-Maguhn recovered the files of already published leaks from Domscheit-Berg and handed them over to an unnamed WikiLeaks staffer, they were posted online and also uploaded to Pirate Bay. Unfortunately, the set included four overlooked, encrypted files that contained the whole set of unredacted cables. The "slip" was disastrously compounded when *The Guardian*'s publisher, David Leigh, used Assange's passphrase to these files as tech "window dressing" for a heading in his book. He had no idea what the phrase was for. None other than John Young picked up on the inadvertent leak, successfully decrypted the files, and spilled them in their entirety on his platform, Cryptome. This forced Assange's hand to release all of the documents. Greenberg, *This Machine Kills Secrets*, 305–307.

Daniel Domscheit-Berg has implied Andy Müller-Maguhn was the unfortunate person who uploaded the four encrypted files. See Schmidt, "Daniel Domscheit-Berg about WikiLeaks"; see also Greenberg, *This Machine Kills Secrets*, 299–300.

43. Manne, "The Cypherpunk Revolutionary."

44. Manne, "The Cypherpunk Revolutionary."

45. Manne, "The Cypherpunk Revolutionary."

46. Rosenbach, "Top German Hacker."

47. Assange, Appelbaum, Müller-Maguhn, and Zimmermann, *Cypherpunks*. The interview was not done at the Norfolk house, however.

48. Julian Assange, "Preface" (dated October 6, 2012), in Assange, Appelbaum, Müller-Maguhn, and Zimmermann, *Cypherpunks*.

49. Assange, Appelbaum, Müller-Maguhn and Zimmermann, *Cypherpunks*, 151.

50. Assange, Appelbaum, Müller-Maguhn and Zimmermann, *Cypherpunks*, 71.

51. Michael B. Kelley, "NSA: Snowden Stole 1.7 Million Documents and Still Has Access to Most of Them," *Business Insider*, December 13, 2013.

52. This section contains paragraphs from an article I wrote for the Quebec-based revue *Relations*: Maureen Webb, "Les nouveaux habits de Big Brother," trans. Catherine Caron, *Relations*, no. 776 (January–February 2015): 14–17.

53. Glenn Greenwald, *No Place to Hide* (Toronto: McClelland & Stewart, 2014), 47–48.

54. Glenn Greenwald, "XKeyscore: NSA Tool Collects 'Nearly Everything a User Does on the Internet,'" *The Guardian*, July 31, 2013.

55. James Risen and Laura Poitras, "NSA Report Outlined Goals for More Power," *New York Times*, November 22, 2013; "A Strategy for Surveillance Powers," *New York Times*, November 23, 2013.

56. See Edward Snowden, "NSA Whistleblower Edward Snowden: 'I Don't Want to Live in a Society That Does These Sorts of Things,'" *The Guardian*, June 9, 2013, video, https://www.theguardian.com/world/video/2013/jun/09/nsa-whistleblower -edward-snowden-interview-video.

57. Gordon S. Wood, *The American Revolution: A History* (New York: Modern Library, 2002), 162.

58. Wood, *The American Revolution*, 160.

59. Wood, *The American Revolution*, 160.

60. Wood, *The American Revolution*, 159. See also Gary Wills, "Evangelical Awakenings," *New York Review of Books*, April 20, 2017, 26, which covers the history of American evangelism "out of doors," a related phenomenon, perhaps, of American culture.

61. Wood, *The American Revolution*, 160.

62. Wood, *The American Revolution*, 154–158.

63. Wood, *The American Revolution*, 159–162. Ironically and to its patrician theorists' dismay, the egalitarian promise of this radical vision of democracy came to fruition with the addition of a Bill of Rights and a political culture in which ordinary men competed successfully for elected office alongside "their betters."

64. Hastings, "Julian Assange."

CHAPTER 4

1. Stuart Braun, *City of Exiles: Berlin from the Outside In* (Berlin: Noctua Press, 2015), 121–122. In this chapter, I have drawn heavily on Braun's excellent cultural history of Berlin.

2. Braun, *City of Exiles*, 123.

3. The line is taken from a poem by Paul Zeck: "Berlin, stop and think! Your dance partner is Death." See the public poster at Beckyhollandi, "Berlin, Your Dance Partner Is Death," Berlin: A Divided City, February 17, 2013, https://berlindividedcity .wordpress.com/2013/02/17/berlin-your-dance-partner-is-death.

4. Lucy Suchman was the leader of the work practice and technology group that prototyped innovative systems developed through close collaboration with their prospective users.

5. Andrew Clement told me that Gotlieb used to tell the story of a massive pile of printouts from this computer that impressed the Americans and helped persuade them to agree to a Canadian plan for the route of the new St. Lawrence Seaway.

6. Eric Lichtblau and James Risen, "Spy Agency Mined Vast Data Trove, Officials Report," *New York Times*, December 24, 2005.

7. See the public archive of published Snowden documents at Snowden Surveillance Archive, https://snowdenarchive.cjfe.org. The archive is a collaborative research effort between the Politics of Surveillance Project at the Faculty of Information at the University of Toronto and Canadian Journalists for Free Expression (CJFE). Partners and supporters of this initiative include the Centre for Free Expression, Faculty of Communications and Design, Ryerson University; the Digital Curation Institute, Faculty of Information, University of Toronto; and the Surveillance Studies Centre, Queen's University.

8. Natalya Viktorovna Hesse and Vladimir Tolz, "The Sakharovs in Gorky," in Robert B. Silvers, ed., *The New York Review Abroad: Fifty Years of International Reportage* (New York: New York Review of Books, 2013), 153–154.

9. Hesse and Tolz, "The Sakharovs in Gorky," 154.

10. The friendship between Frederick, the patron, and Voltaire, the talent, had its tensions, with Voltaire exercising his free speech in the end to write the following about Frederick in *La loi naturelle* (1756):

> Of incongruities a monstrous pile,
> Calling men brothers, crushing them the while;
> With air humane, a misanthropic brute;
> Oft-times impulsive, sometimes over-'cute;
>
> Weak 'midst his choler, modest in his pride;
> Yearning for virtue, lust personified;
> Statesman and author, of the slippery crew;
> My patron, pupil, persecutor too.

11. These paragraphs are based on Braun, *City of Exiles*, 53–65, and the Heinrich Eduard Jacob quote at 65.

12. Braun, *City of Exiles*, 66–67, and the Rosa Luxemburg quote at 64.

13. In fact, 130,000 Berliners courageously turned out to protest his imminent assumption of power in January 1933, hanging a large placard on the Karl Liebknecht house that read: "To advance the spirit of the struggle against war, violence, fascism, hunger and cold, for work, bread, and freedom." Braun, *City of Exiles*, 85.

14. Braun, *City of Exiles*, 135, citing Michel Contad and Michel Ribalka, *The Writings of Jean Paul Sartre* (Evanston, IL: Northwestern University Press, 1974), 200.

15. George Packer, "The Holder of Secrets: Laura Poitras's closeup view of Edward Snowden," *The New Yorker*, October 20, 2014.

16. Packer, "Holder of Secrets."

17. Sara Corbett, "How a Snowdenista Kept the NSA Leaker Hidden in a Moscow Airport," *Vogue*, February 18, 2015, https://www.vogue.com/article/sarah-harrison -edward-snowden-wikileaks-nsa.

18. Corbett, "Snowdenista."

19. Corbett, "Snowdenista."

20. Laura Poitras reveals this fact in her 2017 film, *Risk*.

21. Glenn Greenwald, "The Intercept Is Broadening Access to the Snowden Archive: Here's Why," *The Intercept*, May 16, 2016.

22. Curtis Skinner, "Reporters Who Broke the Snowden Story Return to the US for the First Time," Reuters, April 11, 2014, https://www.yahoo.com/news/reporters -broke-snowden-story-return-u-first-time-172716376--sector.html.

23. Carole Cadwalladr, "Berlin's Digital Exiles: Where Tech Activists Go to Escape the NSA," *The Guardian*, November 9, 2014; Packer, "Holder of Secrets."

24. "Criminal Complaint against Mass Surveillance: We Won't Back Down!," Chaos Communications Club, posted June 4, 2015, https://www.ccc.de/en/updates/2015/gba3.

25. Corbett, "Snowdenista."

26. Corbett, "Snowdenista."

27. Dante wrote about the pain of exile in his *Divine Comedy*. In *Paradiso*, 17 (55–60), his great-great-grandfather warns him what to expect:

> "You shall leave everything you love most:
> this is the arrow that the bow of exile shoots first.
> You are to know the bitter taste
> of others' bread, how salty it is, and know
> how hard a path it is for one who goes
> ascending and descending others' stairs."

28. DefenseSystems.org published this story.

29. Cory Doctorow, "CryptoParty: Like a Tupperware Party for Learning Crypto," *boing boing*, October 12, 2012, http://boingboing.net/2012/10/12/cryptoparty-like-a-tupperware.html.

30. Chris Irvine and Tom Parfitt, "Kremlin Returns to Typewriters to Avoid Computer Leaks," *The Telegraph*, July 11, 2013.

CHAPTER 5

1. Harry Halpin works on standardization working groups that he himself formed— namely, the W3C Web Cryptography and the W3C Web Authentication Working Group. In 2012, W3C sent him to present his work on web cryptography at the Chaos Computer Club congress: Harry Halpin, "Re-igniting the Crypto Wars on the Web," video filmed December 27, 2012, https://media.ccc.de/v/29c3-5374-en-re_igniting_the_crypto_wars_on_the_web_h264#t=547.

2. Paul Syverson of the Naval Research Lab had the idea and obtained the initial grant for Tor. His webpage is at http://www.syverson.org.

3. Even after Chelsea Manning reportedly used Tor to make her leaks, the US government kept funding Tor. Its own diplomatic and security intelligence agents need it, and to be effective it has to be available to everyone. The diversity and number of nodes make it work.

4. Gabriella Coleman, *Hacker, Hoaxer, Whistleblower, Spy: The Many Faces of Anonymous* (London: Verso, 2014).

5. Jonathan Zittrain, "The Web as Random Acts of Kindness," TEDGlobal 2009, July 2009, https://www.ted.com/talks/jonathan_zittrain_the_web_is_a_random_act_of_kindness#t-158022.

6. Zittrain, "The Web."

7. See another entertaining lecture by Jonathan Zittrain on the nature of internet: "Jonathan Zittrain Kicks Off the Berkman Center's 2015–2016 Academic Year," published September 17, 2015, https://www.youtube.com/watch?v=VirAb9QU0Lc.

8. Zittrain does not use the term "connectivity commons," but that is how I picture it.

9. Jonathan Zittrain, *The Future of the Internet and How to Stop It* (New Haven: Yale University Press, 2008), 67–68.

10. Harry later told me that the informal discussions groups known originally as "birds of a feather" (BOF) meetings were now more likely to meet at a bar (a bar BOF) before the "official" BOF meeting.

11. Heidi Boghosian, *Spying on Democracy* (San Francisco: City Lights, 2013), 137.

12. To be fair, Morozov has subsequently written about other topics.

13. Dan Schiller, *Digital Depression: Information Technology and Economic Crisis* (Chicago: University of Illinois Press, 2014), 208, quoting Milton Mueller in Geoff Dyer and Richard Waters, "Spying Threatens Internet, Say Experts," *Financial Times*, November 21, 2013.

14. Schiller, *Digital Depression*, 208, citing ICANN, "Montevideo Statement on the Future of Internet Cooperation," October 7, 2013, https://www.icann.org/news/announcement-2013-10-07-en.

15. See "Terms of Reference," NETmundial Initiative, https://www.netmundial.org/terms-reference (accessed July 28, 2019).

16. Harry told me later that the World Economic Forum (the organization that meets in Davos, Switzerland) got involved in the NETmundial process at its outset and was viewed by some digital rights activists as subverting the process. Nothing significant came of the NETmundial initiative in the end.

17. Thomas Rid, *Rise of the Machines: A Cybernetic History* (New York: Norton, 2016), 334, Kindle.

18. Gabriella Coleman, "From Internet Farming to Weapons of the Geek," *Current Anthropology* 58, no. S15 (February 2017): S91–S102.

19. Early theorists include Julian Assange, Andrew Feenberg, Geert Lovink, and David Cantwell Smith.

20. Gordon S. Wood, *The American Revolution: A History* (New York: Modern Library, 2002), 93.

21. Wood, *The American Revolution*, 94.

22. As Richard Stallman has pointed out, democracy is certainly the opposite of the libertarianism that is practised by many American adherents: "They use the name 'Libertarian' to pass off laissez-faire [economics] as a matter of liberty. I call them 'Antisocialists' because opposing what they call 'Socialism' (meaning any state programs that help people in general) is what they are all about, and because it's a joke as well. But 'laissez-faireists' would fit them too. Or 'laissez-foutrists';)." Richard Stallman, correspondence with the author, January 7, 2018.

23. On this topic, see Thomas Frank, *Listen, Liberal: Or, What Ever Happened to the Party of the People?* (New York: Metropolitan Books, 2016).

CHAPTER 6

1. The hyperlink to the Privacy International letter is broken, but see "Surveillance Company Hacking Team Exposed," Privacy International, posted July 6, 2015, https://www.privacyinternational.org/node/1031.

2. "Ethiopia: Digital Attacks Intensify—Spyware Firm Should Address Alleged Misuse," Human Rights Watch, posted March 9, 2015, https://www.hrw.org/news/2015/03/09/ethiopia-digital-attacks-intensify.

3. Ron Deibert, "Open Letter to Hacking Team," Citizen Lab, posted August 8, 2014, https://citizenlab.ca/2014/08/open-letter-hacking-team; Ron Deibert, "Open Letter

to Hacking Team," Citizen Lab, posted March 5, 2015, https://citizenlab.ca/2015/03/open-letter-hacking-team-march-2015.

4. Alex Hern, "Hacking Team Hacked: Firm Sold Spying Tools to Repressive Regimes, Documents Claim," *The Guardian*, July 6, 2015.

5. Andrew Greenberg, *This Machine Kills Secrets: Julian Assange, the Cypherpunks, and Their Fight to Empower Whistleblowers* (New York: Plume, 2012), 229–230.

6. For the whole story, including the ultimate revocation of the license, see "Hacking Team's Global License Revoked by Italian Export Authorities," Privacy International, posted April 8, 2016, https://www.privacyinternational.org/node/1042.

7. For links to all of its research and articles related to Hacking Team, see "Hacking Team," The Citizen Lab, https://citizenlab.ca/tag/hacking-team.

8. Hern, "Hacking Team."

9. Hern, "Hacking Team"; Mattathias Schwartz, "Cyberwar for Sale," *New York Times Magazine*, January 4, 2017, https://www.nytimes.com/2017/01/04/magazine/cyberwar-for-sale.html.

10. Hern, "Hacking Team." The government of Sudan, a US-designated state sponsor of terrorism, paid Hacking Team nearly one million euros between 2012 and 2014, and the FBI paid the group $700,000. Schwartz, "Cyberwar for Sale."

11. Craig Timberg, "Net of Insecurity: The Kernel of the Argument," *Washington Post*, November 5, 2015.

12. Timberg, "Net of Insecurity."

13. Timberg, "Net of Insecurity."

14. Bill Anderson, "Android and the Linux Kernel Towelroot Exploit," *Android News for Costa Rica*, June 23, 2014, http://www.all-things-android.com/content/android-and-linux-kernel-towelroot-exploit. See also "Hacker Geohot Releases Root Tool for Galaxy S5 and Most Other Android Devices," *Geek.com*, July 16, 2014, https://www.geek.com/android/hacker-geohot-releases-root-tool-for-galaxy-s5-and-most-other-android-devices-1596797.

15. Timberg, "Net of Insecurity."

16. Timberg, "Net of Insecurity." See also the Wikileaks Hacking Team Archive at https://wikileaks.org/hackingteam/emails/emailid/5761.

17. Gianluca gave me permission to print this part of our conversation.

18. Schwartz, "Cyberwar for Sale."

19. Schwartz, "Cyberwar for Sale."

20. "Chaos Computer Club: Staatstrojaner Affair," Wikipedia, https://en.wikipedia.org/wiki/Chaos_Computer_Club (accessed December 30, 2018).

21. Vernon Silver, "The Hackers Russia Proofing Germany's Elections," *Bloomberg Businessweek*, June 26, 2017.

22. "State Trojan Again on Trial in Constitutional Court," Chaos Computer Club, posted July 6, 2015, https://www.ccc.de/en/updates/2015/bkag.

CHAPTER 7

1. Mattathias Schwartz, "Cyberwar for Sale," *New York Times Magazine*, January 4, 2017.

2. Schwartz, "Cyberwar for Sale."

3. Schwartz, "Cyberwar for Sale."

4. Andrew Greenberg, *This Machine Kills Secrets: Julian Assange, the Cypherpunks, and Their Fight to Empower Whistleblowers* (New York: Plume, 2012), 108.

5. "Chat with Prof. Ron Deibert and Edward Snowden," Rights Con 2016, video, published April 12, 2016, https://www.youtube.com/watch?v=l1Hy_OFkZ8s.

6. Bruce Schneier, "NSA Surveillance: A Guide to Staying Secure," *The Guardian*, September 6, 2013, https://www.theguardian.com/world/2013/sep/05/nsa-how-to -remain-secure-surveillance.

7. Yael Grauer, "Staggering Variety of Clandestine Trackers Found in Popular Android Apps," *The Intercept*, November 24, 2017.

8. Grauer, "Staggering Variety."

9. Hacker Kim.dotcom has proposed using the reserve computing power of cell phones to create a decentralized alternative internet: "'By the People, for the People': Kim.dotcom to Launch Alternative Internet," RT, November 22, 2017, https://www .rt.com/news/410606-kim-dotcom-meganet-internet.

10. Ashley Madison was an online service for people looking for adulterous hook-ups. The site was hacked in 2015, and its unencrypted data for more than 32 million members was released on the dark net. In a matter of days, members were receiving blackmail threats. Reportedly, the Chinese government cross-tabulated hacked data on civil servants with Ashley Madison data to find government employees susceptible to being exploited for Chinese espionage. Sue Halpern, "In the Depths of the Net," *New York Review of Books*, October 8, 2015.

11. The implementation of Tor was in 2003, but onion routing was conceived and tested from the mid-1990s.

12. Vint Cerf, "Hangout with Vint Cerf," TWiT Hangouts, video, published April 2, 2014, https://www.youtube.com/watch?v=17GtmwyvmWE&feature=share&t= 23m1s. See also Craig Timberg, "Net of Insecurity: The Kernel of the Argument," *Washington Post*, November 5, 2015.

13. Silkie Carlo, "Protect Your Privacy by Moving to the Dark Web," *Wired*, January 8, 2017.

14. Micha Lee, "Edward Snowden's New App Uses Your Smart Phone to Physically Guard Your Laptop," *The Intercept*, December 22, 2017.

15. Timberg, "Net of Insecurity."

16. See "You Broke the Internet: We'll Make Ourselves a GNU One," Youbroke theinternet.org, http://youbroketheinternet.org.

17. "Youbroketheinternet" presentation filmed at the 2014 ThinkTwice conference, video, https://www.youtube.com/watch?v=iGxjN-lfr_Y.

18. See "The Project Map," Youbroketheinternet.org, http://youbroketheinternet. org/map. See also Christian Grothoff, Bartlomiej Polot, and Carlo Loesch, "The Internet Is Broken: Idealistic Ideas for Building a NEWGNU Network," paper presented at the W3C/IETF Strengthening the Internet Workshop STRINT, March 2014, https://www.w3.org/2014/strint/report.html#idm29683568: "This paper describes issues for security and privacy at all layers of the Internet stack and proposes radical changes to the architecture to build a network that offers strong security and privacy by default."

19. See "About NGI," Next Generation Internet, https://www.ngi.eu/about.

20. European Commission, "Next Generation Internet Initiative," https://ec.europa. eu/digital-single-market/en/policies/next-generation-internet (accessed January 1, 2019).

21. "Next Generation Internet," NLnet Foundation, https://nlnet.nl/NGI (accessed January 1, 2019). NLnet Foundation has been commissioned by the European Commission to write the NGI Vision: "NLnet and Gartner to Write Vision for EC's Next Generaiton Internet Initiative," NLnet Foundation, https://nlnet.nl/news/2017/20170412-EC-NGI.html. See also "NGI Study," Next Generation Internet, https://www.ngi.eu/about/ngi-study.

22. See "You Broke the Internet: We'll Make Ourselves a GNU One," Youbrokethe internet.org, http://youbroketheinternet.org.

CHAPTER 8

1. Adam Nagourney, Ian Lovett, and Richard Perez-Pena, "San Bernardino Shooting Kills at Least Fourteen; Two Suspects Are Dead," *New York Times*, December 2, 2015.

2. Cindy Cohn profile, Electronic Frontier Foundation, https://www.eff.org/about/staff/cindy-cohn (accessed December 30, 2018).

3. David Gilbert, "Going Dark? FBI Not So Blind Despite Apple iPhone and Other Encrypted Devices," *International Business Times*, March 7, 2016. See also James Comey, "Going Dark: Are Technology, Privacy and Public Safety on a Collision Course?," remarks as delivered to the Brookings Institution, Washington, DC, October 16, 2014, https://www.fbi.gov/news/speeches/going-dark-are-technology-privacy-and-public-safety-on-a-collision-course.

4. Samuel Gibbs, "Snowden: FBI's Claim It Can't Unlock the San Bernardino iPhone Is 'Bullshit,'" *The Guardian*, March 9, 2016.

5. Spencer Ackerman, "FBI May Have Found Way to Unlock San Bernardino Shooter's iPhone without Apple," *The Guardian*, March 22, 2016.

6. "Secret Documents Reveal NSA Campaign against Encryption," *New York Times*, September 5, 2013, http://www.nytimes.com/interactive/2013/09/05/us/documents-reveal-nsa-campaign-against-encryption.html (accessedDecember 30, 2018); James Ball, Julian Borger, and Glenn Greenwald, "US and UK Spy Agencies Defeat Privacy and Security on the Internet," *The Guardian*, September 5, 2013.

7. Ackerman, "FBI May Have Found."

8. Bernstein had invented a way of encrypting material that used the algorithm of a hash and was not itself an encryption tool. He wanted to test the logic of the US prohibition on the export of cryptographic tools by applying for permission to publish his results on the internet in five different ways. Steven Levy, *Crypto: How the Code Rebels Beat the Government—Saving Privacy in the Digital Age* (New York: Penguin, 2001), 297.

9. Bernstein v. United States (9th Cir. May 6, 1999). See also Levy, *Crypto*, 297–302.

10. The *Junger* case is citable but not as thrilling.

11. The authors included cypherpunk and Electronic Frontier Foundation (EFF) founder John Gilmore, well-known cryptographic inventors Whitfield Diffie and Ronald L. Rivest, security expert Bruce Schneier, and prominent academics with computer science and policy credentials, including Harold Abelson, Ross Anderson, Steven M. Bellovin, Josh Benaloh, Matt Blaze, Matthew Green, Susan Landau, Peter G. Neumann, Jeffrey I. Schiller, Michael Specter, Daniel J. Weitzner. "Keys under the Doormat: Mandating Insecurity by Requiring Government Access to All Data and Communications," July 7, 2015, https://www.schneier.com/academic/paperfiles/paper-keys-under-doormats-CSAIL.pdf.

12. "Keys under the Doormat," 2.

13. "Tor Is Not as Safe as You May Think," Infosecurity, posted September 2, 2013, https://www.infosecurity-magazine.com/news/tor-is-not-as-safe-as-you-may-think/, cited in Sue Halpern, "In the Depths of the Net," *New York Review of Books*, October 8, 2015.

14. Halpern, "In the Depths."

15. The Tor Project website can be found at https://www.torproject.org/index.html.en.

16. Andrew Greenberg, *This Machine Kills Secrets: Julian Assange, the Cypherpunks, and Their Fight to Empower Whistleblowers* (New York: Plume, 2012), 149.

17. "Join the Tor Challenge," Electronic Frontier Foundation, https://www.eff.org/torchallenge.

18. Greenberg, *This Machine Kills Secrets*, 150.

19. Andrew Lewman, executive director of the Tor Project, quoted in Halpern, "In the Depths."

20. Greenberg, *This Machine Kills Secrets*, 145.

21. Greenberg, *This Machine Kills Secrets*, 150.

22. Gennie Gebhart, "We're Halfway to Encrypting the Entire Web," Electronic Frontier Foundation, posted February 21, 2017, https://www.eff.org/deeplinks/2017/02/were-halfway-encrypting-entire-web.

23. Timothy Snyder, *On Tyranny: Twenty Lessons from the Twentieth Century* (New York: Tim Duggan Books, 2017), 88, Kindle, referring to Hannah Arendt's work, *The Origins of Totalitarianism* (New York: Schocken Books, 1951).

24. Snyder, *On Tyranny*, 88.

25. Julia Angwin, "First Library to Support Anonymous Internet Browsing Effort Stops after DHS Email," *ProPublica*, September 10, 2015.

26. The first Tor relay was set up in Canada at the library of the University of Western Canada, where the legality of it was uncertain. Jordan Pearson, "Can You Be Arrested for Running a Tor Exit Node in Canada? Running a Tor Exit Node Is a Risky Proposition," *Motherboard*, September 25, 2015.

27. Jonathan Zittrain, *The Future of the Internet and How to Stop It* (New Haven: Yale University Press, 2008), 223–228.

28. Dan Farber, "WikiLeaks Is Winning the Info War So Far," December 7, 2010, CBS News, https://www.cbsnews.com/news/wikileaks-is-winning-the-info-war-so-far.

29. Greenberg, *This Machine Kills Secrets*,186.

30. Greenberg, *This Machine Kills Secrets*, 210–216.

31. Greenberg, *This Machine Kills Secrets*, 212–213. In the hack of Barr and HBGary, LulzSec announced themselves as Anonymous.

32. "The HBGary Emails," WikiLeaks, published November 29, 2016, https://wikileaks.org/hbgary-emails/press-release.

33. Farber, "Wikileaks Is Winning."

34. Barton Gellman, "*The One Hundred Most Influential People in the World*," *Time*, April 18, 2012.

35. Andrea Peterson, "WikiLeaks Posts Nearly Twenty Thousand Hacked DNC Emails Online," *Washington Post*, July, 2016.

36. Alana Abramson and Shushanna Walshe, "Emails Released by WikiLeaks Appear to Show DNC Trying to Aid Hillary Clinton," ABC News, July 22, 2016, https://abcnews.go.com/Politics/emails-released-wikileaks-show-dnc-aid-hillary-clinton/

story?id=40815253; Alana Abramson and Shushanna Walshe, "The Four Most Damaging Emails from the DNC WikiLeaks Dump," ABC News, July 25, 2016, https://abcnews.go.com/Politics/damaging-emails-dnc-wikileaks-dump/story?id=40852448.

37. Alex Johnson, "WikiLeaks' Julian Assange: No Proof Hacked DNC Emails Came from Russia," NBC News, July 25, 2017, https://www.nbcnews.com/news/us-news/wikileaks-julian-assange-no-proof-hacked-dnc-emails-came-russia-n616541.

38. Massimo Calabresi, "Inside Russia's Social Media War on America," *Time*, May 18, 2017.

39. Calabresi, "Inside Russia's Social Media War."

40. Calabresi, "Inside Russia's Social Media War."

41. Leslie Shapiro, "Anatomy of a Russian Facebook Ad," *Washington Post*, November 1, 2017.

42. Calabresi, "Inside Russia's Social Media War."

43. Calabresi, "Inside Russia's Social Media War."

44. Calabresi, "Inside Russia's Social Media War."

45. Brian Fung, "Darrell Issa: James Clapper Lied to Congress and Should Be Fired," *Washington Post*, January 27, 2014.

46. Matthew Cole, Richard Esposito, Sam Biddle, and Ryan Grim, "Top Secret NSA Report Details Russian Hacking Effort Days before2016 Election," *The Intercept*, June 5, 2017.

47. Cole, Esposito, Biddle, and Grim, "Top Secret."

48. "Russian President Says 'Patriotic' Hackers May Have Meddled in US Election," Democracy Now, June 2, 2017, https://www.democracynow.org/2017/6/2/headlines/russian_president_says_patriotic_hackers_meddled_in_us_election.

49. Julia Ioffe, "The Secret Correspondence between Donald Trump Jr. and WikiLeaks," *The Atlantic*, November 13, 2017.

50. Ioffe, "The Secret Correspondence."

51. Robert Mackey, "Julian Assange's Hatred of Hillary Clinton Was No Secret. His Advice to Donald Trump Was," *The Intercept*, November 15, 2017.

52. Mackey, "Julian Assange's Hatred."

53. John Swaine and Marc Bennetts, "Mueller Charges Thirteen Russians with Interfering in US Election to Help Trump," *The Guardian*, February 16, 2017.

54. Adrian Chen, "The Agency," *New York Times Magazine*, June 2, 2015.

55. Chen, "The Agency."

56. Adrian Chen (@AdrianChen), tweet, February 20, 2018, https://twitter.com/AdrianChen/status/965962680161980417. Anonymous once made Chen wear a tutu with a shoe on his head before they would cooperate with him for a story he was writing about an alleged hack on the FBI. See photo at Whitney Phillips, "Anonymous, Adrian Chen, and the Shoe," posted September 5, 2012, https://billions-and-billions.com/2012/09/05/anonymous-adrian-chen-and-the-shoe.

57. Author's interview with hacker, May 14, 2018; author's interview with hacker/political staffer at Libre Planet conference, March 2017.

58. Carole Cadwalladr's tweet @carolecadwalla: "Yesterday @facebook threatened to sue us. Today we publish this. Meet the whistleblower blowing the lid off Facebook & Cambridge Analytica," March 17, 2018, tweet, 2008, https://www.theguardian.com/news/2018/mar/17/cambridge-analytica-facebook-influence-us-election?CMP=share_btn_tw.

59. Carole Cadwalladr and Emma Graham-Harrison, "Revealed: Fifty Million Facebook Profiles Harvested for Cambridge Analytica in Massive Data Breach," *The Observer*, March 17, 2018.

60. Manuela Tobias, "Comparing Facebook Use by Obama, Cambridge Analytica," *PolitiFacts*, posted March 22, 2018, http://www.politifact.com/truth-o-meter/statements/2018/mar/22/meghan-mccain/comparing-facebook-data-use-obama-cambridge-analyt. Other reports put the figure at thirty million users: Mattathias Schwartz, "Facebook Failed to Protect Thirty Million Users from Having Their Data Harvested by Trump Campaign Affiliate," *The Intercept*, March 30, 2017.

61. Cadwalladr and Graham-Harrison, "Revealed"; Schwartz, "Facebook Failed."

62. Schwartz, "Facebook Failed."

63. Zeynep Tufekci, "Facebook Doesn't Sell Your Data: It Sells You—Zeynep Tufekci on How Company's Profit Really Works," interview with Amy Goodman, *Democracy Now*, April 11, 2018, video, https://www.democracynow.org/2018/4/11/facebook_doesnt_sell_your_data_it.

64. Haroon Saddique, "Facebook Whistleblower Gives Evidence to MPS on Cambridge Analytica Row: How It Happened," *The Guardian*, March 21, 2018; Paul Lewis, "'Utterly Horrifying': Ex-insider Says Covert Data Harvesting Was Routine," *The Guardian*, March 20, 2018: "Sandy Parakilas, the platform operations manager at Facebook responsible for policing data breaches by third-party software developers between 2011 and 2012, told the *Guardian* he warned senior executives at the company that its lax approach to data protection risked a major breach."

65. Agreement Containing Consent Order, In the Matter of Facebook, Inc., US Federal Trade Commission Agreement, File no. 092 3184 (2011), https://www.ftc.gov/sites/default/files/documents/cases/2011/11/111129facebookagree.pdf.

66. Lewis, "'Utterly Horrifying.'"

67. Tufekci, "Facebook Doesn't Sell."

68. Schwartz, "Facebook Failed."

69. Tobias, "Comparing Facebook."

70. Doc Searles, "Facebook's Cambridge Analytica Problems Are Nothing to What's Coming for All of Online Publishing," posted March 23, 2018, https://blogs.harvard.edu/doc/2018/03/23/nothing.

71. Julian Assange, "Conspiracy as Governance," posted December 3, 2006, me@iq,org, reposted Cryptome, https://cryptome.org/0002/ja-conspiracies.pdf.

72. Snyder, *On Tyranny*. Snyder is the Levin Professor of History at Yale University. He is also author of *Bloodlands: Europe between Hitler and Stalin*, *Black Earth: The Holocaust as History and Warning*, and *The Road to Unfreedom: Russia, Europe, America*.

73. Timothy Snyder, "The Road to Tyranny," interview with Sam Harris, *Waking Up with Sam Harris*, Episode 79, May 30, 2017, audio, https://www.youtube.com/watch?v=gmI_YNGx_jE.

74. Snyder, "The Road to Tyranny."

75. Snyder, "The Road to Tyranny."

76. Snyder, "The Road to Tyranny."

77. Snyder, "The Road to Tyranny."

78. Snyder, "The Road to Tyranny."

79. Snyder, "The Road to Tyranny"; Snyder, *On Tyranny* (see "lessons" 11, 12, and 13).

80. Joint Comments of Internet Engineers, Pioneers, and Technologists on the Technical Flaws in the FCC's Notice of Proposed Rule-Making and the Need for the Light Touch, Bright Lines Rules from the Open Internet Order, In the Matter of Restoring Internet Freedom, Federal Communications Commission, WC Docket No.: 17-108, 3, submitted July 17, 2017, https://ecfsapi.fcc.gov/file/1071761547058/Dkt.%2017-108%20Joint%20Comments%20of%20Internet%20Engineers%2C%20Pioneers%2C%20and%20Technologists%202017.07.17.pdf.

81. Joseph Torres, "FCC set to Roll Back Digital Civil Rights with Tomorrow's Vote to Repeal Net Neutrality," interview with Amy Goodman and Juan Gonzalez, *Democracy Now*, December 13, 2017, video, http://www.truth-out.org/news/item/42898-fcc-set-to-roll-back-digital-civil-rights-with-tomorrow-s-vote-to-repeal-net-neutrality.

82. Swapna Krishna, "Internet Pioneers and Leaders Tell the FCC: You Don't Understand How the Internet Works," Engaget, open letter, December 11, 2017, https://www.engadget.com/2017/12/11/internet-pioneers-fcc-open-letter.

83. Joint Comments of Internet Engineers, 1.

84. Joint Comments of Internet Engineers, 1.

85. Jessica Rosenworcel, "FCC Must Investigate Fraud before Voting on Net Neutrality," *Wired*, December 9, 2017.

86. Cecelia Kang, "FCC Repeals Net Neutrality Rules," *New York Times*, December 14, 2017.

87. Associated Press, "Nearly Two Dozen Attorneys General Sue to Block FCC's Repeal of Net Neutrality Rules," *USA Today*, January 16, 2018.

88. Sean Burch, "Senate Votes to Block FCC's Repeal of Net Neutrality," *The Wrap*, May 16, 2018.

89. Zaid Jilani, "Killing Net Neutrality Has Brought on a New Call for Public Broadband," *The Intercept*, December 15, 2017.

90. Jilani, "Killing Net Neutrality."

91. Dominic Rushe, "Chattanooga's Gig: How One City's Super-fast Internet Is Driving a Tech Boom," *The Guardian*, August 30, 2014.

92. Rushe, "Chattanooga's Gig."

93. Rushe, "Chattanooga's Gig."

94. Dominic Rushe, "US Telecoms Giants Call on FCC to Block Cities' Expansion of High-Speed Internet," *The Guardian*, August 29, 2014.

95. Jilani, "Killing Net Neutrality."

96. People in the digital rights movement generally do not like the name "digital rights management," which is meant to legitimize the regime, so activists often refer to DRM as "digital restrictions management," but that is not its name in legislation and treaties.

97. On the word *creation*, which often is used in connection with copyright, see "Words to Avoid Because They Are Loaded or Confusing," GNU Operating System, Gnu.org, https://gnu.org/philosophy/words-to-avoid.html.

98. Limitations on Exclusive Rights: Fair Use, 17 USC. § 107.

99. "What Is Free Software?," GNU Operating System, Gnu.org, https://www.gnu.org/philosophy/free-sw.en.html (accessed December 30, 2018).

100. This section concerns only copyright. Other restrictions on software include the practice of not releasing source code, imposing end user license agreements, and "tivoization."

101. In traditional copyright law, moral rights are the right of creators to prohibit modification of their work. In a famous Canadian case on moral rights, the department store Eaton's put red ribbons around the necks of the sculptures of flying geese it had installed in the high atrium of its flagship store. The artist, Michael Snow, was not happy with the modification and sued Eaton's successfully for violating the "moral rights" he retained in his artwork. Snow v. Eaton's Ltd., 70 CPR (2d) 105 (1982).

102. I use the term *piracy* not in the sense of limited sharing of copies but in the sense of selling large numbers of copies to seize the commercial value of the original.

103. The "anti-circumvention" provisions (sections 1201 et seq. of the Copyright Act) bar circumvention of access controls and technical protection measures. Electronic Frontier Foundation, "Digital Millennium Copyright Act," Electronic Frontier Foundation, https://www.eff.org/issues/dmca (accessed December 30, 2018).

104. "The 'safe harbor' provisions (section 512) protect service providers who meet certain conditions from monetary damages for the infringing activities of their users and other third parties on the net. ... To receive these protections service providers must comply with the conditions set forth in Section 512, including 'notice and takedown' procedures that give copyright holders a quick and easy way to disable access to allegedly infringing content. Section 512 also contains provisions allowing users to challenge improper takedowns. Without these protections, the risk of potential copyright liability would prevent many online intermediaries from providing services such as hosting and transmitting user-generated content. Thus the safe harbors, while imperfect, have been essential to the growth of the Internet as an engine for innovation and free expression." Electronic Frontier Foundation, "Digital Millennium Copyright Act."

105. John Kennedy, "Lamar Smith Decides to Postpone SOPA 'Indefintely,'" *Silicon Republic*, January 20, 2012.

106. Elaine Burke, "SOPA, PIPA, ACTA and the Battle for Freedom on the Internet," *Silicon Republic*, January 3, 2013.

107. Baker& Hostetler LLP, "The Impact of the TPP on Digital Rights Management," legal opinion, posted January 2016, https://www.bakerlaw.com/files/uploads/Docu ments/News/Articles/LITIGATION/2016/Cohen-ECLP-January2016pg11-12.pdf.

108. Known as the Comprehensive and Progressive Agreement for the Trans Pacific Partnership or CPTPP. See Mike Masnick, "With the US out, Canada Gets Copyright out of TPP, and Moves Closer to Agreement," *TechDirt*, November 13, 2017.

109. Erika Werner, Damian Paletta, and Seung Min Kim, "Trump Weighs Re-joining Trans-Pacific Partnership Amid Trade Dispute with China," *Washington Post*, April 12, 2018.

110. Matt Lee, "GPL Version 3: Background to Adoption," Free Software Foundation, June 9, 2005, https://www.fsf.org/news/gpl3.html.

111. Richard Stallman, communication with the author, April 2017.

112. Read, for example, about the Intel management system debate. Denis Carikli and Molly le Blanc, "The Intel Management Engine: An Attack on Computer Users' Freedom," Free Software Foundation, January 10, 2018, https://www.fsf.org/blogs/sysadmin/the-management-engine-an-attack-on-computer-users-freedom.

113. Kyle Weins, "We Can't Let John Deere Destroy the Very Idea of Ownership," *Wired*, April 21, 2015.

114. Jason Koebler, "Why American Farmers Are Hacking Their Tractors with Ukrainian Firmware," *Vice Motherboard*, March 21, 2017.

115. Koebler, "Why American Farmers."

116. Koebler, "Why American Farmers."

117. Koebler, "Why American Farmers."

118. Weins, "We Can't Let John Deere Destroy."

119. Weins, "We Can't Let John Deere Destroy."

120. Abigail Bessler, "Obama Signs a Bill 'Unlocking' Cell Phones," CBS News, August 1, 2014, https://www.cbsnews.com/news/obama-signs-bill-unlocking-cellphones.

121. See "Measures Governments Can Use to Promote Free Software," GNU Operating System, Gnu.org, https://gnu.org/philosophy/government-free-software.html.

122. Jeremy Rifkin, *The Zero Marginal Cost Society: The Internet of Things, the Collaborative Commons, and the Eclipse of Capitalism* (New York: Palgrave, McMillan, 2015), 14.

123. Rifkin predicts that by 2030, the number of sensors connected to the internet will be 100 trillion. Sensors will be in the roads and public squares, in every store we walk past, in every product and shipping container, in cars and transportation systems, in every device and home appliance, in our clothes and eyeware, in our bodies, and in our children's bodies. This is already happening.

124. John Chambers and Wim Elfrink, "The Future of Cities: The Internet of Everything Will Change How We Live," *Foreign Affairs*, October 31, 2014.

125. Chambers and Elfrink, "The Future of Cities."

126. *The Matrix* is a 1999 film in which artificial intelligence creates a virtual reality world to subdue human beings while actually milking their warehoused bodies as an energy source.

127. Nick Srnicek, *Platform Capitalism* (Cambridge: Polity Press, 2017), 98, Kindle.

128. Srnicek, *Platform Capitalism*, 98–99.

129. Srnicek, *Platform Capitalism*, 98–99.

130. Alex Hern, "Facebook Is Chipping Away at Privacy—and My Profile Has Been Exposed," *The Guardian*, June 29, 2016.

131. Douglas Rushkoff, *Throwing Rocks at the Google Bus: How Growth Became the Enemy of Prosperity* (New York: Portfolio/Penguin, 2016), 49–50.

132. Rushkoff, *Throwing Rocks at the Google Bus*, 48.

133. Chicago Council on Global Affairs, "Big Tech: The Return of Monopolies?," April 18, 2018, video, https://www.thechicagocouncil.org/event/big-tech-return-monopolies. For a slightly different parsing, see Jonathan Taplin, "Is it Time to Break Up Google?," *New York Times*, April 22, 2017, opinion page: "Google has an 88 percent market share in search advertising, Facebook (and its subsidiaries Instagram, WhatsApp and Messenger) owns 77 percent of mobile social traffic and Amazon has a 74 percent share in the e-book market."

134. Dan Schiller, *Digital Depression: Information Technology and Economic Crisis* (Chicago: University of Illinois Press, 2014), 81–82; Rushkoff, *Throwing Rocks at the Google Bus*, 93.

135. Schiller, *Digital Depression*, 227.

136. Rushkoff, *Throwing Rocks at the Google Bus*, 31. That said, the two companies that currently dominate the digital ad market, Google and Facebook, were expected to make $39.9 billion and $21 billion, respectively, in US ad sales in 2018. Total US digital ad sales were expected to rise to $107 billion. Rani Molla, "Google's and Facebook's Share of the US Ad Market Could Decline for the First Time, Thanks to Amazon and Snapchat," *Recode*, March 19, 2018.

137. Rushkoff, *Throwing Rocks at the Google Bus*, 36–37, citing various sources.

138. Rushkoff, *Throwing Rocks at the Google Bus*, 249. He makes the estimate for the year 2015.

139. Srnicek, *Platform Capitalism*, 123.

140. Rushkoff, *Throwing Rocks at the Google Bus*, 37.

141. Chicago Council on Global Affairs, "Big Tech."

142. Tim Higgins, "Tim Cooke's $181 Billion Dollar Headache: Apple's Cash Held Overseas," *Bloomberg News*, July 22, 2015.

143. Nicole Goodkind, "NYC Taxi Drivers Are Killing Themselves and Some Blame Uber and Lyft," *Newsweek*, March 30, 2018.

144. Ben Way, *Jobaclypse: The End of Human Jobs and How Robots Will Replace Them* (Ben Way, 2013), 132, Kindle; Randall Collins, "The End of Middle-Class Work: No More Escapes," in Emmanuel Wallerstein, Randall Collins, Michael Mann, Giorgi Derluguian, and Craig Calhoun, eds., *Does Capitalism Have a Future?* (Oxford: Oxford University Press, 2013), 51. Both Way and Collins are cited in Robert W. McChesney and John Nicols, *People Get Ready: The Fight against a Jobless Economy and a Citizenless Democracy* (New York: Nation Books, 2016), 20.

145. Rushkoff, *Throwing Rocks at the Google Bus*, 92.

146. See Nick Srnicek's book for a full analysis of the process that might bring this about. Srnicek, *Platform Capitalism*.

147. Businesses are already looking at these options. Srnicek, *Platform Capitalism*, 124.

148. Srnicek, *Platform Capitalism*, 125.

149. Caillie Millner, "Why We're Invisible to Google Bus Riders," *San Francisco Chronicle*, April 26, 2013.

150. Rob Wile, "Mark Zuckerberg Has Made More Money Than Anyone Else in 2017—Even Jeff Bezos," *Time*, August 8, 2017.

151. Alana Semuels, "The 'Black Hole' That Sucks Up Silicon Valley's Money," *The Atlantic*, May 14, 2018.

152. Semuels, "The 'Black Hole.'"

153. Semuels, "The 'Black Hole.'"

154. Semuels, "The 'Black Hole.'"

155. Srnicek, *Platform Capitalism*, 97.

156. "History of US Antitrust Law," Wikipedia, https://en.wikipedia.org/wiki/History_of_United_States_antitrust_law (accessed December 30, 2018).

157. "History of US Antitrust Law," Wikipedia.

158. Cathrin Schaer, "Could the EU Really Break Up Facebook's Monopoly?," *Handelsblatt Today*, May 24, 2018, https://global.handelsblatt.com/politics/eu-really -break-facebooks-monopoly-925261.

159. Schaer, "Could the EU."

160. Schaer, "Could the EU."

161. For a good description see, Quora, "What Is General Data Protection Regulation?," *Forbes*, February 14, 2018.

162. David Dayen, "The US Government Is Finally Scrambling to Regulate Facebook," *The Intercept*, April 24, 2018.

163. Kevin Dugan, "Street Artist Taunts Schumer over His Daughter's Facebook Job," *New York Post*, April 3, 2018.

164. Dugan, "Street Artist Taunts Schumer."

165. See Timothy Snyder's Chatham House talk comparing contemporary or postmodern authoritarianism with the modern authoritarianism of the 1930s. Timothy Snyder, "Chatham House Primer: Modern Authoritarianism," video, published October 30, 2013, https://www.youtube.com/watch?v=FMkIYCeybBs.

166. Snyder, On Tyranny, 11–12.

167. Snyder, On Tyranny, 12.

168. In a 1940 speech, Hitler stated that "Nationalism and socialism had to be redefined and they had to be blended into one strong idea to carry new strength which would make Germany great again": David Evon, "Hitler and Trump: Common Slogans?," Snopes.com, https://www.snopes.com/fact-check/make-germany-great-again, March 4, 2016.

169. Milton Mayer, They Thought They Were Free: The Germans 1933–45 (Chicago: University of Chicago Press, 2017). This version is a recent republication with an afterword by Richard J. Evans, a Cambridge historian.

170. Cass Sunstein, "It Can Happen Here," New York Review of Books, June 28, 2018.

171. Andy Müller-Maguhn has said approximately the same thing in Julian Assange, Jacob Appelbaum, Andy Müller-Maguhn, and Jérémie Zimmermann, Cypherpunks: Freedom and the Future of the Internet (New York: OR Books, 2012), 95.

172. Heather Brooke, "Inside the Secret World of Hackers," The Guardian, August 24, 2011.

CHAPTER 9

1. Harry Halpin, email to the author, August 31, 2018. Harry Halpin and Tunisian activist Slim Amamou hosted Julian Assange at the 2015 World Social Forum in Tunis. See https://towardfreedom.org/archives/activism/making-a-better-world-the-2015-world-social-forum-in-tunis.

2. Encryption had not yet taken off among them, though, making them vulnerable to crackdowns. In the Middle East, for example, activists used VIBER, an Israeli messaging app, rather than more secure alternative tools.

3. Jasmine Ryan, "Anonymous and the Arab Uprisings," Al Jazeera, May 19, 2011.

4. Ryan, "Anonymous."

5. Matthias Schwartz, "Pre-Occupied," The New Yorker, November 28, 2011.

6. Andrew Fleming, "Adbusters Spark Wall Street Protest," Vancouver Courier, September 27, 2011.

7. "Anonymous Joins #OCUPYWALLST," Adbusters, posted August 23, 2011, http://www.adbusters.org/blogs/adbusters-blog/anonymous-join.

8. "Occupy Movement," Wikipedia, accessed July 30, 2018, https://en.wikipedia.org/wiki/Occupy_movement.

9. Carmen Pérez-Lanzac, "Democracia Real Ya prepara una convocatoria mundial para el 15 de octubre," El País, May 30, 2011.

10. Chris Barton, "'Occupy Auckland' Protest Speaks with Many Voices," New Zealand Herald, October 29, 2011, https://www.nzherald.co.nz/nz/news/article.cfm?c_id=1&objectid=10762353.

11. Aaron Bady and Mike Konczal, "From Master Plan to No Plan: The Slow Death of Public Higher Education," Dissent, Fall 2012, https://www.dissentmagazine.org/article/from-master-plan-to-no-plan-the-slow-death-of-public-higher-education.

12. Cornel West, "Cornel West on Occupy Wall Street: It's the Making of a US Autumn Responding to the Arab Spring," interview with Amy Goodman, *Democracy Now*, September 29, 2011, https://www.democracynow.org/2011/9/29/cornel_west _on_occupy_wall_street_its_the_makings_of_a_us_autumn_responding_to_the _arab_spring.

13. Hao Li, "Occupy Wall Street Protest Names Single Enemy: 'Neoliberalism,'" *International Business Times*, October 15, 2011, https://www.ibtimes.com/occupy-wall -street-protest-names-single-enemy-neoliberalism-323631.

14. Mattathias Schwartz, "Pre-Occupied," *The New Yorker*, November 28, 2011.

15. Roger Lowenstein, "Occupy Wall Street: It's Not a Hippie Thing," *Bloomberg Business Week*, October 27, 2011.

16. Shannon Bond, "Obama Extends Support for Protesters," *Financial Times*, October 16, 2011.

17. "Occupy Movement," Wikipedia, https://en.wikipedia.org/wiki/Occupy_ movement (accessed July 30, 2018).

18. Robert Pear, "Top Earners Doubled Share of Nation's Income, Study Finds," *New York Times*, October 25, 2011.

19. Li, "Occupy Wall Street Protest."

20. Matthew Stewart, "The 9.9 Percent Is the New American Aristocracy," *The Atlantic*, June 2018.

21. Stewart, "The 9.9 Percent."

22. Aimee Picchi, "A $500 Surprise Expense Would Put Most Americans into Debt," *Moneywatch*, January 12, 2017, https://www.cbsnews.com/news/most-americans -cant-afford-a-500-emergency-expense, cited in Umair Haque, "Why America Is the First Poor Rich Country; Or, How American Collapse Is Made of a New Kind of Poverty," *Eudaimonia*, May 23, 2018, https://eand.co/why-america-is-the-worlds-first -poor-rich-country-17f5a80e444a.

23. Leslie Albrecht, "One-Third of American Households Have Struggled to Afford Either Food, Shelter or Medical Care," Marketwatch, September 27, 2017, https:// www.marketwatch.com/story/one-third-of-american-households-cant-afford-food -shelter-or-medical-care-2017-09-27, cited in Haque, "Why America."

24. David Harvey, *A Brief History of Neoliberalism* (Oxford: Oxford University Press, 2005).

25. David Harvey, "Technology and Post-Capitalism," video, filmed September 25, 2017 at The World Transformed by Novara Media, https://www.youtube.com/ watch?v=g18JoOZsoEMat.

26. Laurie Penny, "Protest by Consensus," *New Statesman*, October 16, 2011.

27. Daniel Cohn-Bendit, interview with Jean-Paul Sartre, recorded in Hervé Bourges, trans. B. R. Brewster, *The Student Revolt: The Activists Speak* (London: Panther Books, 1968), 97–107. This interview originally was published in *Le Nouvel Observateur* on May 20, 1968. The interview also can be found online at https://medium.com/ @AM_HC/jean-paul-sartre-interviews-daniel-cohn-bendit-5cd9ef932514.

28. Lizzy Davies, "Occupy Movement: City-by-City Police Crackdowns So Far," *The Guardian*, November 15, 2011; Tom Burgis, "Authorities Clear St. Paul's Occupy Camp," *Financial Times*, February 28, 2012.

29. "Occupy Homes," Wikipedia, https://en.wikipedia.org/wiki/Occupy_Homes (accessed December 30, 2018). See also "Occupy Our Homes," http://occupyourhomes .org (accessed December 30, 2018).

30. See "Operation Anti-Security," Wikipedia, https://en.wikipedia.org/wiki/Opera tion_AntiSec (accessed December 30, 2018), and sources cited therein. See also Paul Carr, "Watch Out, LulzSec: The CIA Is Adept at Wiping Lulz Off Faces," *The Guardian*, June 22, 2011.

31. Charles Arthur, "LulzSec Members Jailed for a String of Sophisticated Cyber-attacks," *The Guardian*, May 16, 2013.

32. "Operation Anti-Security," Wikipedia.

33. "Anonymous (group)," Wikipedia, https://en.wikipedia.org/wiki/Anonymous _(group) (accessed December 30, 2018).

34. This is what Yascha Mounk, lecturer on political theory at Harvard, has called "illiberal democracy." See Yascha Mounk, *The People vs. Democracy: Why Our Freedom Is in Danger and How to Save It* (Cambridge: Harvard University Press, 2018).

35. Harvey, "Technology and Post-Capitalism."

36. For this primer, I am indebted to Samer Hassan, professor of computer science, Madrid, whom I interviewed at the Berkman Center for Internet & Society, Harvard University, in March 2016.

37. Trebor Scholz, "The State of Platform Cooperativism," filmed at #PDF18, published June 18, 2018, video, https://www.youtube.com/watch?v=qcPUARqRsVM.

38. Trebor Scholz and Nathan Schneider, eds., *Ours to Hack and to Own: The Rise of Platform Cooperativism—A New Vision for the Future of Work and a Fairer Internet* (New York: OR Books, 2016), 11–12.

39. Scholz and Schneider, *Ours to Hack and to Own*, 12 (emphasis added).

40. Scholz and Schneider, *Ours to Hack and to Own*, 12.

41. Scholz, "The State of Platform Cooperativism."

42. See "The Platform Conservatism Consortium," Platform Conservatism Consortium, The New School, https://platform.coop/about/consortium.

43. Scholz, "The State of Platform Cooperativism."

44. Scholz, "The State of Platform Cooperativism."

45. Scholz and Schneider, *Ours to Hack and to Own*, 210.

46. Scholz, "The State of Platform Cooperativism."

47. Scholz, "The State of Platform Cooperativism."

48. Chris Lehmann, "The Populist Morass: Why Liberal Policy Savants Deplore Rule by the People," *The Baffler* no. 42 (November–December 2018):14.

49. "Co-operative Commonwealth Federation," *Encyclopaedia Britannica*, https:// www.britannica.com/topic/Co-operative-Commonwealth-Federation (accessed January 1, 2019).

50. Scholz, "The State of Platform Cooperativism."

51. See "Tool Library," Farm Hack, http://farmhack.org/tools.

52. "The Free Farm Manifesto," Farm Hack, http://farmhack.org/tools/free-farm -manifesto.

53. Scholz, "The State of Platform Cooperativism."

54. I learned about this experiment from Sean O'Brien, visiting fellow at the Yale Privacy Lab, at the March 2016 LibrePlanet conference. See the Anarcho Tech Collective website at https://thebasebk.org/anarcho-tech-collective.

55. See the Enspiral website at https://enspiral.com.

56. Scholz, "The State of Platform Cooperativism."

57. Scholz and Schneider, *Ours to Hack and to Own*, 181.

58. Ben Kersey, "The Troubled History of Diaspora: The $200,000 'Facebook Killer' Launched on Kickstarter," *Motherboard*, October 8, 2012; Casey Newton, "Mastodon. social Is an Open-Source Twitter Competitor That's Growing Like Crazy," *The Verge*, April 4, 2017, https://www.theverge.com/2017/4/4/15177856/mastodon -social-network-twitter-clone.

59. Charley Locke, "Remember Ello? You Abandoned It, But Artists Didn't," *Wired*, May 17, 2016.

60. Casey Newton, "Ello Is the Doomed Utopia We Can't Stop Building," *The Verge*, September 30, 2014, https://www.theverge.com/2014/9/30/6874727/ello-is-the -doomed-utopia-we-cant-stop-building.

61. See the lists of projects on the Redecentralize.org website at https:// redecentralize.org/interviews.

62. See "RSS," Wikipedia, https://en.wikipedia.org/wiki/RSS (accessed December 30, 2018).

63. See "GNU Social," GNU Operating System, https://www.gnu.org/software/ social. According to its website, GNU Social merged with the SatusNet project in 2013.

64. Katrina Brooker, "'I Was Devastated': Tim Berners-Lee, the Man Who Invented the World Wide Web, Has Some Regrets," *Vanity Fair*, July 1, 2018.

65. Newton, "Mastodon.social."

66. Harry Halpin, correspondence with the author, August 31, 2018.

67. "OwnCloud," Wikipedia, https://en.wikipedia.org/wiki/OwnCloud (accessed December 30, 2018). See also Steven Vaughan-Nicols, "OwnCLoud: Build Your Own or Manage Your Public Cloud Storage Services," *ZNet Edition US*, October 11, 2012, https://www.zdnet.com/article/owncloud-build-your-own-or-manage-your-public -cloud-storage-services.

68. "Raspberry Pi," Wikipedia, https://en.wikipedia.org/wiki/Raspberry_Pi (accessed December 30, 2018).

69. The Free Software Foundation webpage on single-board computers warns readers that "Until the nonfree startup program is fully freed, these boards are useless in the free world." "Single-Board Computers," Free Software Foundation, May 15, 2013, https://www.fsf.org/resources/hw/single-board-computers.

70. See the lists of projects on the Redecentralize.org website at https://redecentralize .org/interviews.

71. Michel Bauwens and Vasilis Kastokis, "Peer-to-Peer: A New Opportunity for the Left," *Roar*, January 12, 2017, https://roarmag.org/essays/peer-to-peer-bauwens -kostakis.

72. See the Freenet website at https://freenetproject.org.

73. See "Netsukuku," Source Forge, https://sourceforge.net/projects/netsukuku.

74. "FAROO," Wikipedia, https://en.wikipedia.org/wiki/FAROO (accessed December 30, 2018).

75. See "Osiris," Wikipedia, https://en.wikipedia.org/wiki/Osiris_(software).

76. "Peercasting," Wikipedia, https://en.wikipedia.org/wiki/Peercasting (accessed December 30, 2018).

77. Specifically, a GPLv3 license. See "A Few Questions to Discover PeerTube," PeerTube, https://joinpeertube.org/en/faq.

78. See "Own Your Memories," Textile, https://www.textile.photos.

79. See the lists of projects on the Redecentralize.org website at https://redecentralize .org/interviews.

80. Zoe Corbyn, "Decentralisation: The Next Step for the World Wide Web," *The Guardian*, September 8, 2018.

81. Bauwens and Kastokis, "Peer-to-Peer."

82. Lehmann, "The Populist Morass."

83. Carmela Troncoso, Marios Isaakidis, George Danezis, and Harry Halpin, "Systematizing Decentralization and Privacy: Lessons from Fifteen Years of Research and Deployment," *Proceedings on Privacy Enhancing Technologies*, no. 1 (January 2017): 404–426, https://dblp.uni-trier.de/db/journals/popets/popets2017.html.

84. Christopher Cannucciari, *Banking on Bitcoin* (Studio Gravitas Ventures, 2017).

85. Scholz, "The State of Platform Cooperativism."

86. Louise Matsakis, "Minds Is the Anti-Facebook That Pays You for Your Time," *Wired*, April 19, 2018.

87. Nigel Dollentas, "DTube: Steemit User Builds Foundations of a Decentralized YouTube," *BTC Manager*, August 23, 2017, https://btcmanager.com/steemit-user -builds-decentralized-youtube.

88. See the Twister website at http://twister.net.co.

89. Corbyn, "Decentralisation."

90. Jonathan Nieh, "Brave Browser's ICO Raises $36 Million in Thirty Seconds," *CrowdFund Insider*, June 2, 2017, https://www.crowdfundinsider.com/2017/06/101301 -brave-browsers-ico-raises-36-million-30-seconds.

91. Primavera de Filippi and Samer Hassan, "Blockchain Technology as a Regulatory Technology: from Code Is Law to Law Is Code," *First Mind Journal* 21, no. 12 (December 5, 2016), http://journals.uic.edu/ojs/index.php/fm/article/view/7113.

92. Charles Hoskinson, "The Future Will Be Decentralized," video, filmed at Tedx Talks Bermuda, December 4, 2014, https://www.youtube.com/watch?v=97ufCT6lQ cY.

93. Giulio Prisco, "W3C and MIT Media Lab Host First 'Blockchain and the Web' Workshop," *Bitcoin Magazine*, July 8, 2016, https://bitcoinmagazine.com/articles/the -w-c-and-mit-media-lab-host-first-blockchain-and-the-web-workshop-1467989496.

94. Mike Masnick, "EFF Resigns from W3C after DRM in HTML Is Approved in Secret Vote," *TechDirt*, September 18, 2017.

95. See, for example, MIT Media Lab, public dialogue on DRM, video, filmed April 5, 2016, https://www.youtube.com/watch?v=e3kfXtXRgk0; Richard Stallman, "The W3C's Soul at Stake," Free Software Foundation, posted May 2, 2013, https://www .fsf.org/blogs/rms/w3c-soul-at-stake; Cory Doctorow, "W3C, DRM and the Future of the Open Web," *boing boing*, February 13, 2017, https://boingboing.net/2017/02/13/ the-w3c-drm-and-future-of-th.html; Peter Bright, "Over Many Objections, W3C Approves DRM for HTML5," *Ars Technica*, July 10, 2017, https://arstechnica.com/ information-technology/2017/07/over-many-objections-w3c-approves-drm-for -html5. See also DefectivebyDesign, https://www.defectivebydesign.org.

96. See J. M. Porup, "A Battle Rages for the Future of the Web," *Ars Technica*, February 12, 2017, https://arstechnica.com/information-technology/2017/02/future -of-the-www-timbl-drm.

97. MIT Media Lab, public dialogue on DRM.

98. See Porup, "A Battle Rages"; Masnick, "EFF Resigns." Parties engaged in the debate pointed out that corporate members of W3C paid membership fees of approximately $80,000 but academic and nonprofit groups paid about $8,000.

99. MIT Media Lab, public dialogue on DRM.

100. Richard Stallman, correspondence with the author, September 2, 2018.

101. MIT Media Lab, public dialogue on DRM.

102. MIT Media Lab, public dialogue on DRM.

103. Masnick, "EFF Resigns."

104. Brooker, "'I Was Devastated.'"

105. Giulio Prisco, "The Internet Needs a Solid Re-decentralization: Tim Berners-Lee," CryptoInsider, undated, https://cryptoinsider.21mil.com/internet-needs-solid-re-decen tralization-tim-berners-lee.

106. Brooker, "'I Was Devastated.'"

107. CSAIL, "Web Inventor Tim Berners-Lee's Next Project: A Platform That Gives Users Control of Their Data," posted November 2, 2015, https://www.csail .mit.edu/news/web-inventor-tim-berners-lees-next-project-platform-gives-users -control-their-data. Berners-Lee's "linked data" solution was one issue that helped to derail the W3C Social Web Working Group. Representatives from the Solid team pushed through standards such as Linked Data Notifications, while many others in the developer community preferred a nonlinked data solution. See Harry Halpin, "Semantic Insecurity: Security and the Semantic Web," paper from the Proceedings of the Fifth Workshop on Society, Privacy, and the Semantic Web: Privacy and Technology, PrivOn@ISWC 2017, https://dblp.uni-trier.de/db/conf/semweb/privon 2017.html.

108. CSAIL, "Web Inventor."

109. Prisco, "W3C and MIT Media Lab Host."

110. Brooker, "'I Was Devastated.'"

111. Harry Halpin has criticized its design from a security and privacy point of view. See Halpin, "Semantic Insecurity."

112. Prisco, "The Internet Needs."

113. See Decentralized Web Summit, https://decentralizedweb.net/about.

114. Prisco, "The Internet Needs."

115. See Decentralized Web Summit, https://decentralizedweb.net.

116. Jack Goldsmith and Tim Wu, *Illusions of a Borderless World* (Oxford: Oxford University Press, 2006), 20.

117. John Kennedy, "$1.4bn Investment in Blockchain Start-ups in Last Nine Months, Says PwC Expert," *Silicon Republic*, November 2016, http://linkis.com/Ayjzj.

118. Rob Marvin, "IBM, Microsoft, Are Building Our Blockchain Future: and They're Not Afraid to Butt Heads," *PC Magazine*, August 4, 2016, https://www.pcmag.com/ article/346729/ibm-microsoft-are-building-our-blockchain-future-and-theyr.

119. Michael Halloran, "Blockchain, Mobile and the Internet of Things," *Insight*, March 17, 2016, https://insights.samsung.com/2016/03/17/block-chain-mobile-and-the -internet-of-things.

120. "Perspectives: Break Through with Blockchain: How Can Financial Institutions Leverage a Powerful Technology?," Deloitte, https://www2.deloitte.com/us/en/ pages/financial-services/articles/blockchain-series-deloitte-center-for-financial -services.html (accessed August 3, 2018).

121. "Blockchain Explored by 90% of Major North American and European Banks, Survey Finds," CCN, October 26, 2016, https://www.ccn.com/blockchain-explored -90-major-north-american-european-banks-survey-finds. Blockchain is especially interesting to the financial industry because it is capable of running smart contracts that can execute all kinds of financial transactions, such as options, swaps, coupon bond payments, cross-border transfers, the clearing of over-the-counter derivatives, purchases using escrow, and many other kinds of settlements. Adam Hayes, "Is Ethereum More Important Than Bitcoin?," *Investopedia*, January 4, 2018, https://www .investopedia.com/articles/investing/032216/ethereum-more-important-bitcoin .asp.

122. Hayes, "Is Ethereum."

123. Frank Chaparro, "97% of All Bitcoins Are Held in 4% of Addresses," *Business Insider*, January 11, 2018, https://www.businessinsider.com/bitcoin-97-are-held-by -4-of-addresses-2018-1?op=1.

124. Chaparro, "97% of All Bitcoins."

125. Abhishek Singh, "What Is the Major the Limitation of Blockchain Technology?," Quora, updated January 2, 2018, https://www.quora.com/What-is-the-major-limita tion-of-blockchain-technology?share=1.

126. Elliott Krause, "A Fifth of All Bitcoin Is Missing: These Crypto Hunters Can Help," *Wall Street Journal*, July 5, 2018.

127. See, for example, Neil Gandal and Tyler Moore, "Bitcoin Price Manipulation PutsTrust in Cryptos at Risk," *Asia Times*, June 27, 2018, http://www.atimes.com/ article/bitcoin-price-manipulation-puts-trust-in-cryptos-at-risk. See also Sue Halpern, "Bitcoin Mania," *New York Review of Books*, January 18, 2018.

128. See, for example, The Next System Project, https://thenextsystem.org; The Zeitgeist Movement, https://www.thezeitgeistmovement.com; David Bollier, "The Future Is a Pluriverse," posted December 5, 2017, http://www.bollier.org/ blog/future-pluriverse; The New Economics Foundation, https://neweconomics .org; P2P Foundation, https://p2pfoundation.net; Creative Commons, https:// creativecommons.org; and a host of like-minded discussions.

129. Joe Guinan and Gar Alperovitz, "Democracy and Decentralization: UK Labour Leaders Reframe Socialism for the Twenty-first Century," *Truthout*, February 25, 2016.

130. "Election Results 2017: Jeremy Corbyn Says May 'Underestimated' Voters," *BBC News*, June 9, 2017, https://www.bbc.co.uk/news/election-2017-40208861. Labour won 262 seats to the Conservatives' 318, which left the Conservatives eight seats short of a majority and having to form a coalition government with a small fringe party, the Northern Irish Democratic Unionists (DUP).

131. Guinan and Alperovitz, "Democracy and Decentralization."

132. "Jeremy Corbyn: 'Councils Should Run Local Services,'" BBC News, February 6, 2016, https://www.bbc.com/news/uk-politics-35508740.

133. Guinan and Alperovitz, "Democracy and Decentralization."

134. Guinan and Alperovitz, "Democracy and Decentralization."

CHAPTER 10

1. Anne Koch, "These Spanish Activists Have Taken Punishing Bankers into Their Own Hands," *The Nation*, November 14, 2016.

2. Like SOPA in the United States, the "Sinde" law allowed an administrative commission to shut down, without judicial supervision, any web page that showed links to or allowed irregular downloading of copyrighted content. "Anti Austerity Movement in Spain," Wikipedia, https://en.wikipedia.org/wiki/Anti-austerity_movement_in _Spain (accessed December 30, 2018).

3. Suzanne Daley, "Leading the Charge against Spain's Mortgage Crisis," *New York Times*, December 20, 2013.

4. Ada Colau, "Ada Colau, Barcelona's New Mayor, on Spain's Political Revolution," interview with Amy Goodman, *Democracy Now*, video, June 5, 2015, https://www .democracynow.org/2015/6/5/from_occupying_banks_to_city_hall.

5. Colau interview.

6. See "Ada Colau llama criminal al representante de la banca en el congreso," published on February 6, 2013, https://www.youtube.com/watch?v=Mz175s8gjs0. For translation, listen to the Colau interview.

7. Daley, "Leading the Charge."

8. Colau interview.

9. Colau interview.

10. Colau interview.

11. Colau interview.

12. Colau interview.

13. Sol Trumbo Vila and Matthijs Peters, "The Bail-Out Business," *Transnational Institute*, February 22, 2017, https://www.tni.org/en/publication/the-bail-out-busi ness.

14. See Koch, "These Spanish Activists." See also Trumbo Vila and Peters, "The Bail-Out Business."

15. See Trumbo Vila and Peters, "The Bail-Out Business."

16. For more details, see Koch, "These Spanish Activists."

17. See the @15MpaRato website at https://15mparato.wordpress.com/2014/10/28/ story-citizen-lawsuit.

18. See Koch, "These Spanish Activists."

19. This conversation between Jean-Paul Sartre and Daniel Cohn-Bendit was first published in *Le Nouvel Observateur* on May 20, 1968. The translation by B. R. Brewster was collected in Hervé Bourges, ed., *The Student Revolt: The Activists Speak* (London: Panther Books, 1968). It has also been published online at Medium at https://medium.com/@AM_HC/jean-paul-sartre-interviews-daniel-cohn-bendit -5cd9ef932514.

20. Larry Lessig, *Republic Lost: How Money Corrupts Congress* (New York: Twelve, 2011). See also Larry Lessig, "#OccupyWallSt, Then #OccupyKSt, Then #OccupyMainSt," The Blog, *HuffPost*, October 5, 2011, updated December 6, 2017, https://www .huffingtonpost.com/lawrence-lessig/occupywallst-then-occupyk_b_995547.html . Lessig quotes Thoreau: "there are a thousand hacking at the branches of evil, to one who is striking at the root."

21. *Trumpland*, directed by Michael Moore, distributed by Michael Moore, 2016.

22. I was thinking of Caravaggio's *Cardsharps*, painted around 1594. See https:// en.wikipedia.org/wiki/Cardsharps_(Caravaggio).

23. See, for example, Reilly Jones, "A Critique of Barlow's Declaration of the Independence of Cyberspace," *Extropy* 17, vol. 8. no. 2 (1996).

24. Cristobal Montoro, the Minister of Housing at the relevant time.

25. With the exception of France, no other country had a greater proportion of its population volunteer in Spain than Canada. Adrienne Clarkson, Governor General of Canada, Speech on the Occasion of the Unveiling of the Mackenzie-Papineau Battalion Monument, Ottawa, October 20, 2001, http://archive.gg.ca/media/doc.asp?lang=e&DocID=1331.

26. See Ross Tieman, "Barcelona: Smart City Revolution in Progress," *Financial Times*, October 25, 2017.

27. Decode is one of the projects the Barcelona Initiative for Technological Sovereignty (BITS) is working on with the city of Amsterdam and twelve other partners. It is exploring solutions using blockchain and cryptography that are supposed to give people better control over the data they generate in their homes and cities by setting rules about who can access it, for what purpose, and on what terms. As Francesca Bria, the chief technology and digital innovation officer of the city of Barcelona, has described it, Decode conceives of data as a shared resource to which citizens can contribute, while being able to access it themselves as a common good without proprietary restrictions, to solve problems like traffic congestion and air pollution. The idea is that citizens will set their own anonymity level so that they cannot be identified without explicit consent, and they will keep ownership and control over data even after they share it for the common good. The common data infrastructure, in turn, will be open to local companies, coops, and social organizations to create long-term public value. Francesca Bria, "Our Data Is Valuable: Here's How We Can Take That Value Back," *The Guardian*, April 5, 2018, https://www.theguardian.com/commentisfree/2018/apr/05/data-valuable-citizens-silicon-valley-barcelona. The BITS project has been harshly criticized by citizens and activists. See also the trenchant civic criticism of Google's "smart city" project in Toronto, Canada. Ava Kofman, "Google's 'Smart City of Surveillance' Faces Resistance in Toronto," *The Intercept*, November 13, 2018.

28. See Tieman, "Barcelona." See also Gemma Galdon, "Technological Sovereignty? Democracy, Data and Governance in the Digital Era," CCCBLab, posted April 25, 2017, http://lab.cccb.org/en/technological-sovereignty-democracy-data-and-governance-in-the-digital-era.

29. See Paul Mason, "Technology and Post-Capitalism," video, filmed at The World Transformed by Novara Media, September 25, 2017, https://www.youtube.com/watch?v=g18JoOZsoEM.

30. I later learned that the project ran into challenges in its execution. The giant tech company Cisco became the city's main industry partner, and activists and political allies felt it had become a disaster. The experiment shows the kind of radical agenda citizens might attempt to push through when they gain control of their democratic processes. However, it is also a cautionary tale about how easily the smart city model can work against citizens' interests and raises the question of whether democracies should try to implement it at all. Google's experiments in Toronto offer a similar cautionary tale. See Kofman, "Google's 'Smart City of Surveillance.'"

31. "The Former General Director of the IMF Rodrigo Rato Went to Jail," *Quebec Telegram*, October 26, 2017, https://qtelegram.com/the-former-general-director-of-the-imf-rodrigo-rato-went-to-jail/1600.

32. See Steve Rushton, "Rato Finito: Spanish Citizens Send Most Corrupt Banker-Politician to Jail," PopularResistance.org, posted March 25, 2017, https://popularresistance.org/rato-finito-spanish-citizens-send-most-corrupt-banker-politician-to-jail/, for all the facts in this paragraph.

33. Alexander Stille, "Not So Funny," *New York Review of Books*, May 10, 2018.

34. Stille, "Not So Funny"; Gianroberto Casaleggio and Beppe Grillo, *Siamo in guerra: Per una nuova politica* (We Are at War: For a New Politics) (Milan: Chiarelettere, 2011).

35. Stille, "Not So Funny," citing Oliviero Ponte di Pino, *Comico e politico: Beppe Grillo e la crisi della democrazia* (Comic and Politician: Beppe Grillo and the Crisis of Democracy) (Milan: Raffaello Cortina, 2014).

36. Stille, "Not So Funny."

37. J.H., "*The Economist* Explains Italy's Five Star Movement," *The Economist*, October 24, 2016.

38. Stille, "Not So Funny."

39. Tim Parks, "Italy: Who Ever Wins Won't Govern," *New York Review of Books Daily*, February 14, 2018.

40. J.H., "*The Economist* Explains"; Stille, "Not So Funny."

41. Jan-Werner Müller, "Italy: The Bright Side of Populism?," *New York Review of Books*, June 8, 2018.

42. Stille, "Not So Funny," citing Roberto Biorcio and Paolo Natale, *Politica a Cinque Stelle: Idee, storia e strategie del movimento di Grillo* (Five-Star Politics: Ideas, History and Strategies of the Grillo Movement) (Milan: Feltrinelli, 2013).

43. Müller, "Italy."

44. Stille, "Not So Funny," citing an article by Ponte di Pino from September 2017 in the online magazine *Doppiozero*.

45. Stille, "Not So Funny," citing di Pino, *Comico e politico*. In 2018 more members were purged for failing to have give a third of their salary to the party's microcredit fund for small businesses, as required by Grillo.

46. Stille, "Not So Funny," citing Marco Canestrari and Nicola Biondo, *Supernova: Com'è stato ucciso il movimento Cinque Stelle* (Supernova: How the Five Star Movement Was Killed) (StreetLib ebook).

47. In 2017. Stille, "Not So Funny."

48. Stille, "Not So Funny."

49. Stille, "Not So Funny."

50. Müller, "Italy."

51. Stille, "Not So Funny."

52. Stille, "Not So Funny."

53. Stille, "Not So Funny," for all of the facts in the paragraph.

54. Formerly the Northern League.

55. Sofia Lotto Persio, "Italy's New Government Is Steve Bannon's Dream Come True," *Newsweek*, June 1, 2018.

56. Mark Hume, "Dark Windows Illuminate Problems in Vancouver's Real Estate Market," *Globe & Mail*, updated May 17, 2018, https://www.theglobeandmail.com/real-estate/vancouver/dark-windows-illuminate-problems-in-vancouvers-real-estate-market/article31822833.

57. In a recent dialogue about the experience and effects of the political uprisings of 1968, Daniel Cohn-Bendit juxtaposed the idea of a "a flexibility dictated by capitalism" and "a flexibility enacted by human beings themselves." Daniel Cohn-Bendit and Claus Leggewie, "1968: Power to the Imagination," *New York Review of Books*, May 10, 2018.

CHAPTER 11

1. "End of War Graffiti in Berlin," film clip, http://www.budgetfilms.com/clip/ 12051 (accessed December 30, 2018).

2. Postwar photo of graffiti on the walls of the Chancellery, undated, in Hans Christian Adam, *Berlin: Portrait of a City* (Cologne: Taschen, 2007), 329.

3. Deborah Cole, "Berlin Woman Revives Red Army Ghosts in Reichstag Graffiti," *Times of Israel*, January 11, 2018, https://www.timesofisrael.com/berlin-woman-revives-red -army-ghosts-in-reichstag-graffiti.

4. Cole, "Berlin Woman," for all of the facts in this paragraph.

5. "Berlin Wall and Migration," Mass Migration as a Travel Business, https://www .business-of-migration.com/migration-processes/other-regions/berlin-wall-and -migration (accessed January 1, 2019).

6. Klaus Wiegrefe, "Who Ordered the Construction of the Berlin Wall?," *Der Spiegel*, May 30, 2009.

7. Wiegrefe, "Who Ordered."

8. Wiegrefe, "Who Ordered."

9. Hans-Hermann Hertle, "The Berlin Wall Story: Biography of a Monument" (Berlin: Verlag, 2011), 39.

10. "Berlin Wall," History.com, https://www.history.com/this-day-in-history/berlin -wall-built (accessed December 30, 2018).

11. Hertle, "The Berlin Wall Story," 42.

12. Hertle, "The Berlin Wall Story," 44.

13. John Vinocur, "Soviet and East Germans Sign an Economic Pact," *New York Times*, October 6, 1979.

14. Felix Denk and Sven von Thulen, *Der Klang der Familie: Berlin, Techno and the Fall of the Wall* (Norderstedt: Books on Demand, 2014), 247, quoting DJ Clé.

15. These facts about Friedrichshain were gleaned through observations and con- versations with two residents of the neighborhood, artist Andrea Neuman and her partner, over an evening I shared with them and Heidi Boghosian (former executive director of the American National Lawyers' Guild) at a local restaurant in the area.

16. Eric Hughes, "A Cypherpunk's Manfesto," 1993, https://www.digitalmanifesto .net/manifestos/16.

17. John Perry Barlow, "A Declaration of the Independence of Cyberspace," https:// www.eff.org/cyberspace-independence (accessed December 30, 2018).

18. Garrett Hardin, "The Tragedy of the Commons," *Science, New Series* 162, no. 3859 (December 13, 1968):1243–1248.

19. Hardin, "Tragedy of the Commons," 1245.

20. Hardin, "Tragedy of the Commons," 1245, citing J. Fletcher, *Situation Ethics* (Philadelphia: Westminster, 1966).

21. Hardin, "Tragedy of the Commons," 1246.

22. Andreas Tzortzis, "One Wall Down, Thousands to Paint," *New York Times*, March, 8, 2007.

23. Johnston, Jules, "Donald Trump Kisses Vladimir Putin on Wall of Lithuanian Restaurant," *Politico*, May 14, 2016.

24. Lauren Said-Moorhouse, "Donald Trump and Boris Johnson Pucker Up in Street Art," CNN, May 24, 2016, https://edition.cnn.com/2016/05/24/europe/ donald-trump-boris-johnson-street-art-kissing.

25. Taly Krupkin, "Graffiti of Trump Passionately Kissing Putin Goes Viral," *Haaretz*, May 18, 2016.

26. T. S. Eliot, "The Hollow Men."

27. Timothy C. May, "The Cyphernomicon," version 0.666, September 10, 1994, http://www.kreps.org/hackers/overheads/11cyphernervs.pdf.

28. Stanley Kubrick's 1964 film satire *Dr. Strangelove or How I Learned to Stop Worrying and Love the Bomb*, about the fallacy of nuclear deterrence, depicts a nuclear first-strike attack ordered by a deranged US general, and the comic attempts of the president's war cabinet to stop it. When they summon the Soviet ambassador, they learn the Soviet Union has a "doomsday device" that will launch nuclear weapons against any 'first strike" and cannot be overridden by human command. This fact is supposed to ensure deterrence, except that they omitted to tell the Americans. Peter Sellers plays the president, a nearly unfazeable RAF exchange officer, and the mad nuclear expert and former Nazi, Dr. Strangelove.

29. Bruce Sterling, *The Hacker Crackdown: Law and Disorder on the Electronic Frontier* (Project Gutenberg ebook, 2008), Kindle. Free download at http://www.gutenberg .org/ebooks/101.

30. See Thomas Frank's excellent book, *Listen, Liberal: What Ever Happened to the Party of the People?* (New York: Metropolitan Books, 2016), especially chapter 9, "The Blue State Model," and chapter 10, "The Innovation Class." Frank writes: "Innovation liberalism is a 'liberalism of the rich,' to use the straightforward phrase of local labor leader Harris Gruman. This doctrine has no patience with the idea that everyone should share in society's wealth. What Massachusetts liberals pine for, by and large, is a more perfect meritocracy—a system where everyone gets an equal chance and the truly talented get to rise. Once that requirement is satisfied—once diversity has been achieved and the brilliant people of all races and genders have been identified and credentialed—this species of liberal can't really conceive of any further grievance against the system. The demands of ordinary working-class people, Gruman says, are unpersuasive to them." Frank, *Listen, Liberal*, 196.

31. See the following articles, among many on the topic: Tory Newmyer, "With Uber's New Hire, Obama's Alumni Invade Silicon Valley," *Fortune*, August 19, 2014; Juliet Eilperin, "Why Silicon Valley Is the New Revolving Door for Obama Staffers," *Washington Post*, February 27, 2015; Noah Deponte Smith, "Eric Holder and the New Revolving Door," *National Review*, July 21, 2016.

32. I exaggerate, but see Frank, *Listen, Liberal*, 201–201, 231, and 194. See also David Dayen, "The Android Administration: Google's Remarkably Close Relationship with the Obama White House, in Two Charts," *The Intercept*, April 22, 2016.

33. Frank, *Listen, Liberal*, 201. See Brody Mullins, "Google Makes the Most of Its Close Ties with the White House," *Wall Street Journal*, March 24, 2015, and Google's response reported in Paul Sawyers, "Google Responds to *Wall Street Journal* Allegations," *Venture Beat*, March 201, 2015, https://venturebeat.com/2015/03/27/ google-responds-to-wsj-allegations-microsoft-visited-the-white-house-more-than-us.

34. See discussion of this topic in Molly Sauter, *The Coming Storm: DDoS Actions, Hacktivism, and Civil Disobedience on the Internet* (New York: Bloomsbury Academic, 2014), 137–140.

35. Author's interview with an anonymous Anon.

36. Sauter, *The Coming Storm*, 63.

37. Gabriella Coleman, *The Hacker Wars: The Battlefield Is the Internet*, directed by Vivian Lesnick Weisman, a Vivian Lesnick Weisman film, 2014. See http:// thehackerwars.com.

38. Sauter, *The Coming Storm*, 68.

39. Jasmine Ryan, "Anonymous and the Arab Uprisings," *Al Jazeera*, May 19, 2011.

40. Ryan, "Anonymous."

41. Ayesha Kazmi, "How Anonymous Emerged to Occupy Wall Street," *The Guardian*, September 27, 2011.

42. From an Anonymous press release quoted in full in Abby Zimet, "OpWisconsin: Anonymous Takes Down Koch Brothers," *Common Dreams*, February 28, 2011.

43. See "Operation Anti-Security," Wikipedia, https://en.wikipedia.org/wiki/Operation_AntiSec (accessed January 1, 2019), and sources cited therein. See also Paul Carr, "Watch out, LulzSec: The CIA Is Adept at Wiping Lulz off Faces," *The Guardian*, June 22, 2011.

44. Charles Arthur, "LulzSec Members Jailed for a String of Sophisticated Cyber-attacks," *The Guardian*, May 16, 2013.

45. "Operation Anti-Security," Wikipedia; Josh Halliday, "Serious Organised Crime Agency Takes Down Website after Hacking Attack," *The Guardian*, June 21, 2011.

46. "Operation Anti-Security," Wikipedia.

47. Andrew Greenberg, *This Machine Kills Secrets: Julian Assange, the Cypherpunks, and Their Fight to Empower Whistleblowers* (New York: Plume, 2013), 215–216.

48. Arthur, "LulzSec Members Jailed."

49. See "LulzSec," Wikipedia, https://en.wikipedia.org/wiki/LulzSec (accessed January 1, 2019).

50. See hqanon, "Being an Anonymous Hacker: In the Eyes of Jeremy Hammond," January 1, 2015, Anonhq.com, https://anonhq.com/anonymous-hacker-eyes-jeremy-hammond.

51. Mike Masnick, "LulzSec Jeremy Hammond Pleads Guilty to CFAA Charges; Faces Ten Years," *TechDirt*, May 28, 2013.

52. "Anonymous (group)," Wikipedia, https://en.wikipedia.org/wiki/Anonymous_(group) (accessed January 1, 2019).

53. Sauter, *The Coming Storm*, 141.

54. US Code, title 18, section 1030.

55. Greenberg, *This Machine Kills Secrets*, 197.

56. Sauter, *The Coming Storm*, 142.

57. Sauter, *The Coming Storm*, 144.

58. Ryan J. Reilly, "Loading Koch Industries Website Too Many Times in One Minute Just Cost This Truck Driver $183,000," *HuffPost*, December 2, 2013.

59. Jane Mayer, *Dark Money: The Hidden History of the Billionaires behind the Radical Right* (New York: Anchor Books, 2017).

60. Reilly, "Loading Koch Industries."

61. Sauter, *The Coming Storm*, 144.

62. Sauter, *The Coming Storm*, 140–141.

63. See Molly Sauter's thorough research on this early history and the different philosophies of these groups in Sauter, *The Coming Storm*.

64. To December 2005.

65. James Risen, "My Life as a *New York Times* Reporter in the Shadow of the War on Terror," *The Intercept*, January 3, 2018.

66. Risen, "My Life.

67. Adam Liptak, "Gonzalez Says Prosecutions of Journalists Are Possible," *New York Times*, May 22, 2016.

68. Risen, "My Life." See also Lee Ferran, "Federal Prosecutors Try to Force *New York Times* Reporter to Reveal Sources," ABC News, May 25, 2011, https://abcnews .go.com/Blotter/james-risen-subpoenaed-jeffrey-sterling-case/story?id=13684074.

69. Risen, "My Life."

70. Risen, "My Life."

71. Emily Bazelon, "Why Eric Holder Won't Send James Risen to Jail," *Slate*, June 2, 2014.

72. Risen, "My Life."

73. Timothy M. Phelps, "Atty. Gen. Tightens Limits on US Subpoenas of Journalists," *Los Angeles Times*, January 4, 2015.

74. Ed Pilkington, "Bradley Manning's Treatment Was Cruel and Inhuman, U.N. Torture Chief Rules," *The Guardian*, March 12, 2012.

75. Jennifer Rizzo, "Bradley Manning Charged," CNN, February 23, 2012, http:// security.blogs.cnn.com/2012/02/23/bradley-manning-charged; Luis Martinez and Steven Portnoy, "Bradley Manning Guilty on Most Charges, But Not Aiding the Enemy," ABC News, July 30, 2013, https://abcnews.go.com/Blotter/bradley -manning-guilty-charges-aiding-enemy/story?id=19797378. See also "United States v. Manning," Wikipedia, https://en.wikipedia.org/wiki/United_States_v._Manning (accessed January 1, 2019).

76. Adam Liptak, "Court Rulings Blur the Line between a Spy and a Leaker," *New York Times*, August 2, 2013.

77. Charlie Savage, "Chelsea Manning to Be Released Early as Obama Commutes Sentece," *New York Times*, January 17, 2017.

78. "Julian Assange Arrested in UK, Denied Bail," CBS New, December 7, 2010, https://www.cbsnews.com/news/julian-assange-arrested-in-uk-denied-bail.

79. Madeline Conway, "Clinton: I Don't Recall Joking about Droning Julian Assange," *Politico*, October 4, 2010.

80. Gonzalo Solano, Raphael Satter, and Sylvia Hui, "WikiLeaks Founder Seeks Asylum at Ecuador Embassy," *Associated Press*, June 20, 2012.

81. Peter Ludlow, "The Strange Case of Barret Brown," *The Nation*, June 18, 2013.

82. Barrett Brown, "Anonymous, Australia, and the Inevitable Fall of the Nation-State," posted April 13, 2010, https://www.huffingtonpost.com/barrett-brown/ anonymous-australia-and-t_b_457776.html.

83. "Free Barrett," The Courage Foundation, https://freebarrettbrown.org/ project-pm (accessed January 1, 2019).

84. Ludlow, "The Strange Case."

85. Ludlow, "The Strange Case."

86. hqanon, "Being an Anonymous Hacker."

87. Ludlow, "The Strange Case"; Greenberg, *This Machine Kills Secrets*, 214.

88. Michael Riley and Ashlee Vance, "Cyber Weapons: The New Arms Race," *Bloomberg Business Week*, July 21, 2011.

89. Ludlow, "The Strange Case."

90. Ludlow, "The Strange Case."

91. hqanon, "Being an Anonymous Hacker"; Dell Cameron, "How an FBI Informant Orchestrated the Stratfor Hack," *The Daily Dot*, June 5, 2014, https://www.dailydot. com/layer8/hammond-sabu-fbi-stratfor-hack.

92. Ludlow, "The Strange Case."

93. The Courage Foundation, "Free Barrett."

94. Ludlow, "The Strange Case."

95. "Aaron Swartz," Wikipedia, https://en.wikipedia.org/wiki/Aaron_Swartz (accessed January 1, 2019). See also, the documentary film *The Internet's Own Boy: The Story of Aaron Swartz*, directed by Brian Knappenberger, Participant Media, 2014.

96. *The Internet's Own Boy.*

97. "Aaron Swartz," Wikipedia.

98. *The Internet's Own Boy.*

99. Aaron Swartz, "Guerilla Open Access Manifesto," July 2008, Eremo, Italy, https://archive.org/stream/GuerillaOpenAccessManifesto/Goamjuly2008_djvu.txt.

100. Nadine Bloch, "The Day Aaron Swartz Helped Make the Internet Go Dark," Waging Non Violence: People Powered News & Analysis, posted January 18, 2013, https://wagingnonviolence.org/feature/the-day-aaron-swartz-helped-make-the -internet-go-dark.

101. "Aaron Swartz," Wikipedia.

102. *The Internet's Own Boy.*

103. *The Internet's Own Boy*; Owen Thomas, "Family of Aaron Swartz Blame MIT, Prosecutors for His Death," *Business Insider*, January 12, 2013, http://www.businessinsider .com/statement-family-aaron-swartz-2013-1?op=1.

104. "Aaron Swartz," Wikipedia.

105. Journalist David Sirota in *The Internet's Own Boy.*

106. *The Internet's Own Boy.*

107. Quinn Norton, "The Internet's Own Boy," *The Message*, June 27, 2014, https:// medium.com/message/the-internets-own-boy-c815ae07a417.

108. Charlie Savage, "Chelsea Manning to Be Released Early as Obama Commutes Sentece," *New York Times*, January 17, 2017.

109. Julia Ioffe, "The Secret Correspondence between Donald Trump Jr. and WikiLeaks," *The Atlantic*, November 13, 2017.

110. Mike Pompeo, "Edward Snowden on Privacy in the Age of Trump and Facebook," *Deconstructed*, May 25, 2018, audio, https://theintercept.com/2018/05/25/ deconstructed-the-edward-snowden-interview.

111. Sam Biddle, "Even WikiLeaks Haters Shouldn't Want It Labeled as a 'Hostile Intelligence Agency,'" *The Intercept*, August 25, 2017." CIA Director Mike Pompeo said, "WikiLeaks walks like a hostile intelligence service and talks like a hostile intelligence service, and has encouraged its followers to find jobs at the CIA in order to obtain intelligence. It's time to call out WikiLeaks for what it really is—a non-state hostile intelligence service, often abetted by state actors like Russia. We have to recognize that we can no longer allow Assange and his colleagues the latitude to use free speech values against us, to give them the space to crush us with misappropriated secrets as a perversion of what our great Constitution stands for. It ends now."

112. Biddle, "Even WikiLeaks Haters."

113. Biddle, "Even WikiLeaks Haters."

114. Ewan MacAskill, Sam Thielman, and Philip Ottermann, "WikiLeaks Publishes 'Biggest Ever Leak of Secret CIA Documents,'" *The Guardian*, March 7, 2017.

115. See, for example, the commentary in Robert Mackey, "What Julian Assange's War on Hillary Clinton Says about WikiLeaks," *The Intercept*, August 6, 2016. See also the early, insightful 2010 analysis of Geert Lovink (with Patrice Riemens),

"Twelve Theses on WikiLeaks," posted August 30, 2010, http://networkcultures.org/geert/2010/12/07/twelve-theses-on-wikileaks-with-patrice-riemens (updated version of Lovink's "Ten Theses on Wikileaks").

116. Richard Perez-Pena and Iliana Magra, "Julian Assange's Arrest Warrant Is Again Upheld by UK Judge," *New York Times*, February 13, 2018.

117. *The Guardian* staff and agencies, "Ecuador to Remove Julian Assange's Extra Security from London Embassy," *The Guardian*, May 18, 2018.

118. Casey Michel, "Julian Assange's Strange New Obsession: The WikiLeaks Founder Turns His Sights on Breaking Up Spain," *Think Progress*, September 25, 2017, https://thinkprogress.org/assange-catalonia-independence-0a83cd016972.

119. William Booth and Karla Adam, "Assange Loses Interent Access," *Washington Post*, March 29, 2018.

120. *The Guardian* staff and agencies, "Ecuador to Remove."

121. Oliver J. J. Lane, "Julian Assange 'Assassination' Claimed after Foiled Ecuadorian Embassy Break-In," *Breitbart News*, August 22, 2016.

122. Suzanne Daley, "Leading the Charge against Spain's Mortgage Crisis," *New York Times*, December 20, 2013.

123. The referendum was not directly related to the breakout of populist agitation in Catalonia. It had a longer, more complicated genesis, although Spain's financial crisis certainly deepened Catalonians' resentment against the central Spanish government. Omar G. Encarnación, "Homage to Catalonia?," *New York Review of Books*, November 9, 2017.

124. Charles Penty, "Rajoy Falls, Paying Price for Generation of Corruption in Spain," *Bloomberg News*, May 31, 2018.

125. Jan-Werner Müller, "Italy: The Bright Side of Populism?," *New York Review of Books*, June 8, 2018.

126. *Reference re Secession of Quebec*, [1998] 2 S.C.R. 217.

127. Gerard Alberto and Ruth Oldenzeil, eds., *Hacking Europe: From Computer Cultures to Demoscenses* (London: Springer-Verlag, 2014), 173, citing Protocol of the Committee for Legal Affairs, Parliamentary Archives (PA-DBT 3109 A 10/6), Prot. 26.

128. Alberto and Oldenzeil, *Hacking Europe*, 174.

129. Alberto and Oldenzeil, *Hacking Europe*, 174.

130. Alberto and Oldenzeil, *Hacking Europe*, 170.

131. Vernon Silver, "The Hackers Russia Proofing Germany's Elections," *Bloomberg Businessweek*, June 26, 2017.

132. Silver, "The Hackers Russia Proofing."

133. "Chaos Computer Club: Staatstrojaner Affair," Wikipedia, https://en.wikipedia.org/wiki/Chaos_Computer_Club (accessed Janary 1, 2019).

134. Silver, "The Hackers Russia Proofing."

135. "State Trojan Again on Trial in Constitutional Court," Chaos Computer Club, July 6, 2015, https://www.ccc.de/en/updates/2015/bkag.

136. See, as an example, their statement on their "You Broke the Internet" webpage: "Others focus on anarchic technologies designed to undermine democracy, as if it was democracy's fault that digital offences produce no evidence. They thereby foster platforms for bypassing social obligations like contributing taxes, but taxes are fundamental in order to produce infrastructure and social security for the weak. It is

impressive how many people have been fooled into thinking negatively about taxes when they in fact depend on them for their own well-being. Only a tiny minority pays more taxes than it enjoys advantages from them. This project is for those who want to look into a future of an Internet, which actually respects constitutional principles and returns democracy to a mostly functional condition." "You Broke the Internet," http://youbroketheinternet.org (accessed February 1, 2018).

137. Jennifer Baker, "German Prosecutor Given Das Boot over Netzpolitik Treason Charge," *The Register*, August 5, 2015, http://www.theregister.co.uk/2015/08/05/netzpolitik_treason_charges_chief_prosecutor_quits.

138. Staff, "Ex-federal Prosecutor Range Defends Conduct in Netzpolitik Scandal," *DW*, August 7, 2015, http://www.dw.com/en/ex-federal-prosecutor-range-defends-conduct-in-netzpolitik-scandal/a-18633505; Baker, "German Prosecutor."

139. Baker, "German Prosecutor." See also "Our Statement," Netzpolitik, https://netzpolitik.us.

140. Staff, "Ex-federal Prosecutor."

141. Staff, "German Prosecutor's Sacking over Netzpolitik Sparks Anger," *DW*, August 5, 2015, http://www.dw.com/en/german-prosecutor-sacking-over-netzpolitik-sparks-anger/a-18628768. Technically the prosecutor resigned, but he was forced out after criticizing the minister for interference. See also Baker, "German Prosecutor."

142. Baker, "German Prosecutor."

143. Staff, "Critics Say Maas Sacked Prosecutor on Political Grounds," *DW*, August 5, 2015, http://www.dw.com/en/critics-say-maas-sacked-prosecutor-on-political-grounds/a-18628274.

144. Tom Barfield, "Prosecutors Drop Netzpolitik Treason Probe," *The Local*, August 10, 2015, https://www.thelocal.de/20150810/prosectors-drop-netzpolitik-treason-probe.

145. Barfield, "Prosecutors Drop."

CHAPTER 12

1. Walter Frick, "Boston: The Start-Up Revolution Reviving its Tech Cred," BBC, September 4, 2013, http://www.bbc.com/future/story/20130903-boston-restoring-its-tech-cred.

2. The Mayflower Compact, essentially a social contract for the new colony, was signed on board ship in November 1620. "Mayflower Compact," Wikipedia, https://en.wikipedia.org/wiki/Mayflower_Compact (accessed January 1, 2019).

3. "A Model of Christian Charity," sermon by Governor John Winthrop delivered on board the *Arbella* in 1630, Winthrop Society, https://www.winthropsociety.com/doc_charity.php (accessed January 1, 2019).

4. Winthrop Society, "A Model of Christian Charity."

5. "Congregationalism," *Encyclopaedia Britannica*, https://www.britannica.com/topic/Congregationalism (accessed January 1, 2019).

6. They were settled in 1620, 1628, 1636, 1636, and 1681, respectively. "Plymouth Colony," Wikipedia, https://en.wikipedia.org/wiki/Plymouth_Colony (accessed January 1, 2019).

7. "Making Democracy Work," Harvard Kennedy School, https://www.hks.harvard.edu/research-insights/policy-topics/democracy/making-democracy-work (accessed January 1, 2018).

8. "Hack4Congress," Harvard Kennedy School, https://ash.harvard.edu/hack4con gress (accessed December 17, 2017).

9. Steven Levy, *Hackers: Heroes of the Computer Revolution* (Sebastopol: O'Reilly, [1984] 2010), 447–451.

10. For those interested in the full geneology, Patrick Henry Winston (Ford Professor of Artificial Intelligence and Computer Science at MIT) has informed me that "Marvin Minsky led the AI Group, which was a substantial part of Project MAC since Project MAC was established in 1963. In 1970, the AI Group, then led by Minsky and Seymour Papert, became an independent MIT Laboratory. Minsky's AI Group in Project MAC had antecedents in the AI Project started by John McCarthy in the Research Laboratory of Electronics in the late 1950s."

11. Levy, *Hackers*, 16–17.

12. Glyn Moody, "A Lawyer Who Is Also Idealist—How Refreshing," *The Guardian*, March 30, 2006.

13. Emacs is a text editor—a program that edits plain text files. GNU Emacs, created by Richard Stallman, is a major element of GNU and one of the most powerful and most ported text editors available, noted for its extensibility.

14. Citing, for illustration, the balkanized, state-controlled internet that the Chinese government has imposed on a fifth of the world's population; the apparent policy of the Indian government to create a biometrically registered, cashless society that would impose total social control on another large chunk of the world's population; and the ascension to power of Donald Trump in the United States, "among the most dangerous men on earth to have any power and he is the most powerful man on earth."

15. Stallman says that he suggests not using Trump's name because it gratifies Trump's narcissism. He says Trump *ostensibly* won the election with the most votes in the Electoral College. Stallman's point is that Trump "won" some states' electoral votes through cheating (voter suppression). With an honest election, Stallman contends, Trump would have lost in the Electoral College. Stallman, communication with author, March 4, 2019. https://us4.campaign-archive.com/?u =33e4ec877eed6a43863a4a92e&id=3a5e219073&e=8283eff9b8; https://theintercept .com/2016/10/27/voter-suppression-is-the-real-election-scandal.

16. Vernon Silver, "The Hackers Russia-Proofing Germany's Elections," *Bloomberg Businessweek*, June 28, 2017.

17. See "Disobedience Award," MIT Media Lab, https://www.media.mit.edu/posts/ disobedience-award.

18. Minow was Dean of Harvard Law School at the time of the video. She stepped down from that post in 2017. https://hls.harvard.edu/faculty/directory/10589/ Minow.

19. Ito would later complete a PhD in Media and Governance at Keio Univeristy in 2018. Wikipedia, "Joi Ito."

20. As a child growing up in Detroit, he was the protégé of his mother's employer— the technologist and social activist Stanford Ovshinsky, who also is a self-taught technologist. "Joi Ito," Wikipedia, https://en.wikipedia.org/wiki/Joi_Ito (accessed January 1, 2019).

21. "Joi Ito," Wikipedia.

22. "The FP One Hundred Top Global Thinkers," *Foreign Policy*, November 28, 2011.

23. Author's interview with Joi Ito, May 24, 2019.

24. Two years later, in April–May 2019, when this book was about to go into production, I had occasion to be grateful for all of these functions. Media Lab staff generously fact-checked and helped to improve this chapter. I also had the opportunity to interview Joi Ito by phone and experience that friendly, accessible way he talks to everyone that seems to make him such a successful catalyst.

25. "Chat with Prof Ron Deibert and Edward Snowden," RightsCon2016 Silicon Valley, video, published April 12, 2016, https://www.youtube.com/watch?v=l1Hy_OFkZ8s. At about thirty-nine minutes into the discussion, Snowden observes, "And that's because many universities are reliant on government funding, government grants. And even outside the United States, because of the international nature of the collaboration that happened against the public here, where many of these documents don't just implicate the United States government, they implicate what's called the Five Eyes Network—the US, the UK, Canada, New Zealand, and Australia—in addition to wider groups of third-party partners. You start to see that it's quite difficult find an institution that's both got the credibility publicly to handle this in an appropriate way and the capability that they can protect this from the charges that national security officials will level that. Look, these are academics. They don't know what they're doing. They can't fight against Chinese spies. They can't fight against Russian spies and so on and so forth. ..."

26. Mark Herz, "Harvard Withdraws Chelsea Manning's Fellowship after CIA Director Backlash," *All Things Considered*, NPR, September 15, 2015, transcript, https://www.npr.org/2017/09/15/551339949/harvard-withdraws-chelsea-mannings-fellowship-after-cia-director-backlash.

27. See a conversation between Reid Hoffman and Joi Ito in "The Future of Work," video, filmed November 8, 2017, at EM Tech 2017, https://events.technologyreview.com/video/watch/joi-ito-reid-hoffman-future-of-work. Although more than half the money raised has gone to entities other than MIT and Harvard: for example to seed funding Julia Angwin's new media enterprise, The Markup, and the ACLU's (Mass.) Digital Liberties project, before it got a $10 million anonymous gift. Author's interview with Joi Ito, May 24, 2019.

28. See a conversation between Reid Hoffman and Joi Ito about Ito's new book *Whiplash*, video, published December 4, 2016, https://www.youtube.com/watch?v=Ak2Chkhn87o.

29. Hoffman and Ito, conversation about *Whiplash*.

30. For the "ninety companies" figure, see Steven Levy, "Joi Ito Explains Why Donald Trump Is Like the Sex Pistols," *Wired*, December 6, 2016, https://www.wired.com/2016/12/joi-ito-explains-why-donald-trump-is-like-the-sex-pistols. See also "Media Lab Membership: Becoming a Member Company," MIT, https://www.media.mit.edu/members/becoming-a-member-company (accessed February 18, 2018).

31. Joi Ito, "Whiplash: How to Survive Our Faster Future," December 14, 2017, lecture at the Japan Society, New York City, video, https://www.youtube.com/watch?v=TTCwaOvSf24. See also MIT Media Lab, "Membership Levels," post, accessed May 18, 2019, https://www.media.mit.edu/posts/membership-levels. Membership entails a minimum three-year commitment. Members are not all corporations. The ML Benefits document states: "Media Lab Members share free, non-exclusive licenses to all of the intellectual property developed during their time at the Lab. Non-Members may purchase licenses to Media Lab IP, but are excluded from doing so for a period of two years after disclosure. Members also have the option of purchasing an 'except for Media Lab Members' license, excluding Non-Members from licensing a specific invention. Members cannot exclude other Members from the shared pool of IP developed during their time."

32. Levy, *Hackers*, 48.

33. Levy, "Joi Ito Explains."

34. See "About the Lab: Mission and History," MIT Media Lab, https://www.media.mit.edu/about/mission-history.

35. "Alex 'Sandy' Pentland: Ethics, Human Dynamics," MIT Media Lab, https://www.media.mit.edu/people/sandy/overview.

36. See idcubed.org.

37. John Henry Clippinger and David Bollier, "The Rise of Digital Common Law: An Argument for Trust Frameworks, Digital Common Law, and Digital Forms of Governance," http://idcubed.org/digital-law/the-rise-of-digital-common-law (accessed July 28, 2019).

38. John Henry Clippinger and David Bollier, "The Social Stack for New Social Contracts," 2012, https://idcubed.org/digital-law/socialstack (accessed March 17, 2017).

39. John Perry Barlow and John Clippinger, speaking at the Stanford Blockchain Workshops, "Blockchain: Law, Regulation, Policy, the Law of the Horse," published November 6, 2015, https://www.youtube.com/watch?v=wtMezbrA3gw.

40. David Cole, "Taxing the Poor," *New York Review of Books*, May 10, 2018, https://www.nybooks.com/articles/2018/05/10/taxing-the-poor.

41. Leslie Albrecht, "One-Third of American Households Have Struggled to Afford Either Food, Shelter or Medical Care," *Marketwatch*, September 27, 2017, cited in Umair Haque, "Why America Is the First Poor Rich Country; Or, How American Collapse Is Made of a New Kind of Poverty," *Eudaimonia*, May 23, 2018, https://eand.co/why-america-is-the-worlds-first-poor-rich-country-17f5a80e444a.

42. Trebor Scholz and Nathan Schneider, eds., *Ours to Hack and to Own: The Rise of Platform Cooperativism—A New Vision for the Future of Work and a Fairer Internet* (New York: OR Books, 2016), 22.

43. Twice the poverty line was about $24,000 per year for the individual and $48,500 per year for a family of four. Of the 42.5 percent, 12.7 percent lived on less than $24,340 for a family of four (the poverty line), and 5.8 percent lived on less than $12,170 for a family of four. Jessica L. Semega, Kayla R. Fontenot, and Melissa A. Kollar, "Income and Poverty in the United States: 2016," US Census Bureau, United States Department of Commerce, issued September 2017, https://www.census.gov/content/dam/Census/library/publications/2017/demo/P60-259.pdf.

44. Richard Stallman has pointed out that exponential growth is very common in nature and human activities. Exponential growth means that the increase in something is proportional to how big the thing already is and can involve rates as low as 1 percent (or less). The hypothetical technological "singularity" implies a growth rate that goes to infinity. The website https://freedom-to-tinker.com/2018/01/03/why-the-singularity-is-not-a-singularity explains this clearly. Vernor Vinge's science fiction book *Marooned in Real Time* also shows what a technological singularity implies. Richard Stallman, correspondence with the author, January 7, 2018.

45. Joi Ito, "Resisting Reduction: A Manifesto," Joi Ito's Web, posted December 20, 2017, https://joi.ito.com/weblog/2017/12/20/resisting-reduction.html.

46. Ito, "Resisting Reduction."

47. Ito tells the story in a blog post: "When Chelsea Manning's fellowship at the Harvard Kennedy School was rescinded, she emailed me and asked if she could speak at the Media Lab. I was thinking about it, and I asked the administration what they thought, and they thought it was a terrible idea. And when they told me that I said, 'You know, now that means I have to invite her.' I remember our Provost Marty

[Schmidt] saying, 'I know.' And that's what I think is wonderful about being here at MIT: the fact that the administration understands that faculty must be allowed to act independently of the Institute." Joi Ito, "My Talk at the MIT-Harvard Conference on the Uyghur Human Rights Crisis," posted May 2, 2019, transcript, https://joi.ito .com/weblog/2019/05/02/my-talk-at-the-.html.

48. "Open code" is a catchier term but could mean either free software or open-source software, which as described in earlier chapters, are two different things politically.

49. The Berkman Center for Internet & Society, "Open Code Open Content Open Law: Building a Digital Commons," Strategic Planning Session Paper, Harvard Law School, 1999, https://cyber.harvard.edu/sites/cyber.law.harvard.edu/files/opencode .session.pdf.

50. See "About Us," Berkman Klein Center for Internet & Society, https://cyber .harvard.edu/about.

51. See "Network of Interdisciplinary Internet & Society Research Centers," Berkman Klein Center for Internet & Society, https://cyber.harvard.edu/research/ network_of_centers. See also "Towards a Global Network of Internet and Society Centers," Alexander von Humboldt Institut für Internet und Gesellschaft, https:// www.hiig.de/en/towards-a-global-network-of-internet-and-society-centers.

52. Jake Shapiro, former associate director and Berkman fellow, "Berkman@10 Report," 2007, https://cyber.harvard.edu/sites/cyber.harvard.edu/files/Berkmanat10 report.pdf.

53. Such as Eldred v. Ashcroft, 537 US 186 (2003), a challenge to the constitutionality of the Sonny Bono Copyright Term Extension Act, which extended US copyright terms by twenty years and increased penalties for infringement. Larry Lessig was lead counsel. The Court decided against the challenge.

54. Fab Labs are cooperative spaces that provide computer-assisted tools and materials for making just about anything that can be mass produced. The concept began as a project between the Grassroots Invention Group and the Center for Bits and Atoms at the MIT Media Lab with a grant from the National Science Foundation in 2001. An MIT course called "How to Make (Almost) Anything" was an inspiration. Fab Labs have subsequently sprouted up in many other places. The Vigyan Ashram in India was one of the first to be set up outside MIT. "Fab Lab," Wikipedia, https:// en.wikipedia.org/wiki/Fab_lab (accessed January 1, 2019).

55. It opened as a community-squatted space not long before the 15M encampment and movement of spring 2011. In May 2015, the Spanish government finally ceded the building to the community. Gloria D. Durán and Andrew W. Moore, "The Tabacalera of Lavapiés: Social Experiment or a Work of Art?," Field (Winter 2015): 49, http://field-journal.com/wp-content/uploads/2016/10/FIELD-02-Duran-Moore-La-Tabacalera.pdf.

56. Heather Brooke, "Inside the Secret World of Hackers," The Guardian, August 24, 2011, https://www.theguardian.com/technology/2011/aug/24/inside-secret-world-of -hackers.

57. Yochai Benkler, The Penguin and the Leviathan: How Cooperation Triumphs over Self-Interest (New York: Crown Business, 2011), 251.

58. Yochai Benkler, "The Idea of the Commons and the Future of Capitalism," video, filmed at the Creative Commons Global Summit held in Seoul, Korea, October 15, 2015, https://www.youtube.com/watch?v=58s100KuAa0.

59. Samer Hassan's project would win the largest individual research funding grant from the EU in spring 2018. Its name is "Decentralized Blockchain-Based Organizations for Bootstrapping the Collaborative Economy."

60. David Harvey, "Marx, Capital and the Madness of Economic Reason," London School of Economics lecture, video, filmed September 18, 2017, https://davidharvey .org/2017/09/video-audio-lse-lecture-marx-capital-madness-economic-reason-18 -september-2017.

61. Sheldon Wolin, "Can Capitalism and Democracy Co-Exist?," interview with Chris Hedges, *The Real News*, November 14, 2014, https://www.youtube.com/ watch?v=LGc8DMHMyi8.

62. Yochai Benkler, *The Wealth of Networks: How Social Production Transforms Markets and Freedoms* (New Haven: Yale University Press, 2006), xii.

63. See the work of Gerald Davis of the Michigan University Business School.

64. Tuition and fees at Harvard are north of $45,000 per year, although Harvard has gone to considerable lengths in the last decade to make its costs more affordable to both American and foreign students, based on need. See Sarah Rimer and Alan Finder, "Harvard Steps Up Financial Aid," *New York Times*, December 10, 2017. See also "Costs of Attendance," Harvard University, https://college.harvard.edu/ financial-aid/how-aid-works/cost-attendance, and "International Students," https:// college.harvard.edu/financial-aid/applying-aid/international-students (accessed January 1, 2019).

65. Moglen does not use these words. "Condition of freedom" is my paraphrase.

66. Eben Moglen, "Snowden and the Future: Westward the Course of Empire," part 1 of a four-part lecture delivered at Columbia University October 9, 2013, in association with Software Freedom Law Center, http://snowdenandthefuture.info.

INDEX